ertain
ENTIFIC
Railgun

Vol. 6

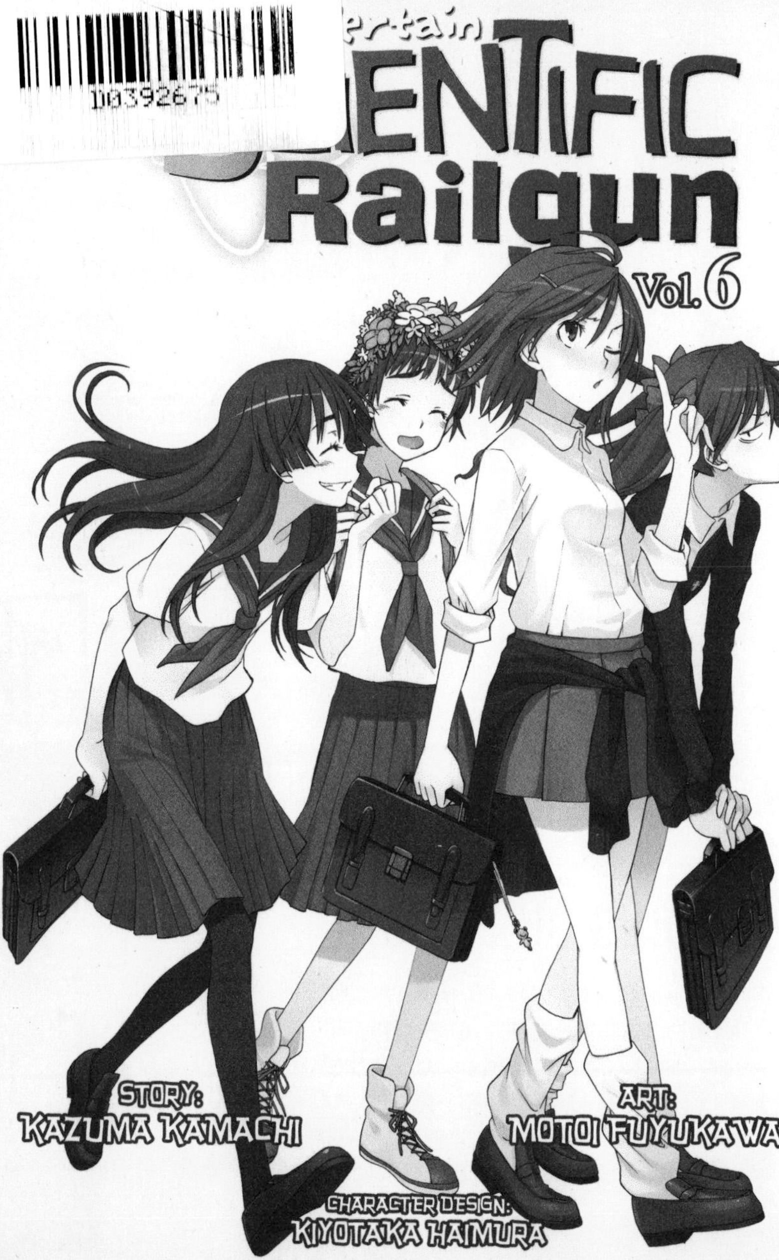

STORY:
KAZUMA KAMACHI

ART:
MOTOI FUYUKAWA

CHARACTER DESIGN:
KIYOTAKA HAIMURA

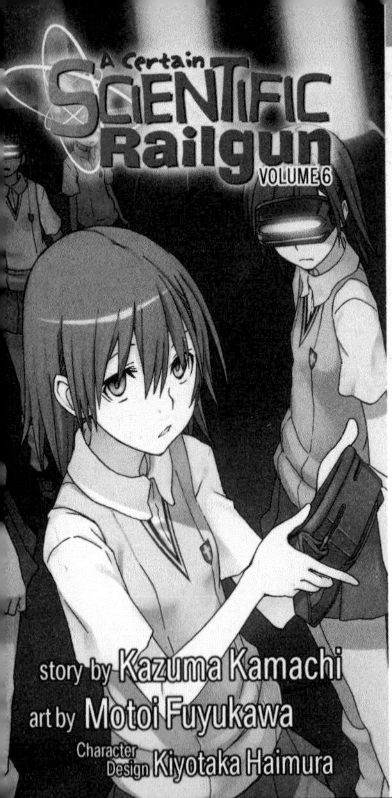
A Certain
SCIENTIFIC
Railgun
VOLUME 6
story by Kazuma Kamachi
art by Motoi Fuyukawa
Character Design Kiyotaka Haimura

STAFF CREDITS

translation Nan Rymer
adaptation Maggie Danger
lettering Roland Amago
layout Bambi Eloriaga-Amago
cover design Nicky Lim
copy editor Shanti Whitesides
assistant editor Alexis Roberts
editor Jason DeAngelis

publisher Seven Seas Entertainment

A CERTAIN SCIENTIFIC RAILGUN VOL. 6

ISBN: 978-1-937867-03-4

Printed in Canada

First Printing: December 2012

10 9 8 7 6 5 4 3 2 1

READING DIRECTIONS

This book reads from ***right to left***, Japanese style. If this is your first time reading manga, you start reading from the top right panel on each page and take it from there. If you get lost, just follow the numbered diagram here. It may seem backwards at first, but you'll get the hang of it! Have fun!!

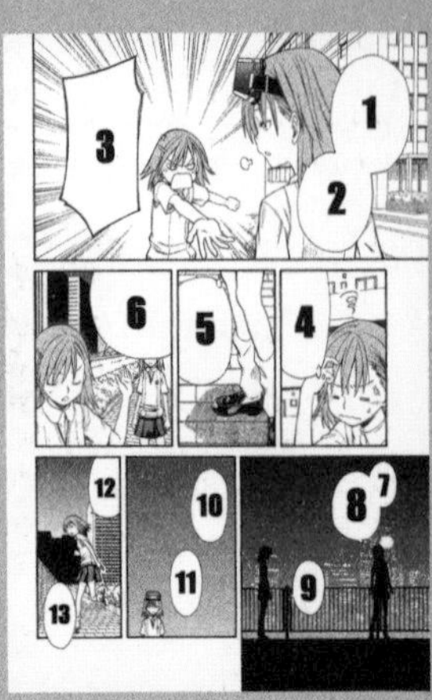
1
2
3
4
5
6
7
8
9
10
11
12
13

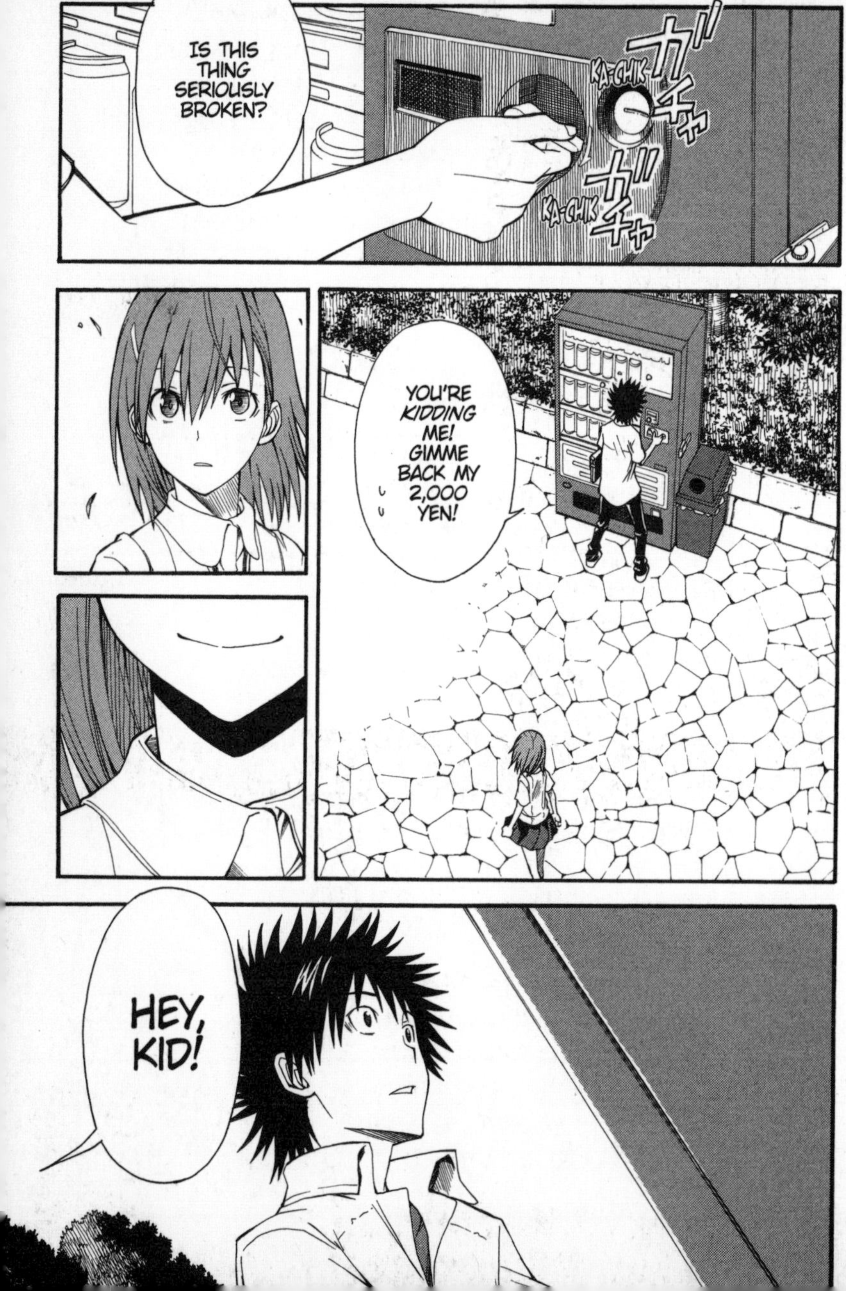

KA-CHIK
KA-CHIK
IS THIS THING SERIOUSLY BROKEN?
YOU'RE KIDDING ME! GIMME BACK MY 2,000 YEN!
HEY, KID!

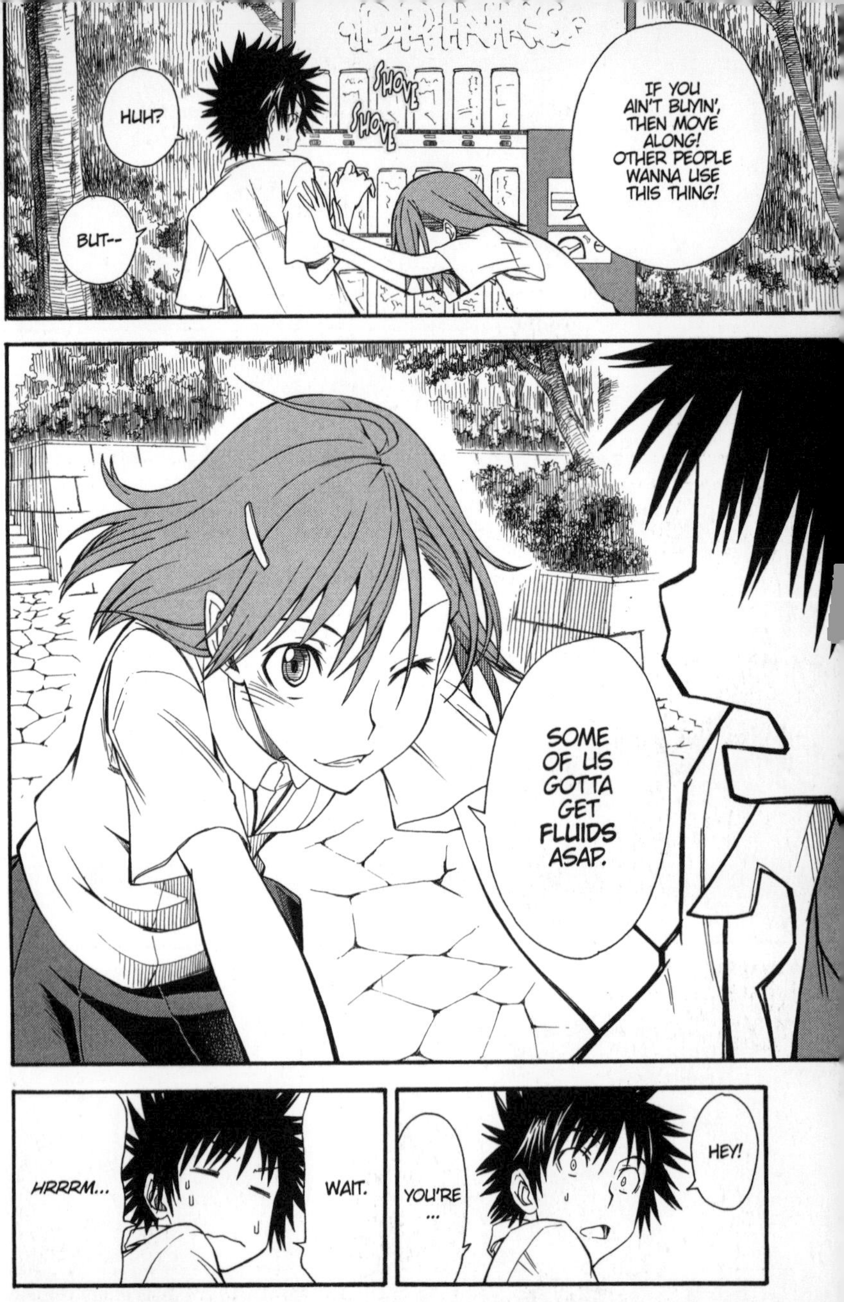
IF YOU AIN'T BUYIN', THEN MOVE ALONG! OTHER PEOPLE WANNA USE THIS THING!
SHOVE
SHOVE
HUH?
BUT--
SOME OF US GOTTA GET FLUIDS ASAP.
HEY!
YOU'RE ...
WAIT.
HRRRM...

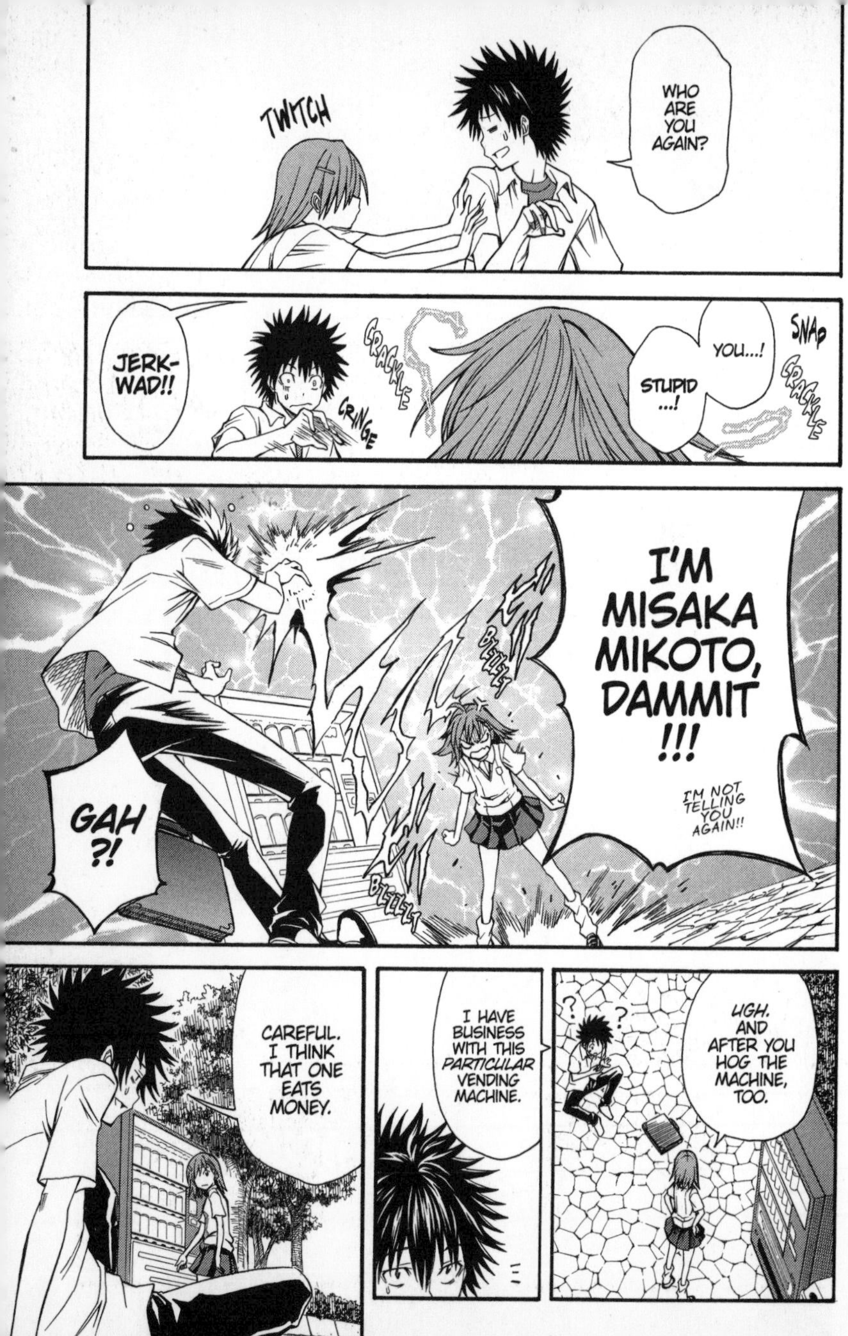
WHO ARE YOU AGAIN?
TWITCH
SNAP
CRACKLE
YOU...!
STUPID ...!
CRACKLE
CRINGE
JERK-WAD!!
I'M MISAKA MIKOTO, DAMMIT!!!
I'M NOT TELLING YOU AGAIN!!
GAH?!
UGH. AND AFTER YOU HOG THE MACHINE, TOO.
I HAVE BUSINESS WITH THIS *PARTICULAR* VENDING MACHINE.
CAREFUL. I THINK THAT ONE EATS MONEY.

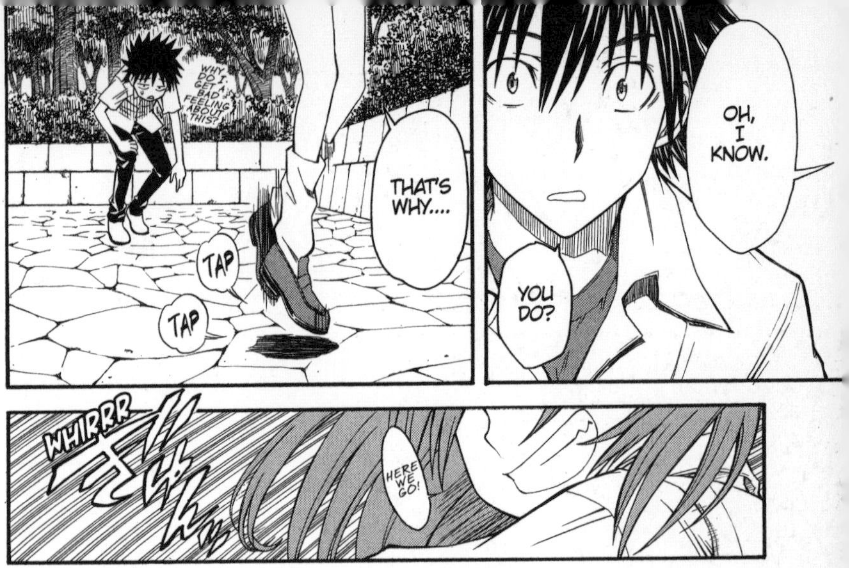
OH, I KNOW.
YOU DO?
THAT'S WHY....
WHY DO I GET A BAD FEELING ABOUT THIS?
TAP
TAP
HERE WE GO!
WHIRRR

CHAPTER 31: AUGUST 20TH (1)

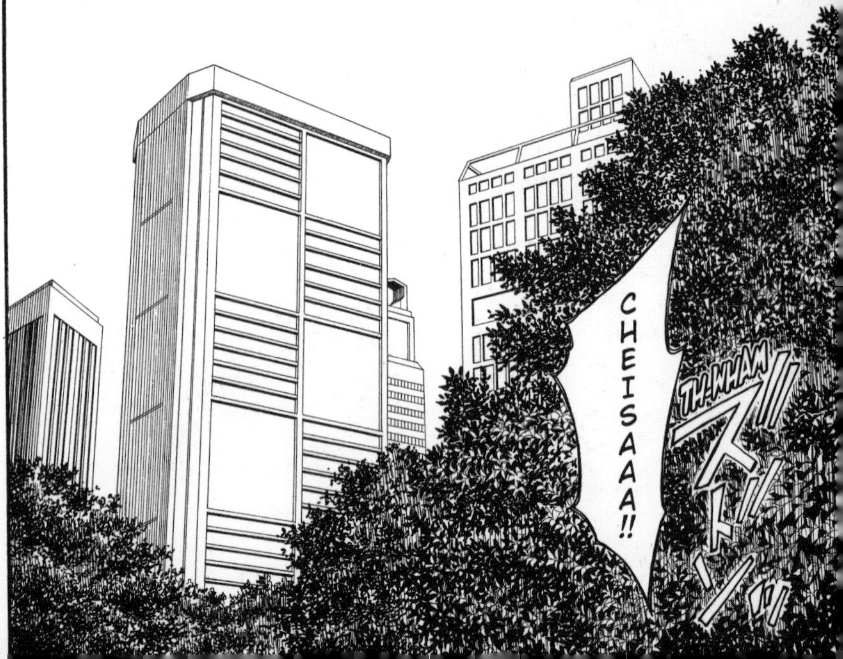
TH-WHAM
CHEISAAAA!!

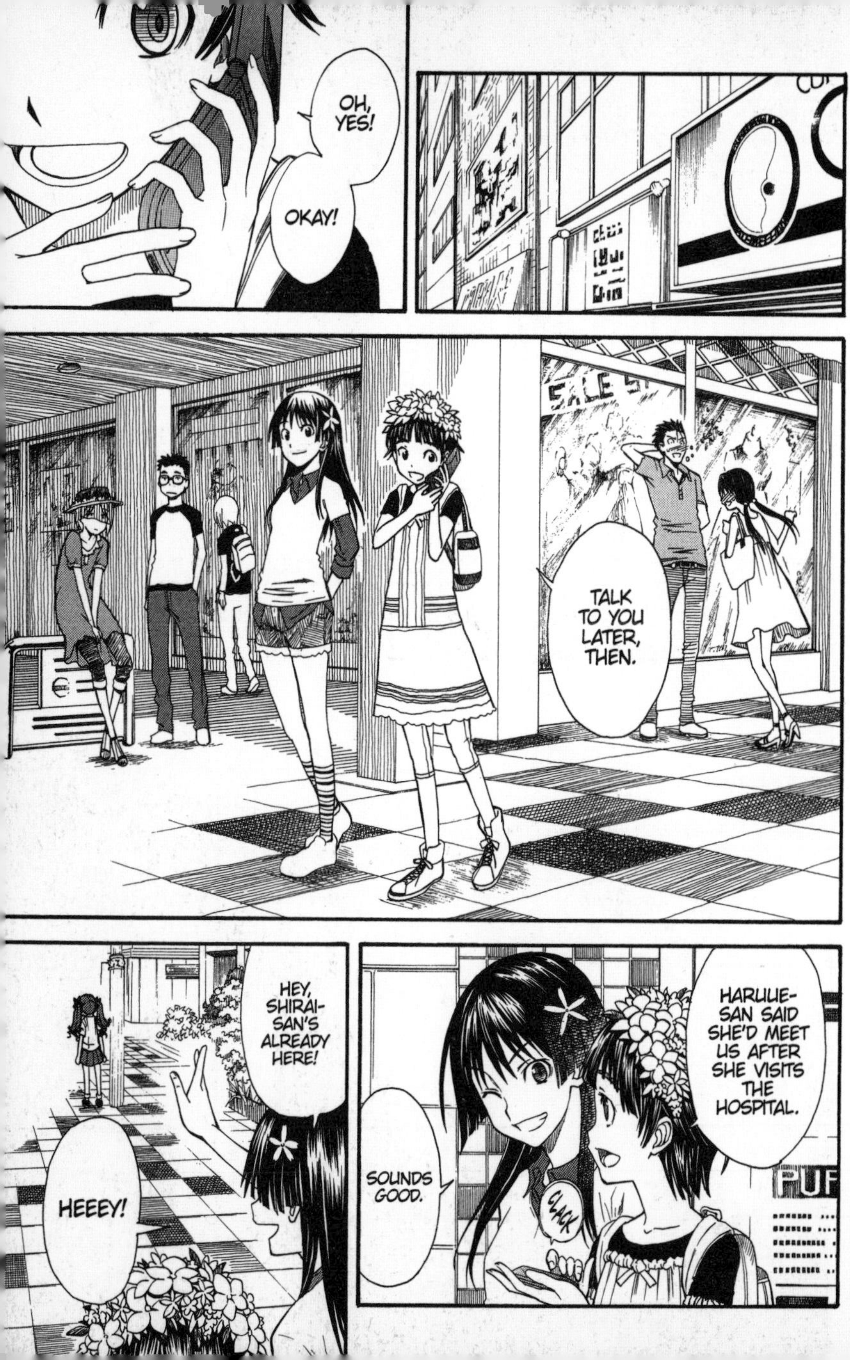
OH, YES!
OKAY!
TALK TO YOU LATER, THEN.
HARUUE-SAN SAID SHE'D MEET US AFTER SHE VISITS THE HOSPITAL.
SOUNDS GOOD.
CLACK
HEY, SHIRAI-SAN'S ALREADY HERE!
HEEEY!

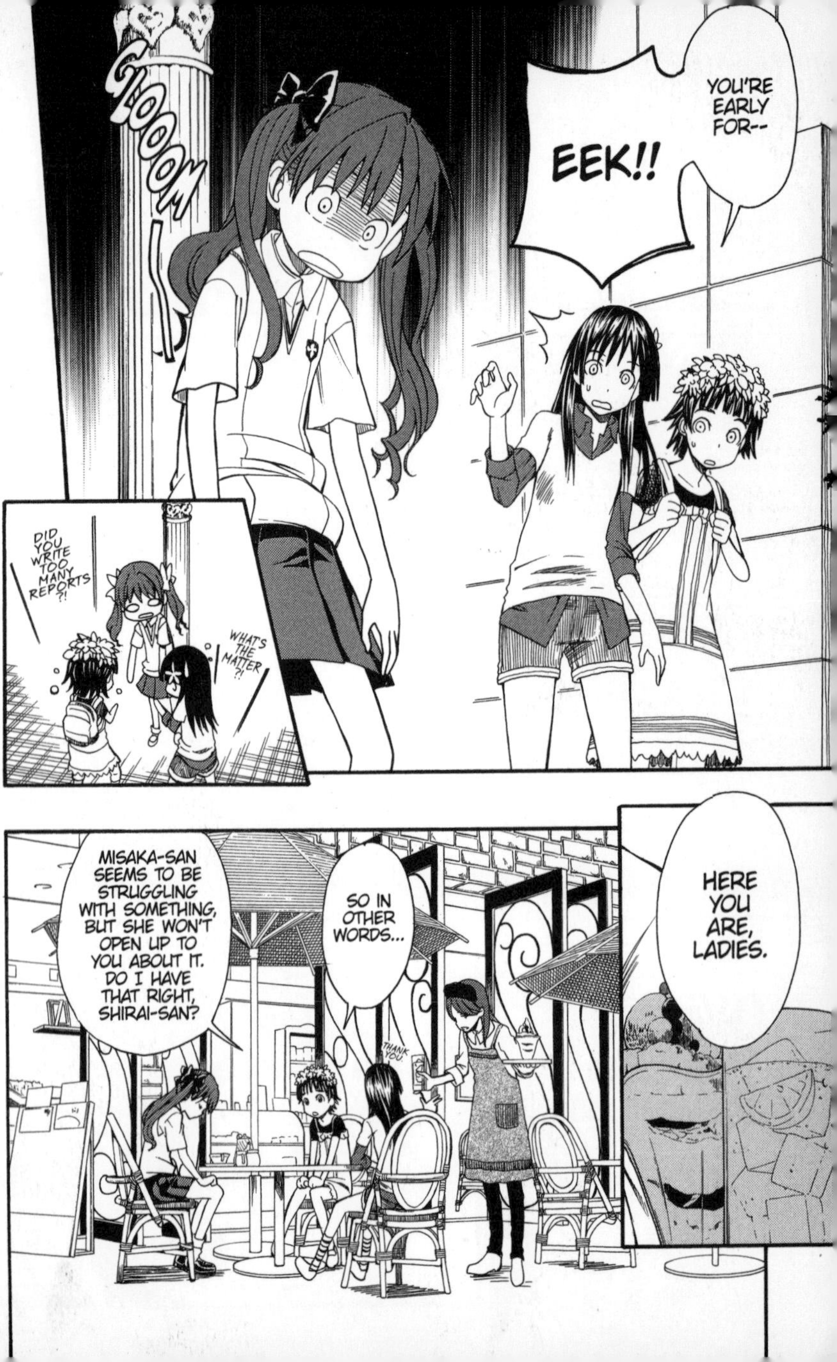
YOU'RE EARLY FOR--
EEK!!
GLOOOM
WHAT'S THE MATTER?!
DID YOU WRITE TOO MANY REPORTS?!
HERE YOU ARE, LADIES.
SO IN OTHER WORDS...
MISAKA-SAN SEEMS TO BE STRUGGLING WITH SOMETHING, BUT SHE WON'T OPEN UP TO YOU ABOUT IT. DO I HAVE THAT RIGHT, SHIRAI-SAN?
THANK YOU.

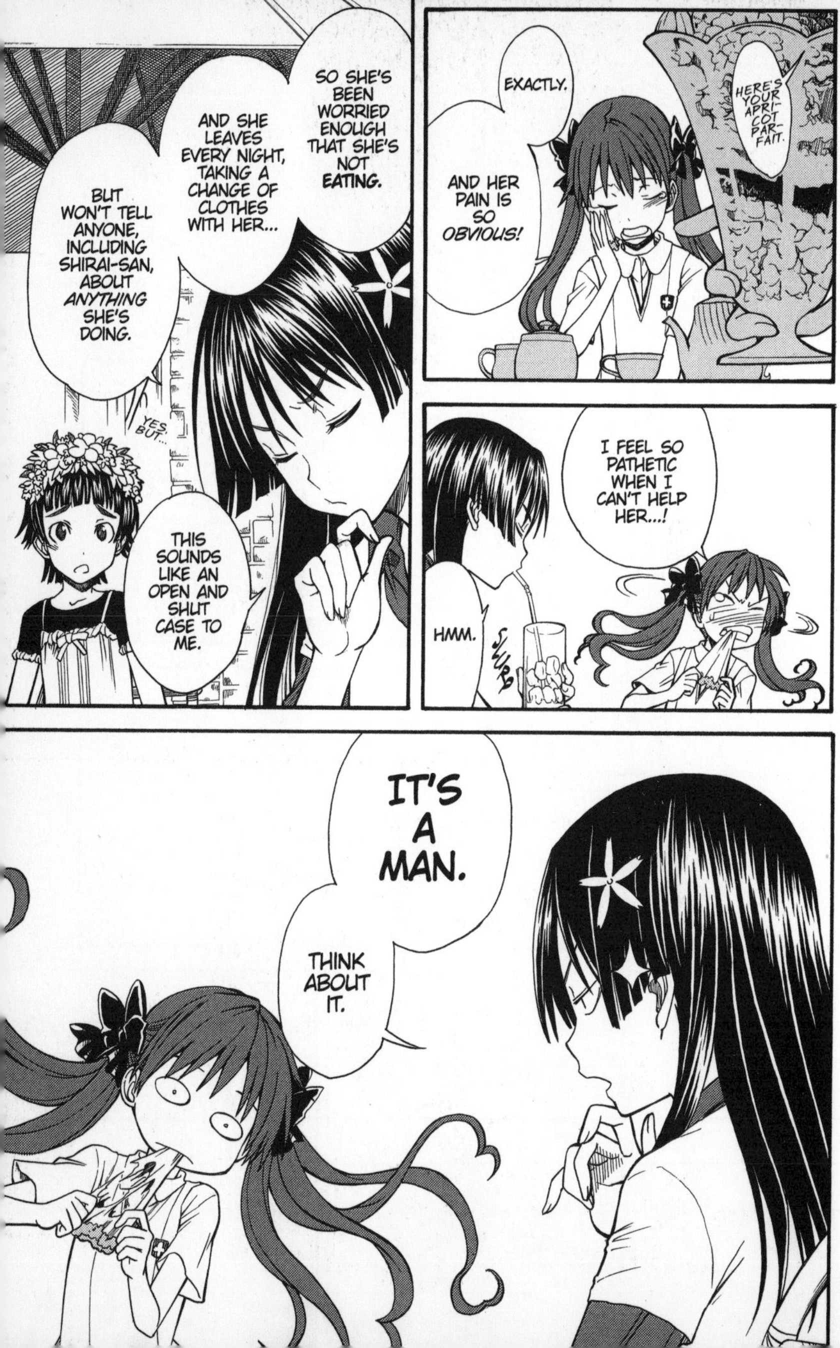
HERE'S YOUR APRICOT PARFAIT.
EXACTLY.
AND HER PAIN IS SO *OBVIOUS!*
I FEEL SO PATHETIC WHEN I CAN'T HELP HER...!
HMM.
SO SHE'S BEEN WORRIED ENOUGH THAT SHE'S NOT **EATING.**
AND SHE LEAVES EVERY NIGHT, TAKING A CHANGE OF CLOTHES WITH HER...
BUT WON'T TELL ANYONE, INCLUDING SHIRAI-SAN, ABOUT *ANYTHING* SHE'S DOING.
THIS SOUNDS LIKE AN OPEN AND SHUT CASE TO ME.
YES, BUT...
IT'S A MAN.
THINK ABOUT IT.

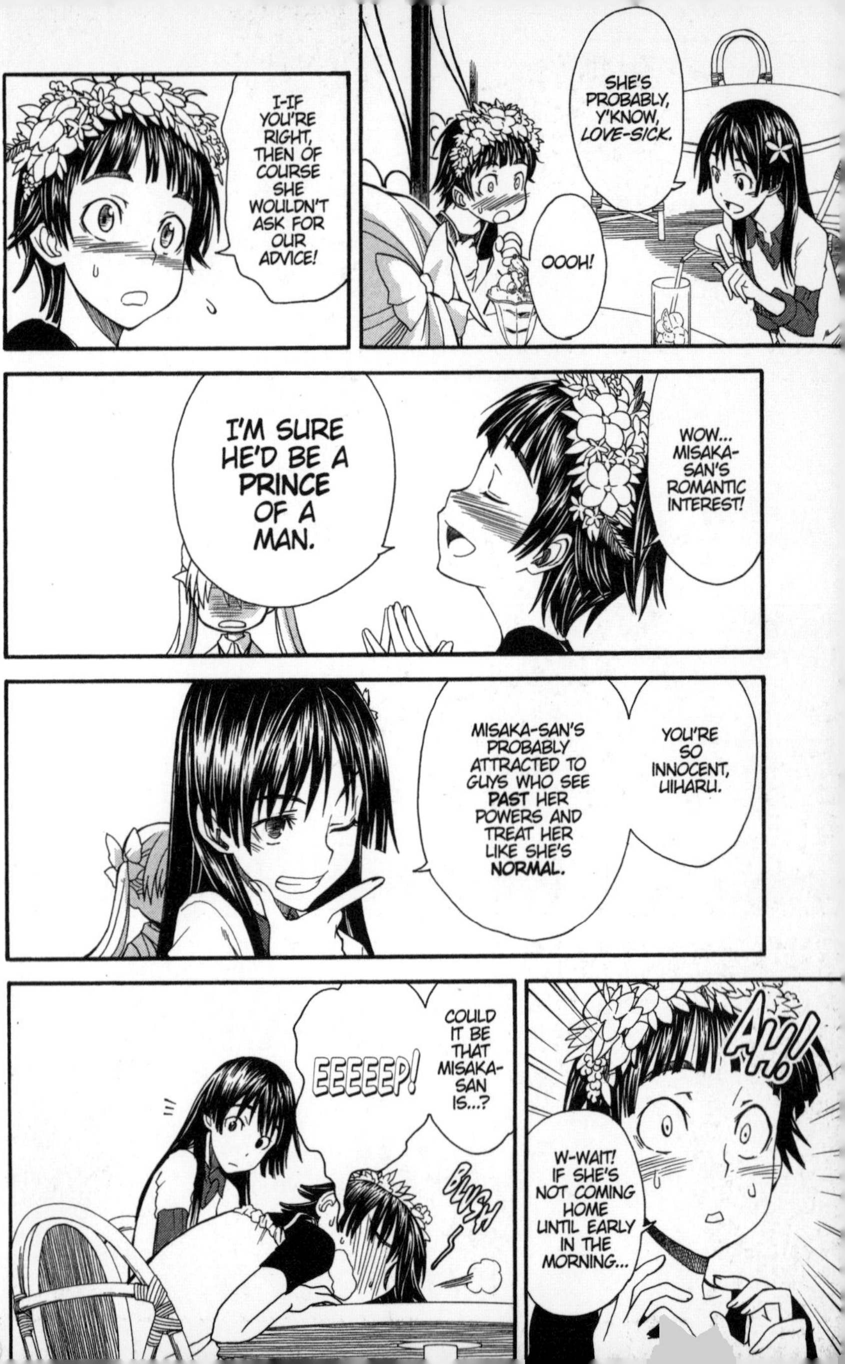
SHE'S PROBABLY, Y'KNOW, LOVE-SICK.
OOOH!
I-IF YOU'RE RIGHT, THEN OF COURSE SHE WOULDN'T ASK FOR OUR ADVICE!
WOW... MISAKA-SAN'S ROMANTIC INTEREST!
I'M SURE HE'D BE A PRINCE OF A MAN.
YOU'RE SO INNOCENT, UIHARU.
MISAKA-SAN'S PROBABLY ATTRACTED TO GUYS WHO SEE PAST HER POWERS AND TREAT HER LIKE SHE'S NORMAL.
AH!
W-WAIT! IF SHE'S NOT COMING HOME UNTIL EARLY IN THE MORNING...
COULD IT BE THAT MISAKA-SAN IS...?
EEEEEEP!

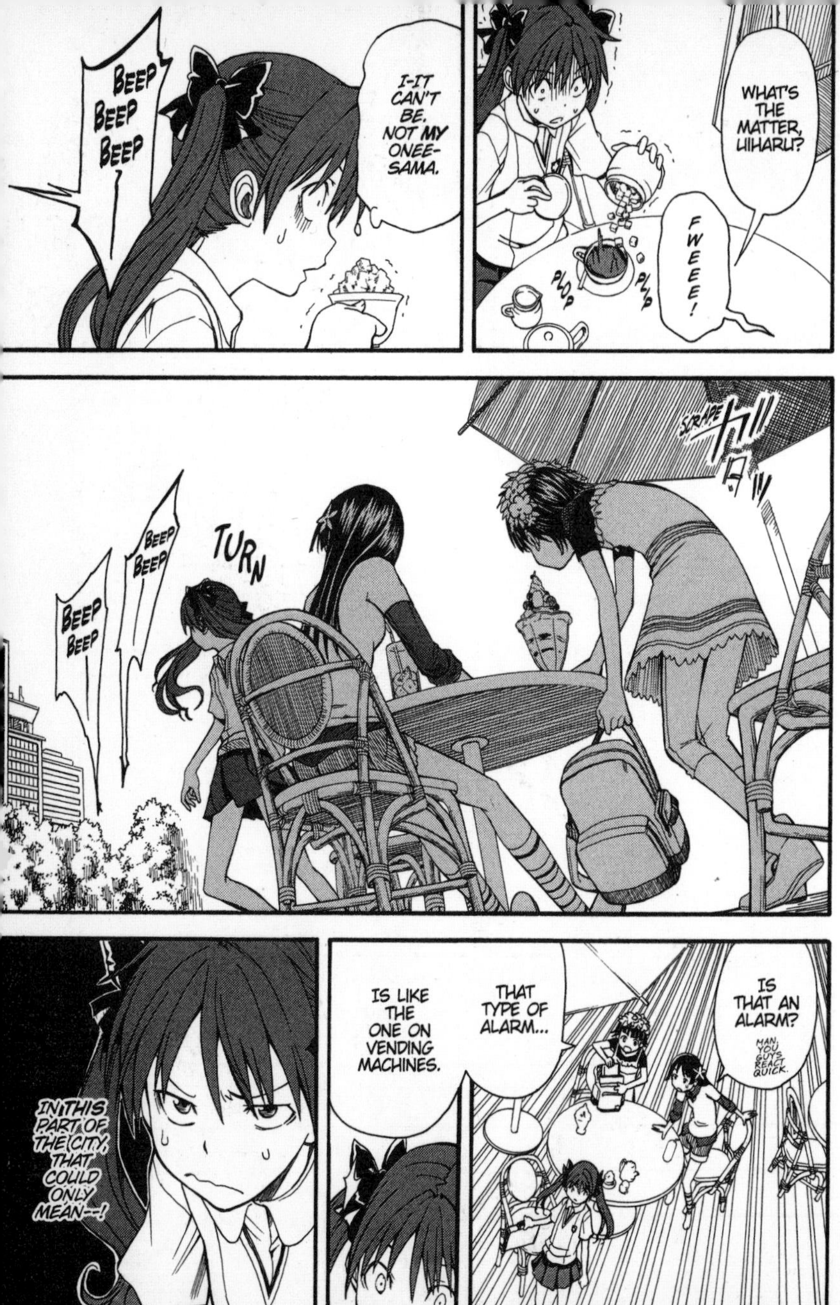
WHAT'S THE MATTER, UIHARU?
FWEEE!
PLOP
PLOP
I-IT CAN'T BE. NOT MY ONEE-SAMA.
BEEP BEEP BEEP
SCRAPE
TURN
BEEP BEEP
BEEP BEEP
IS THAT AN ALARM?
MAN, YOU GUYS REACT QUICK.
THAT TYPE OF ALARM...
IS LIKE THE ONE ON VENDING MACHINES.
IN THIS PART OF THE CITY, THAT COULD ONLY MEAN--!

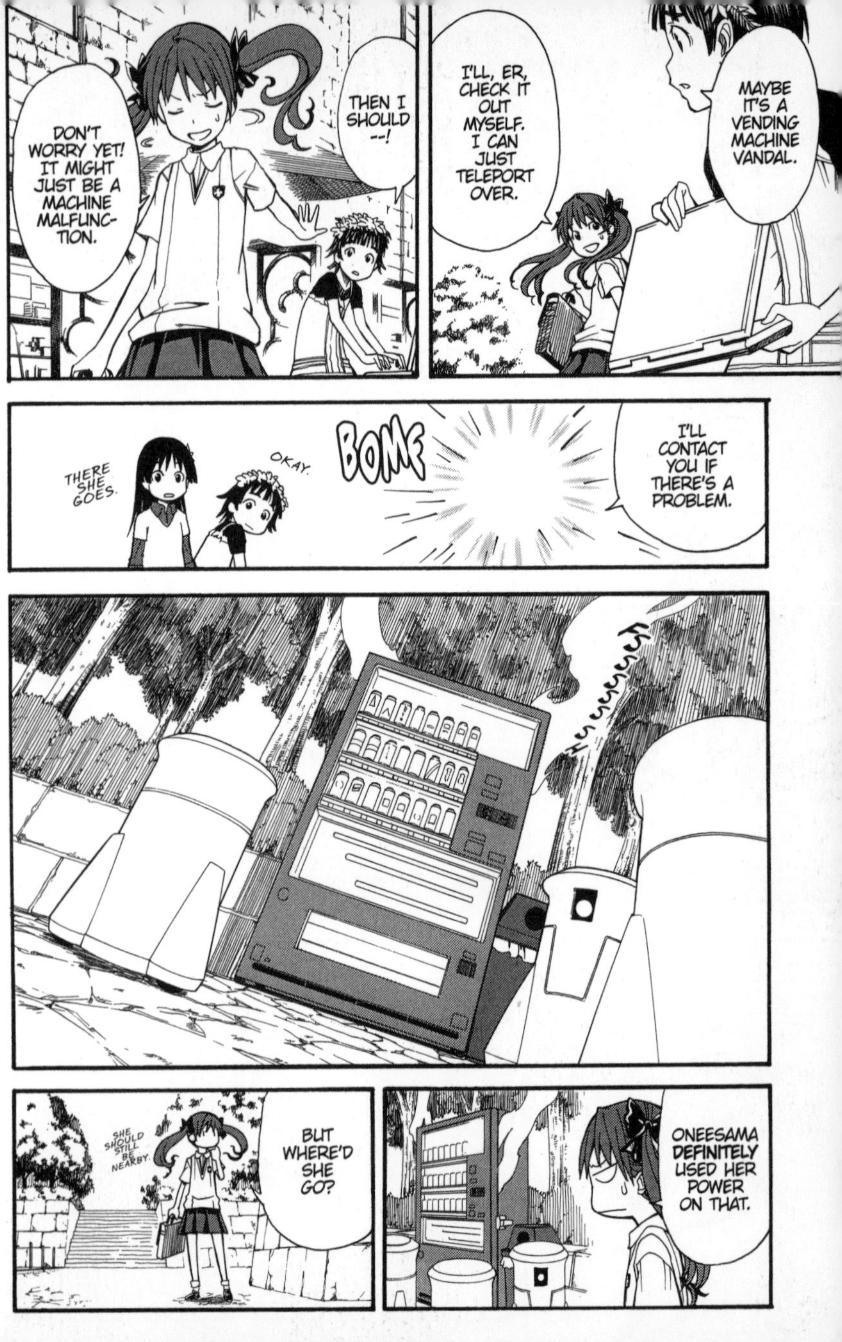

MAYBE IT'S A VENDING MACHINE VANDAL.
I'LL, ER, CHECK IT OUT MYSELF. I CAN JUST TELEPORT OVER.
THEN I SHOULD --!
DON'T WORRY YET! IT MIGHT JUST BE A MACHINE MALFUNCTION.
I'LL CONTACT YOU IF THERE'S A PROBLEM.
BOMF
OKAY.
THERE SHE GOES.
ONEESAMA DEFINITELY USED HER POWER ON THAT.
BUT WHERE'D SHE GO?
SHE SHOULD STILL BE NEARBY.

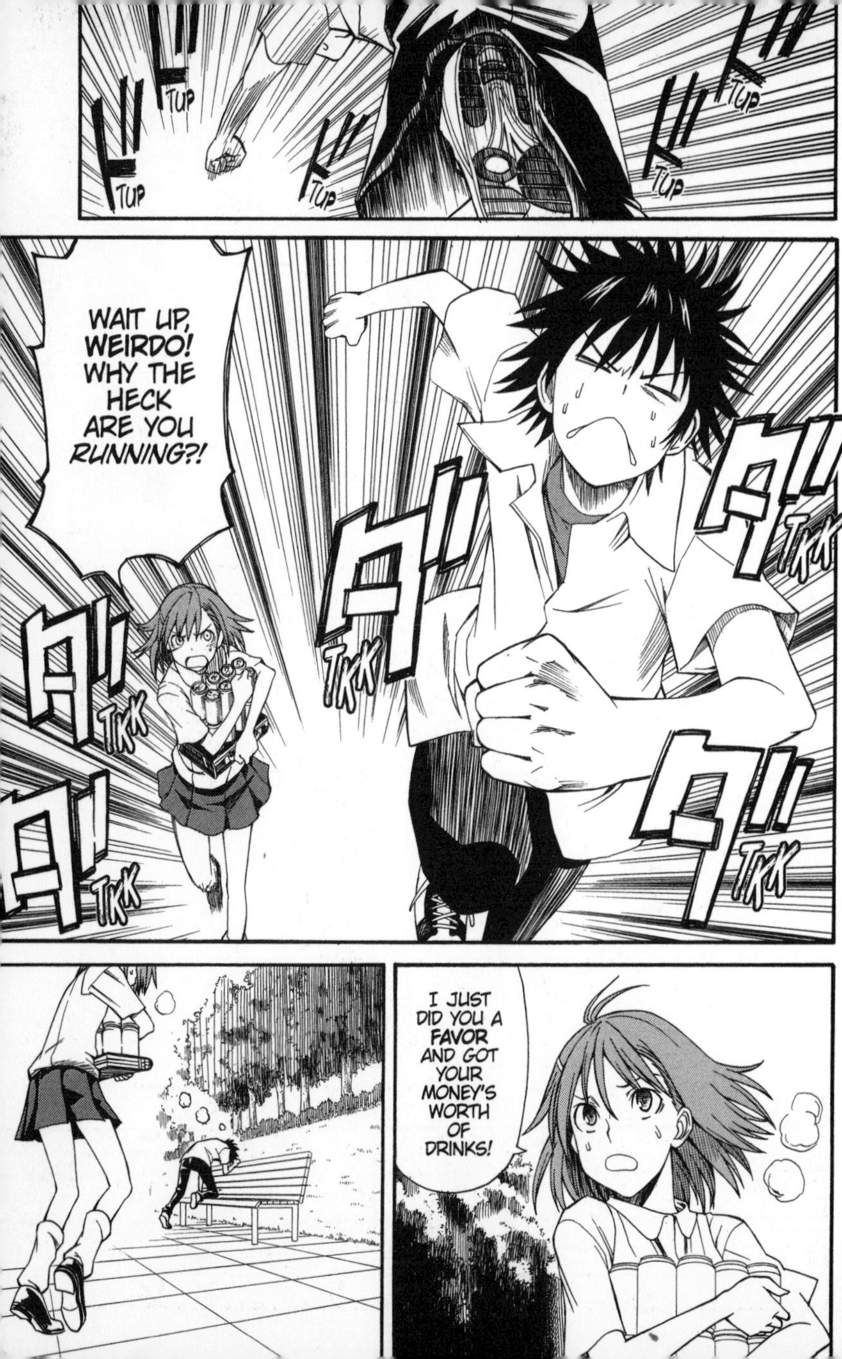
TUP
TUP
TUP
TUP
TUP
TUP
WAIT UP, WEIRDO! WHY THE HECK ARE YOU *RUNNING?!*
TKK
TKK
TKK
TKK
TKK
I JUST DID YOU A **FAVOR** AND GOT YOUR MONEY'S WORTH OF DRINKS!

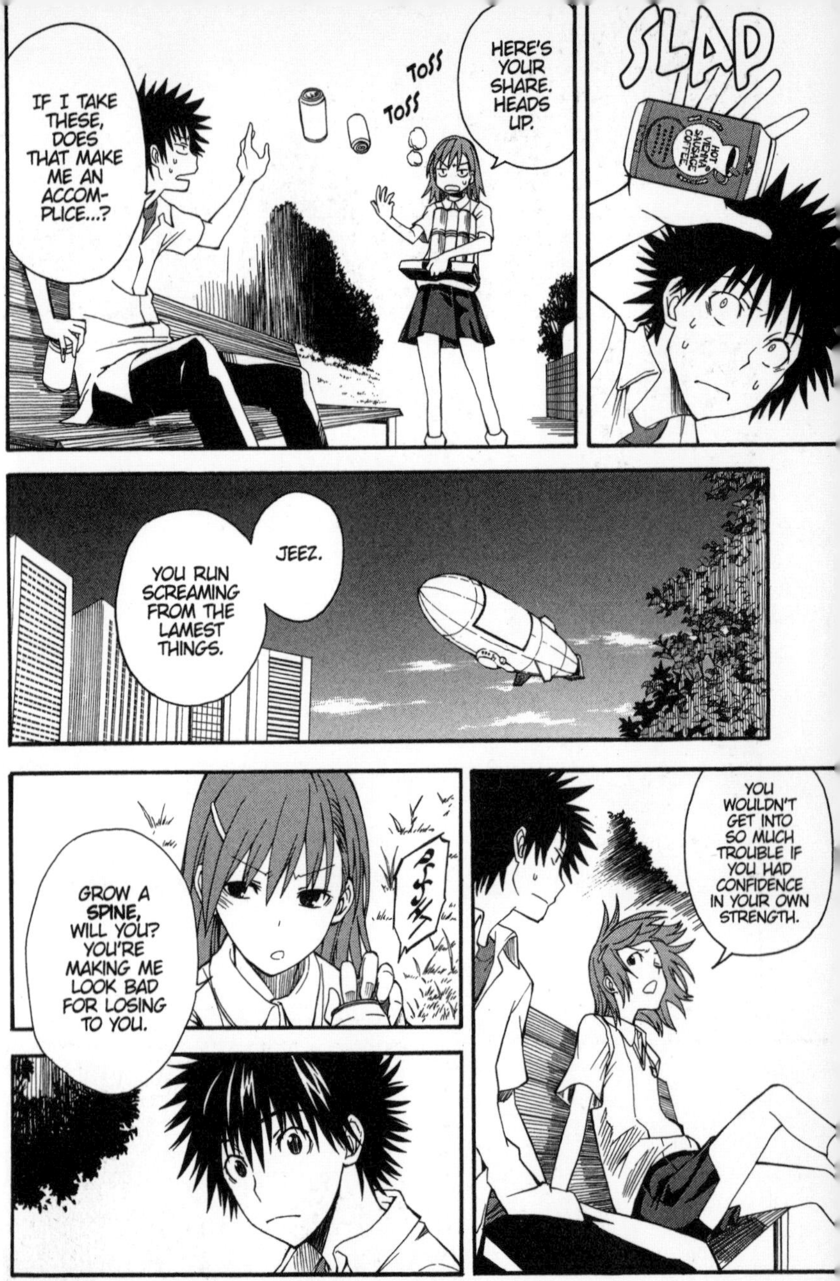
SLAP
HOT VIENNA SAUSAGE COFFEE
HERE'S YOUR SHARE. HEADS UP.
TOSS
TOSS
IF I TAKE THESE, DOES THAT MAKE ME AN ACCOMPLICE...?
JEEZ.
YOU RUN SCREAMING FROM THE LAMEST THINGS.
YOU WOULDN'T GET INTO SO MUCH TROUBLE IF YOU HAD CONFIDENCE IN YOUR OWN STRENGTH.
GROW A **SPINE**, WILL YOU? YOU'RE MAKING ME LOOK BAD FOR LOSING TO YOU.

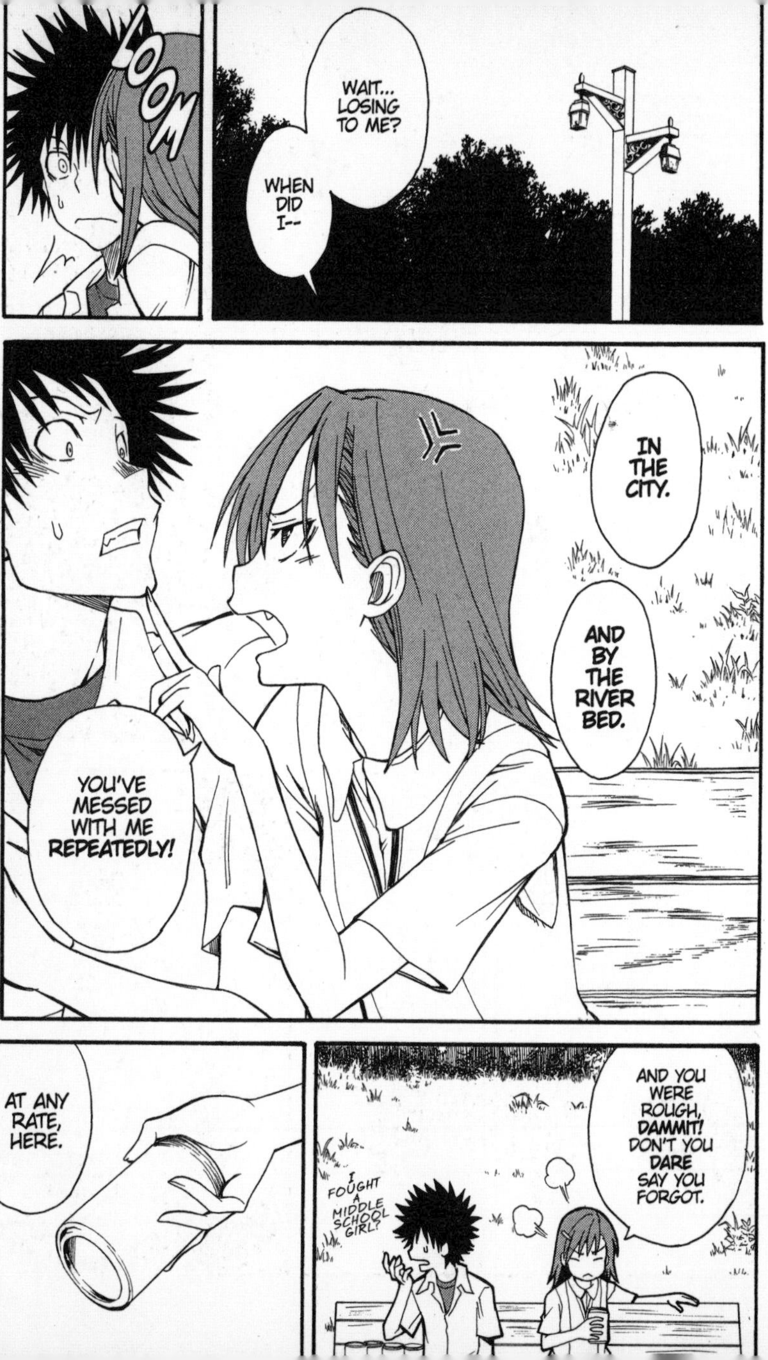

WAIT... LOSING TO ME?
WHEN DID I--
BOOM
IN THE CITY.
AND BY THE RIVER BED.
YOU'VE MESSED WITH ME REPEATEDLY!
AND YOU WERE ROUGH, DAMMIT! DON'T YOU DARE SAY YOU FORGOT.
I FOUGHT A MIDDLE SCHOOL GIRL?
AT ANY RATE, HERE.

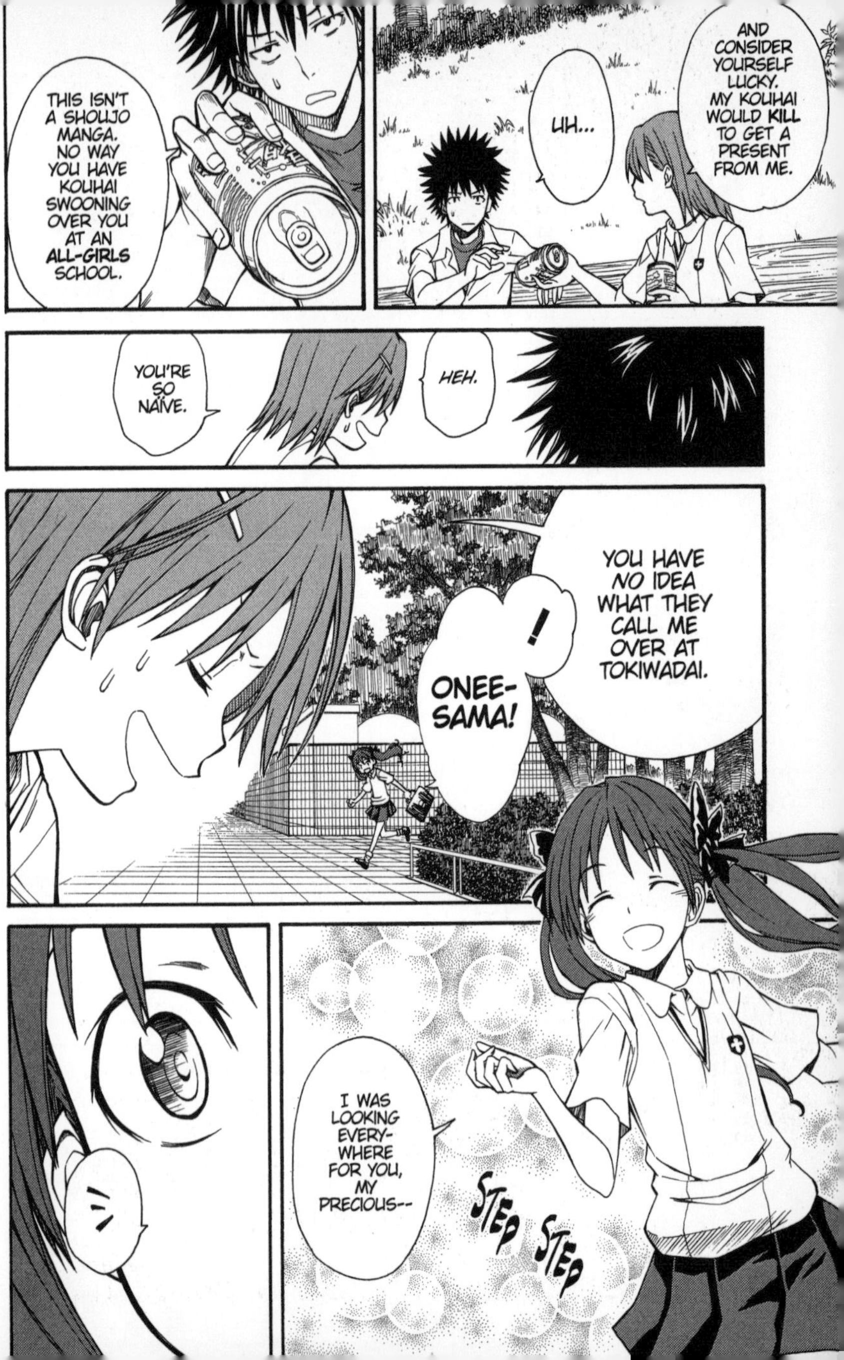
AND CONSIDER YOURSELF LUCKY. MY KOUHAI WOULD KILL TO GET A PRESENT FROM ME.
UH...
THIS ISN'T A SHOUJO MANGA. NO WAY YOU HAVE KOUHAI SWOONING OVER YOU AT AN ALL-GIRLS SCHOOL.
HEH.
YOU'RE SO NAÏVE.
YOU HAVE NO IDEA WHAT THEY CALL ME OVER AT TOKIWADAI.
!
ONEE-SAMA!
I WAS LOOKING EVERY-WHERE FOR YOU, MY PRECIOUS--
STEP STEP

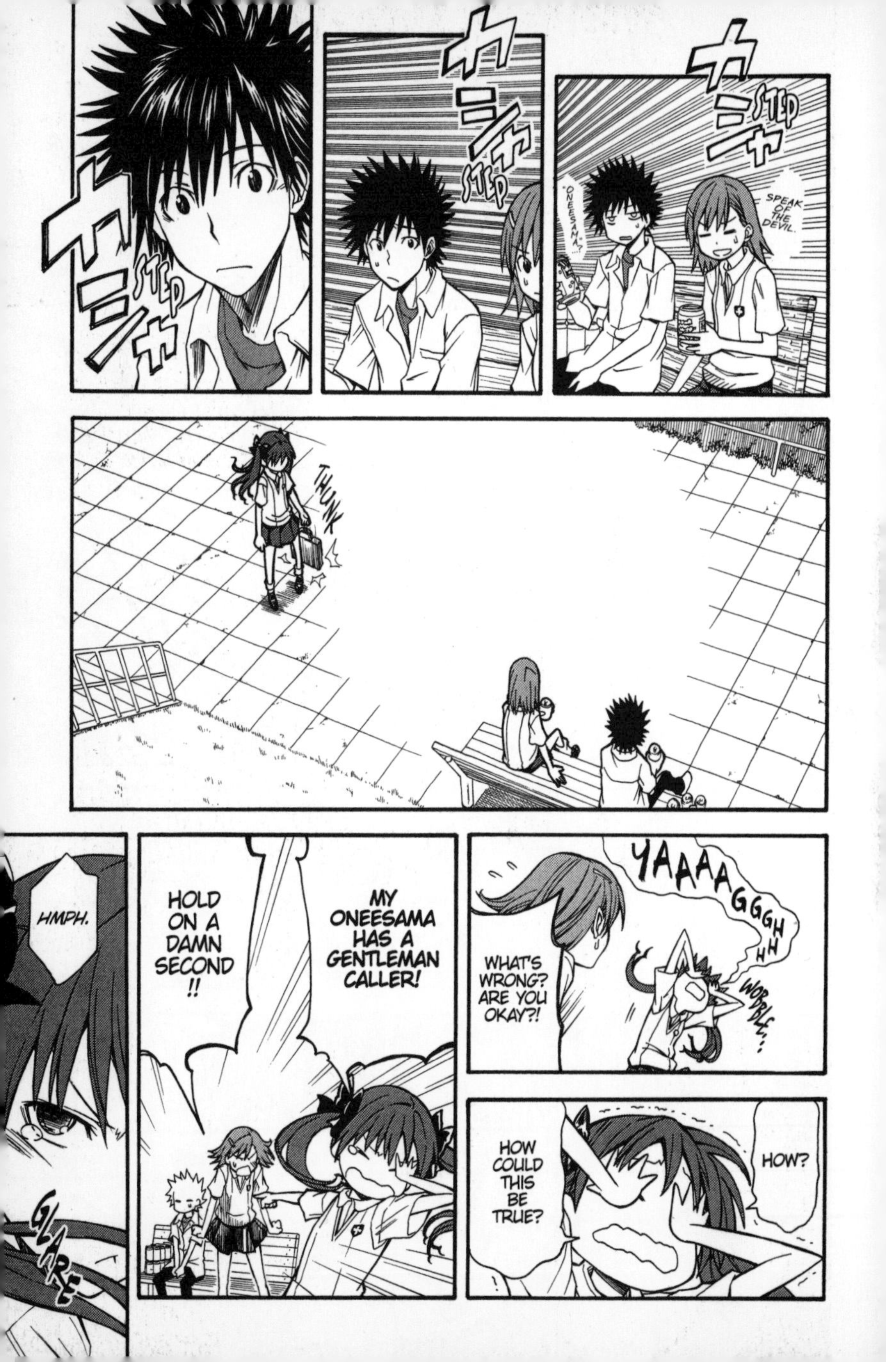

カシャ
STEP
SPEAK OF THE DEVIL.
"ONEESAMA"...?
カシャ
STEP
カシャ
STEP
THUNK
YAAAAGGGHHH
WHAT'S WRONG? ARE YOU OKAY?!
WOBBLE...
HOW?
HOW COULD THIS BE TRUE?
MY ONEESAMA HAS A GENTLEMAN CALLER!
HOLD ON A DAMN SECOND!!
HMPH.
GLARE

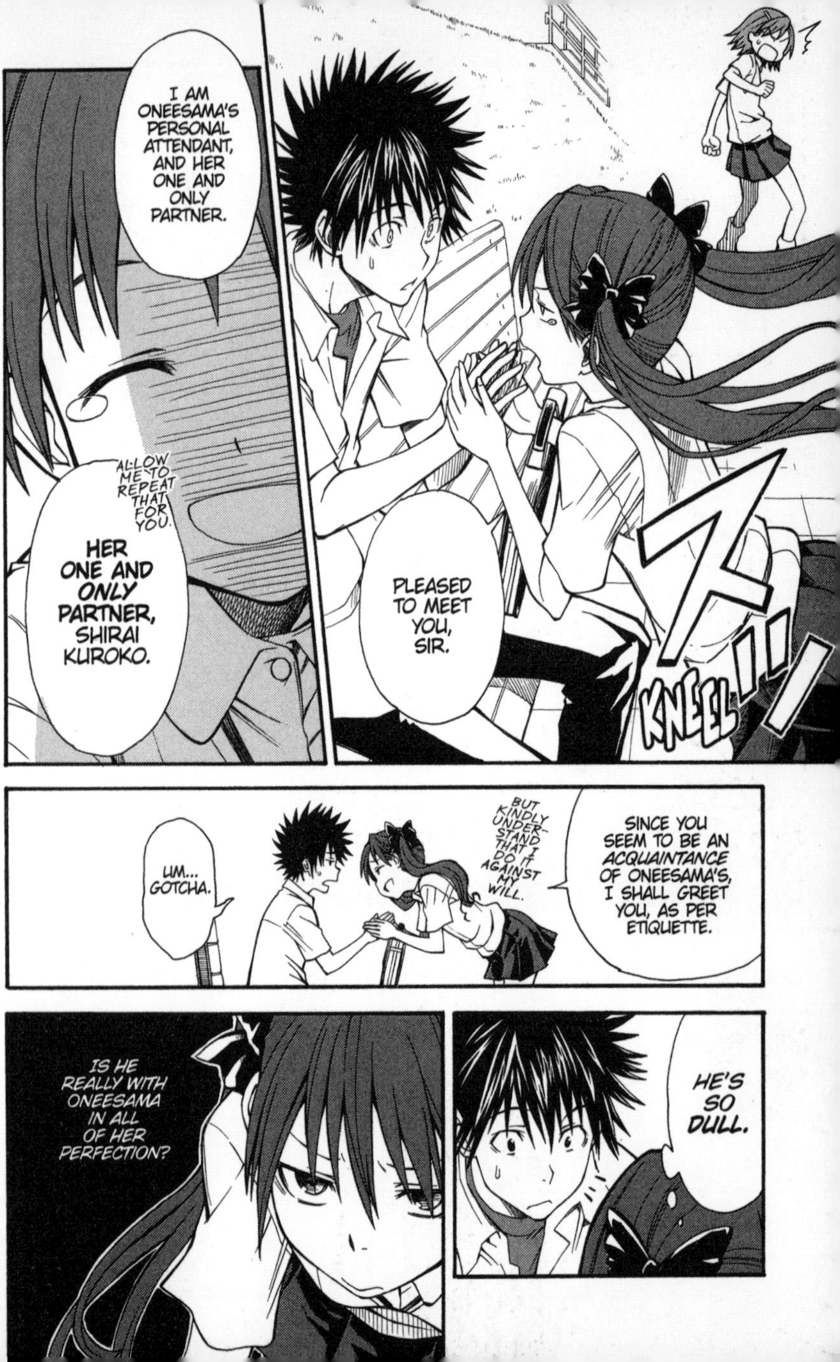
KNEEL!!
PLEASED TO MEET YOU, SIR.
I AM ONEESAMA'S PERSONAL ATTENDANT, AND HER ONE AND ONLY PARTNER.
ALLOW ME TO REPEAT THAT FOR YOU.
HER ONE AND ONLY PARTNER, SHIRAI KUROKO.
SINCE YOU SEEM TO BE AN ACQUAINTANCE OF ONEESAMA'S, I SHALL GREET YOU, AS PER ETIQUETTE.
BUT KINDLY UNDER-STAND THAT I DO IT AGAINST MY WILL.
UM... GOTCHA.
HE'S SO DULL.
IS HE REALLY WITH ONEESAMA IN ALL OF HER PERFECTION?

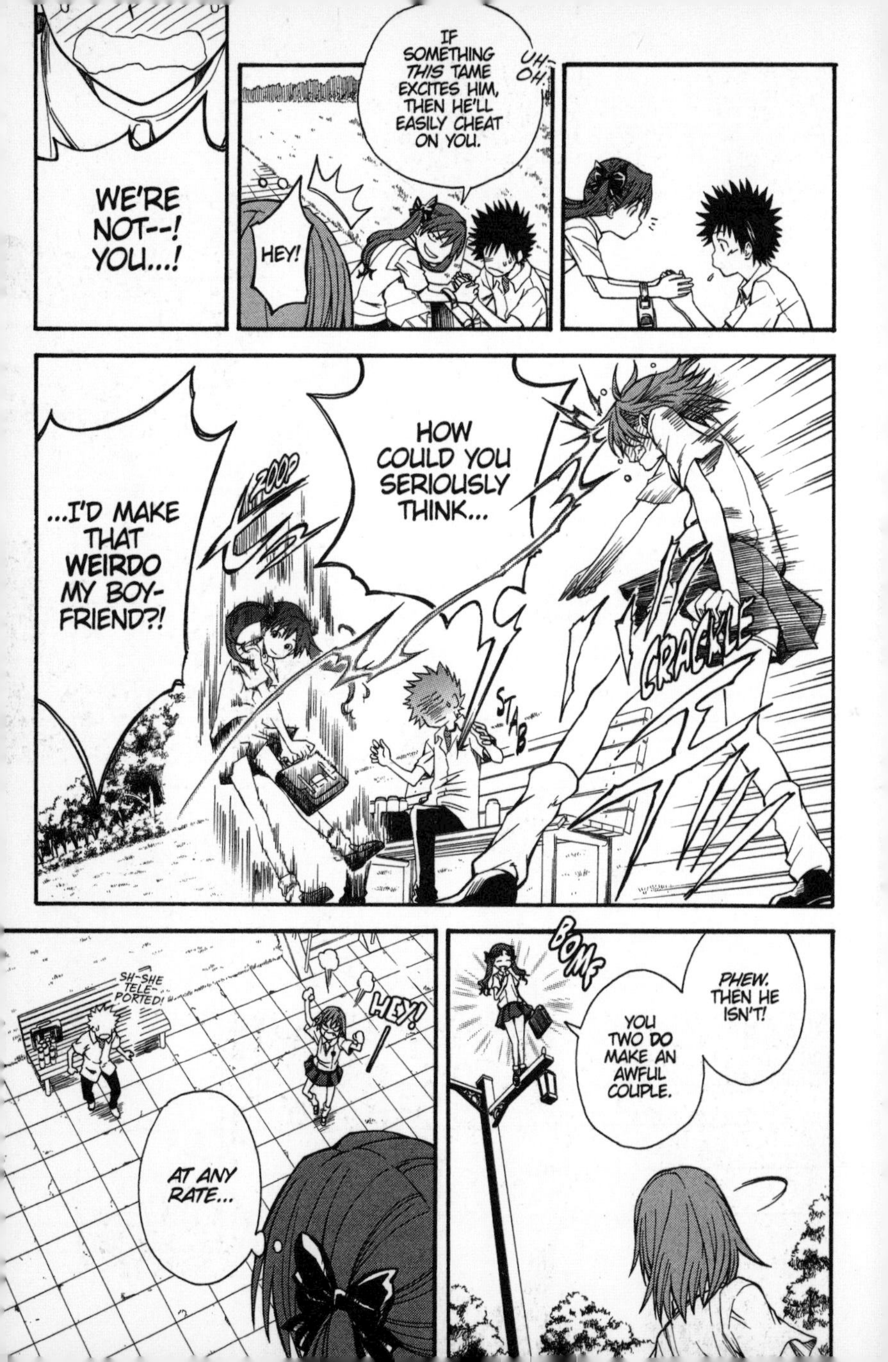
UH-OH.
IF SOMETHING THIS TAME EXCITES HIM, THEN HE'LL EASILY CHEAT ON YOU.
HEY!
WE'RE NOT--! YOU...!
HOW COULD YOU SERIOUSLY THINK...
CRACKLE
STAB
ZOOP
...I'D MAKE THAT WEIRDO MY BOY-FRIEND?!
BOMF
PHEW. THEN HE ISN'T!
YOU TWO DO MAKE AN AWFUL COUPLE.
HEY!
SH-SHE TELE-PORTED!
AT ANY RATE...

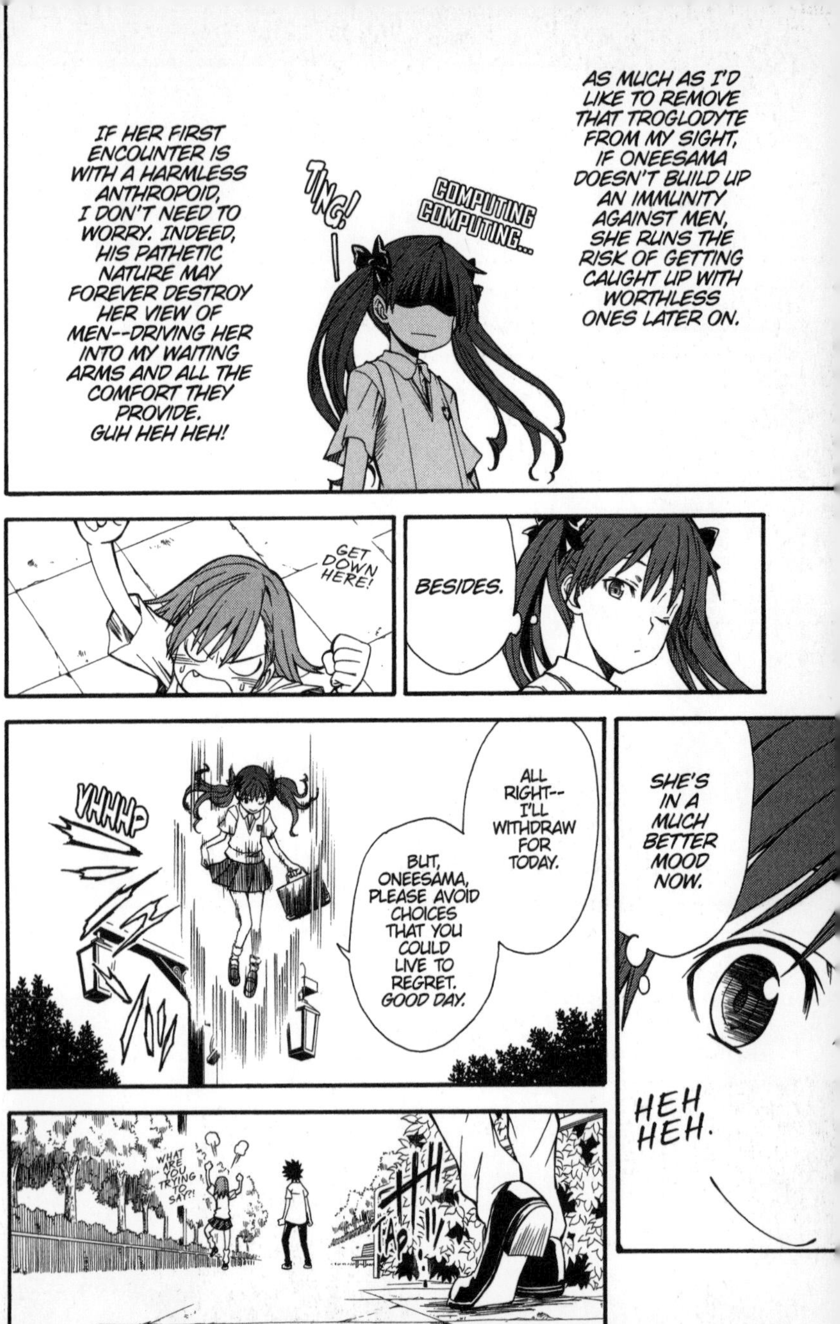
AS MUCH AS I'D LIKE TO REMOVE THAT TROGLODYTE FROM MY SIGHT, IF ONEESAMA DOESN'T BUILD UP AN IMMUNITY AGAINST MEN, SHE RUNS THE RISK OF GETTING CAUGHT UP WITH WORTHLESS ONES LATER ON.
COMPUTING COMPUTING...
TING!
IF HER FIRST ENCOUNTER IS WITH A HARMLESS ANTHROPOID, I DON'T NEED TO WORRY. INDEED, HIS PATHETIC NATURE MAY FOREVER DESTROY HER VIEW OF MEN--DRIVING HER INTO MY WAITING ARMS AND ALL THE COMFORT THEY PROVIDE. GUH HEH HEH!
BESIDES.
GET DOWN HERE!
SHE'S IN A MUCH BETTER MOOD NOW.
HEH HEH.
ALL RIGHT-- I'LL WITHDRAW FOR TODAY.
BUT, ONEESAMA, PLEASE AVOID CHOICES THAT YOU COULD LIVE TO REGRET. GOOD DAY.
YHHHP
TAP!!
WHAT ARE YOU TRYING TO SAY?!

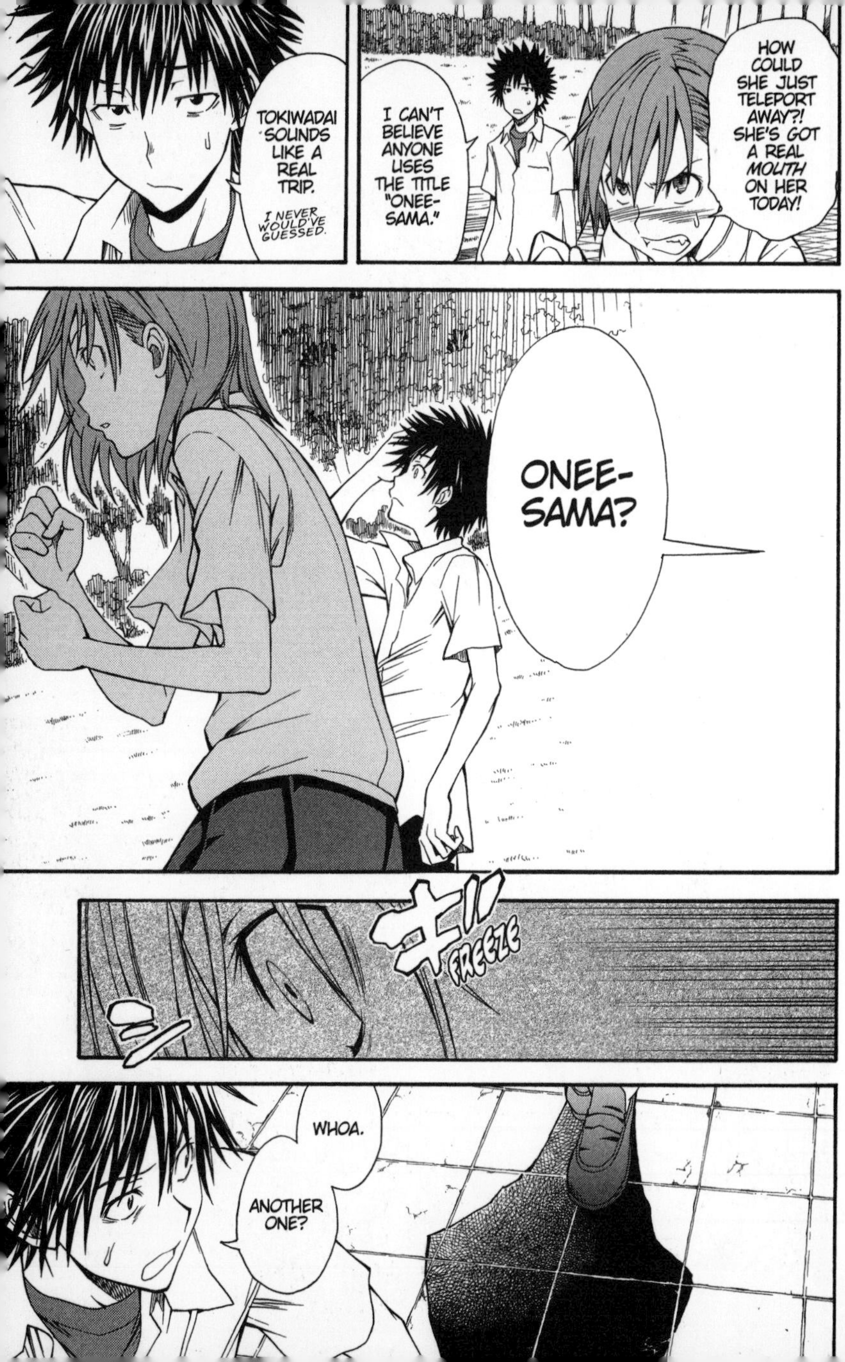
HOW COULD SHE JUST TELEPORT AWAY?! SHE'S GOT A REAL *MOUTH* ON HER TODAY!
I CAN'T BELIEVE ANYONE USES THE TITLE "ONEE-SAMA."
TOKIWADAI SOUNDS LIKE A REAL TRIP.
I NEVER WOULD'VE GUESSED.
ONEE-SAMA?
FREEZE
WHOA.
ANOTHER ONE?

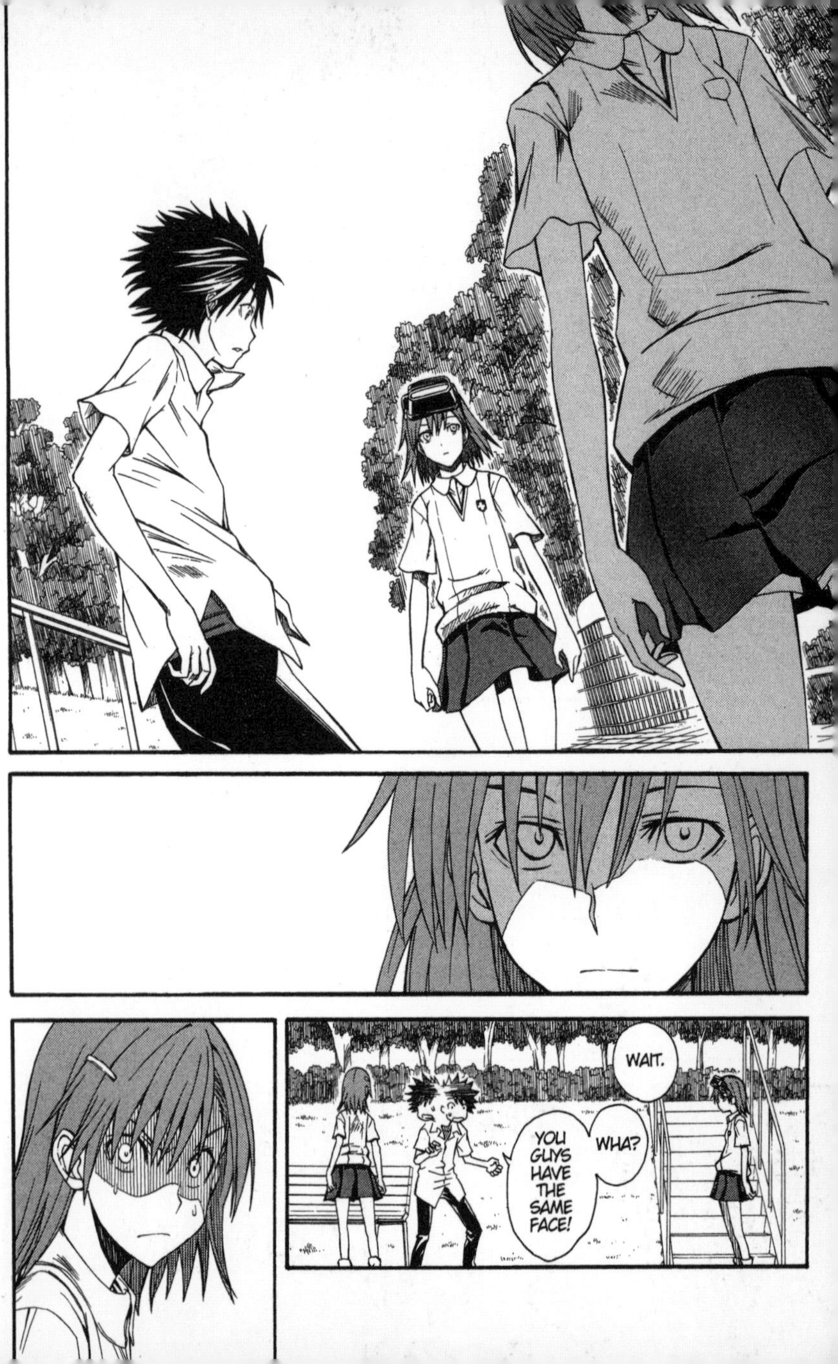
WAIT.
WHA?
YOU GUYS HAVE THE SAME FACE!

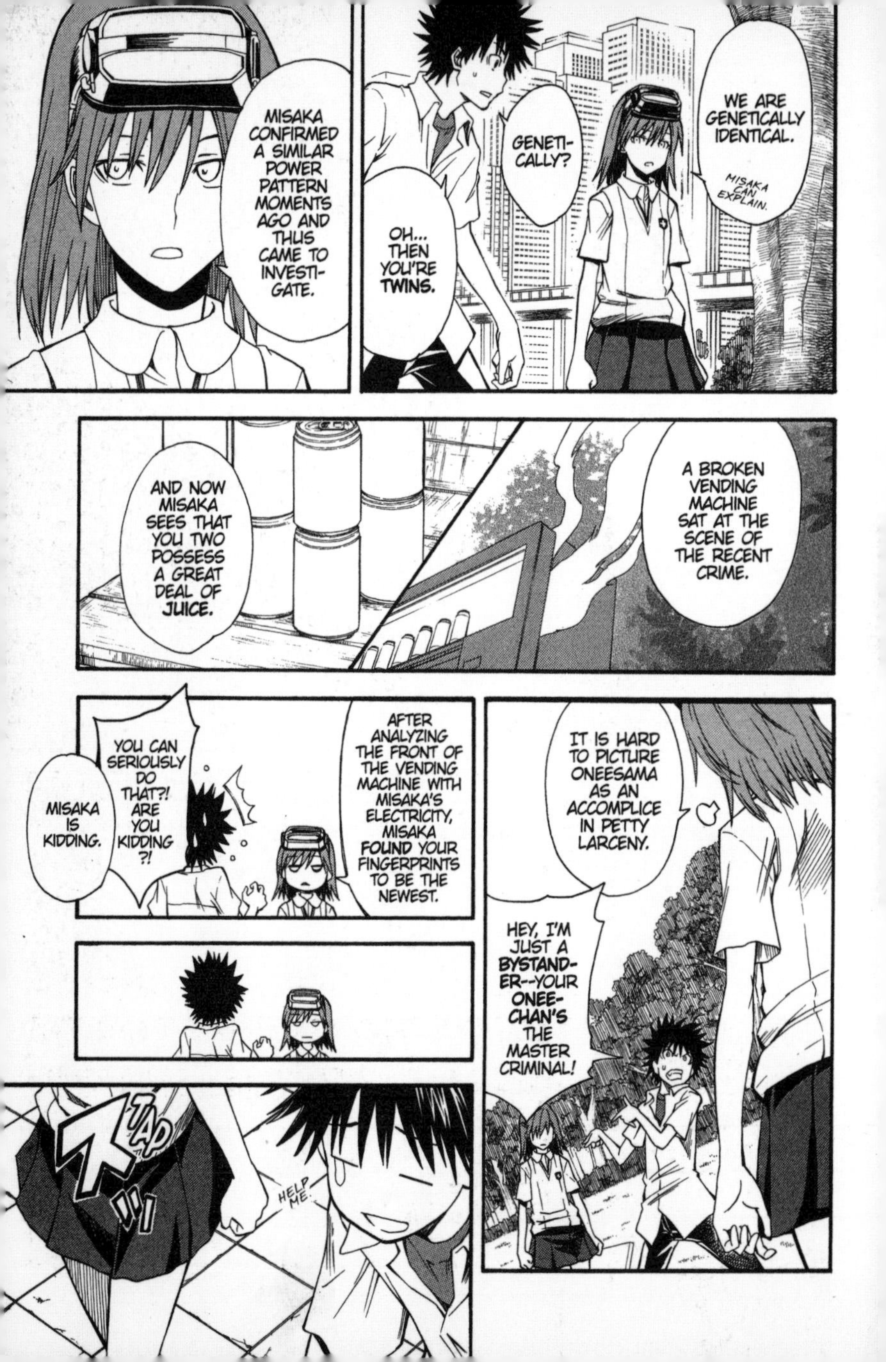
WE ARE GENETICALLY IDENTICAL.
MISAKA CAN EXPLAIN.
GENETI-CALLY?
OH... THEN YOU'RE TWINS.
MISAKA CONFIRMED A SIMILAR POWER PATTERN MOMENTS AGO AND THUS CAME TO INVESTI-GATE.
A BROKEN VENDING MACHINE SAT AT THE SCENE OF THE RECENT CRIME.
AND NOW MISAKA SEES THAT YOU TWO POSSESS A GREAT DEAL OF JUICE.
IT IS HARD TO PICTURE ONEESAMA AS AN ACCOMPLICE IN PETTY LARCENY.
HEY, I'M JUST A BYSTAND-ER--YOUR ONEE-CHAN'S THE MASTER CRIMINAL!
AFTER ANALYZING THE FRONT OF THE VENDING MACHINE WITH MISAKA'S ELECTRICITY, MISAKA FOUND YOUR FINGERPRINTS TO BE THE NEWEST.
YOU CAN SERIOUSLY DO THAT?! ARE YOU KIDDING ?!
MISAKA IS KIDDING.
TAP
HELP ME.

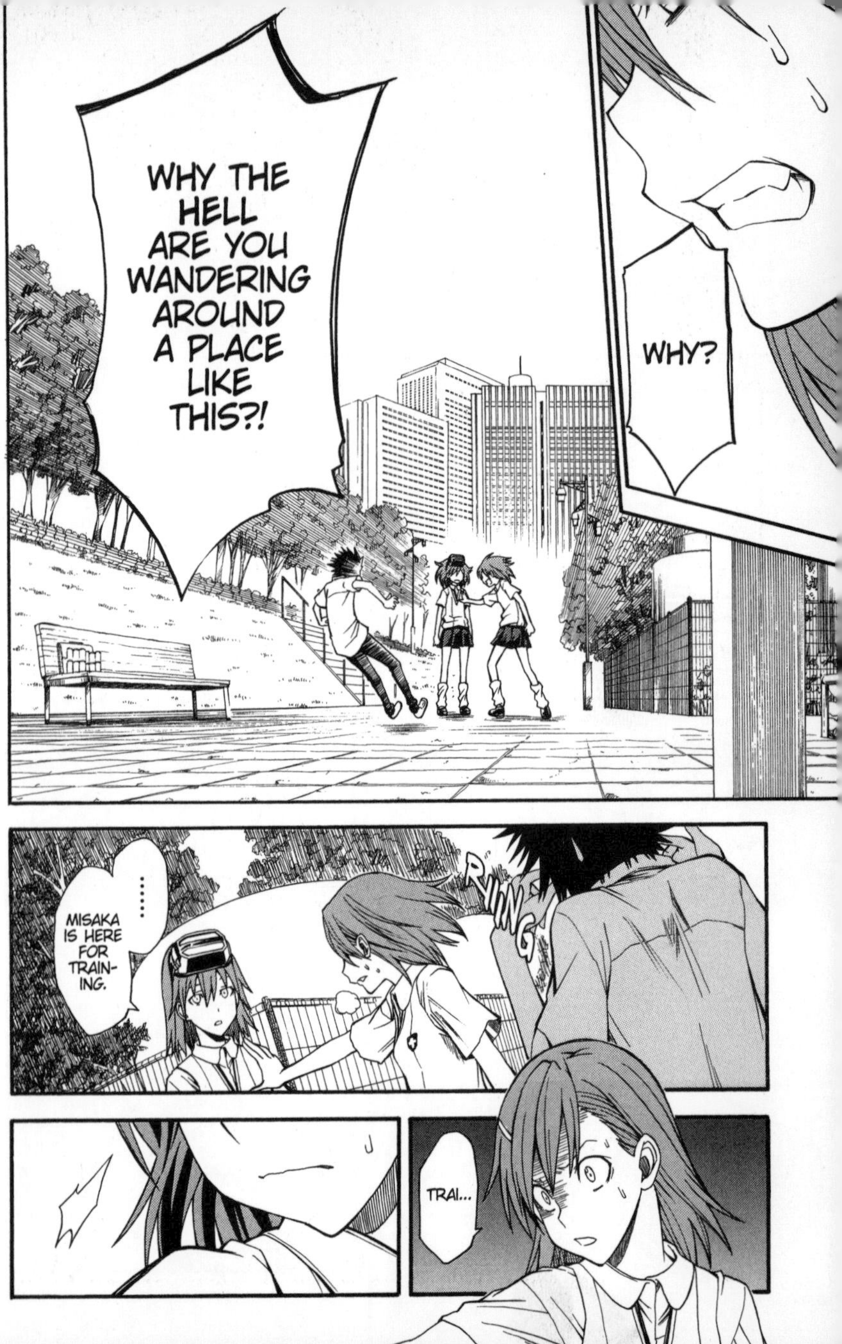
WHY?
WHY THE HELL ARE YOU WANDERING AROUND A PLACE LIKE THIS?!
RYING
......
MISAKA IS HERE FOR TRAIN-ING.
TRAI...

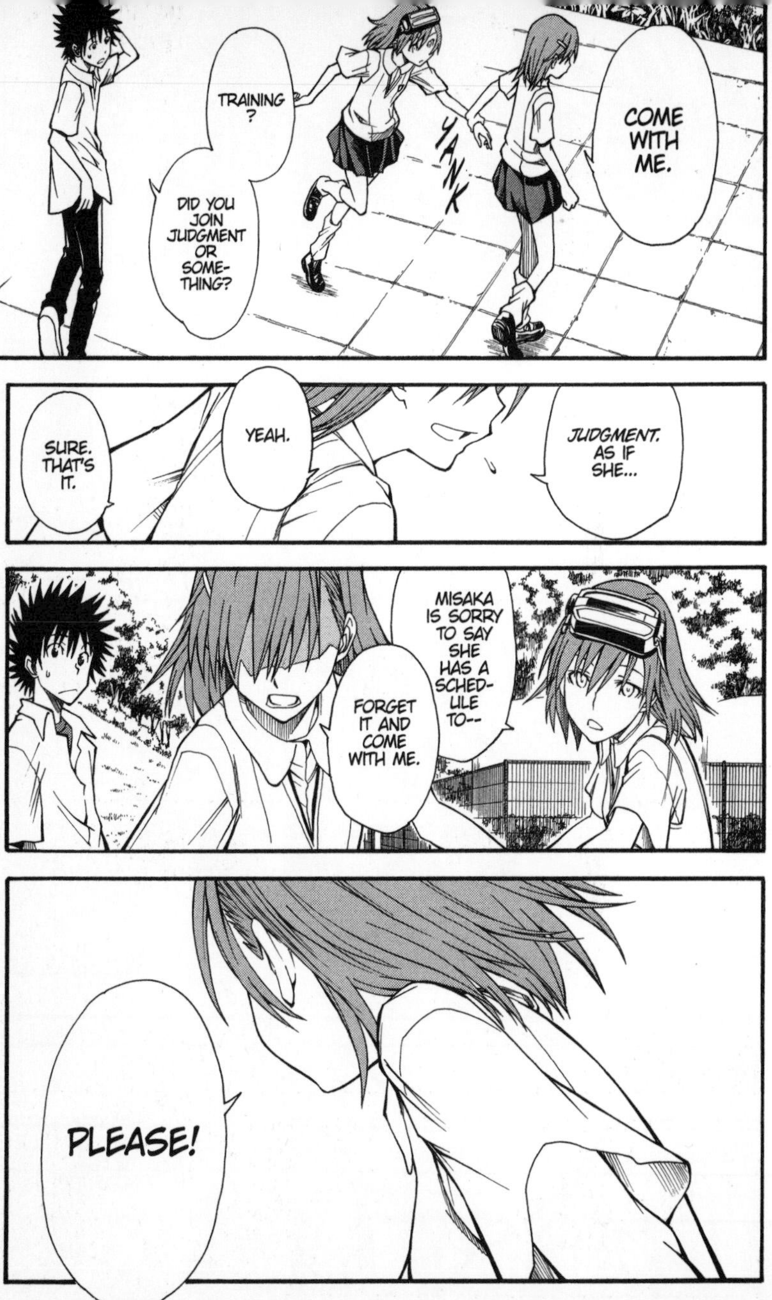
COME WITH ME.
YANK
TRAINING?
DID YOU JOIN JUDGMENT OR SOME-THING?
JUDGMENT. AS IF SHE...
YEAH.
SURE. THAT'S IT.
MISAKA IS SORRY TO SAY SHE HAS A SCHED-ULE TO--
FORGET IT AND COME WITH ME.
PLEASE!

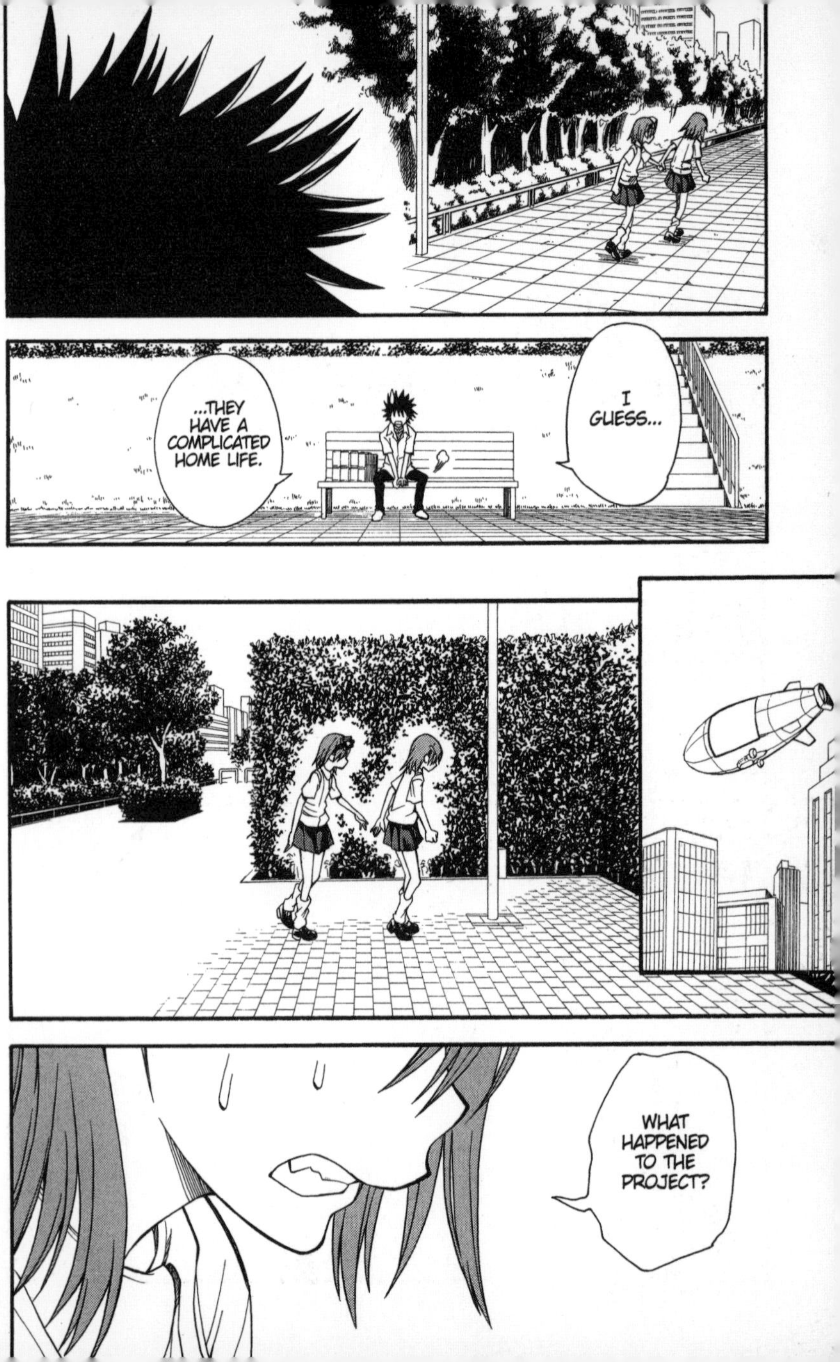
I GUESS...
...THEY HAVE A COMPLICATED HOME LIFE.
WHAT HAPPENED TO THE PROJECT?

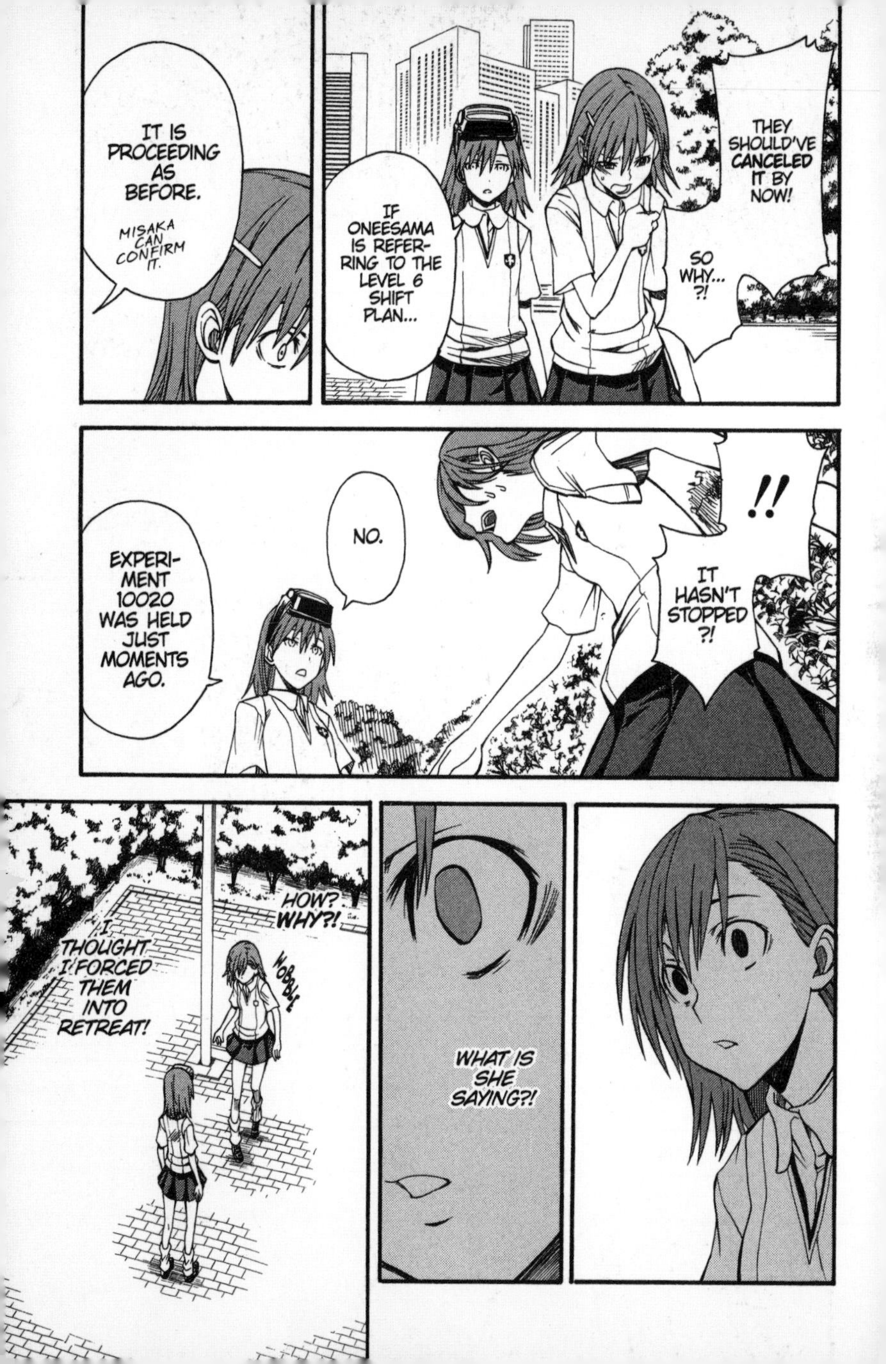
THEY SHOULD'VE CANCELED IT BY NOW!
SO WHY...?!
IF ONEESAMA IS REFERRING TO THE LEVEL 6 SHIFT PLAN...
IT IS PROCEEDING AS BEFORE.
MISAKA CAN CONFIRM IT.
!!
IT HASN'T STOPPED?!
NO.
EXPERIMENT 10020 WAS HELD JUST MOMENTS AGO.
WHAT IS SHE SAYING?!
HOW? WHY?!
WOBBLE
I THOUGHT I FORCED THEM INTO RETREAT!

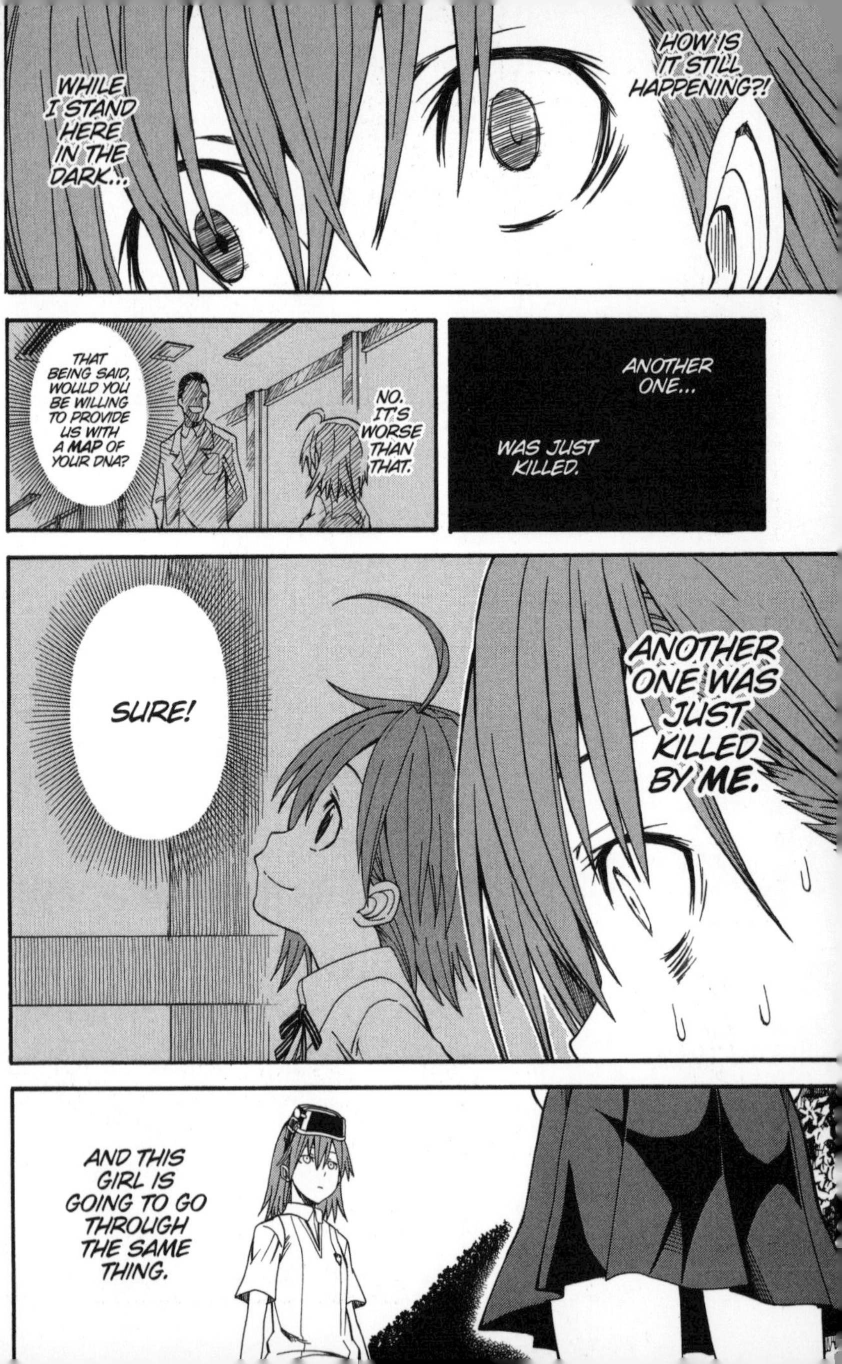
HOW IS IT STILL HAPPENING?!
WHILE I STAND HERE IN THE DARK...
ANOTHER ONE...
WAS JUST KILLED.
NO. IT'S WORSE THAN THAT.
THAT BEING SAID, WOULD YOU BE WILLING TO PROVIDE US WITH A MAP OF YOUR DNA?
ANOTHER ONE WAS JUST KILLED BY ME.
SURE!
AND THIS GIRL IS GOING TO GO THROUGH THE SAME THING.

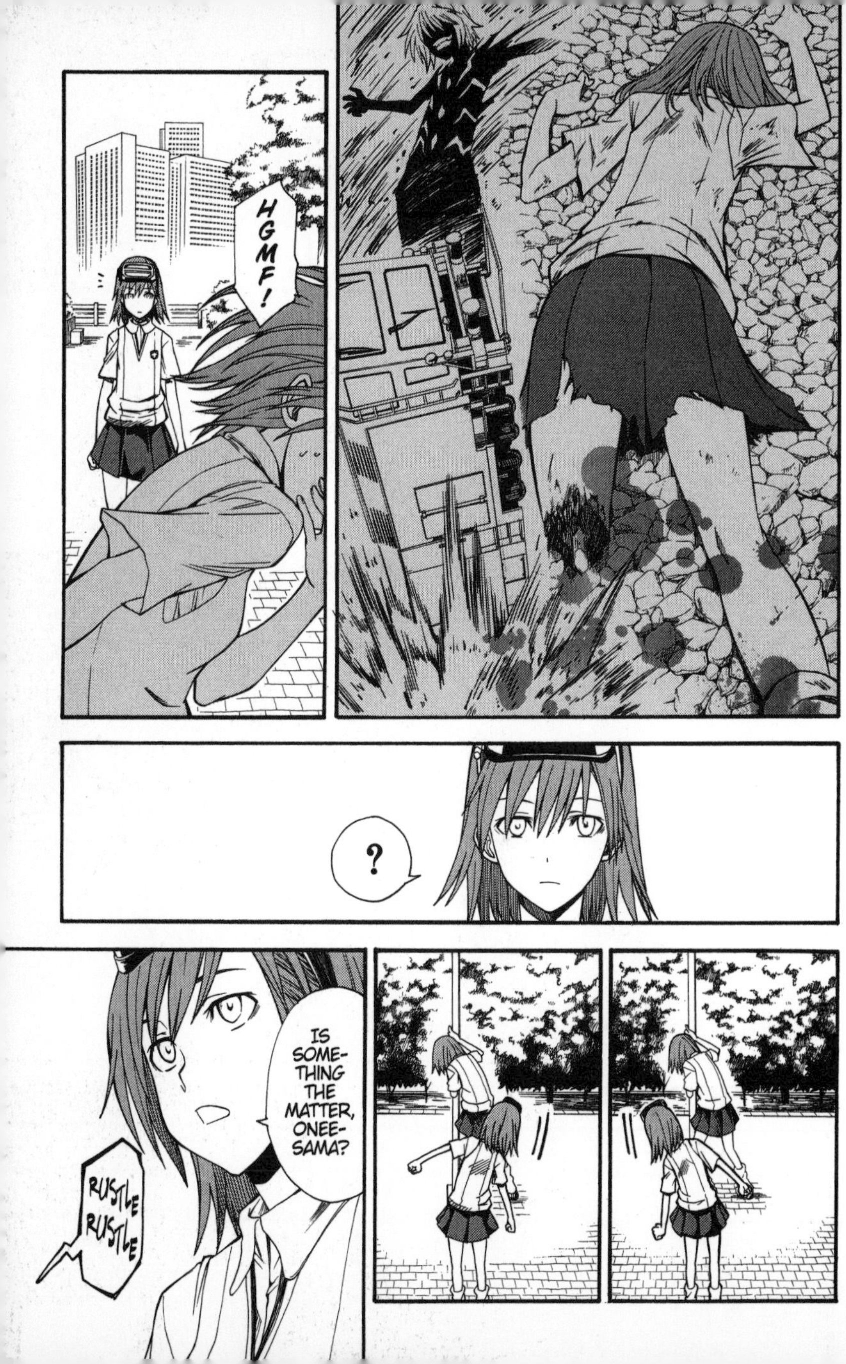
HGMF!
?
IS SOMETHING THE MATTER, ONEE-SAMA?
RUSTLE RUSTLE

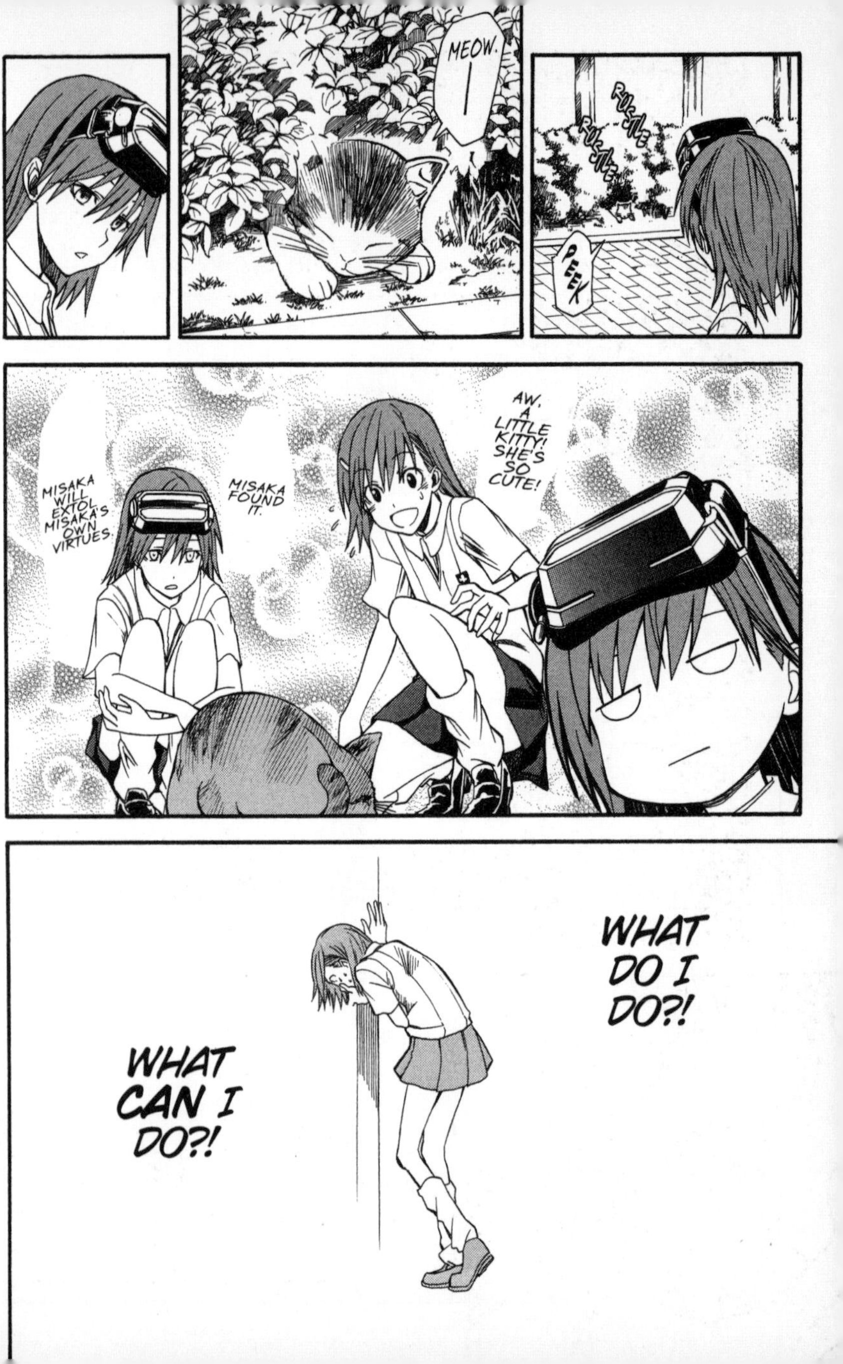
RUSTLE
RUSTLE
PEEK
MEOW.
AW, A LITTLE KITTY! SHE'S SO CUTE!
MISAKA FOUND IT.
MISAKA WILL EXTOL MISAKA'S OWN VIRTUES.
WHAT DO I DO?!
WHAT CAN I DO?!

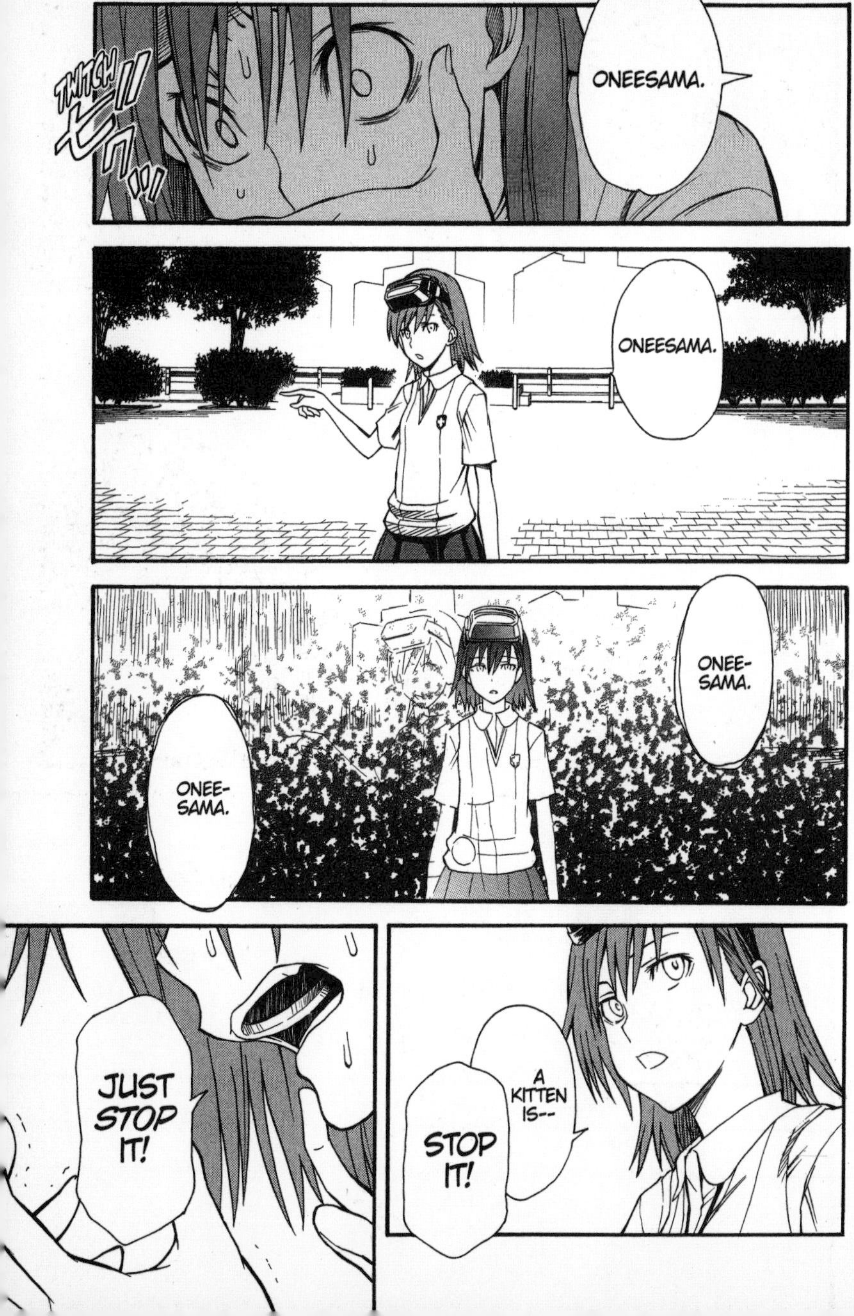
ONEESAMA.
TWITCH
ONEESAMA.
ONEE-SAMA.
ONEE-SAMA.
A KITTEN IS--
STOP IT!
JUST STOP IT!

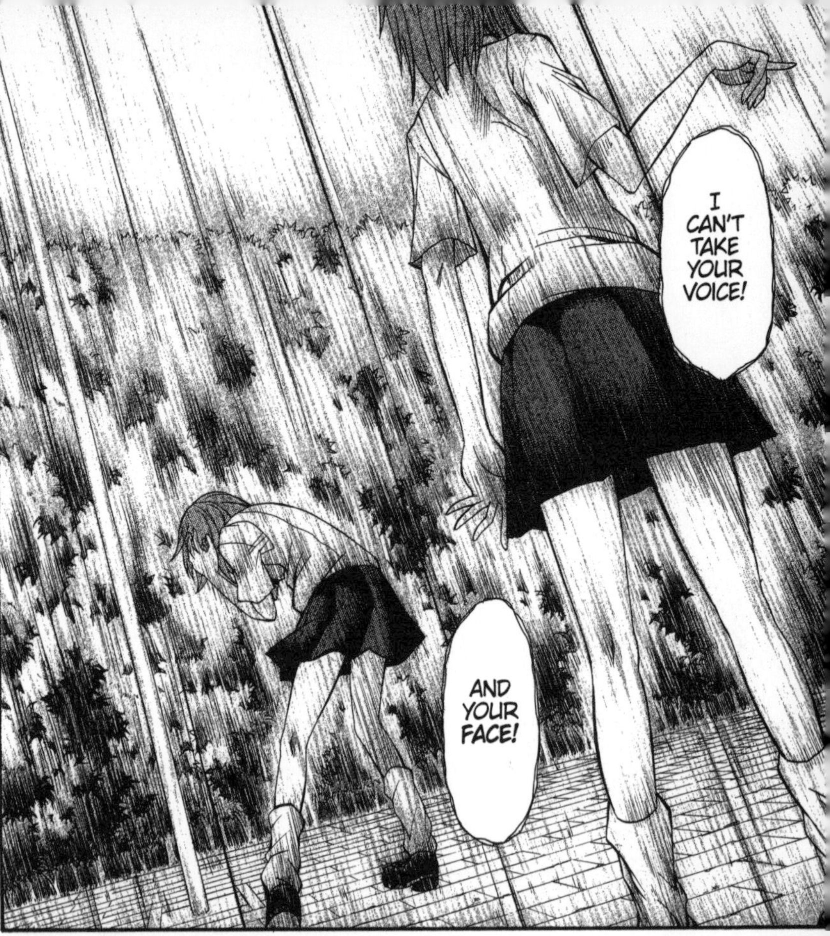
I CAN'T TAKE YOUR VOICE!
AND YOUR FACE!

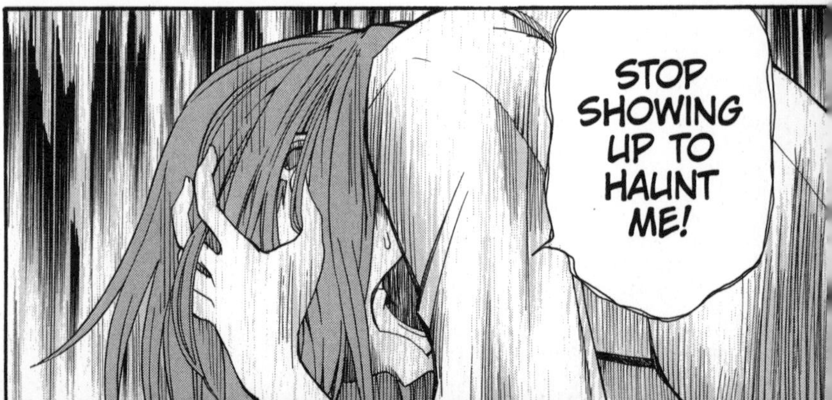
STOP SHOWING UP TO HAUNT ME!

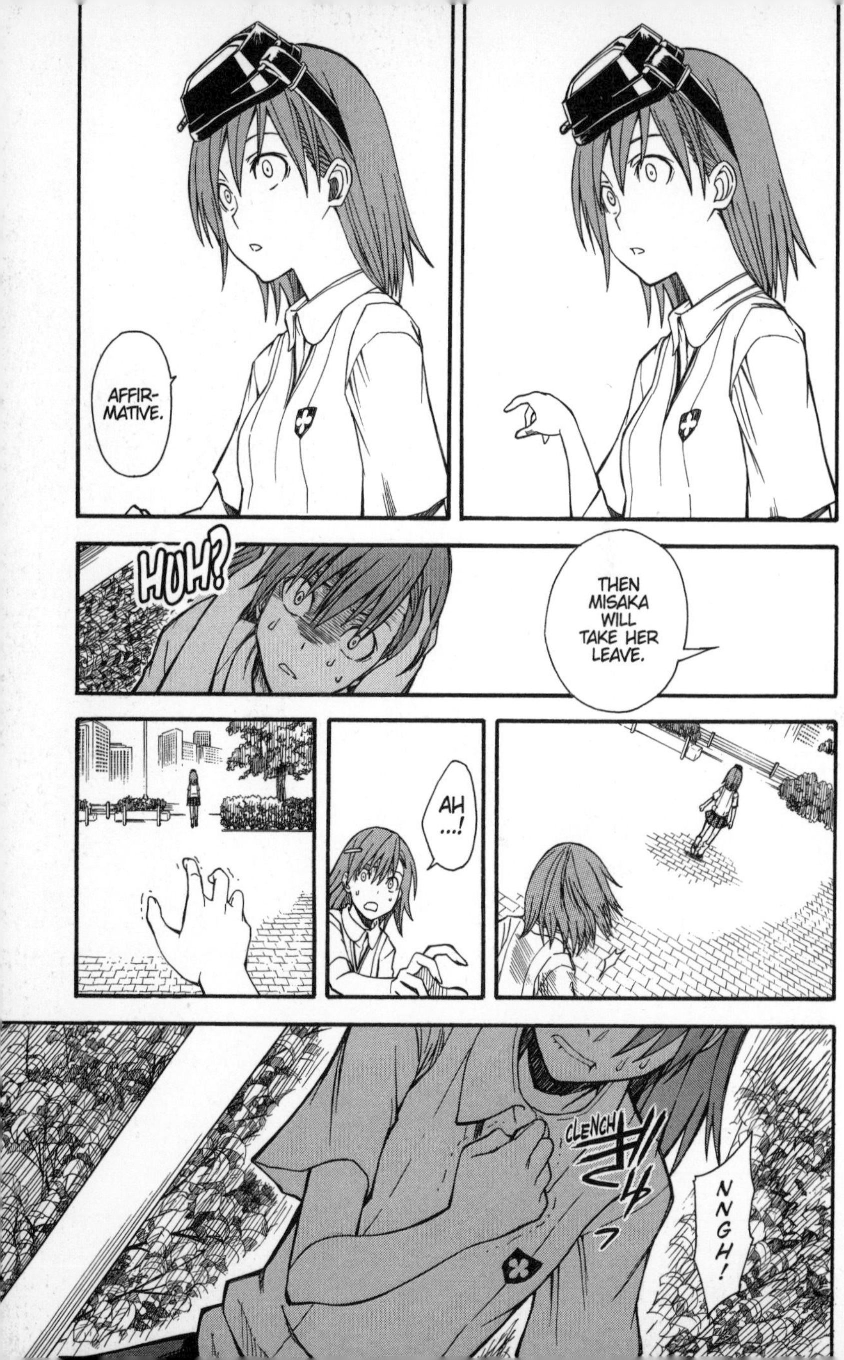
AFFIR-MATIVE.
THEN MISAKA WILL TAKE HER LEAVE.
HUH?
AH ...!
CLENCH
NNGH!

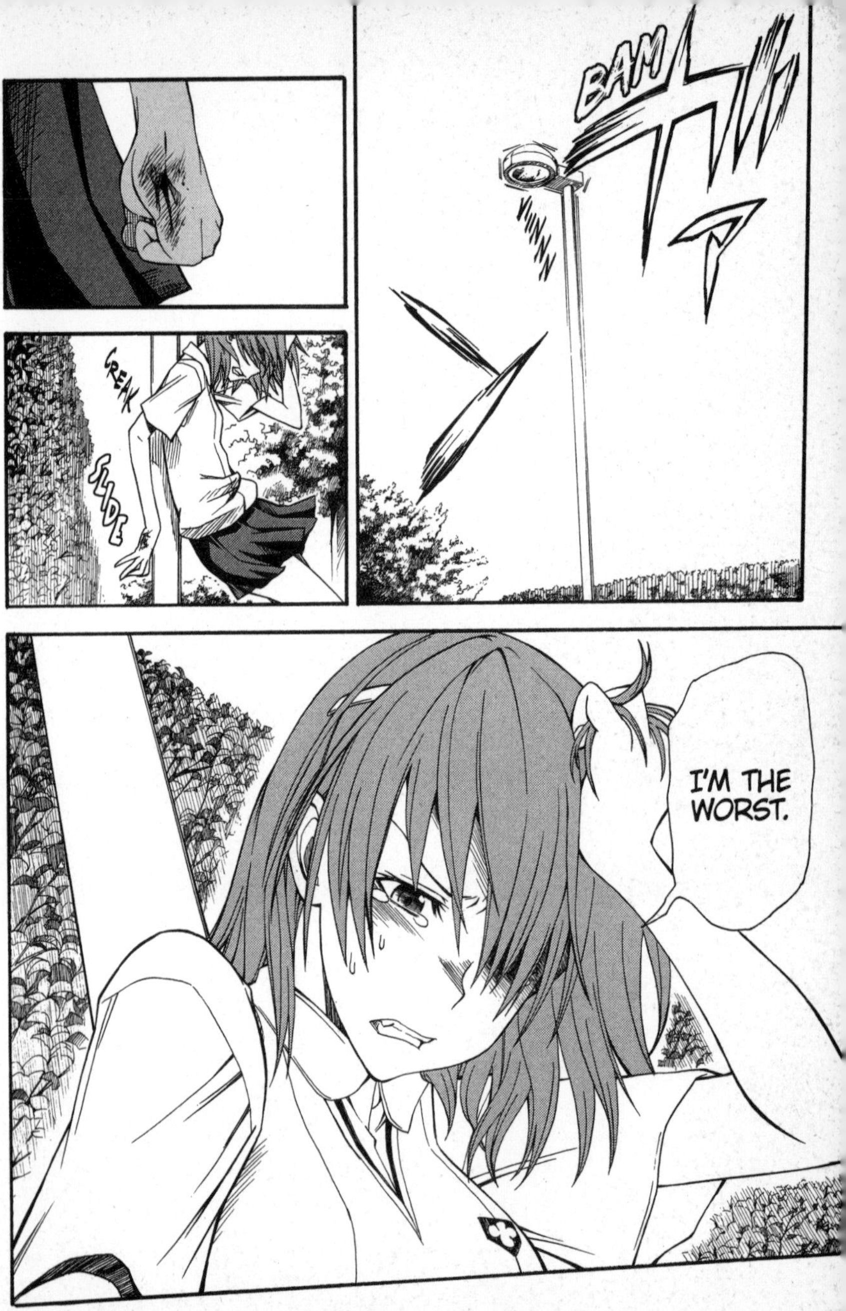
BAM
VIINNN
CREAK
SLIDE
I'M THE WORST.

A Certain
SCIENTIFIC
Railgun

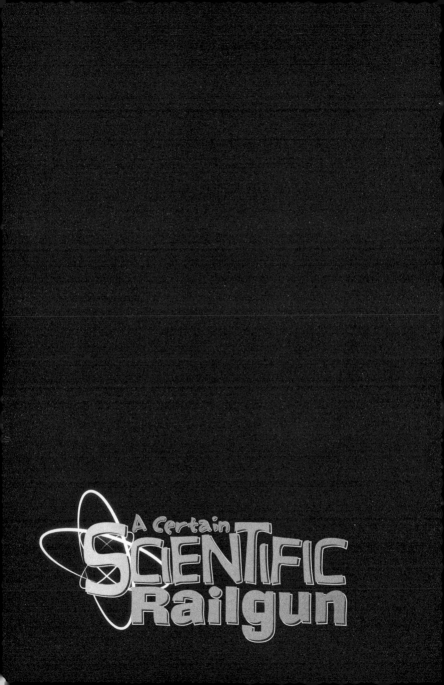

A Certain Boy's Proposal

IN THE CITY.
AND BY THE RIVER BED.
YOU'VE MESSED WITH ME REPEATEDLY!
HUH?
HANG ON--MESSED WITH HER? DOES SHE MEAN MESSED AROUND WITH HER? IF SHE'S THIS DIRECT, DOES THAT MEAN WE'RE INVOLVED?! BUT SHE JUST BLASTED ME WITH HER ELECTRICITY! UNLESS I CAME ON TOO STRONG OR SOMETHING... WHOA, WHOA! WHAT THE HELL HAVE I BEEN UP TO? IN THE CITY AND BY THE RIVER BED?! HOW COULD I TOUCH SOME MIDDLE SCHOOL KID?! I'M LIKE A PREDATOR! WHAT THE HELL DO I DO ABOUT IT?! IF I FOOLED AROUND WITH A LITTLE GIRL WITH A BRIGHT FUTURE AHEAD OF HER... I'VE GOTTA BE RESPONSIBLE. RESPONSIBLE.RESPONSIBLE.
HEY.
HELLO, DUFUS!
PUFF
PLEASE MARRY ME.
TWITCH
FUNYAA ?!

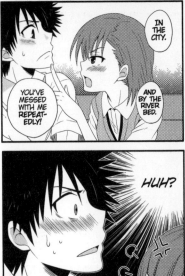

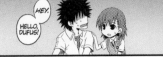

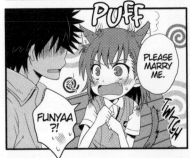

CHAPTER 32: AUGUST 20TH (2)

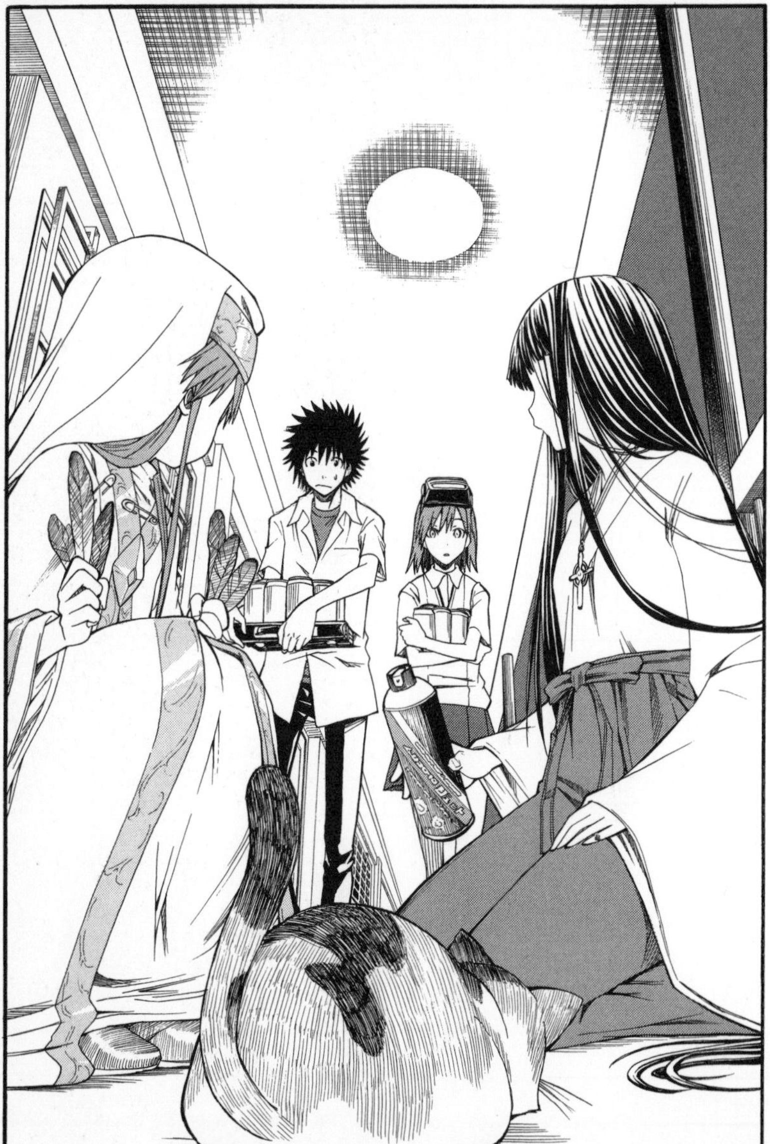

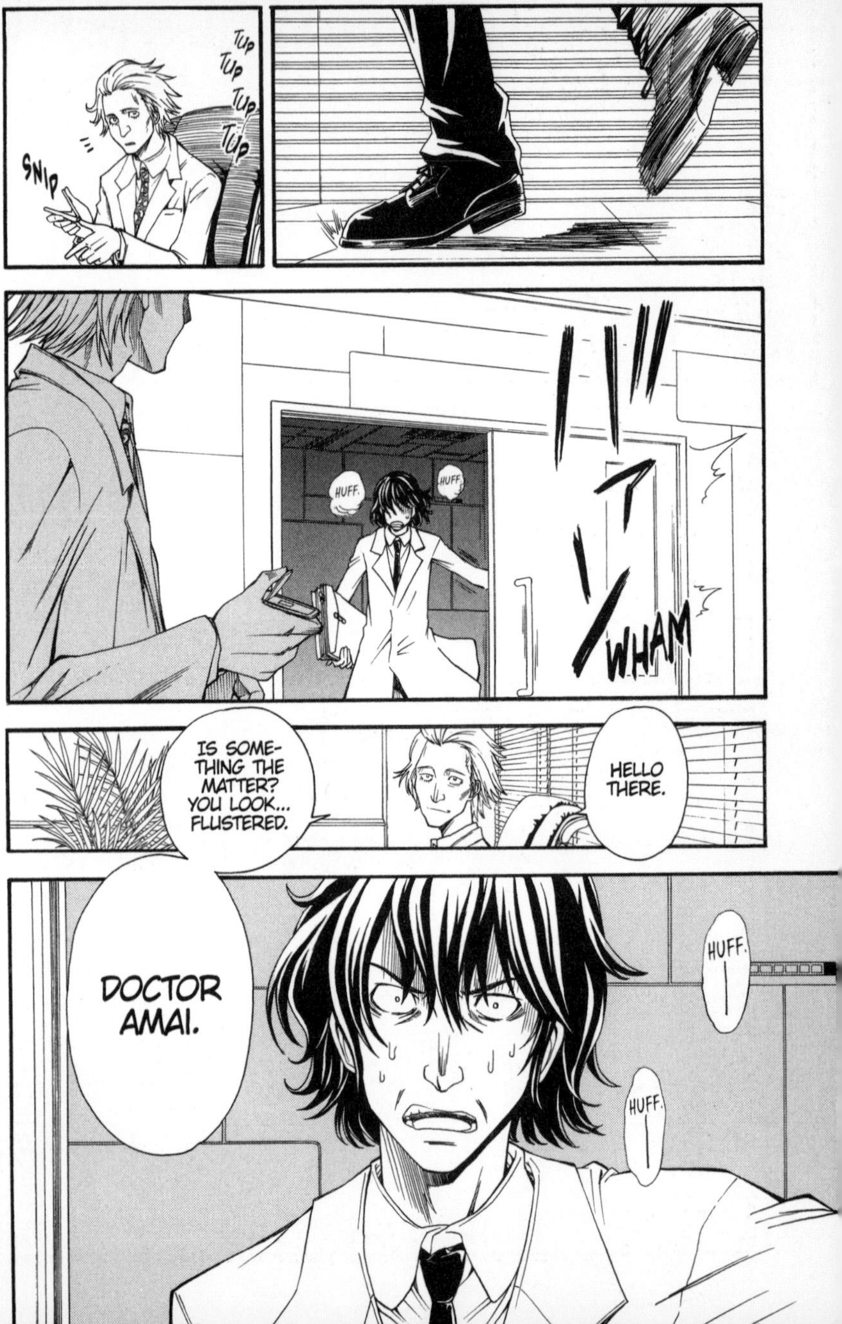
TUP
TUP
TUP
TUP
SNIP
HUFF.
HUFF.
WHAM
HELLO THERE.
IS SOMETHING THE MATTER? YOU LOOK... FLUSTERED.
HUFF.
HUFF.
DOCTOR AMAI.

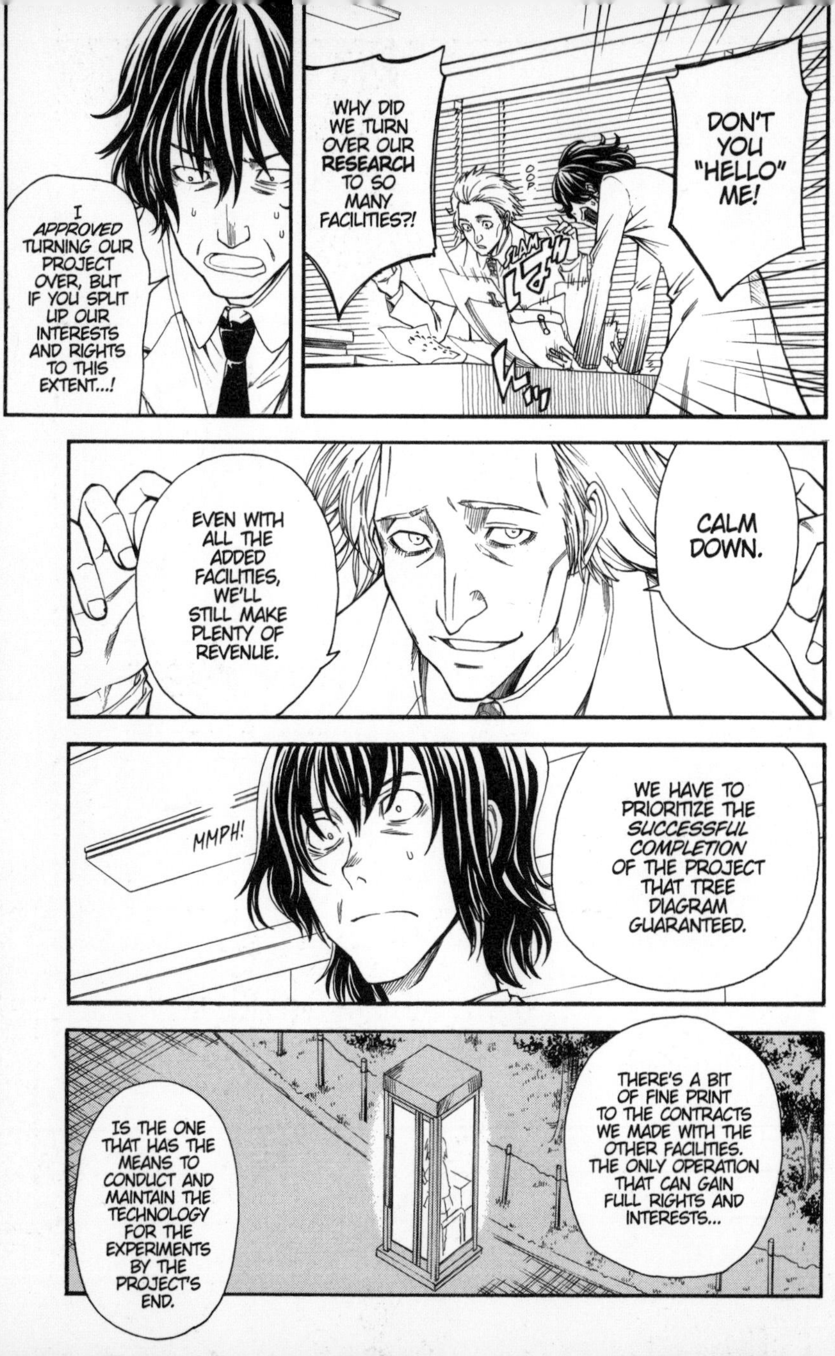
DON'T YOU "HELLO" ME!
WHY DID WE TURN OVER OUR RESEARCH TO SO MANY FACILITIES?!
OOP
SLAM
I APPROVED TURNING OUR PROJECT OVER, BUT IF YOU SPLIT UP OUR INTERESTS AND RIGHTS TO THIS EXTENT...!
CALM DOWN.
EVEN WITH ALL THE ADDED FACILITIES, WE'LL STILL MAKE PLENTY OF REVENUE.
WE HAVE TO PRIORITIZE THE SUCCESSFUL COMPLETION OF THE PROJECT THAT TREE DIAGRAM GUARANTEED.
MMPH!
THERE'S A BIT OF FINE PRINT TO THE CONTRACTS WE MADE WITH THE OTHER FACILITIES. THE ONLY OPERATION THAT CAN GAIN FULL RIGHTS AND INTERESTS...
IS THE ONE THAT HAS THE MEANS TO CONDUCT AND MAINTAIN THE TECHNOLOGY FOR THE EXPERIMENTS BY THE PROJECT'S END.

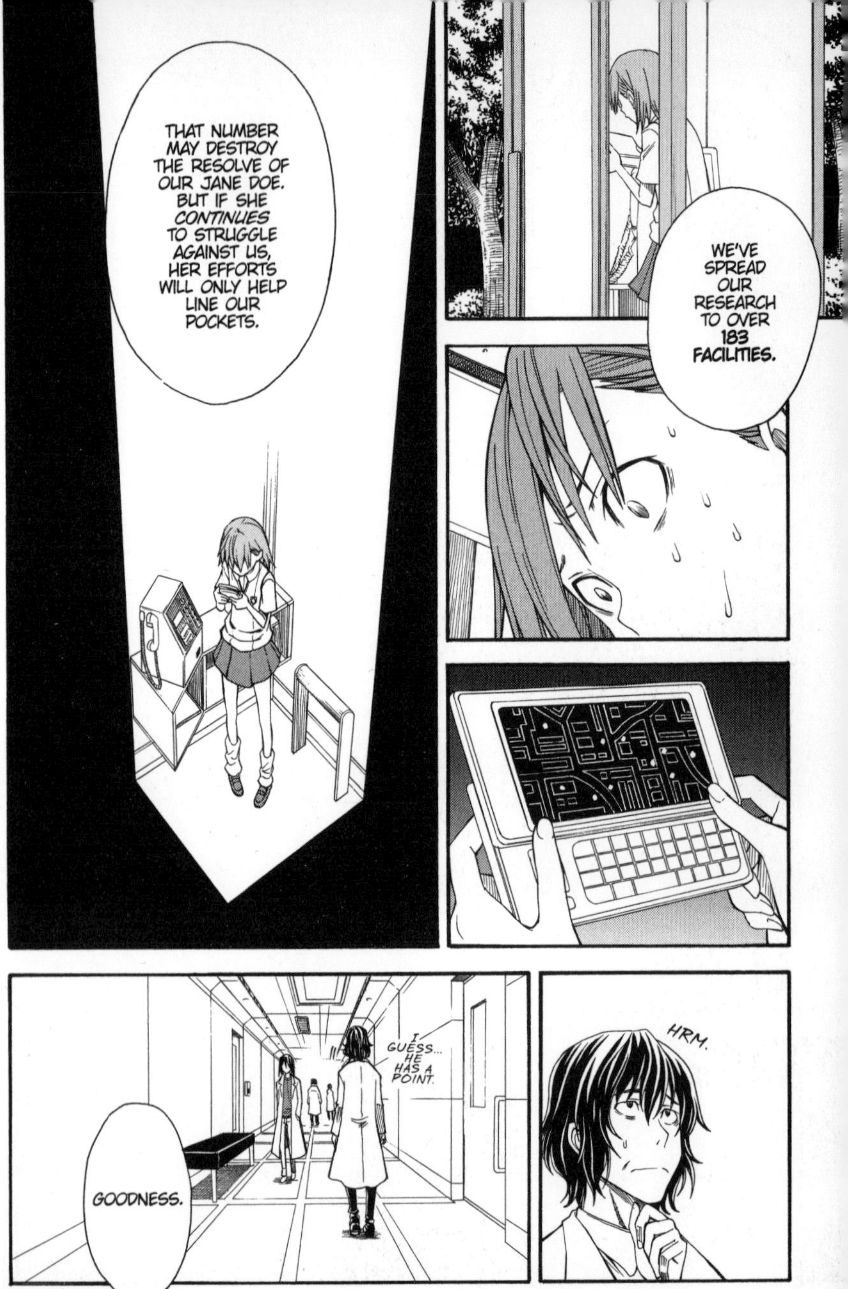

WE'VE SPREAD OUR RESEARCH TO OVER 183 FACILITIES.
THAT NUMBER MAY DESTROY THE RESOLVE OF OUR JANE DOE. BUT IF SHE *CONTINUES* TO STRUGGLE AGAINST US, HER EFFORTS WILL ONLY HELP LINE OUR POCKETS.
HRM.
I GUESS... HE HAS A POINT.
GOODNESS.

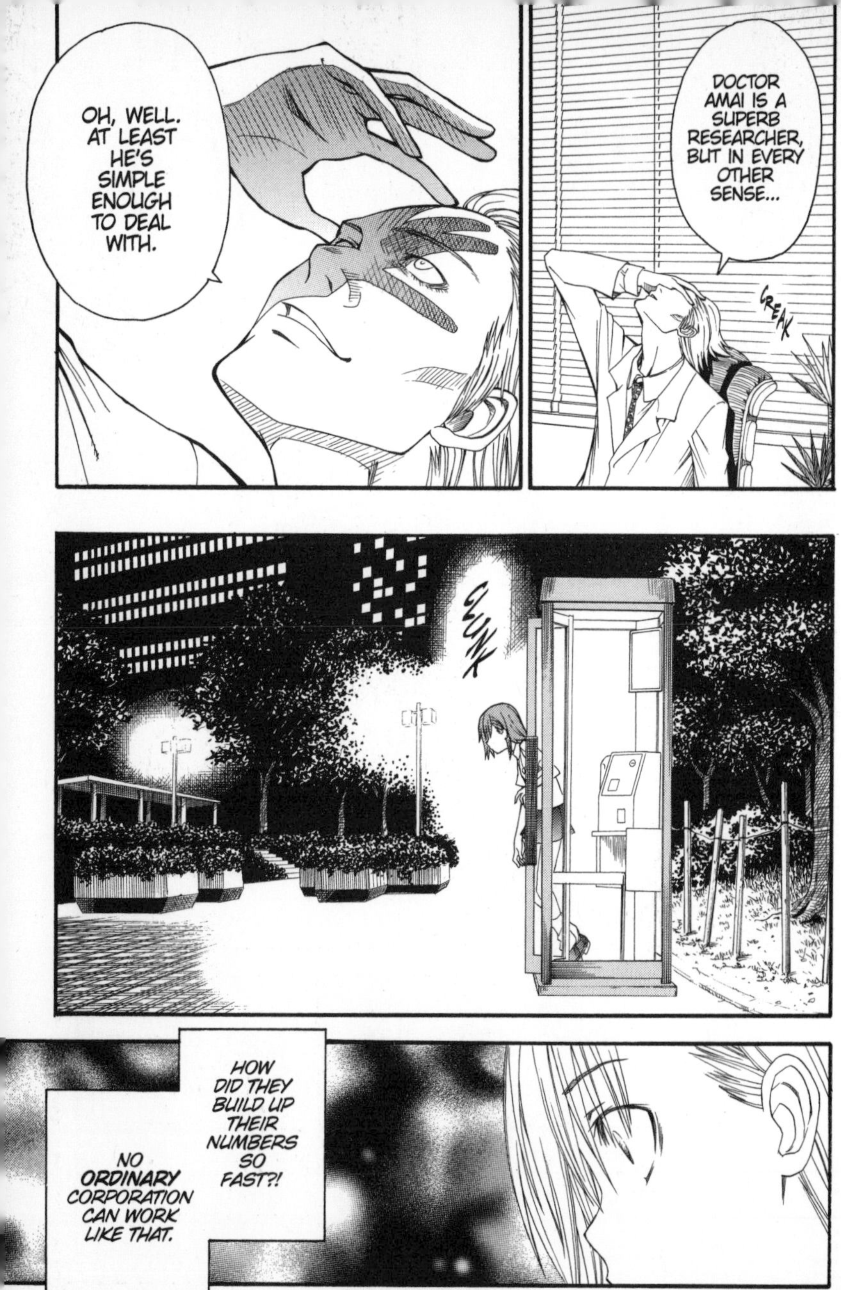
DOCTOR AMAI IS A SUPERB RESEARCHER, BUT IN EVERY OTHER SENSE...
CREAK
OH, WELL. AT LEAST HE'S SIMPLE ENOUGH TO DEAL WITH.
CLUNK
HOW DID THEY BUILD UP THEIR NUMBERS SO FAST?!
NO ORDINARY CORPORATION CAN WORK LIKE THAT.

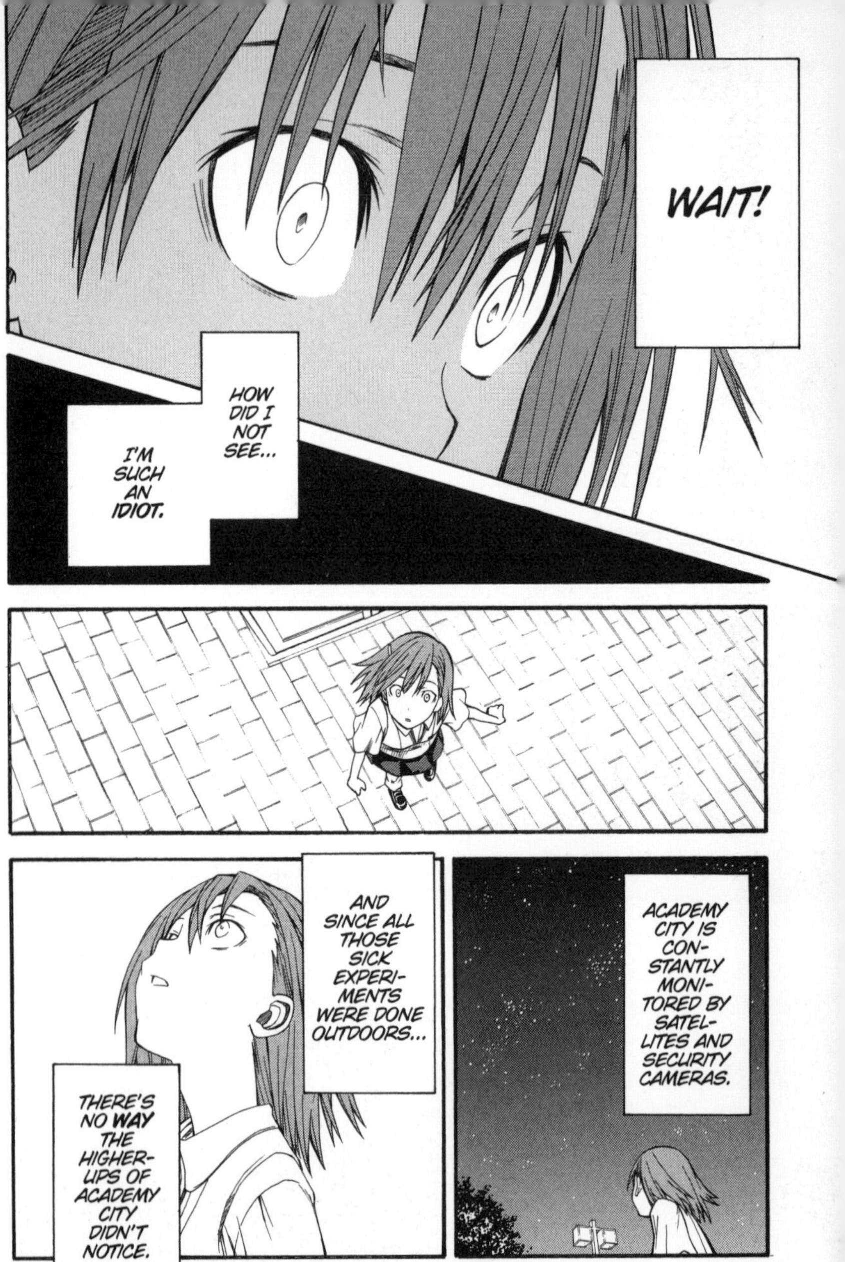
WAIT!
HOW DID I NOT SEE...
I'M SUCH AN IDIOT.
ACADEMY CITY IS CONSTANTLY MONITORED BY SATELLITES AND SECURITY CAMERAS.
AND SINCE ALL THOSE SICK EXPERIMENTS WERE DONE OUTDOORS...
THERE'S NO WAY THE HIGHER-UPS OF ACADEMY CITY DIDN'T NOTICE.

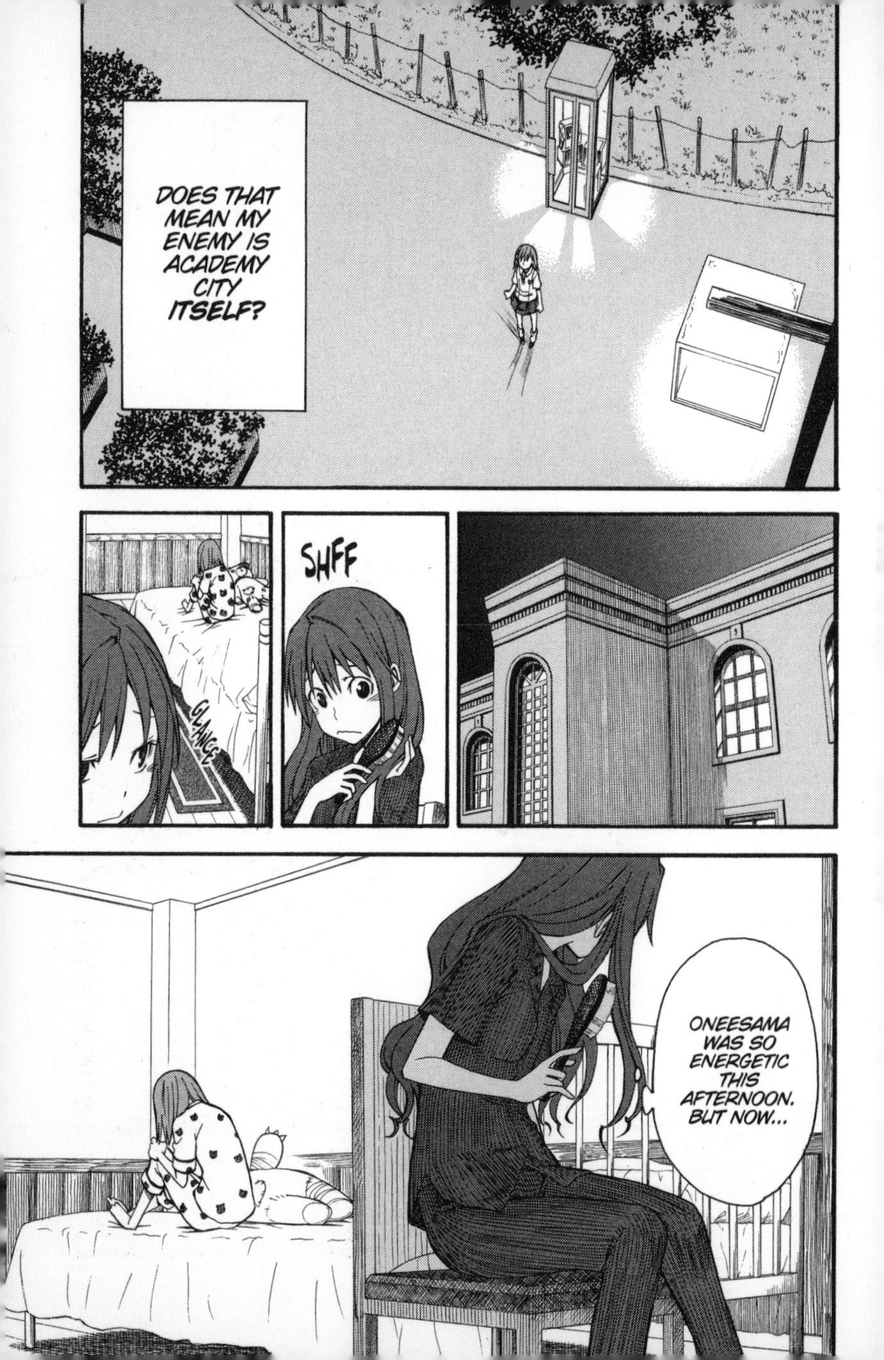
DOES THAT MEAN MY ENEMY IS ACADEMY CITY ITSELF?
SHFF
GLANCE
ONEESAMA WAS SO ENERGETIC THIS AFTERNOON. BUT NOW...

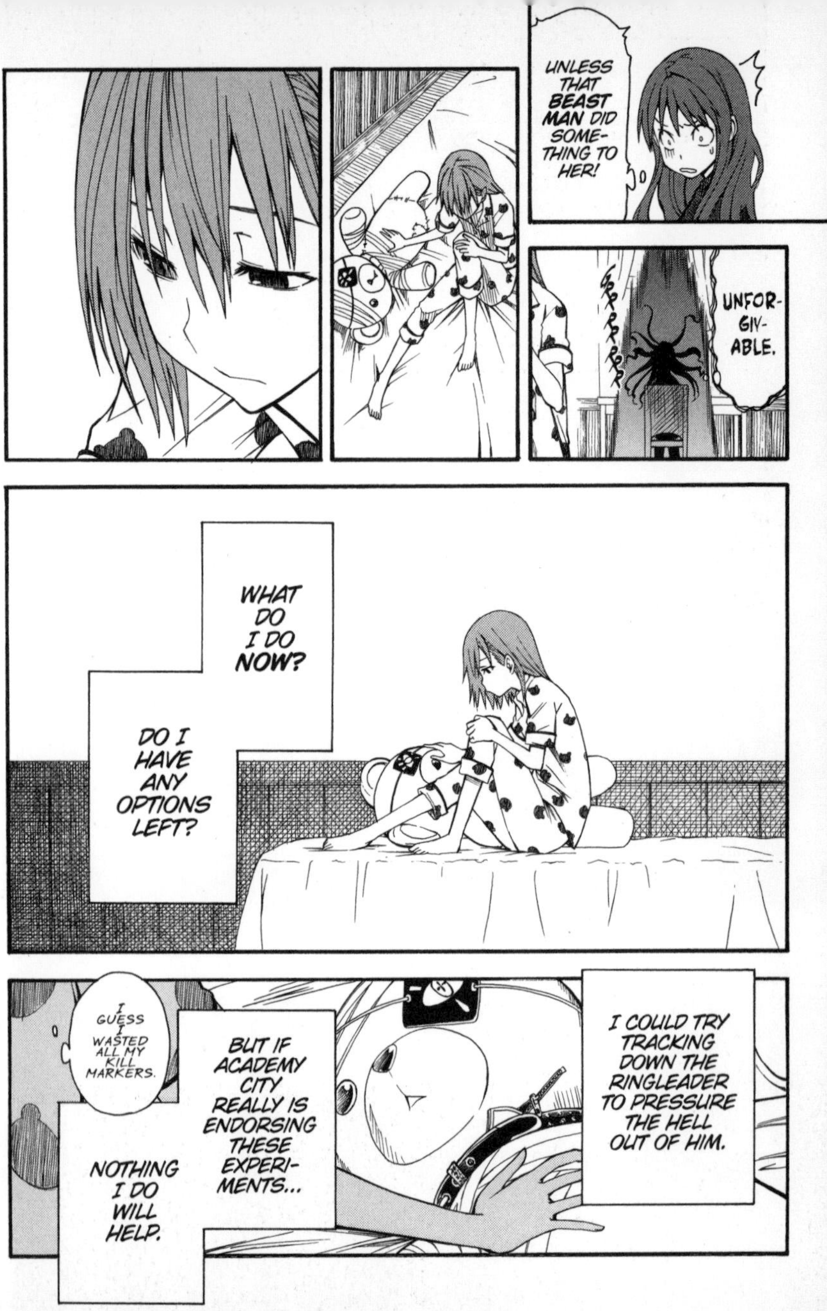
UNLESS THAT BEAST MAN DID SOME-THING TO HER!
GRRRRRR
UNFOR-GIV-ABLE.
WHAT DO I DO NOW?
DO I HAVE ANY OPTIONS LEFT?
I COULD TRY TRACKING DOWN THE RINGLEADER TO PRESSURE THE HELL OUT OF HIM.
BUT IF ACADEMY CITY REALLY IS ENDORSING THESE EXPERI-MENTS...
NOTHING I DO WILL HELP.
I GUESS I WASTED ALL MY KILL MARKERS.

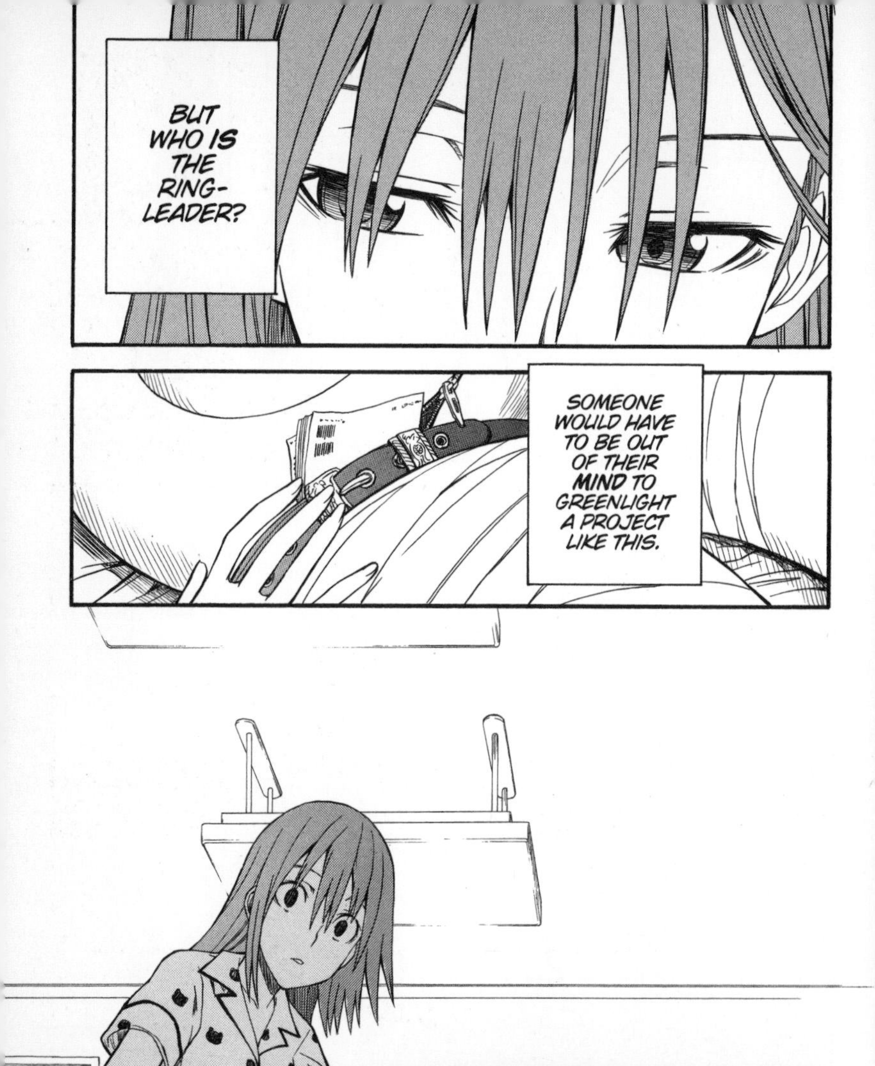
BUT WHO IS THE RING-LEADER?
SOMEONE WOULD HAVE TO BE OUT OF THEIR MIND TO GREENLIGHT A PROJECT LIKE THIS.

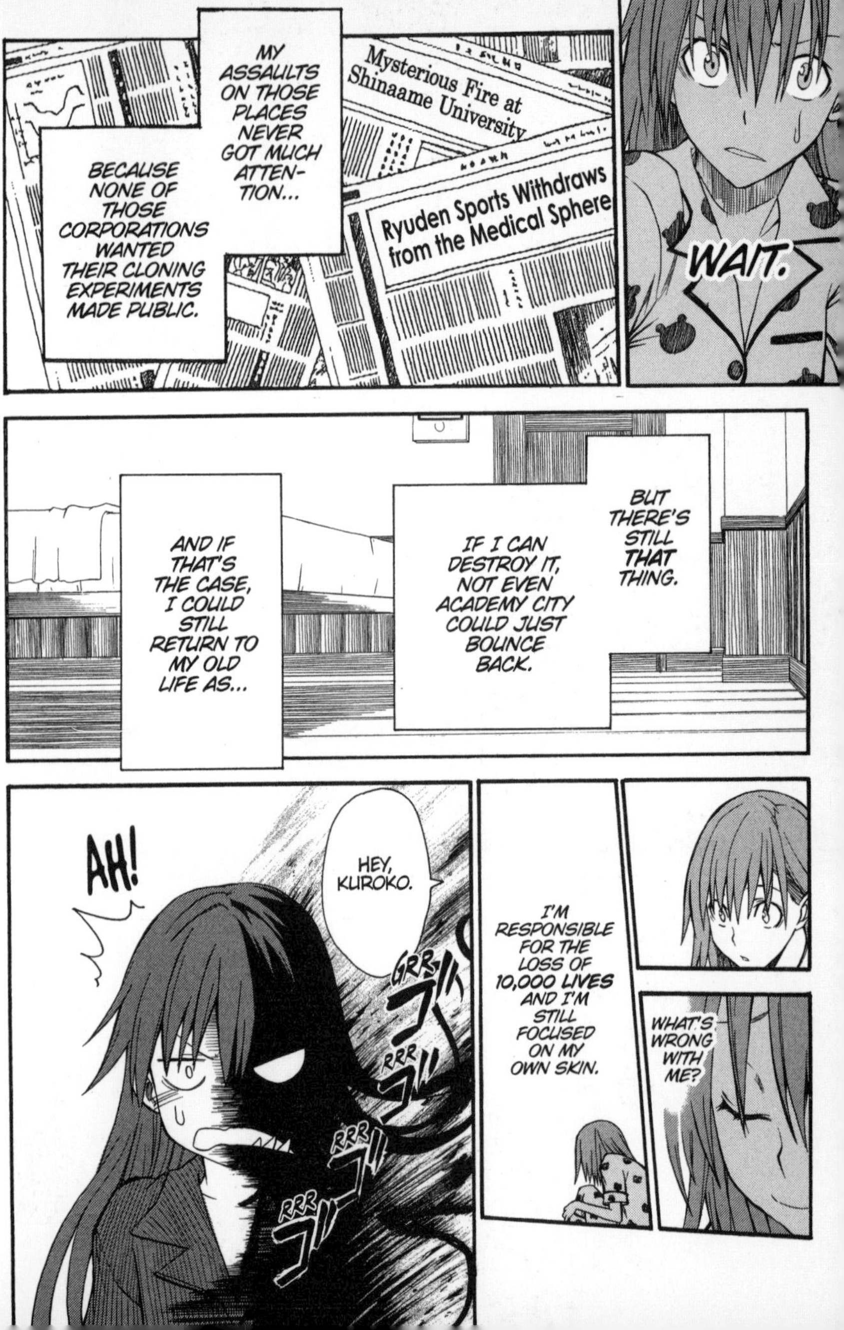
WAIT.
Mysterious Fire at Shinaame University
MY ASSAULTS ON THOSE PLACES NEVER GOT MUCH ATTEN-TION...
Ryuden Sports Withdraws from the Medical Sphere
BECAUSE NONE OF THOSE CORPORATIONS WANTED THEIR CLONING EXPERIMENTS MADE PUBLIC.
BUT THERE'S STILL THAT THING.
IF I CAN DESTROY IT, NOT EVEN ACADEMY CITY COULD JUST BOUNCE BACK.
AND IF THAT'S THE CASE, I COULD STILL RETURN TO MY OLD LIFE AS...
WHAT'S WRONG WITH ME?
I'M RESPONSIBLE FOR THE LOSS OF 10,000 LIVES AND I'M STILL FOCUSED ON MY OWN SKIN.
HEY, KUROKO.
AH!
GRR
RRR
RRR
RRR

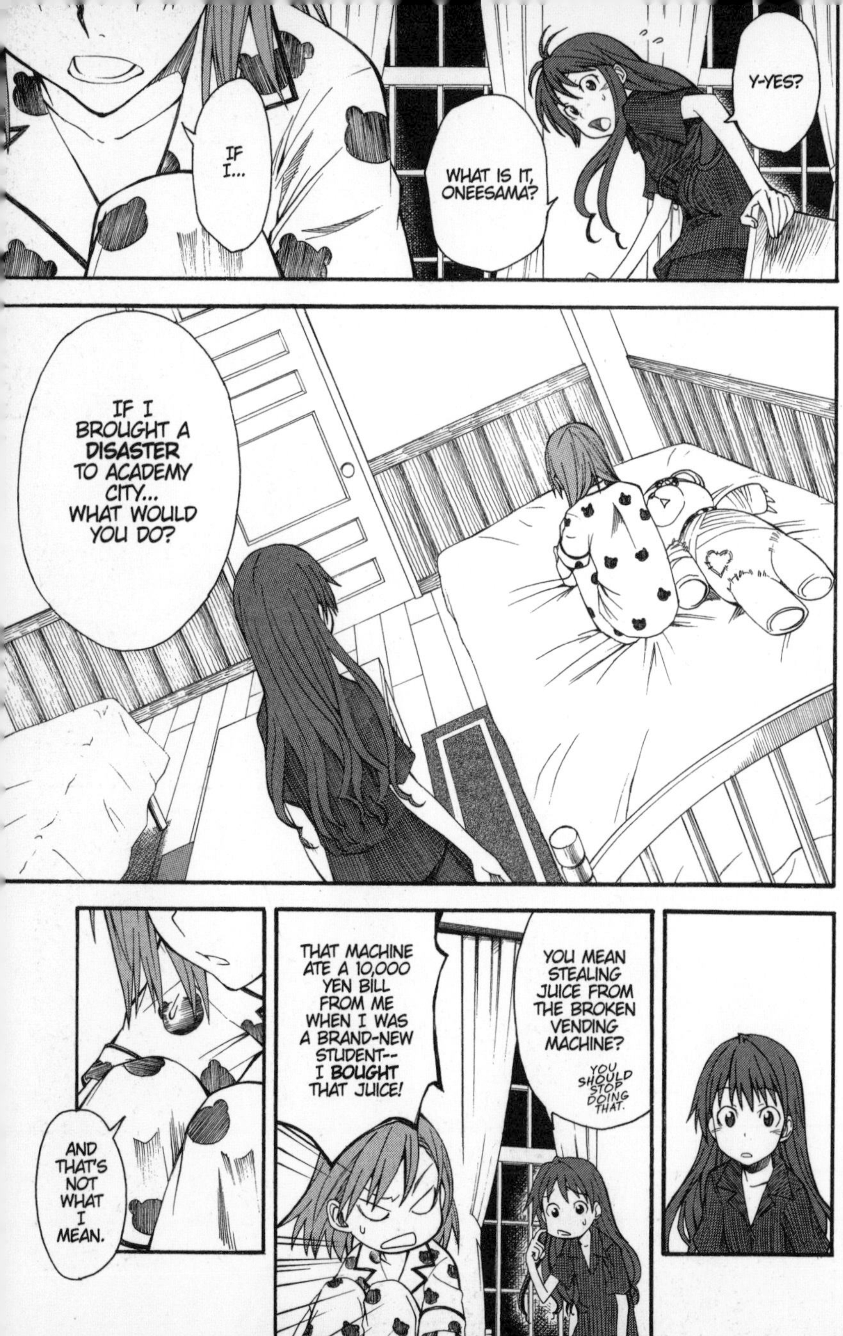
Y-YES?
WHAT IS IT, ONEESAMA?
IF I...
IF I BROUGHT A DISASTER TO ACADEMY CITY... WHAT WOULD YOU DO?
YOU MEAN STEALING JUICE FROM THE BROKEN VENDING MACHINE?
YOU SHOULD STOP DOING THAT.
THAT MACHINE ATE A 10,000 YEN BILL FROM ME WHEN I WAS A BRAND-NEW STUDENT-- I BOUGHT THAT JUICE!
AND THAT'S NOT WHAT I MEAN.

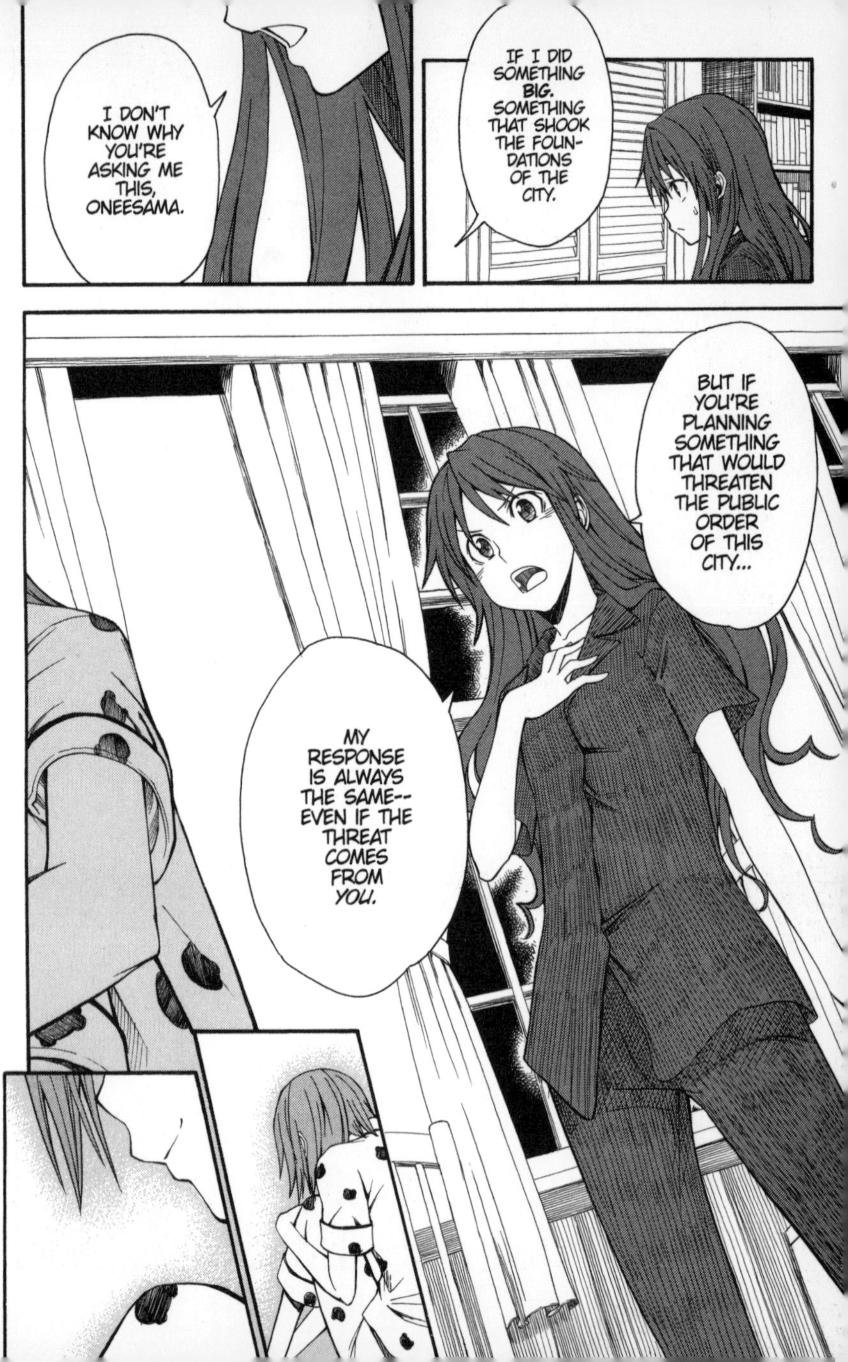

IF I DID SOMETHING BIG. SOMETHING THAT SHOOK THE FOUN- DATIONS OF THE CITY.
I DON'T KNOW WHY YOU'RE ASKING ME THIS, ONEESAMA.
BUT IF YOU'RE PLANNING SOMETHING THAT WOULD THREATEN THE PUBLIC ORDER OF THIS CITY...
MY RESPONSE IS ALWAYS THE SAME-- EVEN IF THE THREAT COMES FROM YOU.

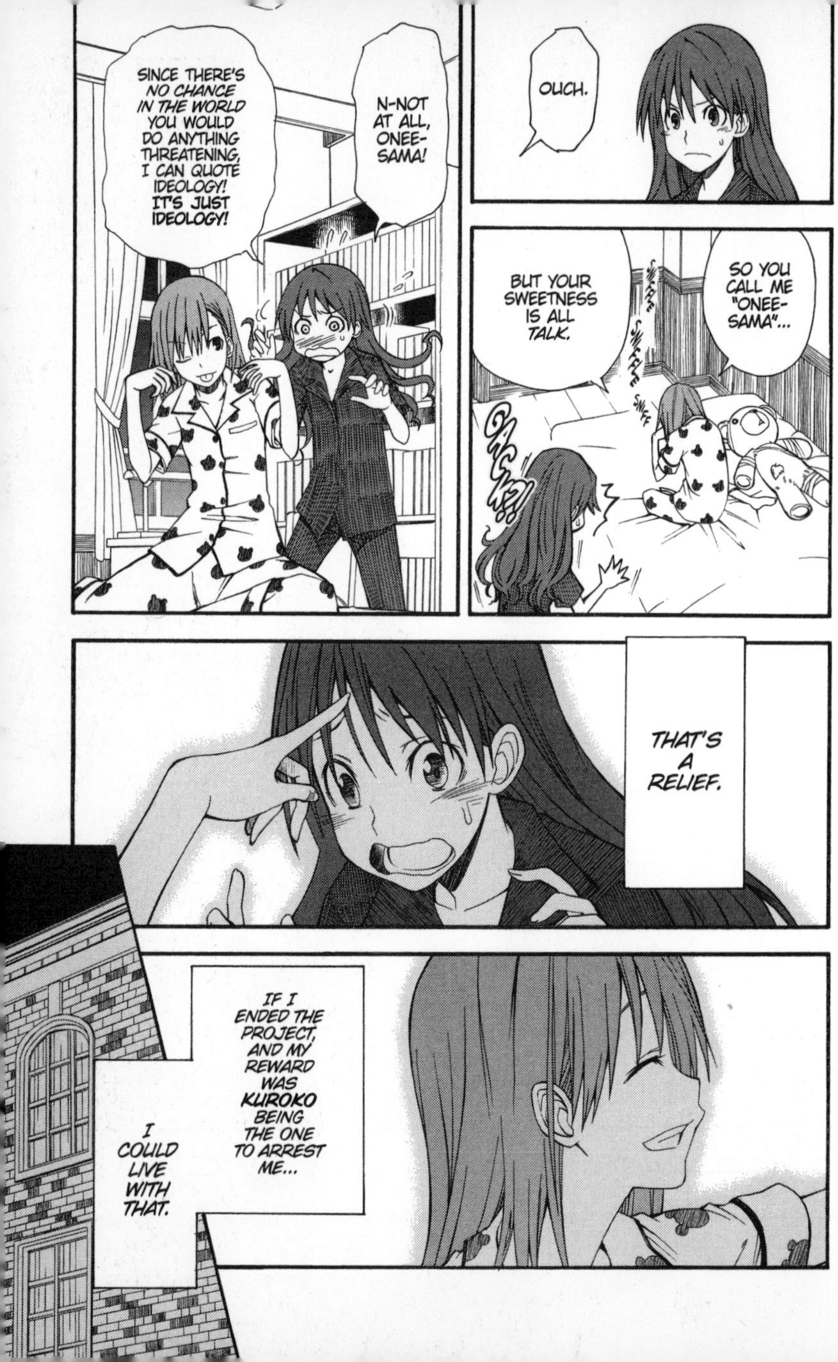
OUCH.
SO YOU CALL ME "ONEE-SAMA"...
BUT YOUR SWEETNESS IS ALL TALK.
SNIFFLE
SNIFFLE
SNIFF
N-NOT AT ALL, ONEE-SAMA!
SINCE THERE'S NO CHANCE IN THE WORLD YOU WOULD DO ANYTHING THREATENING, I CAN QUOTE IDEOLOGY! IT'S JUST IDEOLOGY!
THAT'S A RELIEF.
IF I ENDED THE PROJECT, AND MY REWARD WAS KUROKO BEING THE ONE TO ARREST ME...
I COULD LIVE WITH THAT.

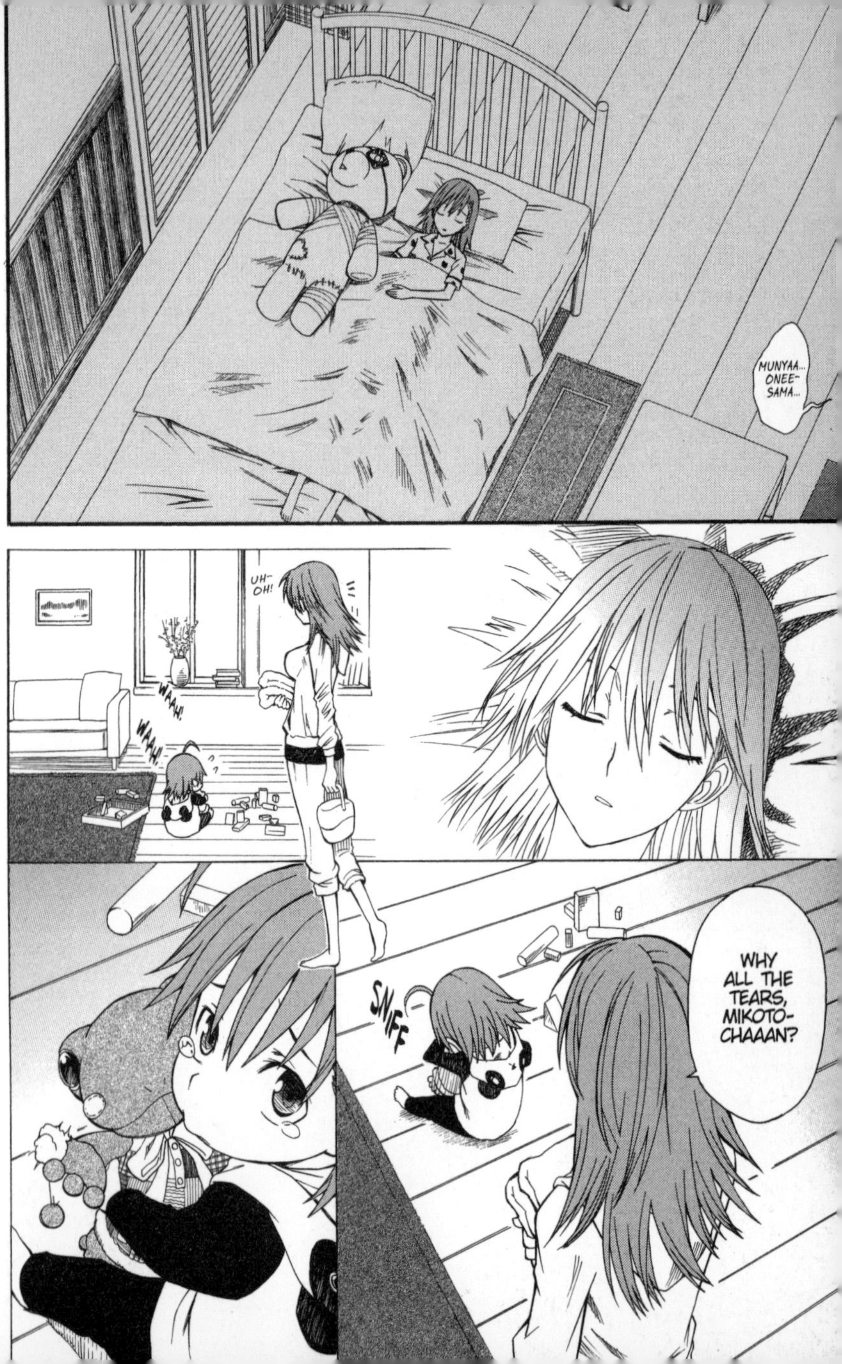
MUNYAA... ONEE-SAMA...
UH-OH!
WAAH!
WAAH!
WHY ALL THE TEARS, MIKOTO-CHAAAN?
SNIFF

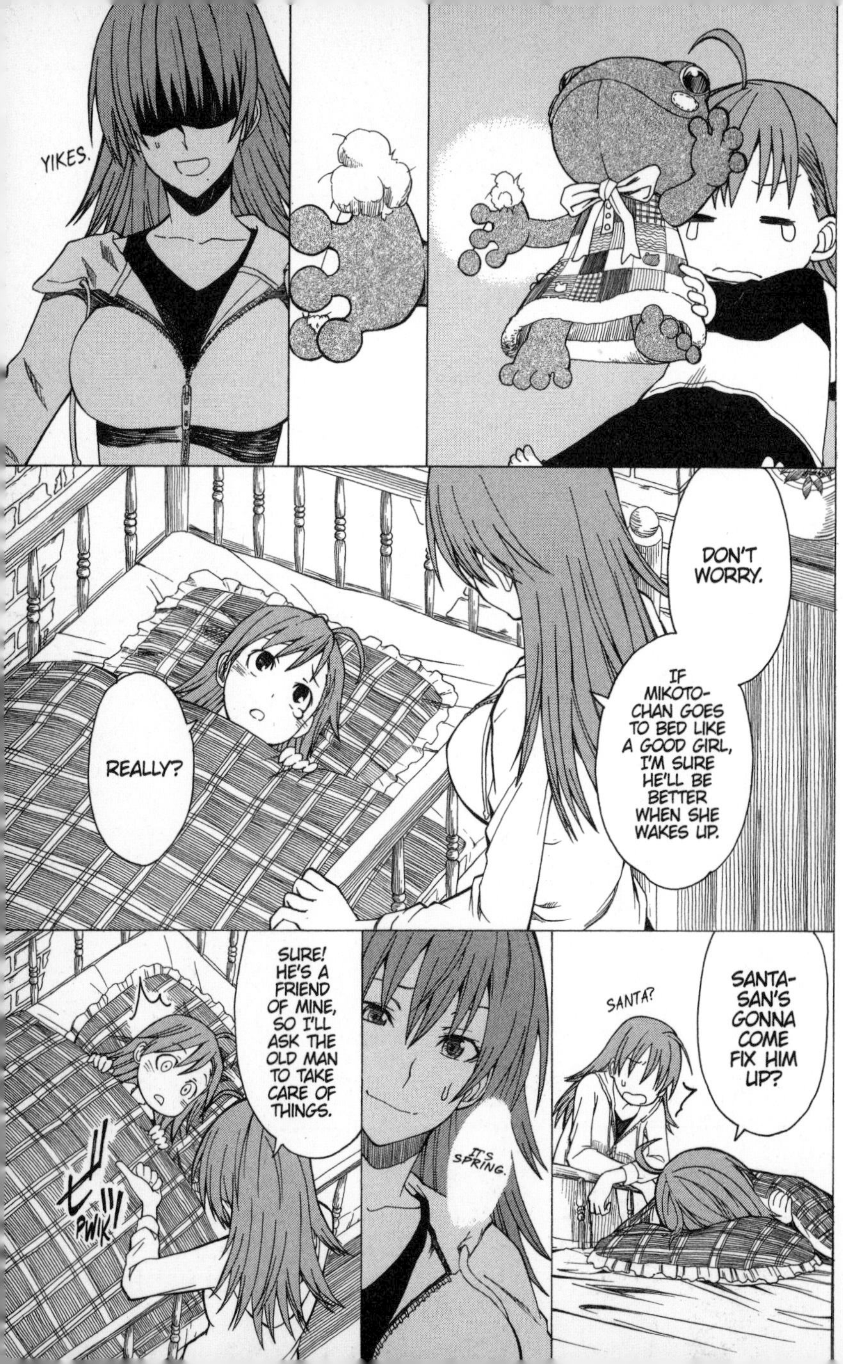
YIKES.
DON'T WORRY.
IF MIKOTO-CHAN GOES TO BED LIKE A GOOD GIRL, I'M SURE HE'LL BE BETTER WHEN SHE WAKES UP.
REALLY?
SANTA-SAN'S GONNA COME FIX HIM UP?
SANTA?
SURE! HE'S A FRIEND OF MINE, SO I'LL ASK THE OLD MAN TO TAKE CARE OF THINGS.
IT'S SPRING.
PWIK!

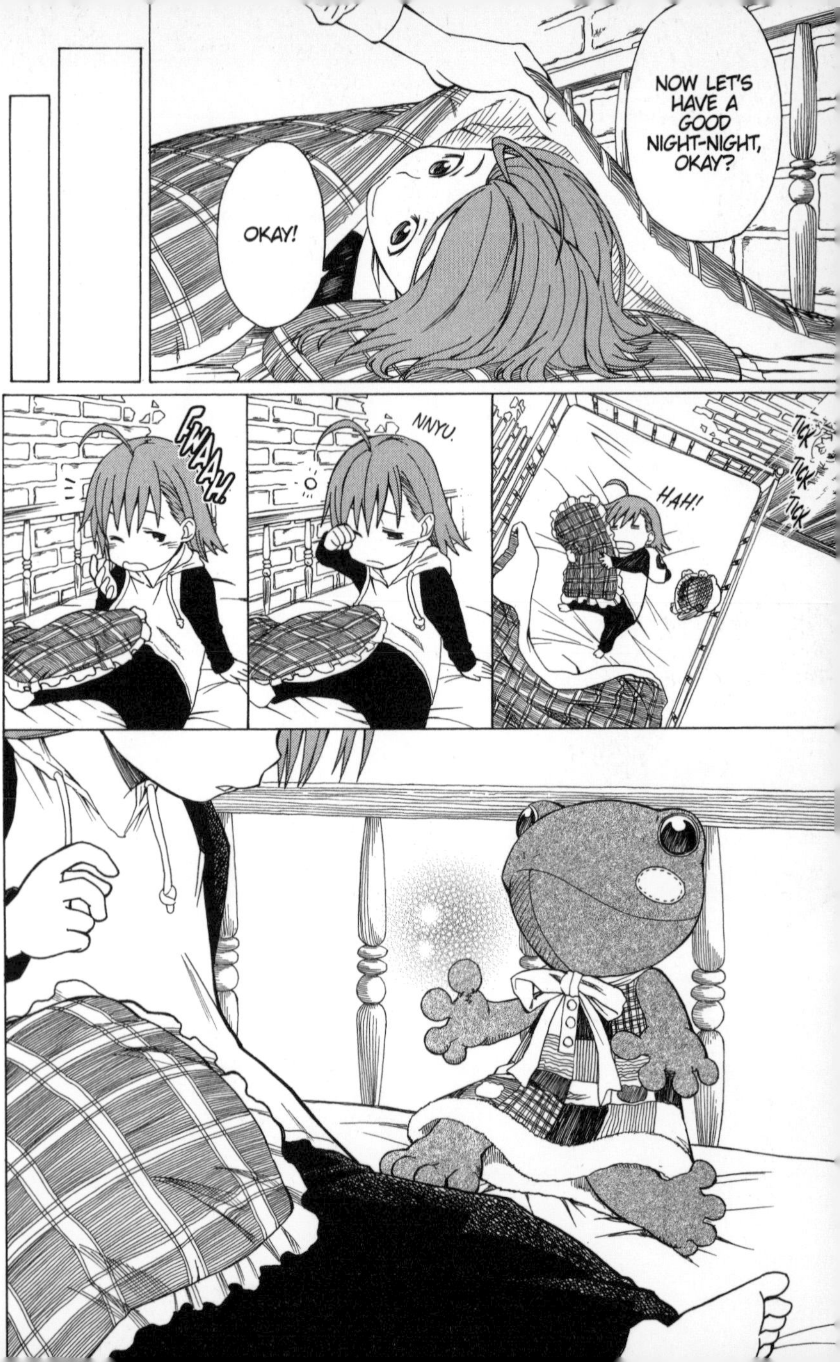
NOW LET'S HAVE A GOOD NIGHT-NIGHT, OKAY?
OKAY!
TICK TICK TICK
HAH!
NNYU.
FWAAH!

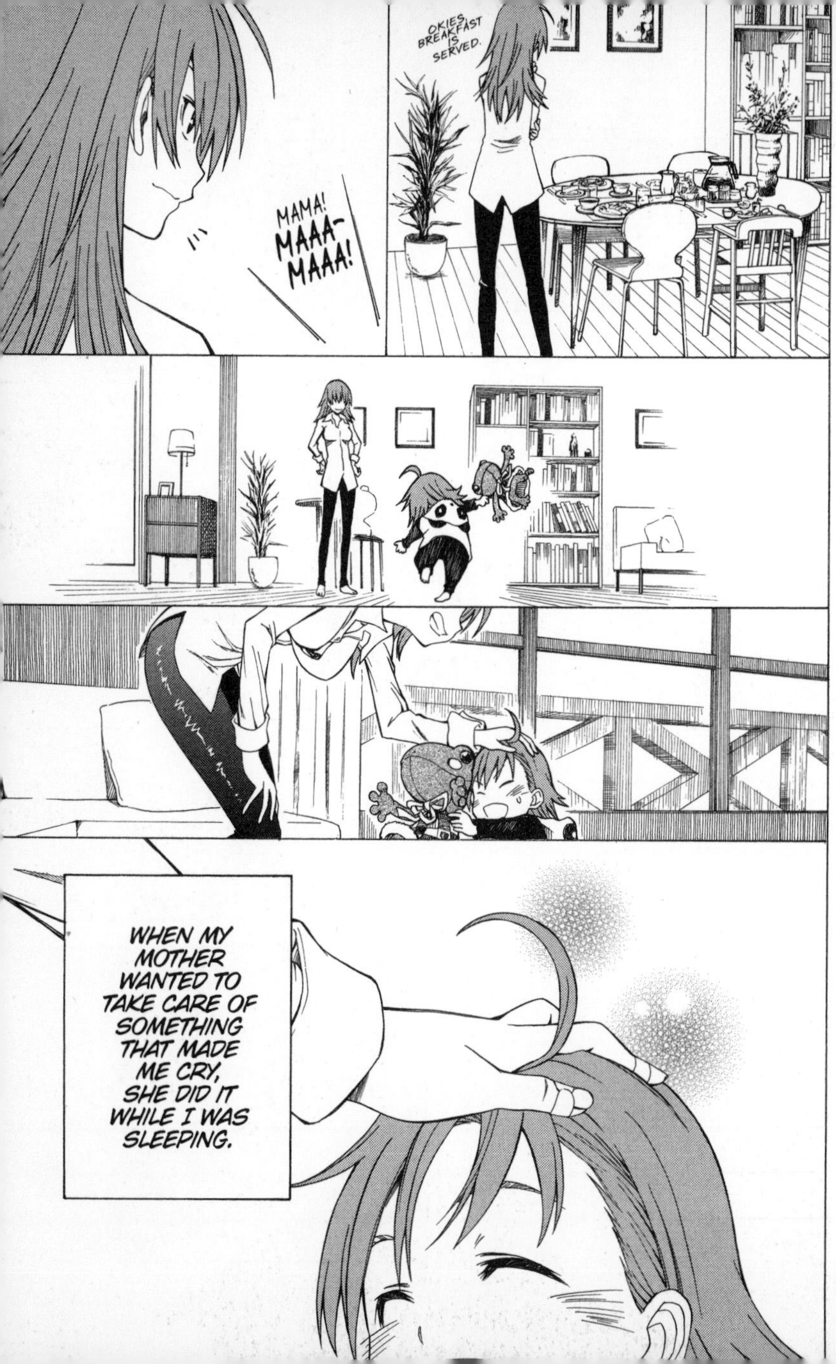
OKIES, BREAKFAST IS SERVED.
MAMA! MAAA-MAAA!
WHEN MY MOTHER WANTED TO TAKE CARE OF SOMETHING THAT MADE ME CRY, SHE DID IT WHILE I WAS SLEEPING.

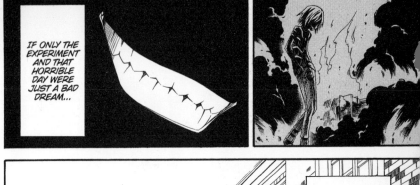

IF ONLY THE EXPERIMENT AND THAT HORRIBLE DAY WERE JUST A BAD DREAM...

...I'D BE FINE IN THE MORNING, JUST LIKE I USED TO BE.

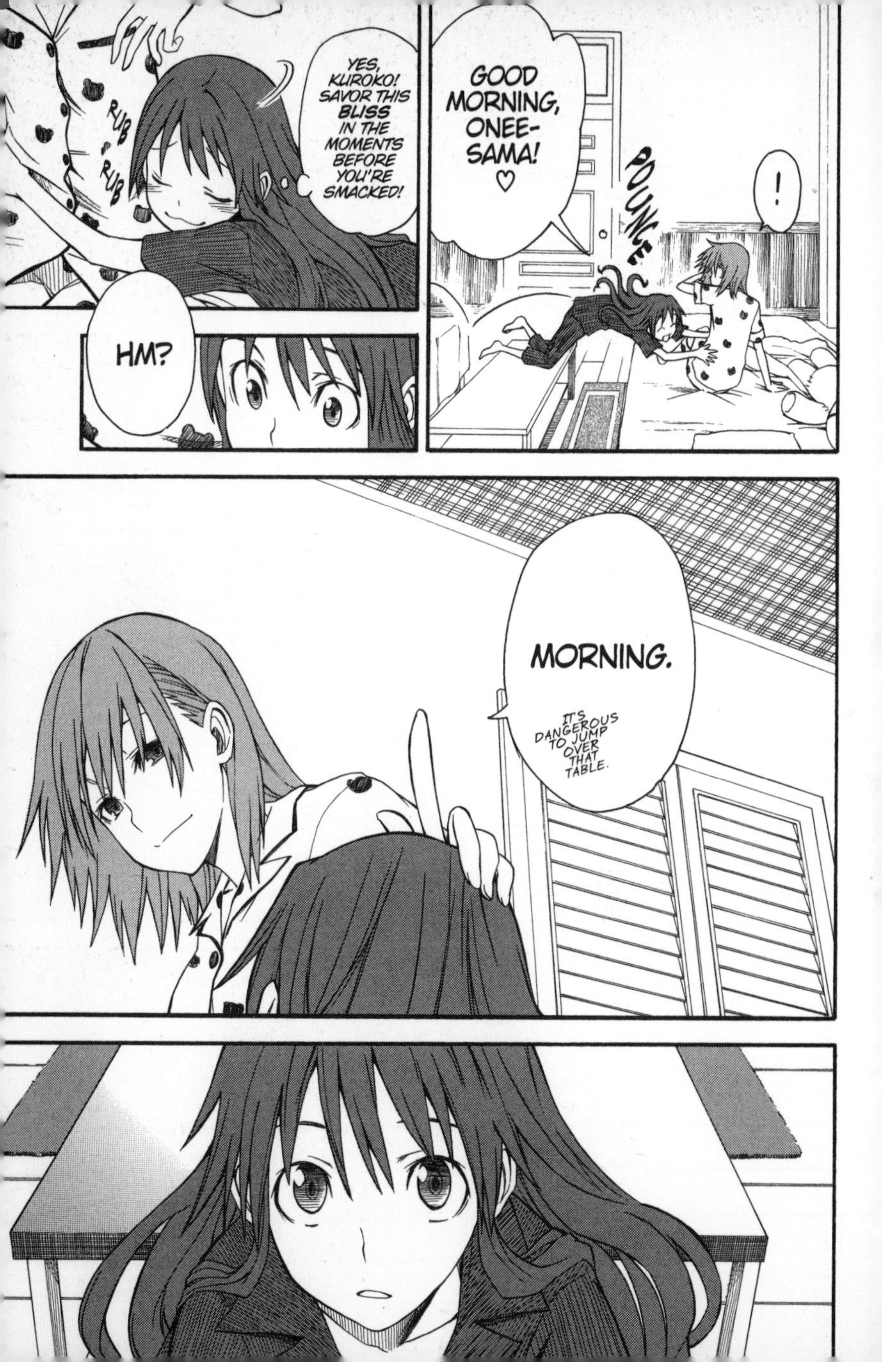
GOOD MORNING, ONEE-SAMA! ♡
POUNCE
!
YES, KUROKO! SAVOR THIS BLISS IN THE MOMENTS BEFORE YOU'RE SMACKED!
RUB RUB
HM?
MORNING.
IT'S DANGEROUS TO JUMP OVER THAT TABLE.

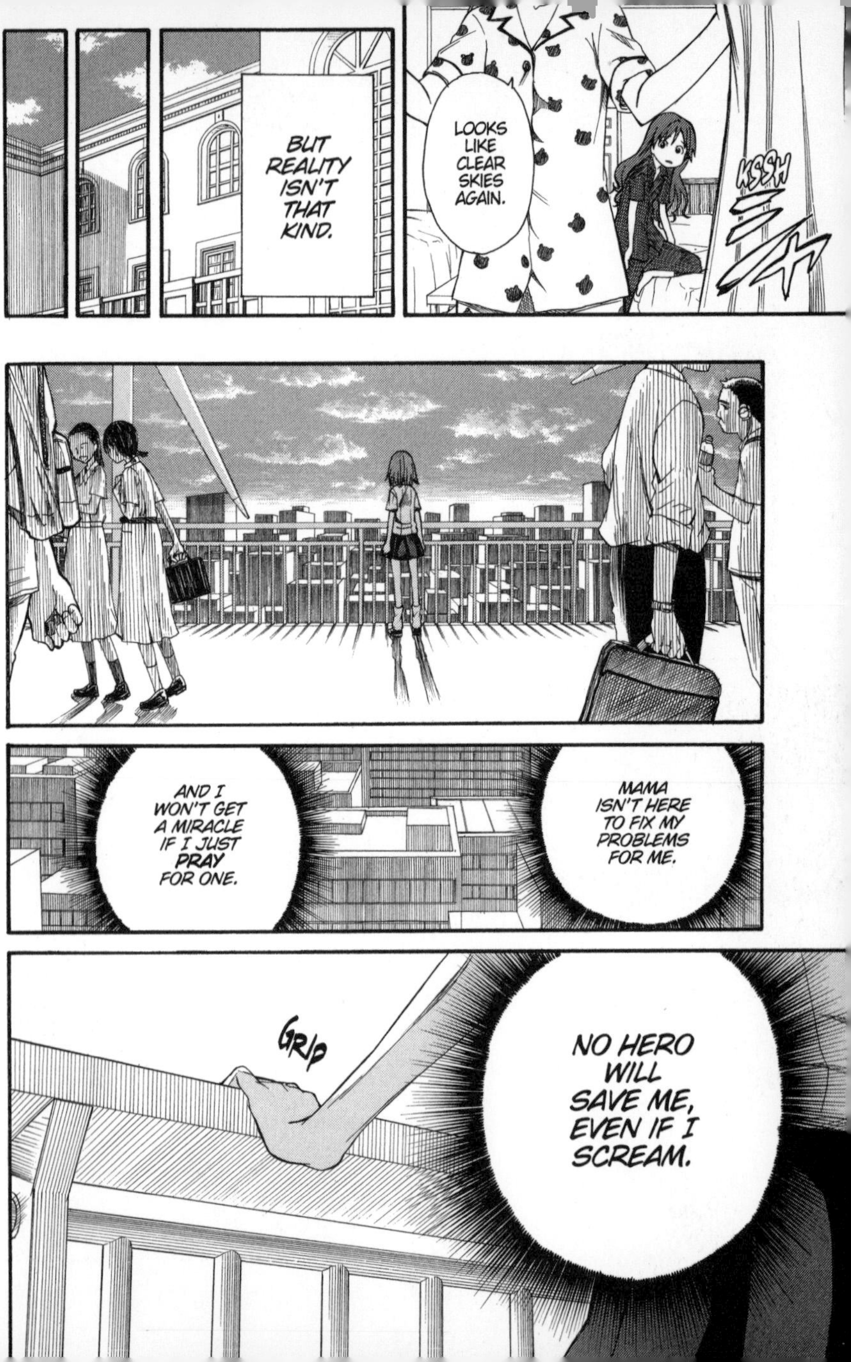

LOOKS LIKE CLEAR SKIES AGAIN.
KSSH
BUT REALITY ISN'T THAT KIND.
MAMA ISN'T HERE TO FIX MY PROBLEMS FOR ME.
AND I WON'T GET A MIRACLE IF I JUST PRAY FOR ONE.
NO HERO WILL SAVE ME, EVEN IF I SCREAM.
GRIP

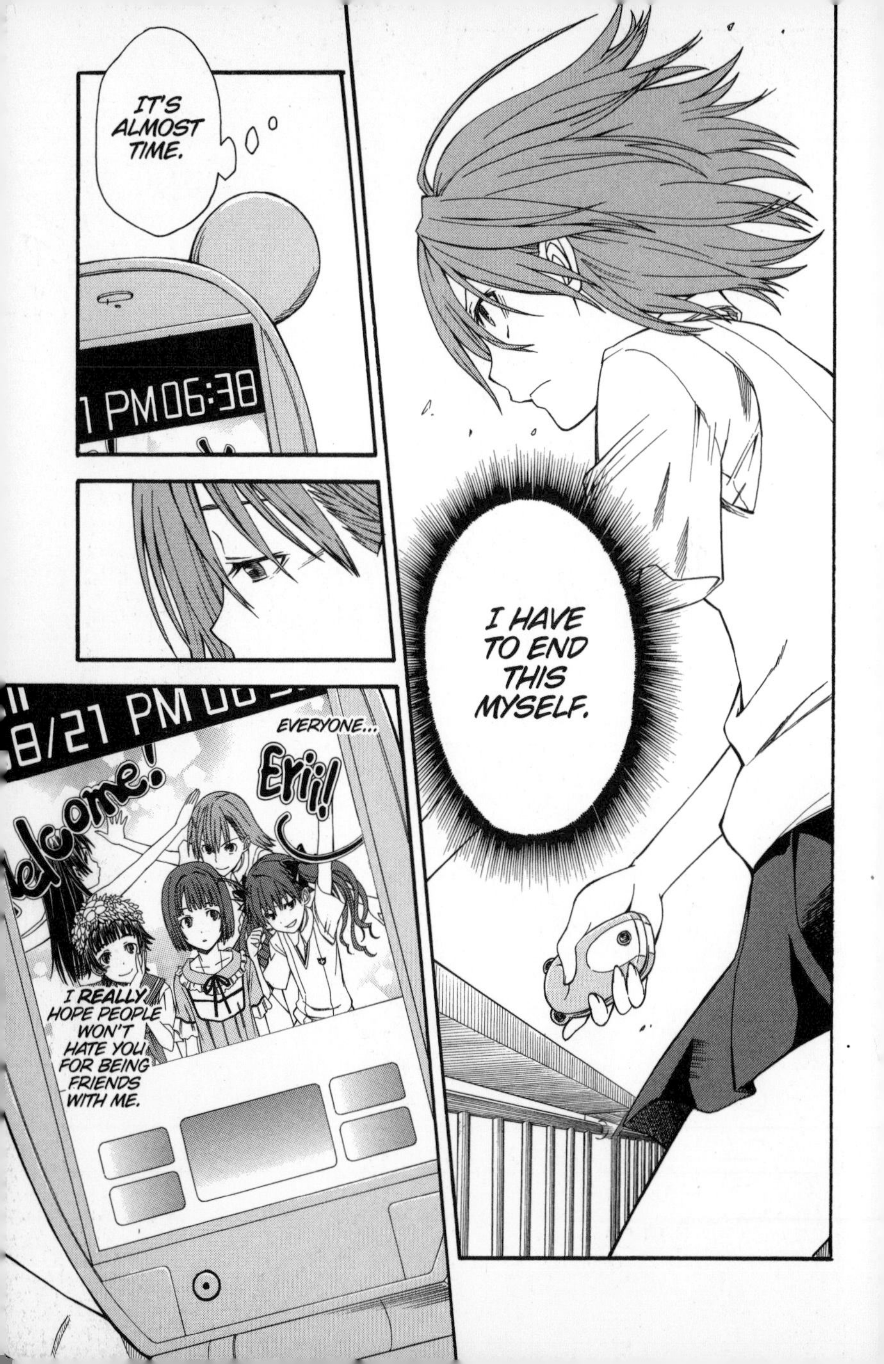
I HAVE TO END THIS MYSELF.
IT'S ALMOST TIME.
1 PM06:38
EVERYONE...
Erii!
I REALLY HOPE PEOPLE WON'T HATE YOU FOR BEING FRIENDS WITH ME.

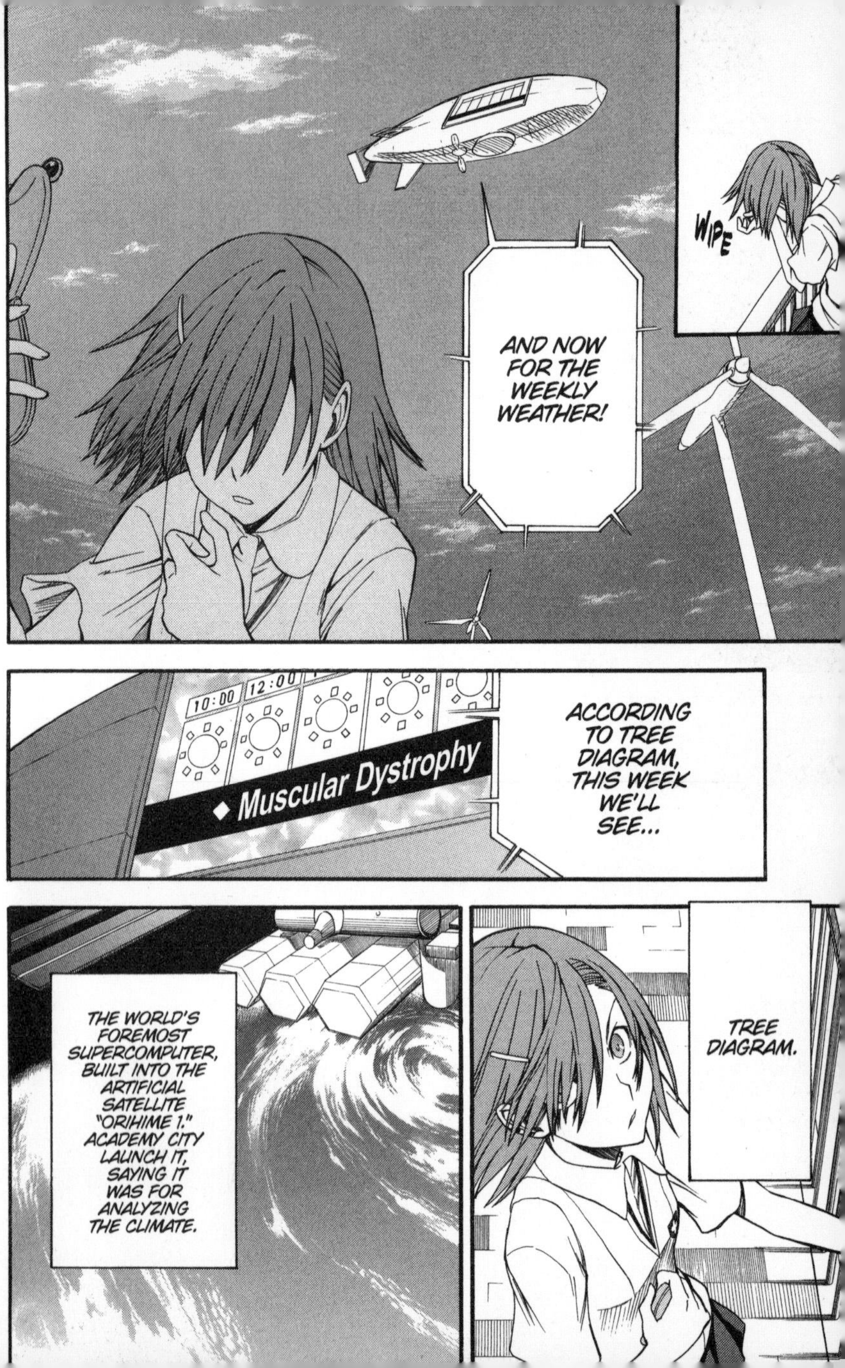
WIPE
AND NOW FOR THE WEEKLY WEATHER!
ACCORDING TO TREE DIAGRAM, THIS WEEK WE'LL SEE...
10:00
12:00
◆ Muscular Dystrophy
TREE DIAGRAM.
THE WORLD'S FOREMOST SUPERCOMPUTER, BUILT INTO THE ARTIFICIAL SATELLITE "ORIHIME 1." ACADEMY CITY LAUNCH IT, SAYING IT WAS FOR ANALYZING THE CLIMATE.

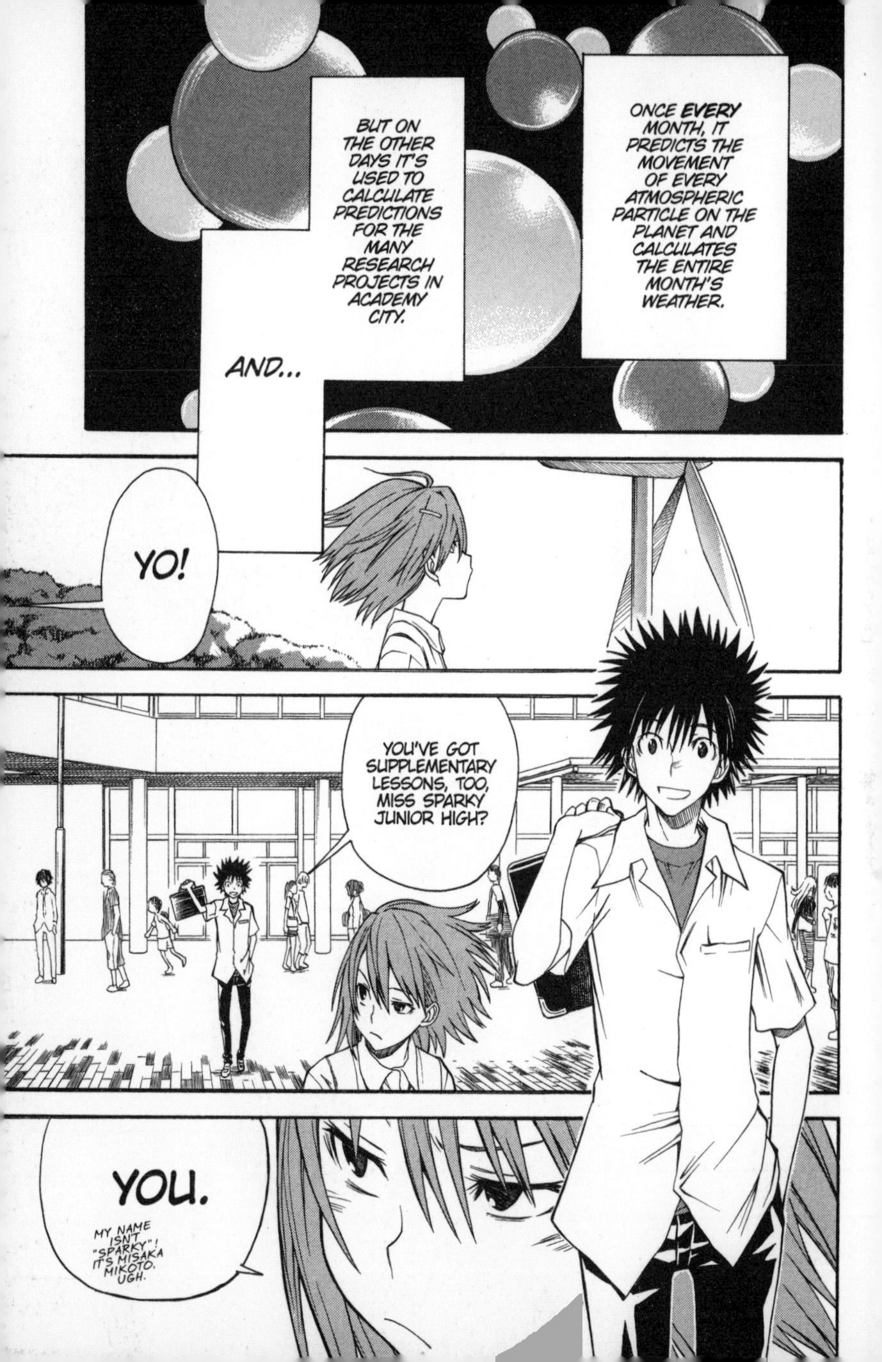
ONCE EVERY MONTH, IT PREDICTS THE MOVEMENT OF EVERY ATMOSPHERIC PARTICLE ON THE PLANET AND CALCULATES THE ENTIRE MONTH'S WEATHER.
BUT ON THE OTHER DAYS IT'S USED TO CALCULATE PREDICTIONS FOR THE MANY RESEARCH PROJECTS IN ACADEMY CITY.
AND...
YO!
YOU'VE GOT SUPPLEMENTARY LESSONS, TOO, MISS SPARKY JUNIOR HIGH?
YOU.
MY NAME ISN'T "SPARKY"! IT'S MISAKA MIKOTO. UGH.

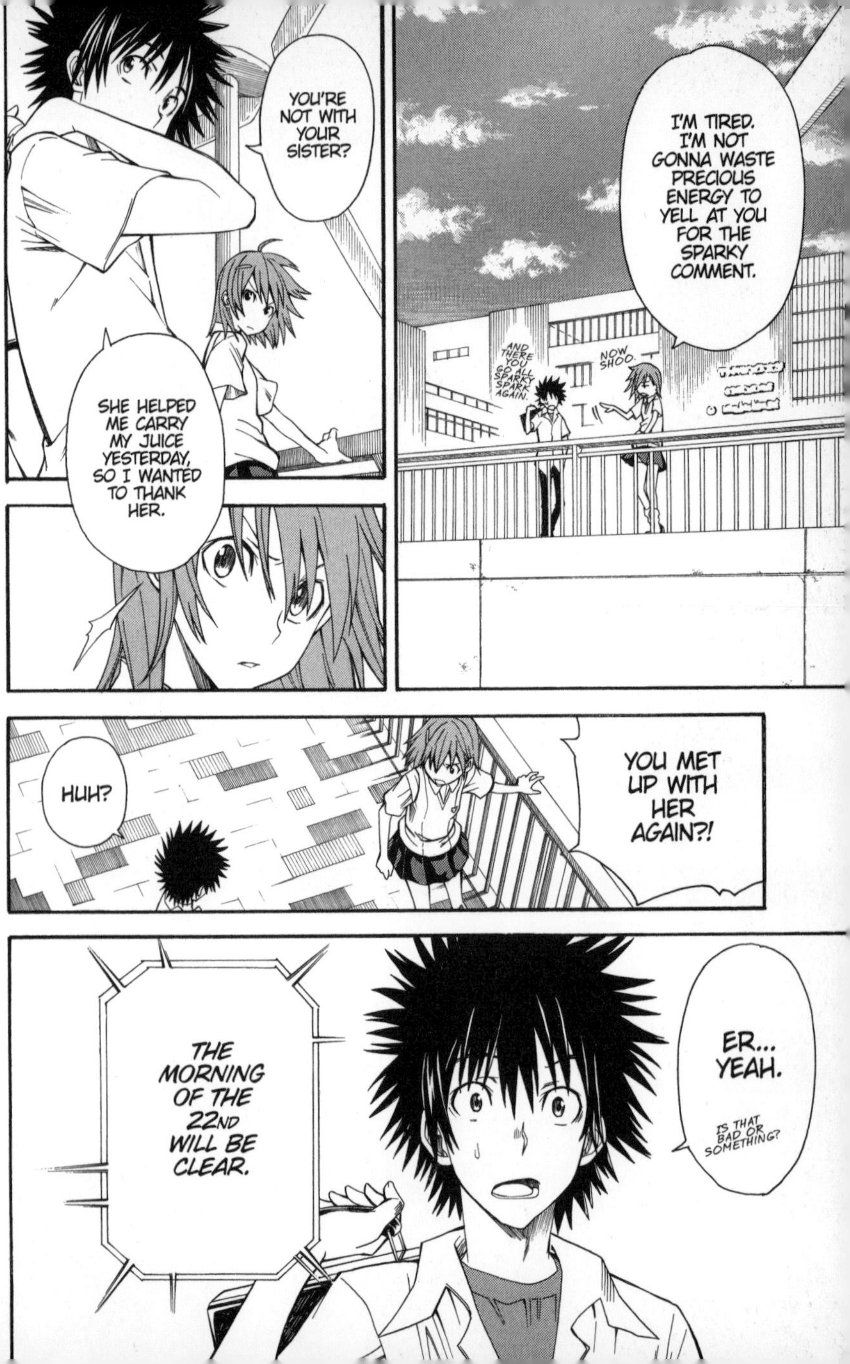
I'M TIRED. I'M NOT GONNA WASTE PRECIOUS ENERGY TO YELL AT YOU FOR THE SPARKY COMMENT.
NOW SHOO.
AND THERE YOU GO ALL SPARKY SPARKY AGAIN.
YOU'RE NOT WITH YOUR SISTER?
SHE HELPED ME CARRY MY JUICE YESTERDAY, SO I WANTED TO THANK HER.
YOU MET UP WITH HER AGAIN?!
HUH?
ER... YEAH.
IS THAT BAD OR SOMETHING?
THE MORNING OF THE 22ND WILL BE CLEAR.

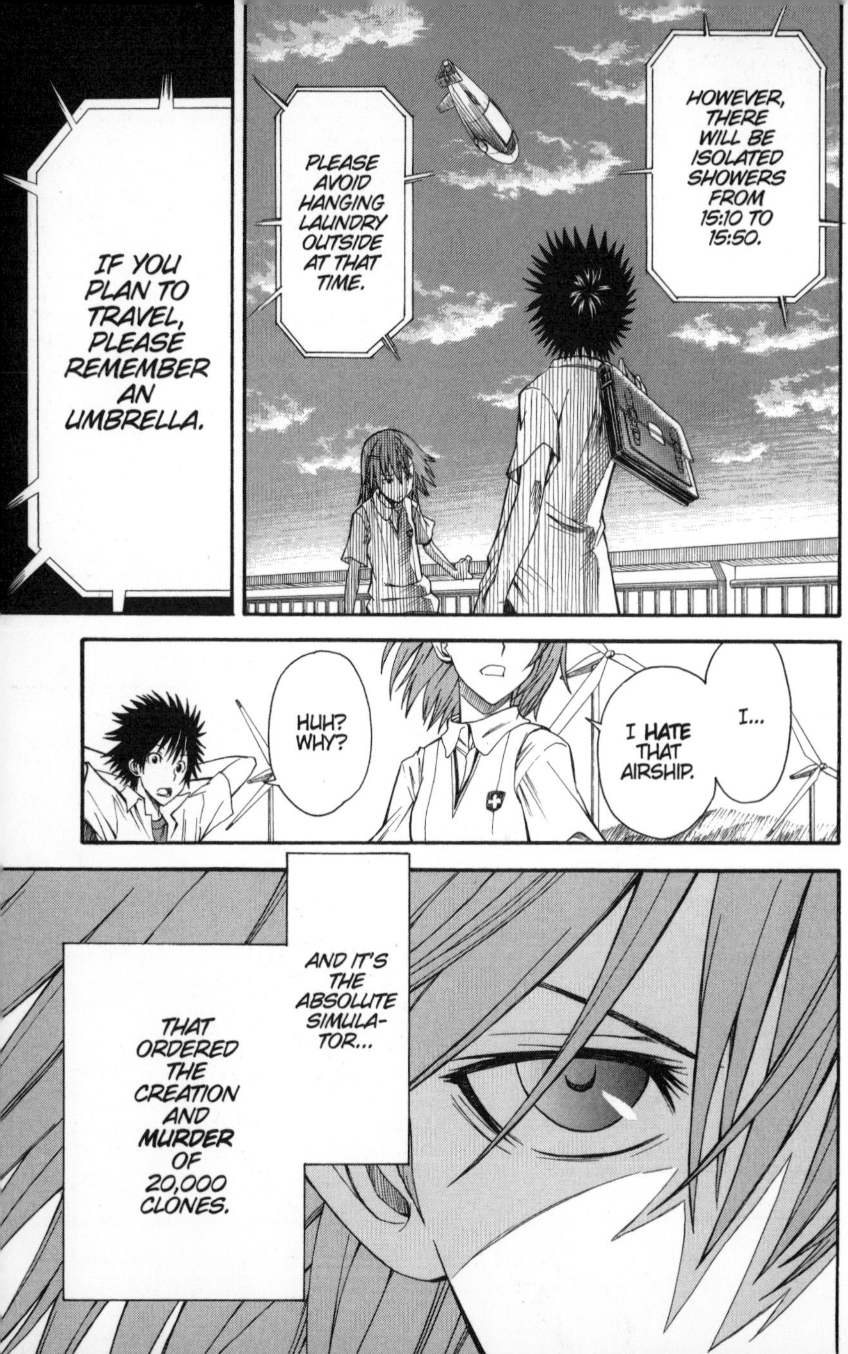
HOWEVER, THERE WILL BE ISOLATED SHOWERS FROM 15:10 TO 15:50.
PLEASE AVOID HANGING LAUNDRY OUTSIDE AT THAT TIME.
IF YOU PLAN TO TRAVEL, PLEASE REMEMBER AN UMBRELLA.
I...
I HATE THAT AIRSHIP.
HUH? WHY?
AND IT'S THE ABSOLUTE SIMULATOR...
THAT ORDERED THE CREATION AND MURDER OF 20,000 CLONES.

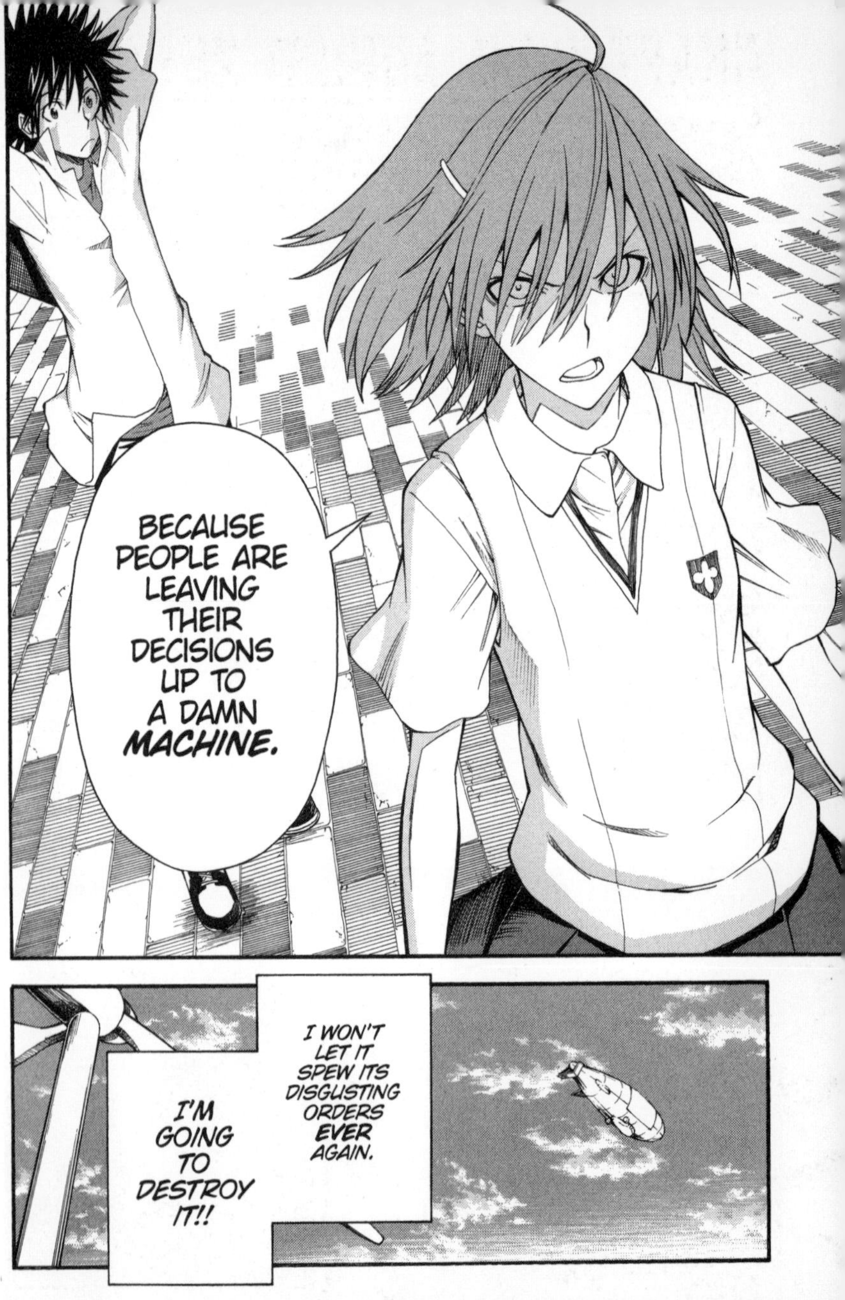
BECAUSE PEOPLE ARE LEAVING THEIR DECISIONS UP TO A DAMN *MACHINE.*
I WON'T LET IT SPEW ITS DISGUSTING ORDERS **EVER** AGAIN.
I'M GOING TO DESTROY IT!!

CHAPTER 33: AUGUST 21ST (1)

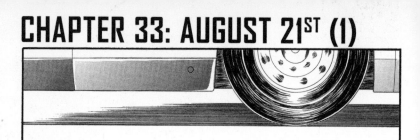

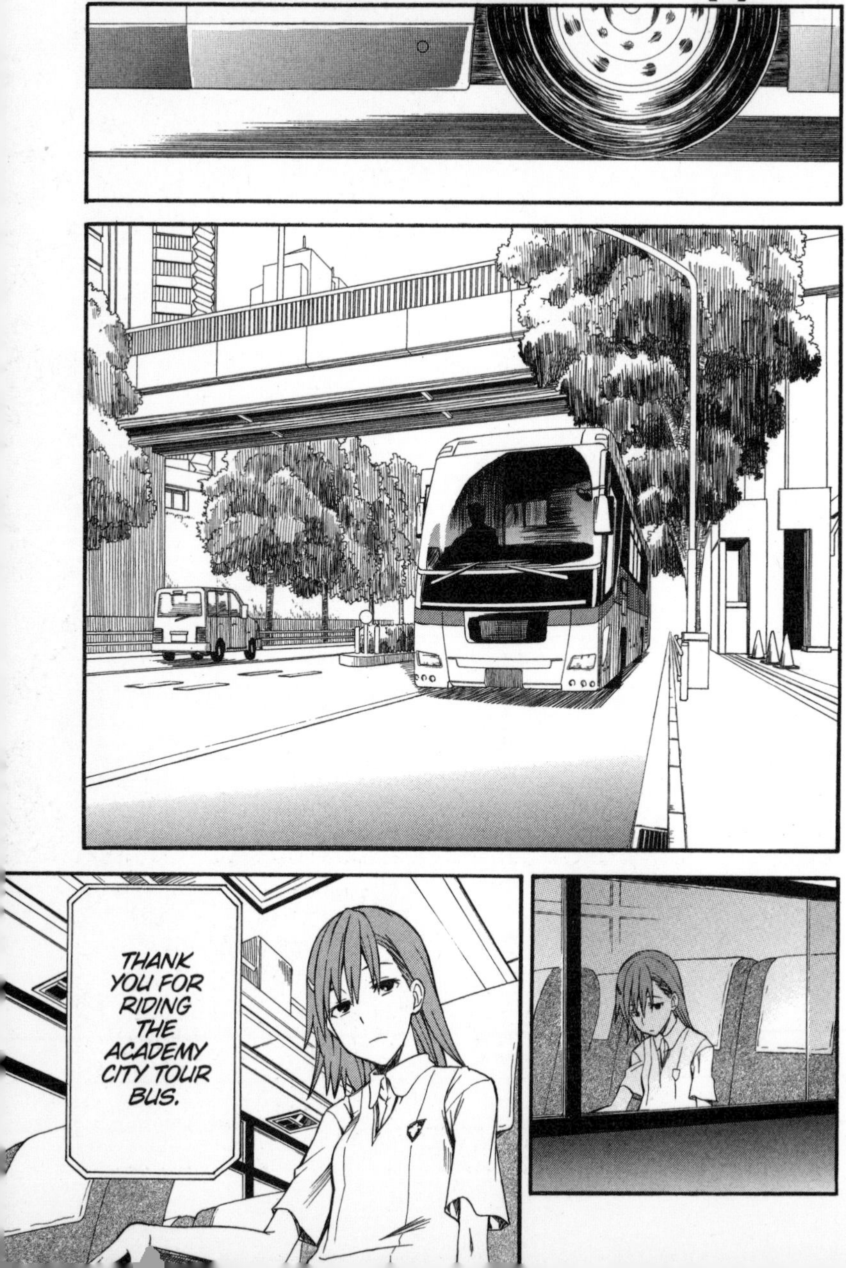
THANK YOU FOR RIDING THE ACADEMY CITY TOUR BUS.

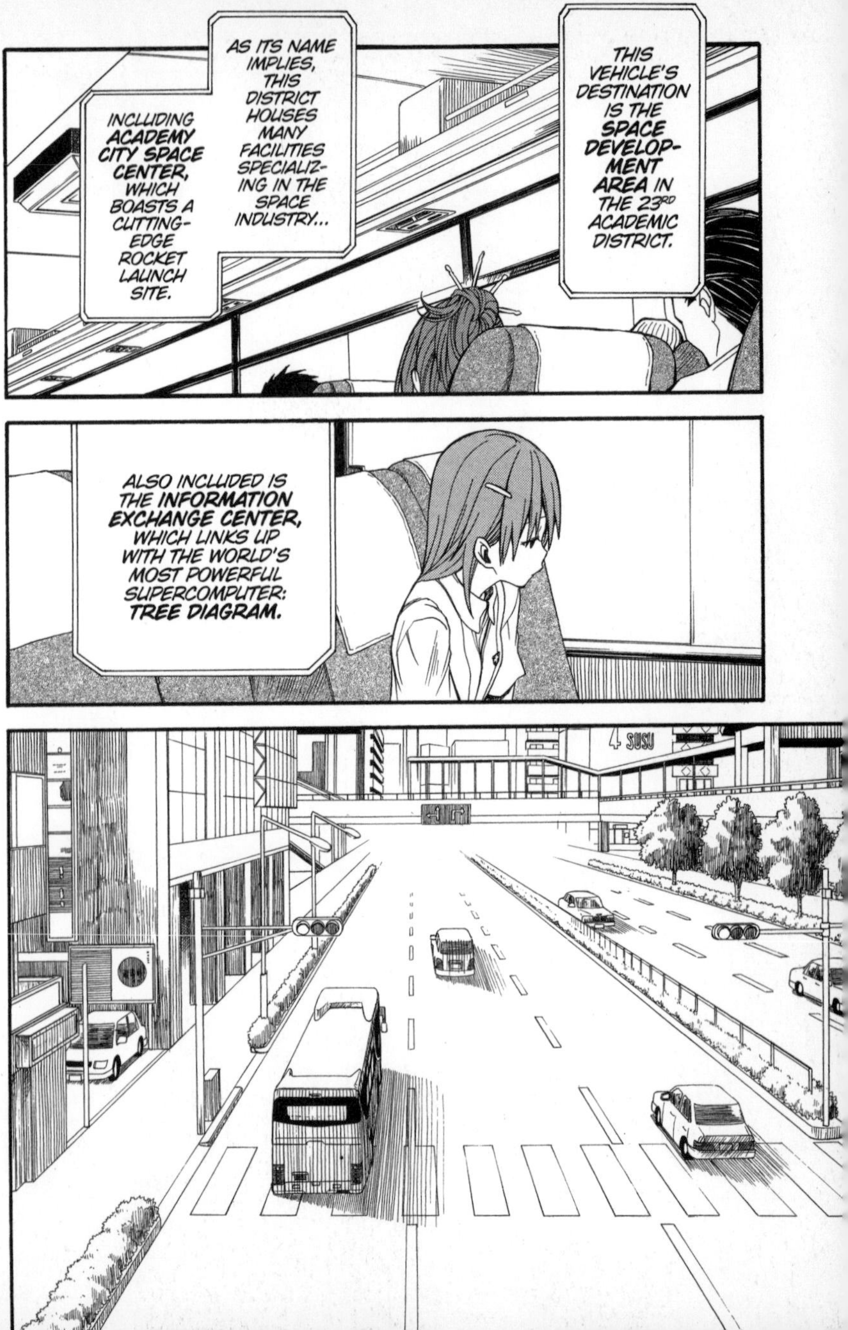
THIS VEHICLE'S DESTINATION IS THE **SPACE DEVELOPMENT AREA** IN THE 23RD ACADEMIC DISTRICT.
AS ITS NAME IMPLIES, THIS DISTRICT HOUSES MANY FACILITIES SPECIALIZING IN THE SPACE INDUSTRY...
INCLUDING **ACADEMY CITY SPACE CENTER,** WHICH BOASTS A CUTTING-EDGE ROCKET LAUNCH SITE.
ALSO INCLUDED IS THE **INFORMATION EXCHANGE CENTER,** WHICH LINKS UP WITH THE WORLD'S MOST POWERFUL SUPERCOMPUTER: **TREE DIAGRAM.**
4 SUSU

CHAPTER 33: AUGUST 21ST (1)

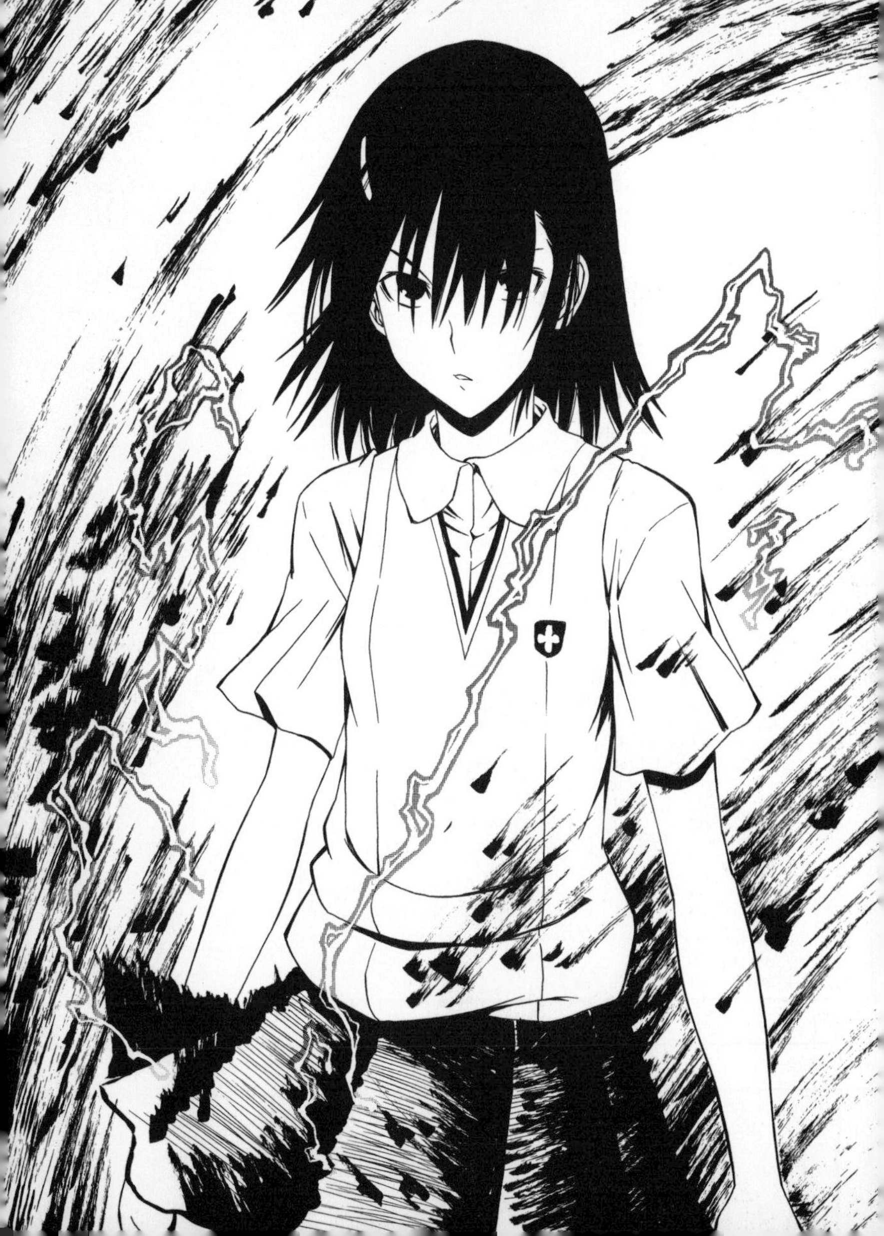

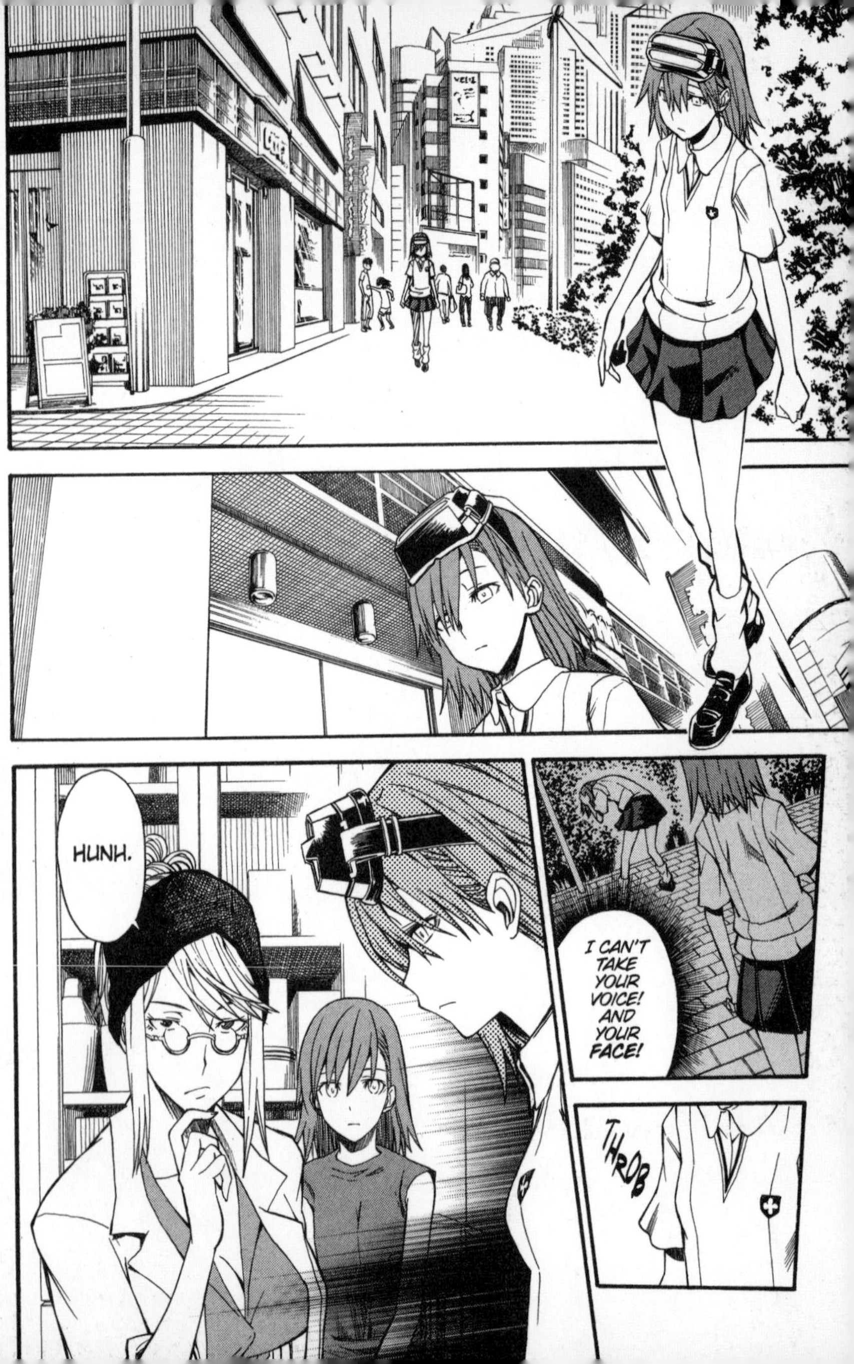
I CAN'T TAKE YOUR VOICE! AND YOUR FACE!
THROB
HUNH.

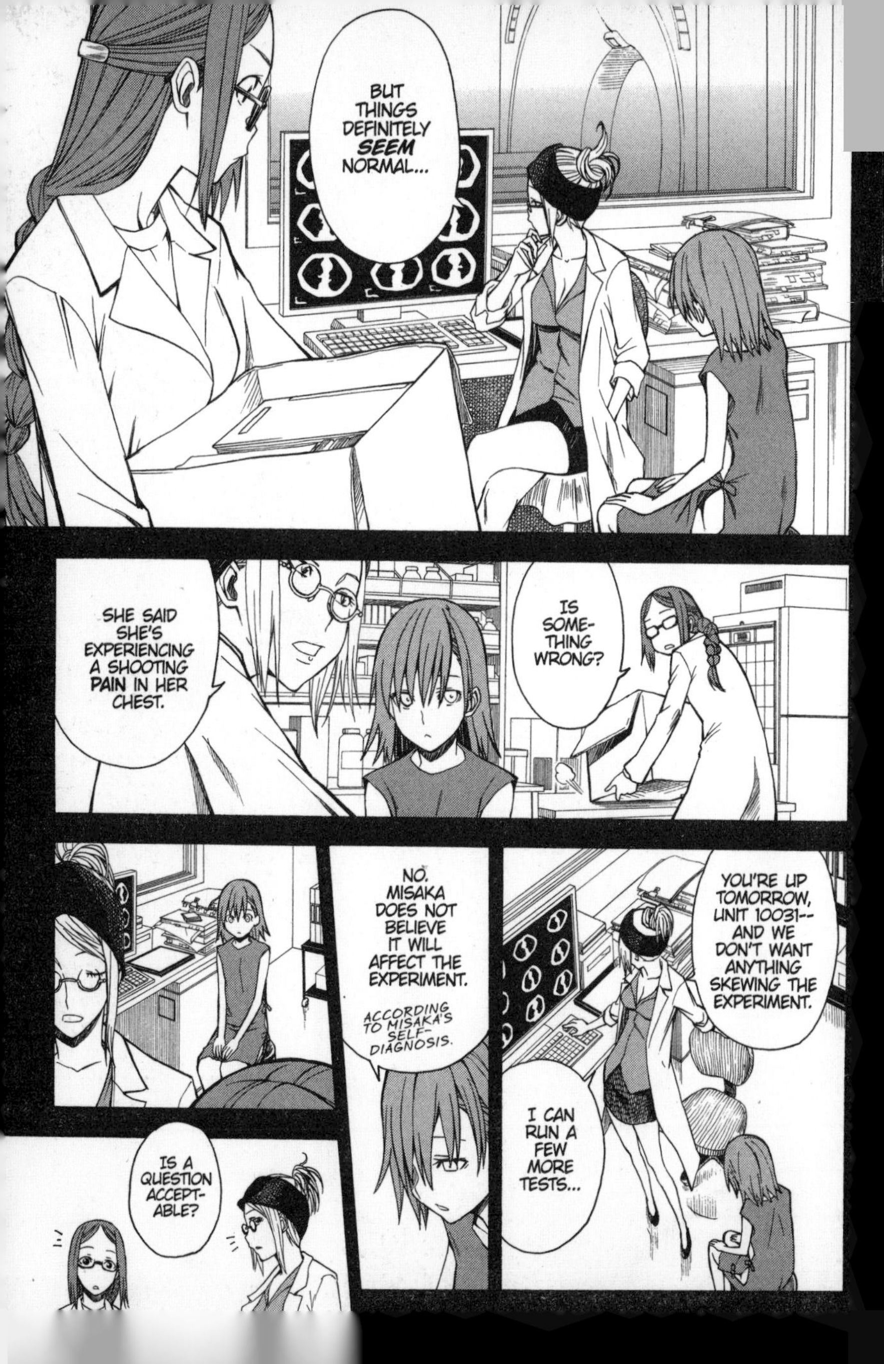
BUT THINGS DEFINITELY **SEEM** NORMAL...
IS SOME-THING WRONG?
SHE SAID SHE'S EXPERIENCING A SHOOTING PAIN IN HER CHEST.
YOU'RE UP TOMORROW, UNIT 10031-- AND WE DON'T WANT ANYTHING SKEWING THE EXPERIMENT.
I CAN RUN A FEW MORE TESTS...
NO. MISAKA DOES NOT BELIEVE IT WILL AFFECT THE EXPERIMENT.
ACCORDING TO MISAKA'S SELF-DIAGNOSIS.
IS A QUESTION ACCEPT-ABLE?

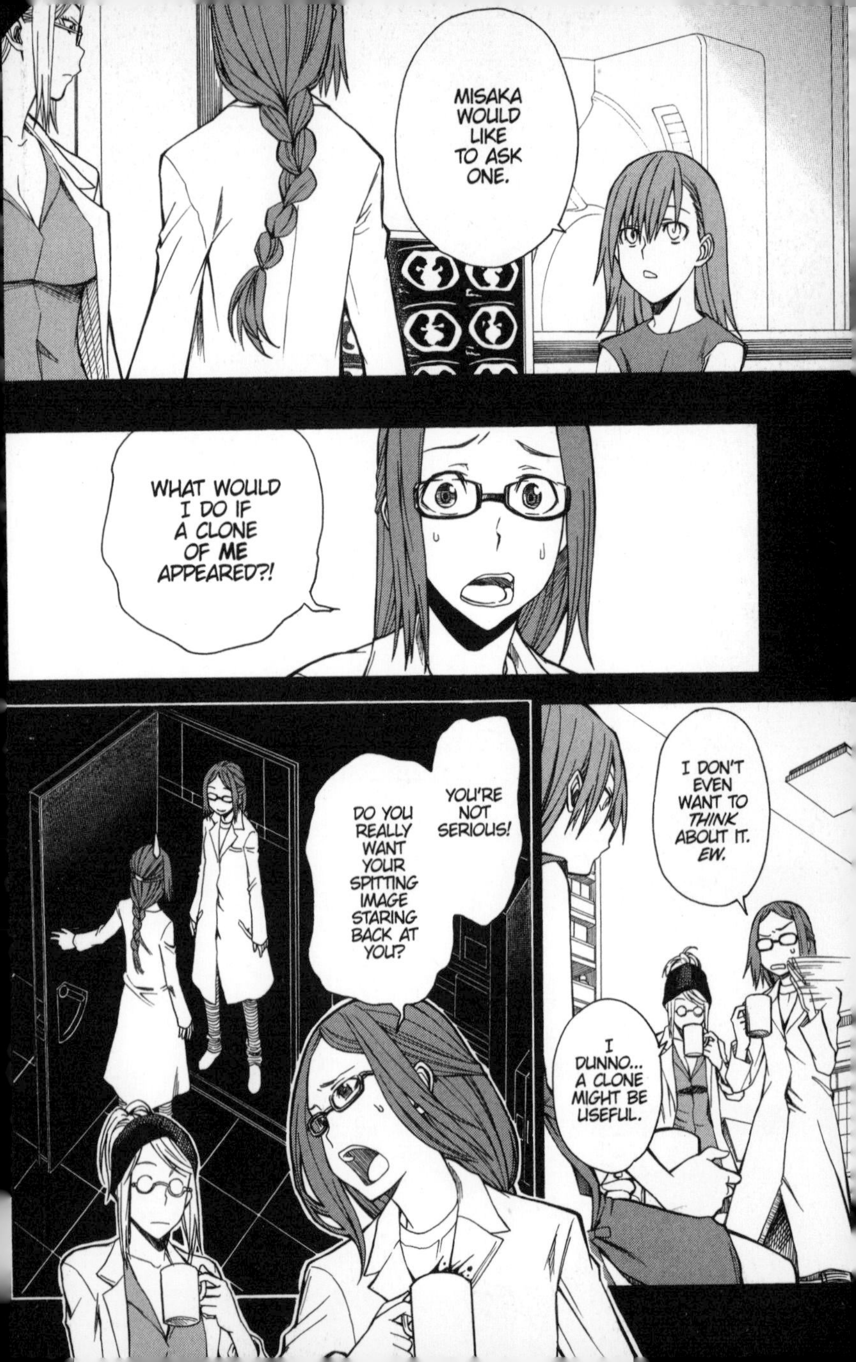
MISAKA WOULD LIKE TO ASK ONE.
WHAT WOULD I DO IF A CLONE OF ME APPEARED?!
I DON'T EVEN WANT TO *THINK* ABOUT IT. *EW.*
I DUNNO... A CLONE MIGHT BE USEFUL.
YOU'RE NOT SERIOUS!
DO YOU REALLY WANT YOUR SPITTING IMAGE STARING BACK AT YOU?

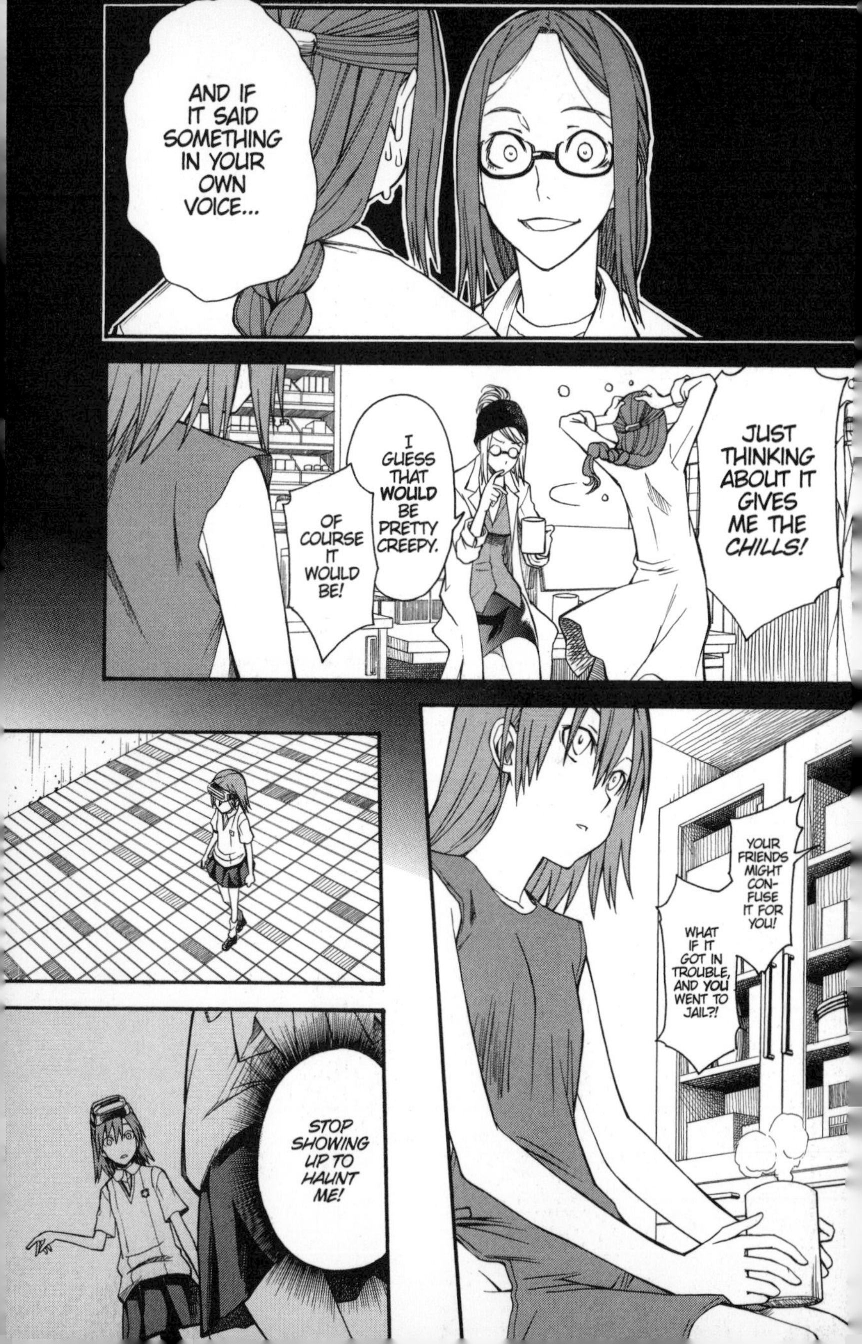
AND IF IT SAID SOMETHING IN YOUR OWN VOICE...
JUST THINKING ABOUT IT GIVES ME THE *CHILLS!*
I GUESS THAT **WOULD** BE PRETTY CREEPY.
OF COURSE IT WOULD BE!
YOUR FRIENDS MIGHT CON-FUSE IT FOR YOU!
WHAT IF IT GOT IN TROUBLE, AND **YOU** WENT TO JAIL?!
STOP SHOWING UP TO HAUNT ME!

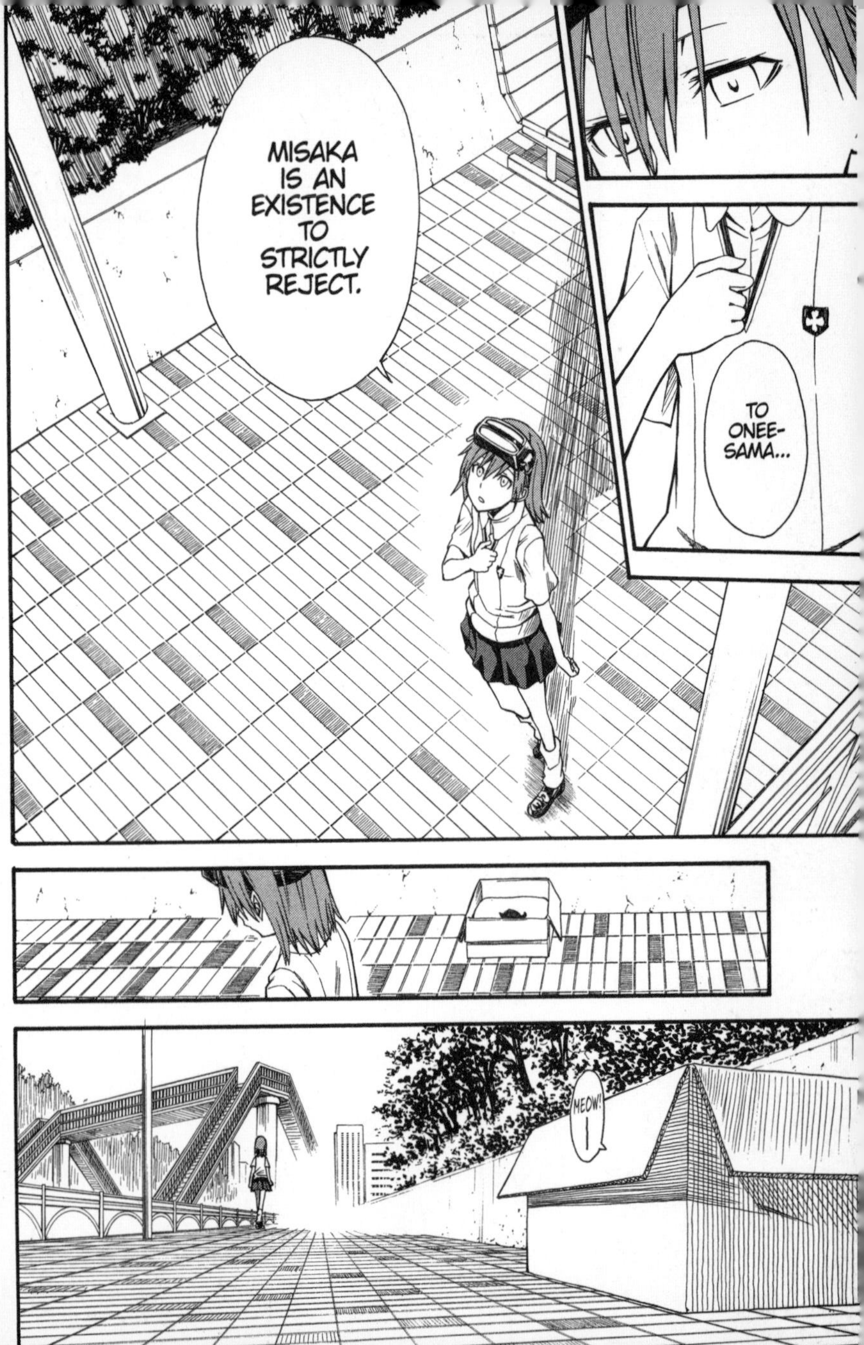
TO ONEE-SAMA...
MISAKA IS AN EXISTENCE TO STRICTLY REJECT.
MEOW!

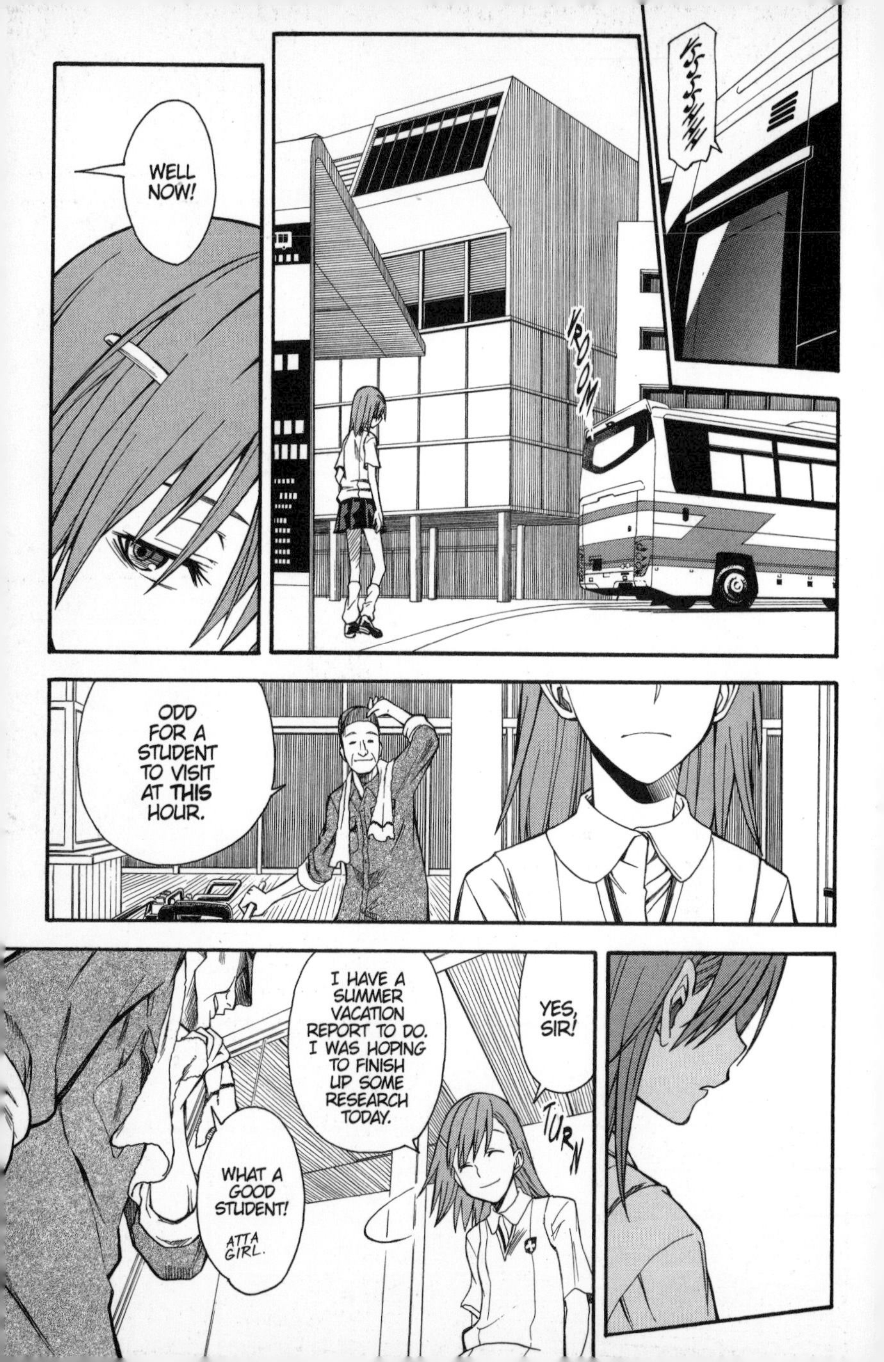
VROOM
WELL NOW!
ODD FOR A STUDENT TO VISIT AT THIS HOUR.
YES, SIR!
I HAVE A SUMMER VACATION REPORT TO DO. I WAS HOPING TO FINISH UP SOME RESEARCH TODAY.
TURN
WHAT A GOOD STUDENT!
ATTA GIRL.

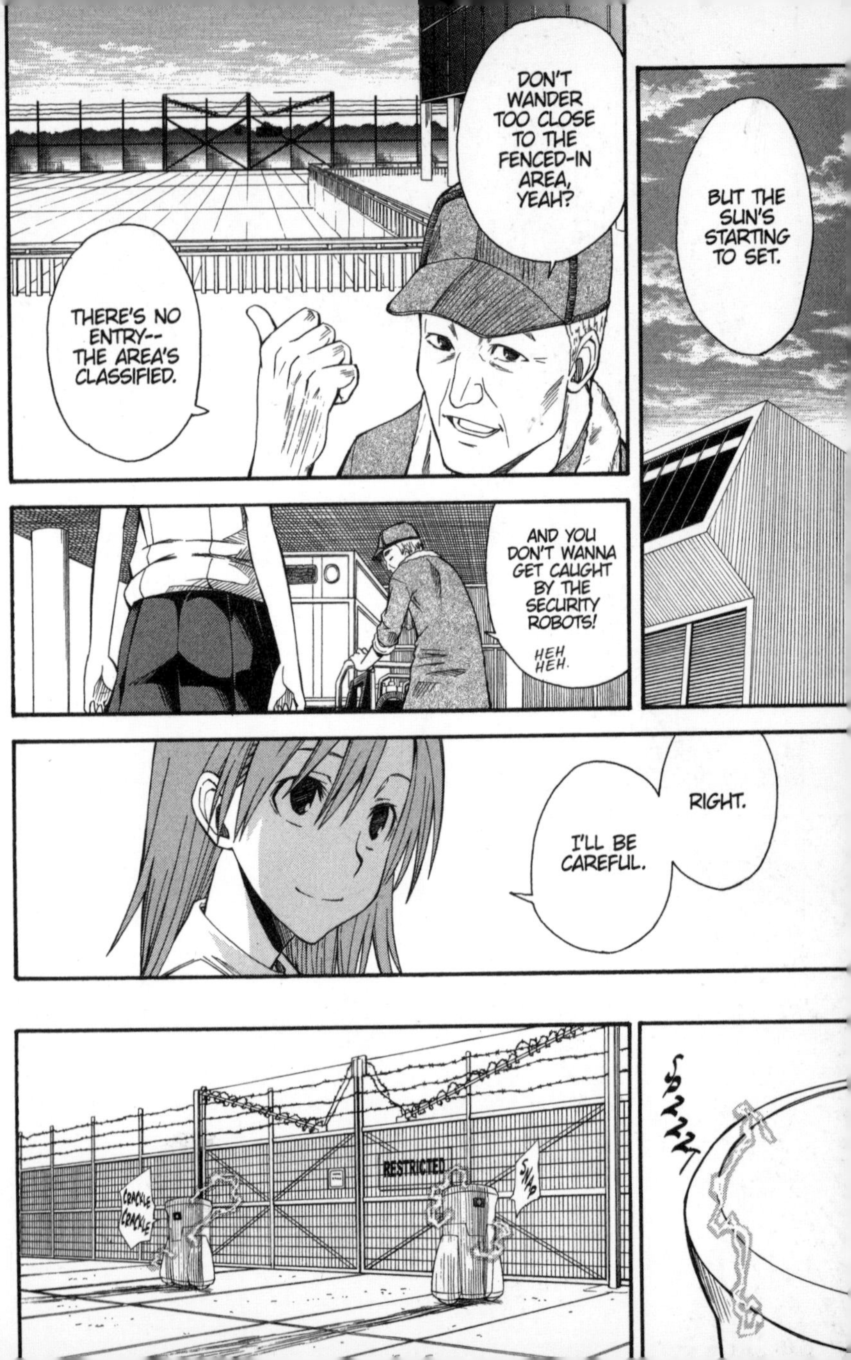
BUT THE SUN'S STARTING TO SET.
DON'T WANDER TOO CLOSE TO THE FENCED-IN AREA, YEAH?
THERE'S NO ENTRY-- THE AREA'S CLASSIFIED.
AND YOU DON'T WANNA GET CAUGHT BY THE SECURITY ROBOTS!
HEH HEH.
RIGHT.
I'LL BE CAREFUL.
SPZZZT
SNAP
RESTRICTED
CRACKLE CRACKLE

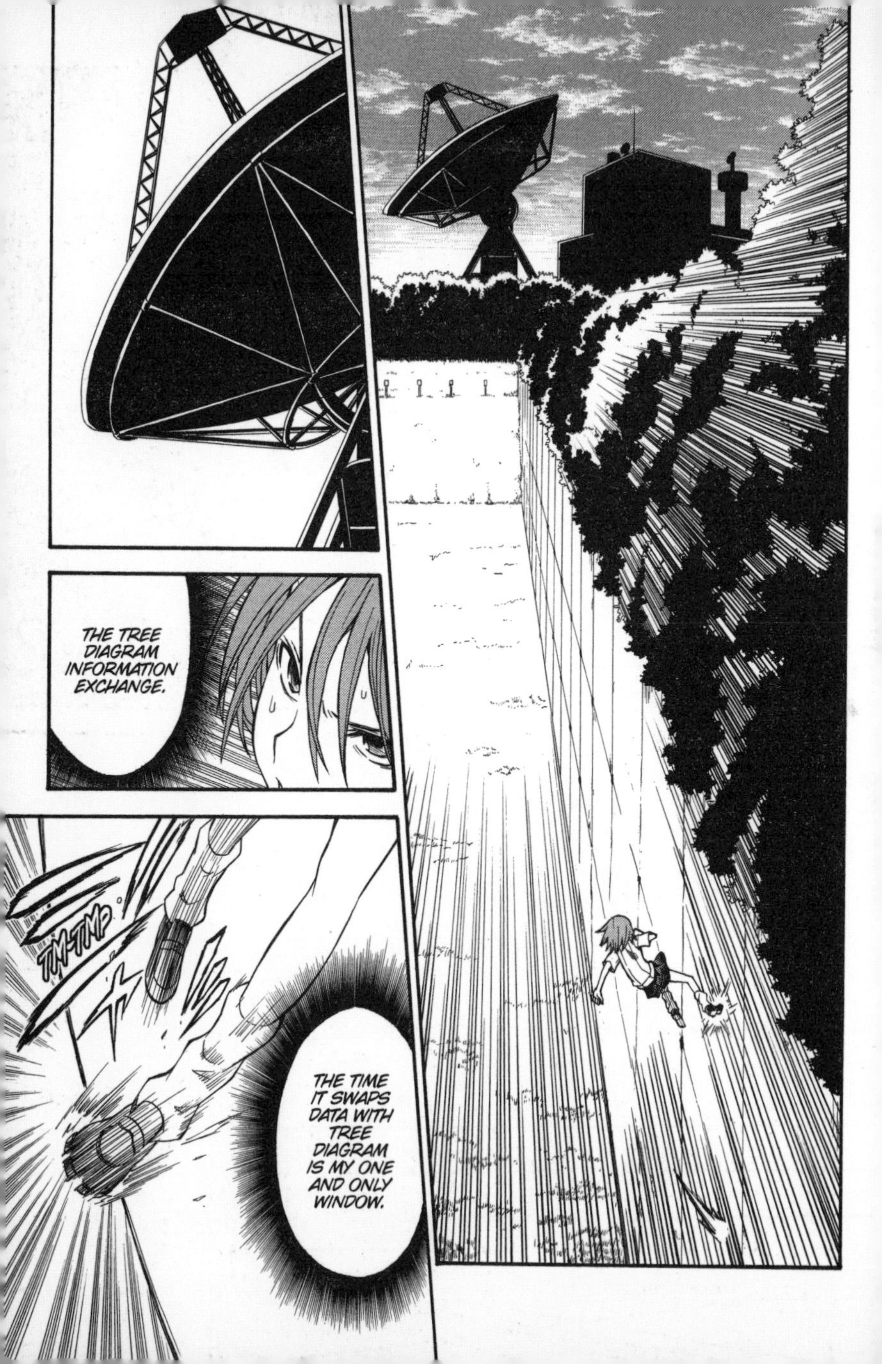
THE TREE DIAGRAM INFORMATION EXCHANGE.
TIM-TIMP
THE TIME IT SWAPS DATA WITH TREE DIAGRAM IS MY ONE AND ONLY WINDOW.

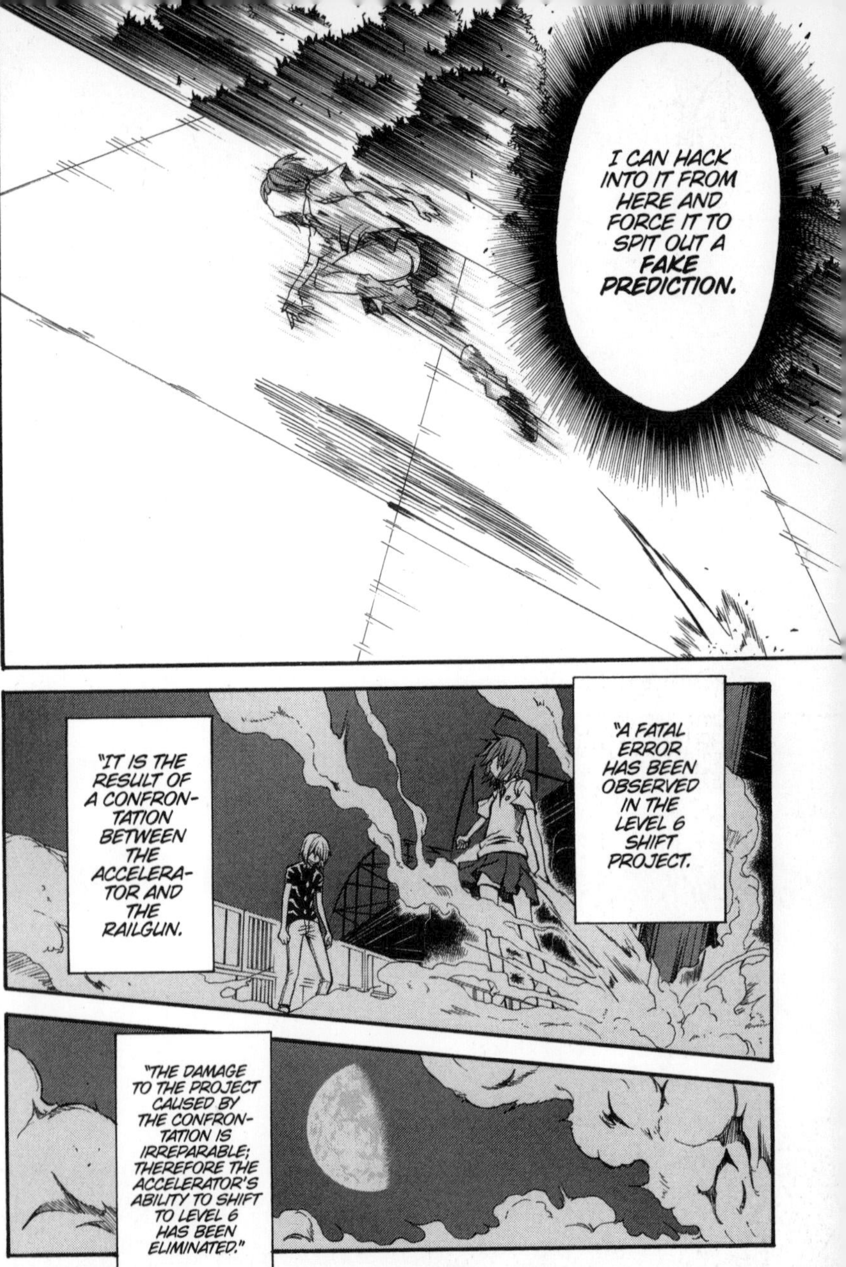
I CAN HACK INTO IT FROM HERE AND FORCE IT TO SPIT OUT A **FAKE PREDICTION.**
"A FATAL ERROR HAS BEEN OBSERVED IN THE LEVEL 6 SHIFT PROJECT.
"IT IS THE RESULT OF A CONFRONTATION BETWEEN THE ACCELERATOR AND THE RAILGUN.
"THE DAMAGE TO THE PROJECT CAUSED BY THE CONFRONTATION IS IRREPARABLE; THEREFORE THE ACCELERATOR'S ABILITY TO SHIFT TO LEVEL 6 HAS BEEN ELIMINATED."

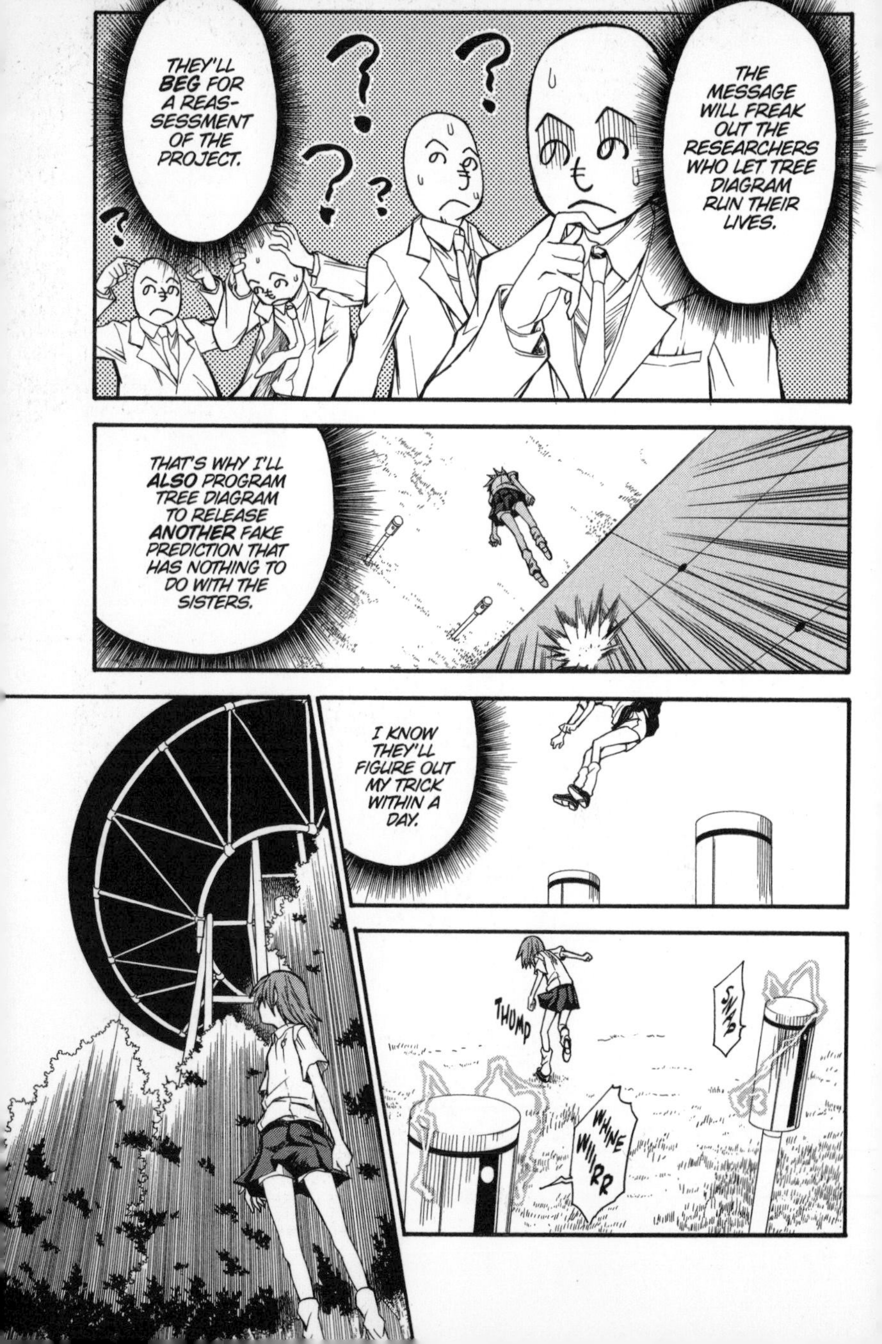
THE MESSAGE WILL FREAK OUT THE RESEARCHERS WHO LET TREE DIAGRAM RUN THEIR LIVES.
THEY'LL **BEG** FOR A REAS-SESSMENT OF THE PROJECT.
THAT'S WHY I'LL **ALSO** PROGRAM TREE DIAGRAM TO RELEASE **ANOTHER** FAKE PREDICTION THAT HAS NOTHING TO DO WITH THE SISTERS.
I KNOW THEY'LL FIGURE OUT MY TRICK WITHIN A DAY.
SNAP
THUMP
WHINE
WIIIRR

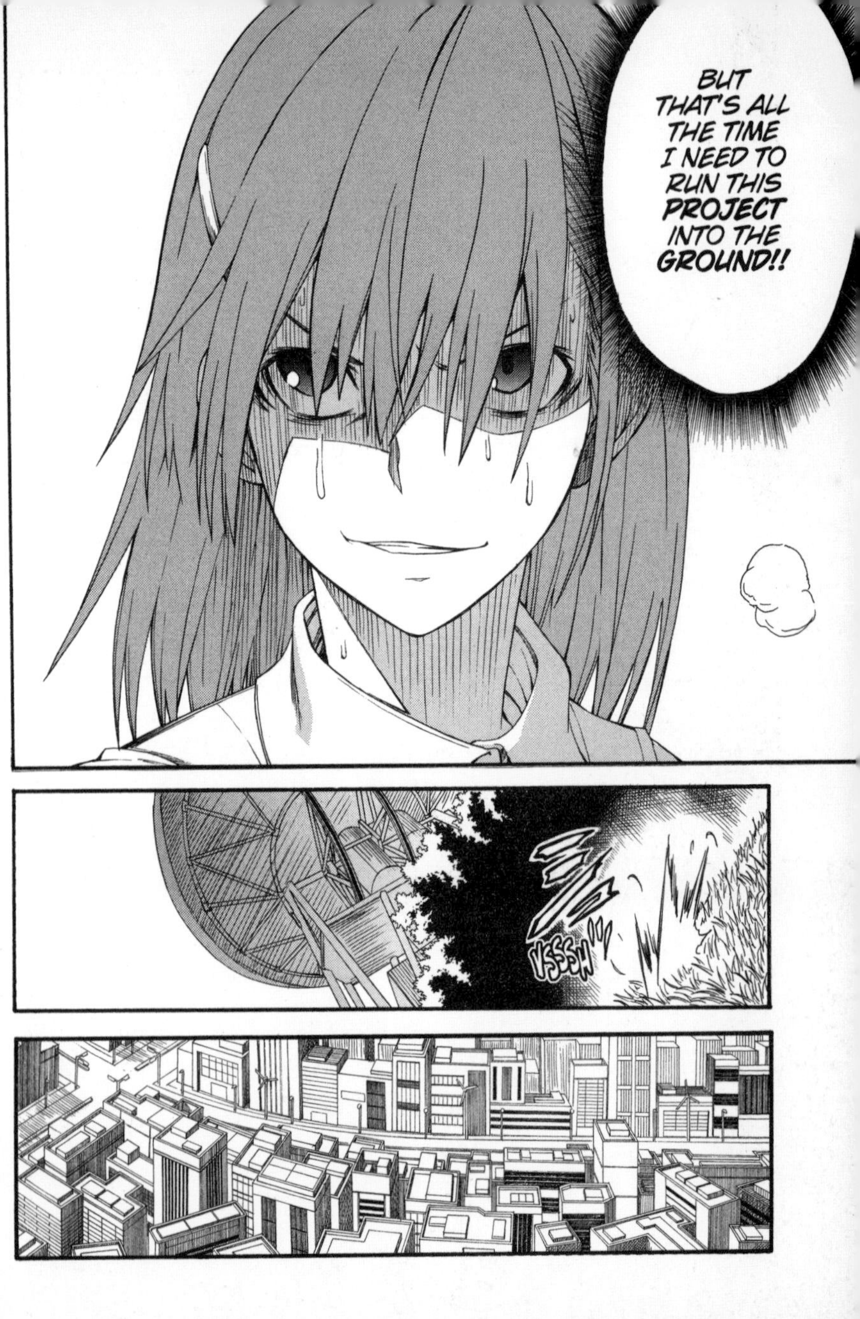
BUT THAT'S ALL THE TIME I NEED TO RUN THIS PROJECT INTO THE GROUND!!
VSSSSH

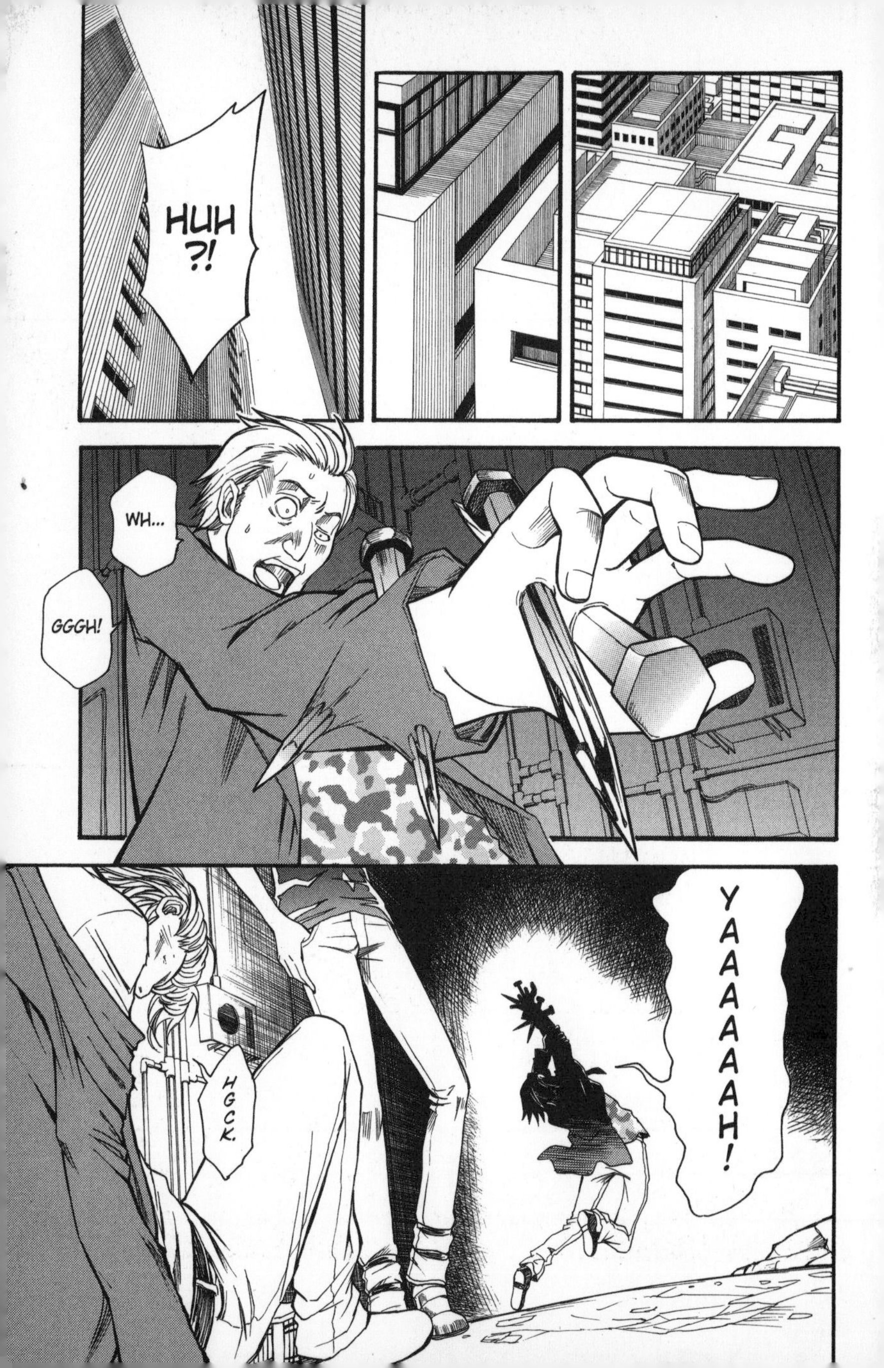
HUH ?!
WH...
GGGH!
YAAAAAAAH!
HGCK.

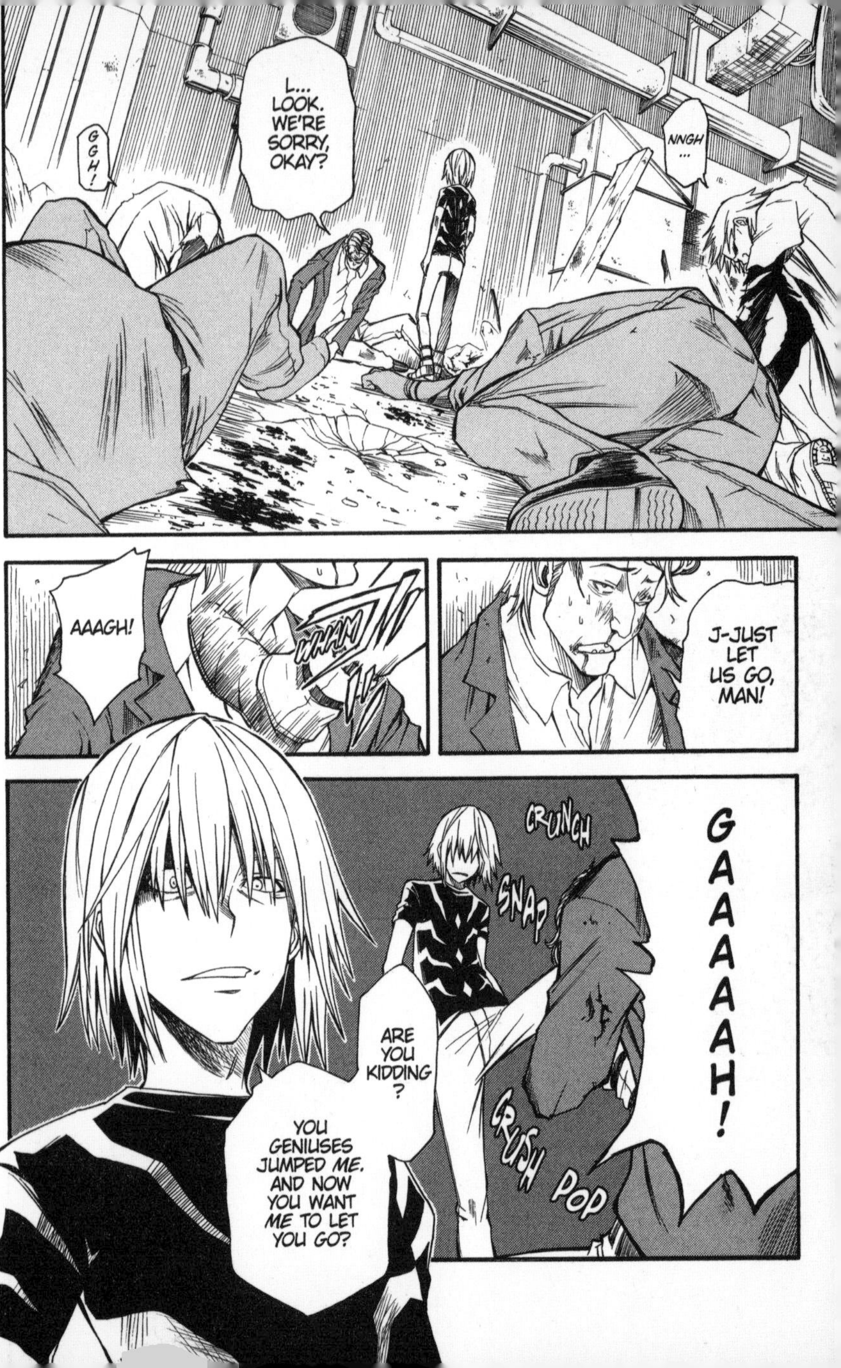
NNGH ...
L... LOOK. WE'RE SORRY, OKAY?
GGH!
J-JUST LET US GO, MAN!
WHAM
AAAGH!
GAAAAAAH!
CRUNCH
SNAP
CRUSH
POP
ARE YOU KIDDING?
YOU GENIUSES JUMPED ME. AND NOW YOU WANT ME TO LET YOU GO?

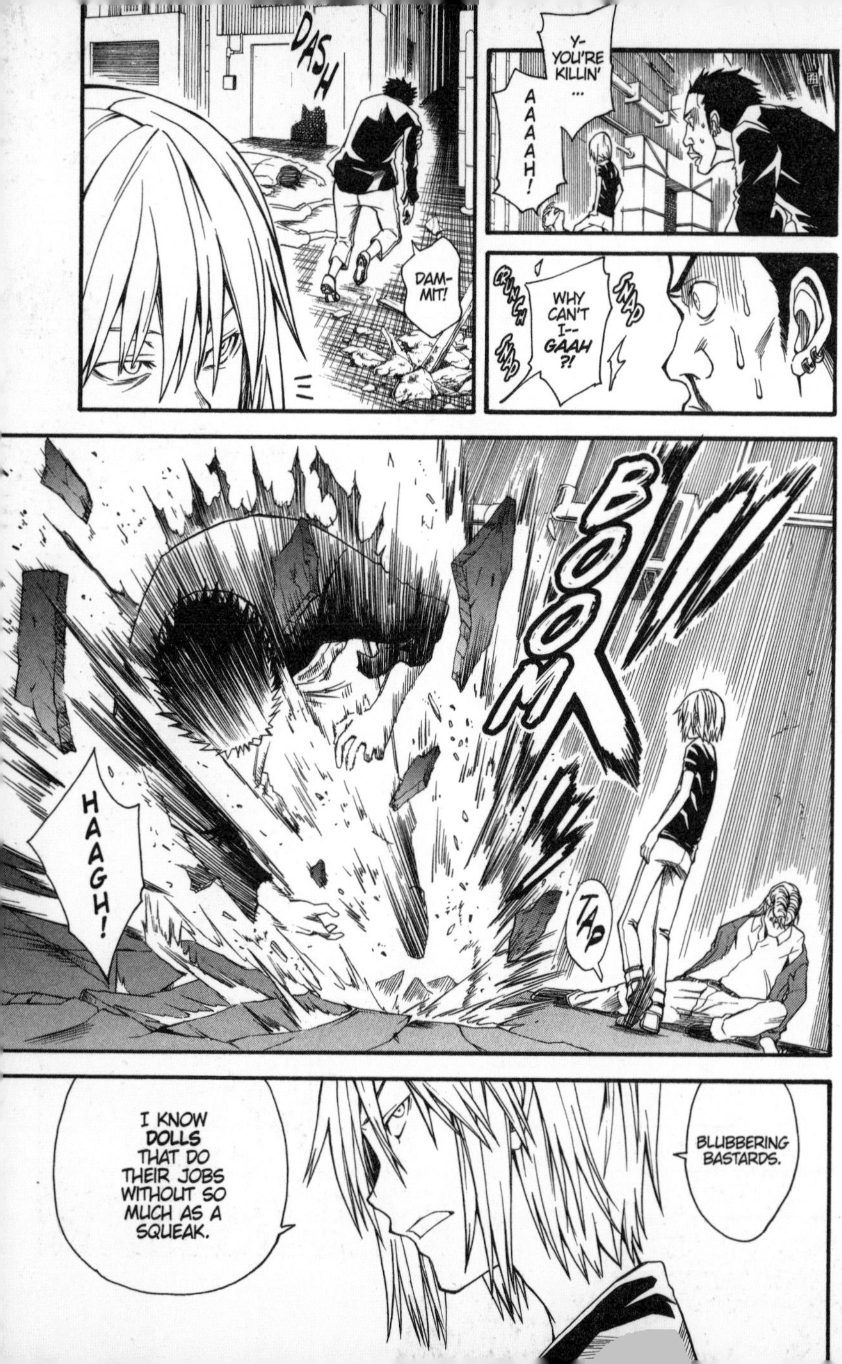
Y-YOU'RE KILLIN'...
AAAAAAH!
SNAP
WHY CAN'T I-- GAAH?!
CRUNCH
SNAP
DASH
DAM-MIT!
BOOM
TAP
HAAGH!
BLUBBERING BASTARDS.
I KNOW DOLLS THAT DO THEIR JOBS WITHOUT SO MUCH AS A SQUEAK.

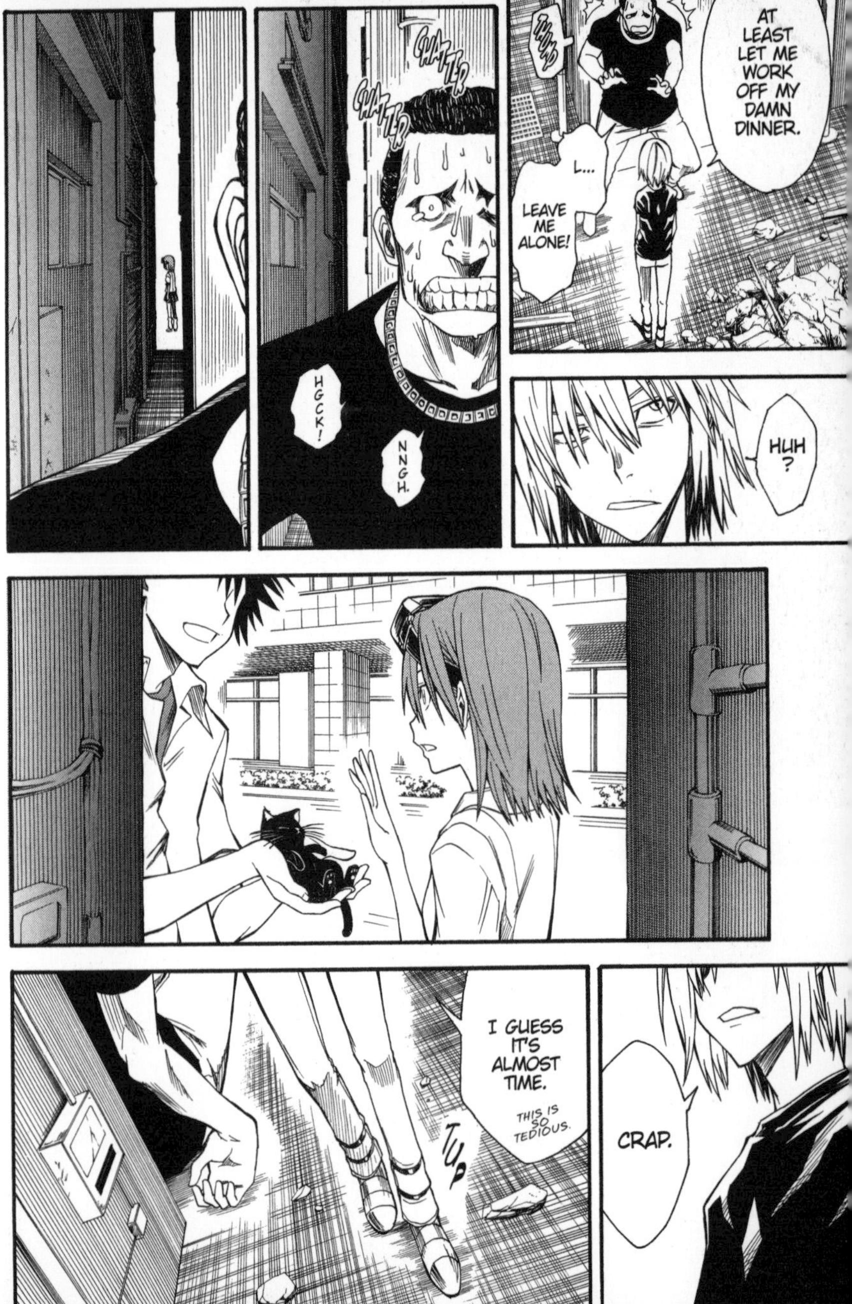
AT LEAST LET ME WORK OFF MY DAMN DINNER.
THUMP
L...
LEAVE ME ALONE!
HUH?
CHATTER
CHATTER
HGCK!
NNGH.
CRAP.
I GUESS IT'S ALMOST TIME.
THIS IS SO TEDIOUS.
TUP

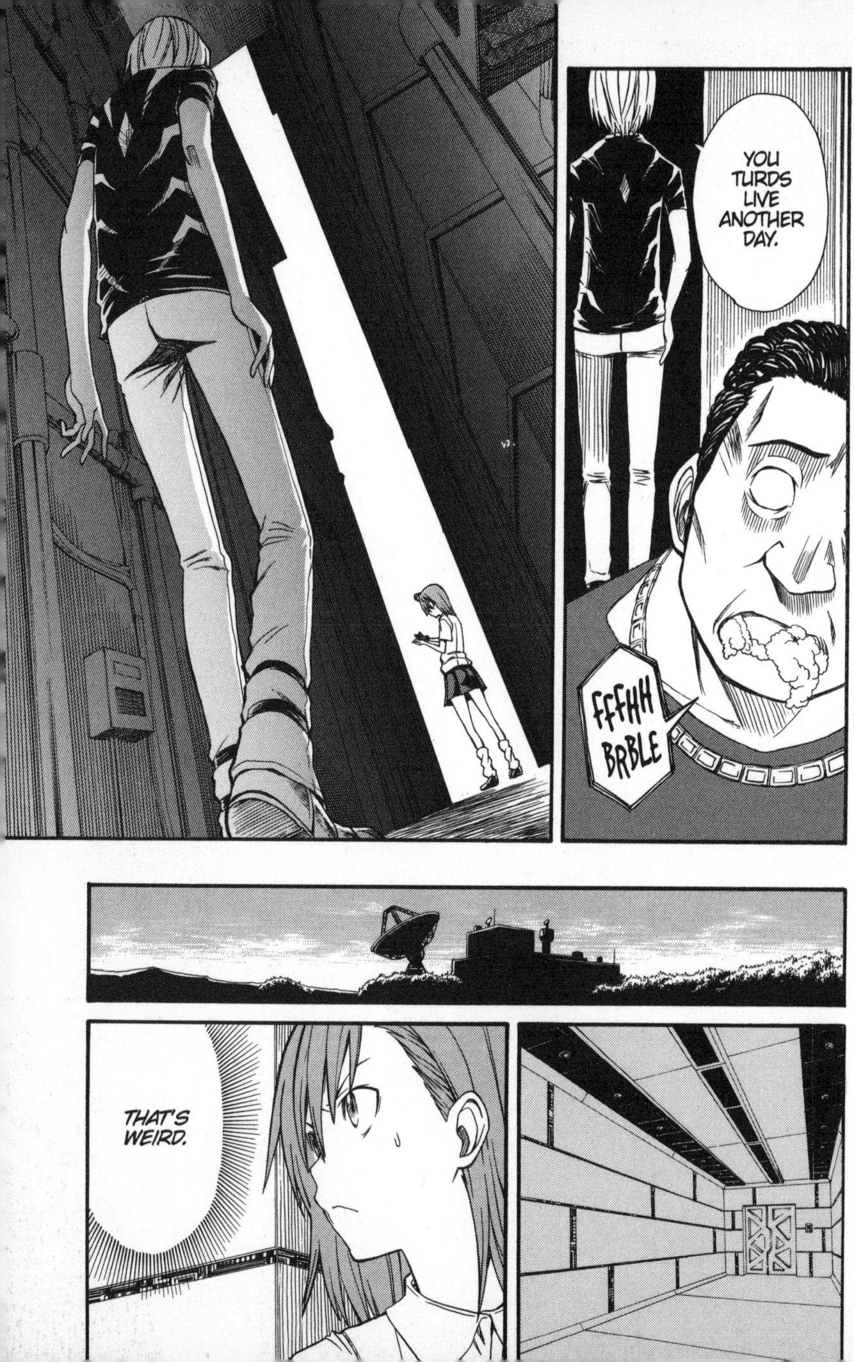
YOU TURDS LIVE ANOTHER DAY.
FFFHH BRBLE
THAT'S WEIRD.

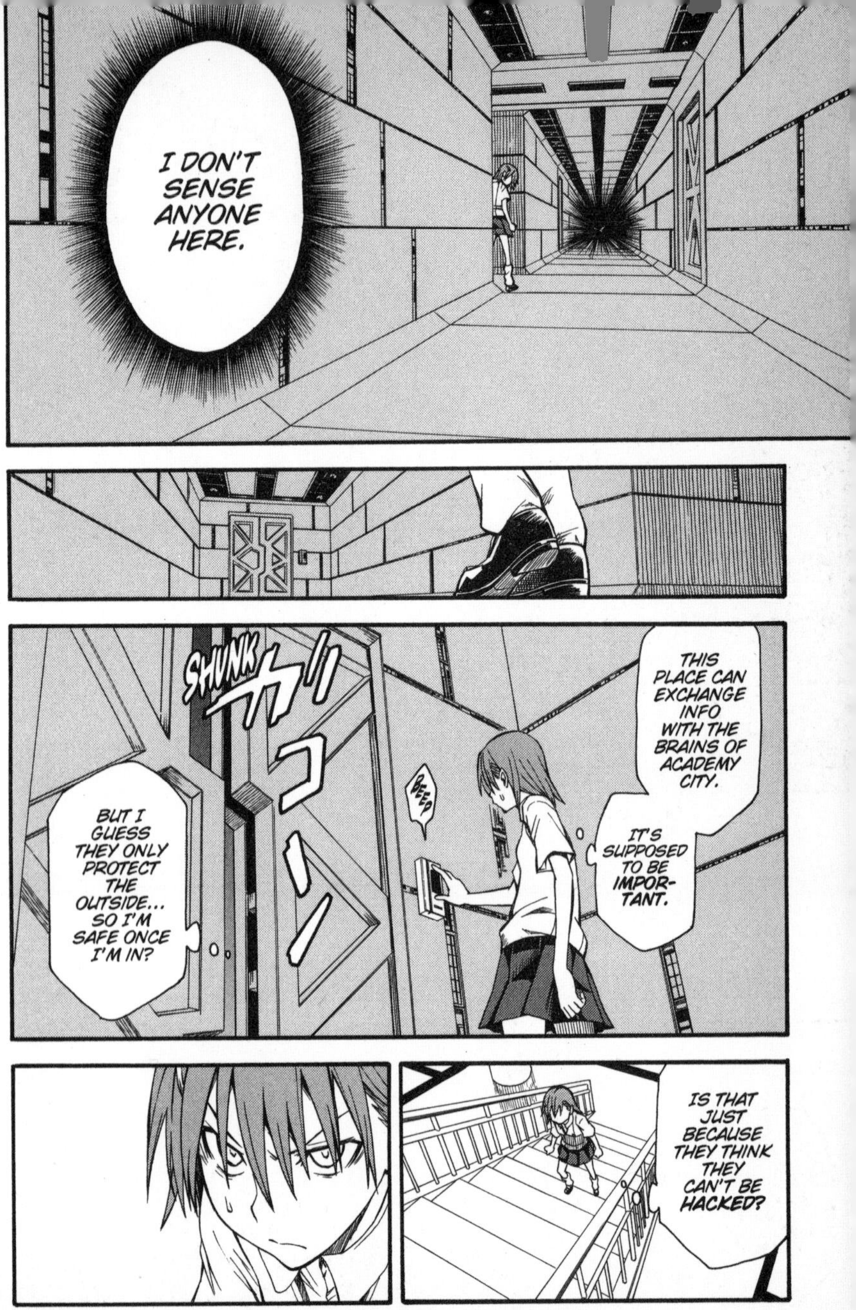
I DON'T SENSE ANYONE HERE.
THIS PLACE CAN EXCHANGE INFO WITH THE BRAINS OF ACADEMY CITY.
SHUNK
BEEP
IT'S SUPPOSED TO BE IMPOR-TANT.
BUT I GUESS THEY ONLY PROTECT THE OUTSIDE... SO I'M SAFE ONCE I'M IN?
IS THAT JUST BECAUSE THEY THINK THEY CAN'T BE HACKED?

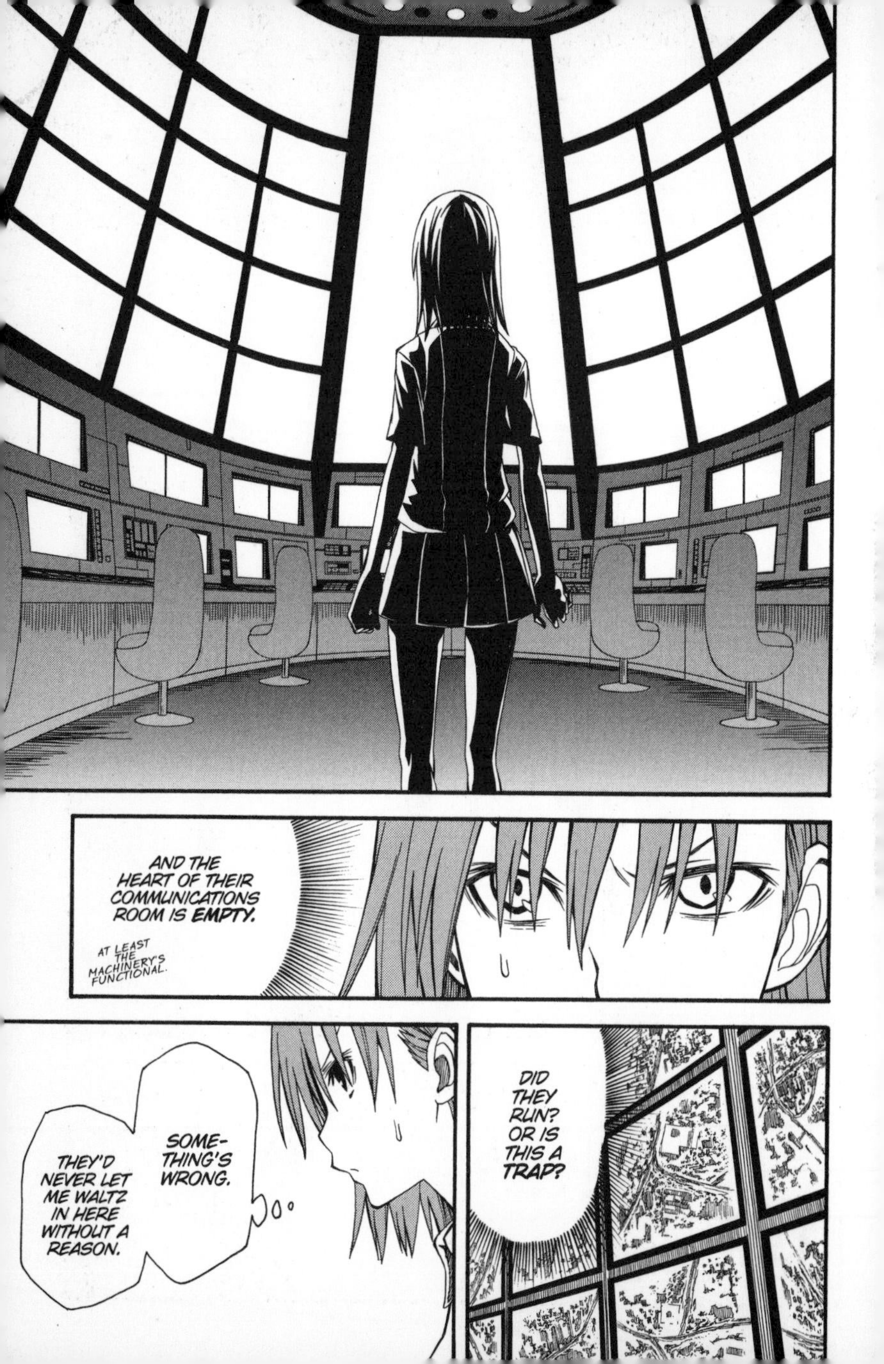
AND THE HEART OF THEIR COMMUNICATIONS ROOM IS **EMPTY.**
AT LEAST THE MACHINERY'S FUNCTIONAL.
DID THEY RUN? OR IS THIS A **TRAP?**
SOME-THING'S WRONG.
THEY'D NEVER LET ME WALTZ IN HERE WITHOUT A REASON.

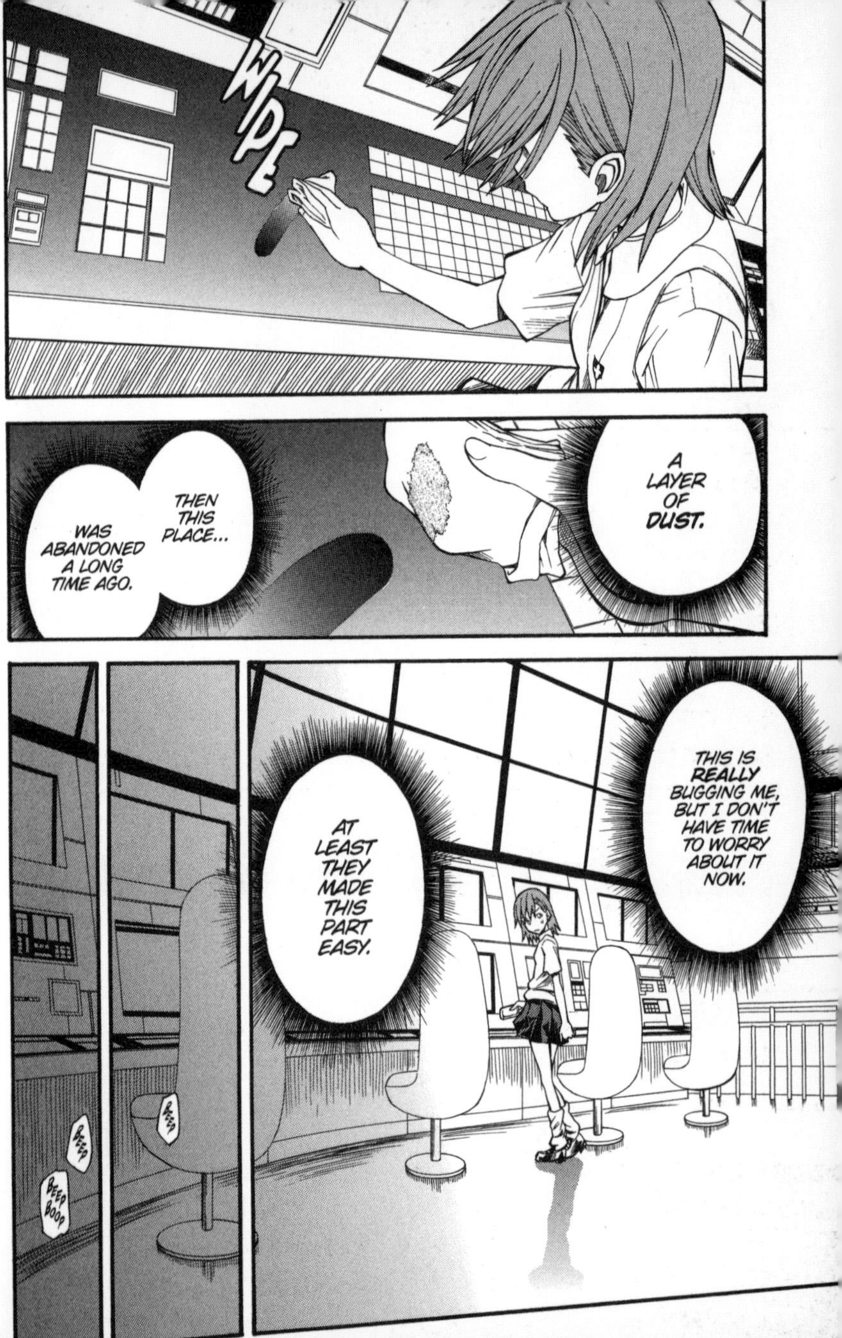
WIPE
A LAYER OF DUST.
THEN THIS PLACE...
WAS ABANDONED A LONG TIME AGO.
THIS IS REALLY BUGGING ME, BUT I DON'T HAVE TIME TO WORRY ABOUT IT NOW.
AT LEAST THEY MADE THIS PART EASY.
BEEP
BEEP
BEEP BEEP BOOP

BEEP

BEEP
BEEP
BEEP

NO WAY.

THERE HAVEN'T BEEN ANY COMMUNI-CATIONS TODAY?!

BUT I THOUGHT THERE WERE *HUNDREDS* OF REQUESTS MADE TO TREE DIAGRAM EVERY DAY!

AND IT'S BEEN LIKE THAT A WHILE.

of dialysis in

"Research on transitional movement mode
Skill Regular distrib
SCIENCE WORSHI

"Influence the stress
institution gives to
CHILD ERROR.

"The color of pan

saka

WAIT. IT LOOKS LIKE SOME PETITIONS WERE SENT HERE...

BUT NONE OF THEM HAVE BEEN PRO-CESSED.

RATTLE
RATTLE

BEEP
BEEP
BEEP
BEEP
BEEP

The report to
SCIENCE WORSHIP UNIFIED COUNCIL.

—CONFIDENTIAL—

"A FINAL REPORT CONCERNING THE MIA TREE DIAGRAM.

"ON JULY 28TH AT 00:22 HOURS, TREE DIAGRAM DISAPPEARED FROM ORBIT.

"AT 01:15 HOURS, THE FIRST SEARCH TEAM WAS DISPATCHED.

"AT 02:40 HOURS, A PORTION OF ITS REMNANTS WAS RECOVERED.

"BASED ON THE RESULTING ANALYSIS...

TREE DIAGRAM lost on the
22:00 minut orbiting sat
sight of the DIAGRAM.
sent primary. 21:4
reco The REMNA round. A
resu

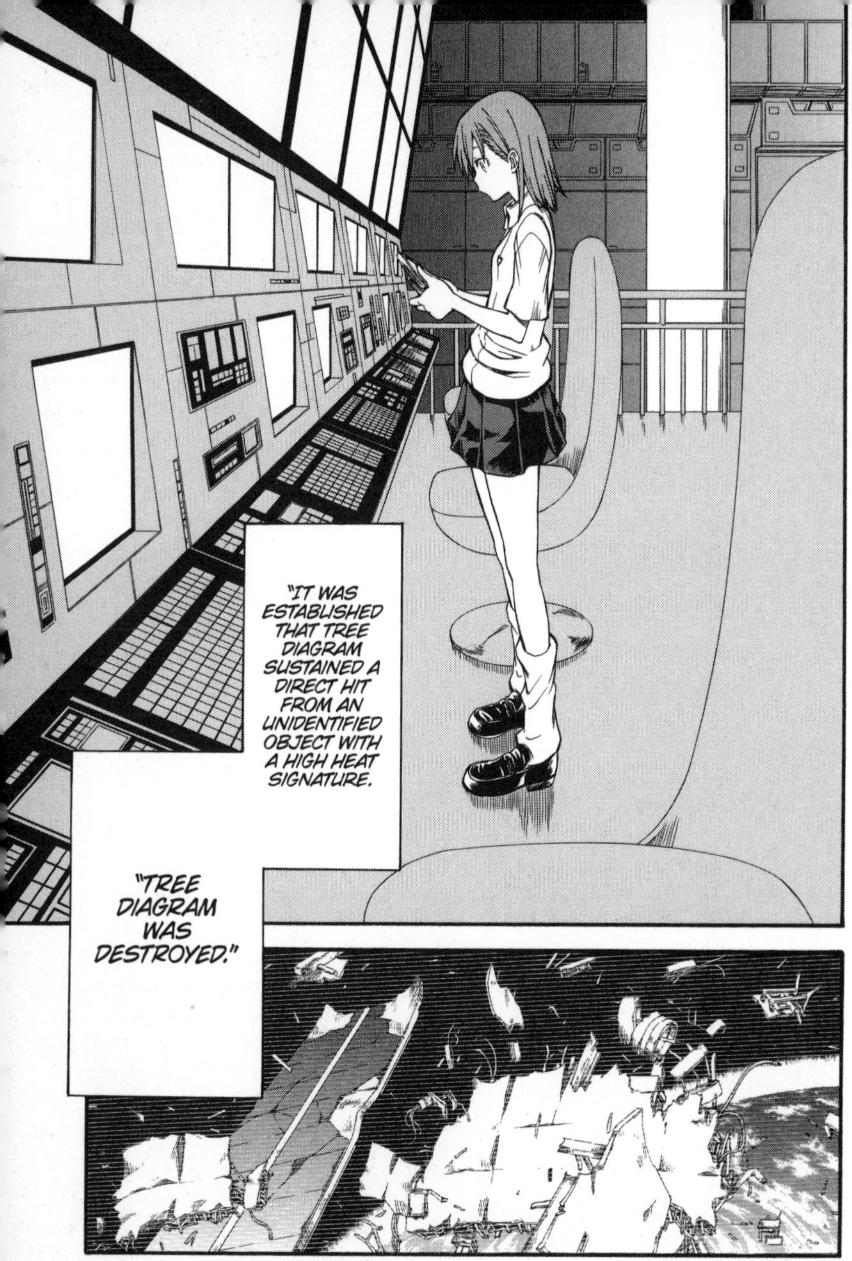
"IT WAS ESTABLISHED THAT TREE DIAGRAM SUSTAINED A DIRECT HIT FROM AN UNIDENTIFIED OBJECT WITH A HIGH HEAT SIGNATURE.
"TREE DIAGRAM WAS DESTROYED."

A Certain Sisters' Enquête

IF A CLONE OF ME SUDDENLY APPEARED?
YOU SURE ASK WEIRD QUES-TIONS.
MY CLONE...
EGGS ARE ONLY 50 YEN A PACK? LIMIT TWO?!
Special Sale
BUT SINCE THERE'S TWO OF ME, I CAN BUY FOUR! ☆
DASH
WOO!
LET'S GO, ME.
GOT-CHA, ME!
WOO!
A CLONE WOULD BE AWE-SOME.
...!
SIGH...

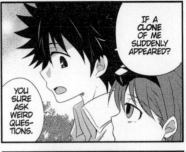

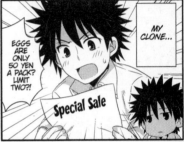

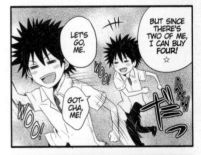

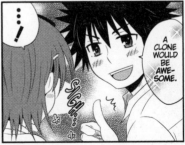

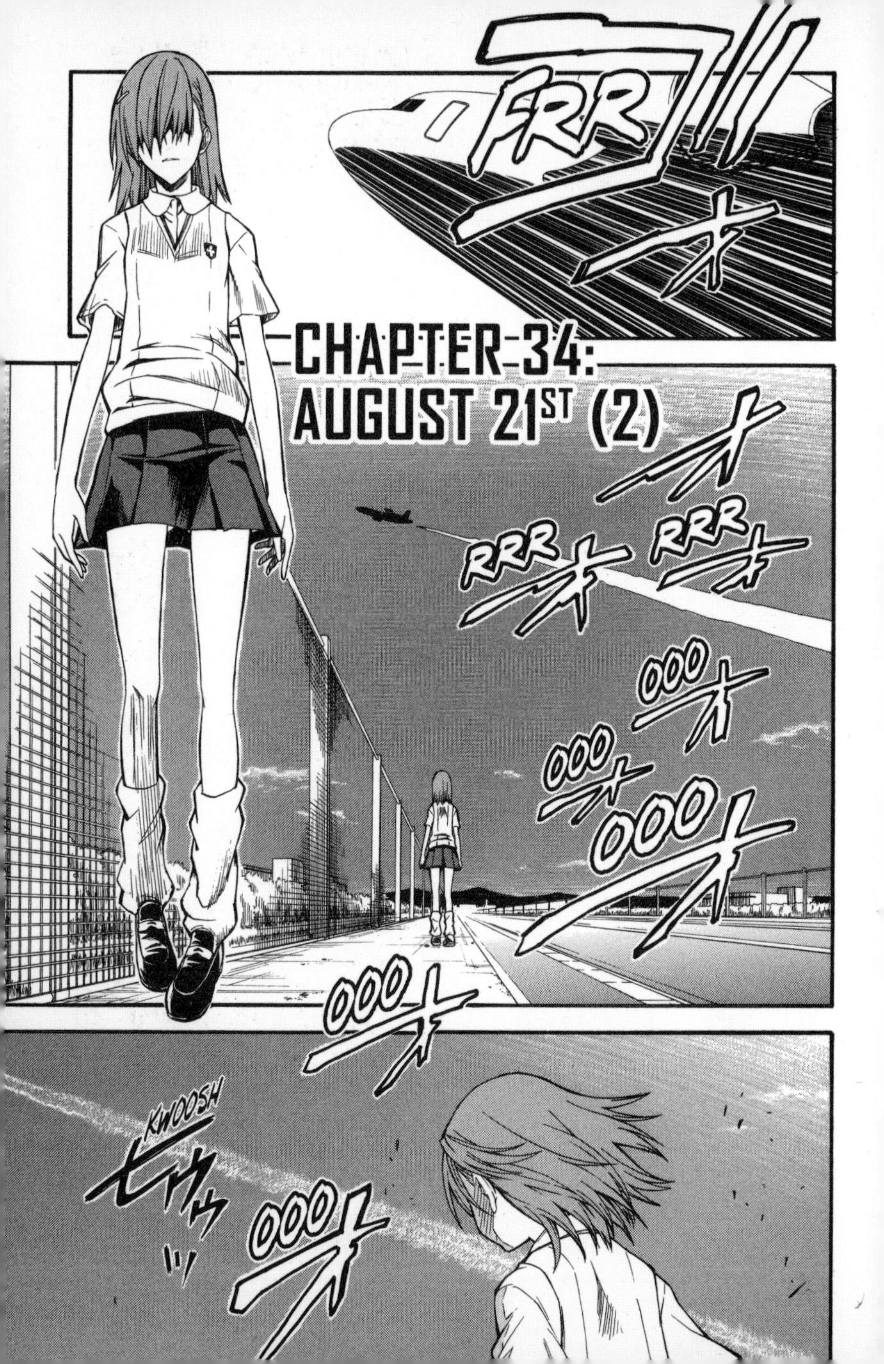
FRR
CHAPTER 34:
AUGUST 21ST (2)
RRR
RRR
OOO
OOO
OOO
OOO
KWOOSH
OOO

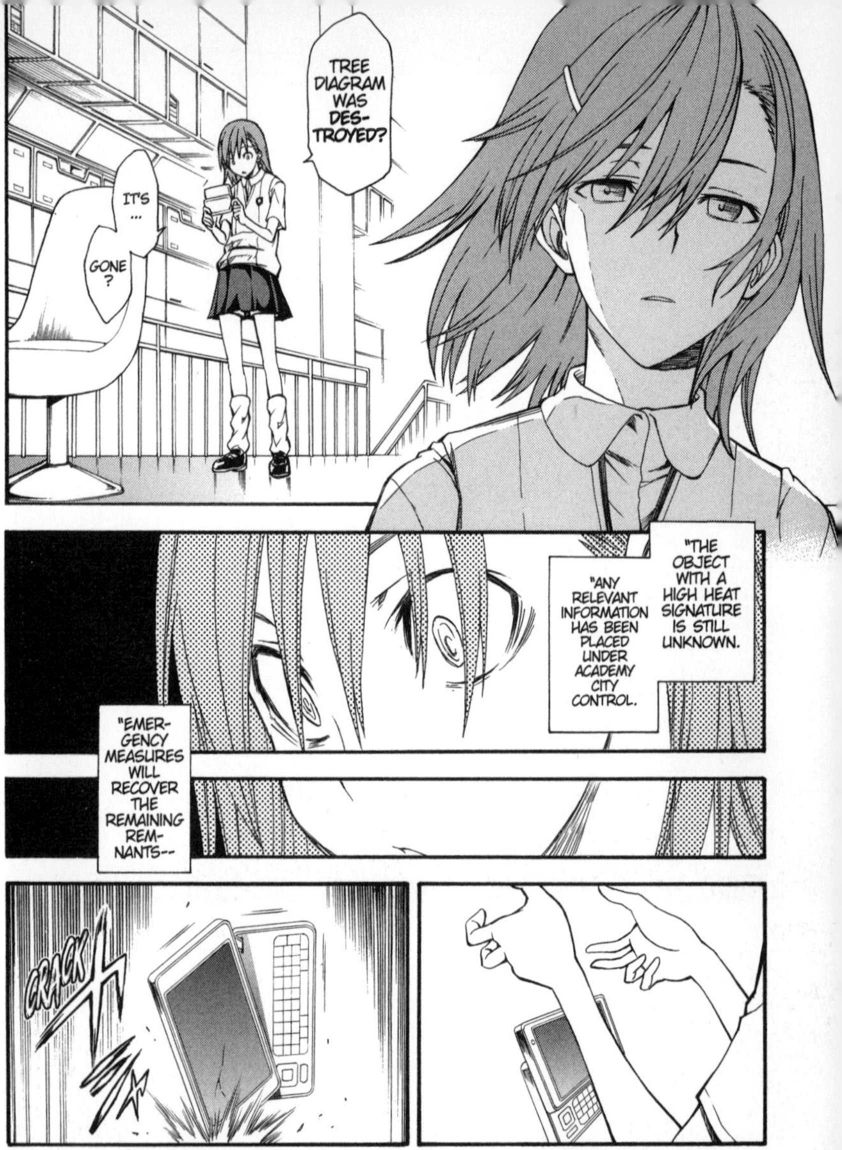
TREE DIAGRAM WAS DES-TROYED?
IT'S ... GONE?
"THE OBJECT WITH A HIGH HEAT SIGNATURE IS STILL UNKNOWN.
"ANY RELEVANT INFORMATION HAS BEEN PLACED UNDER ACADEMY CITY CONTROL.
"EMER-GENCY MEASURES WILL RECOVER THE REMAINING REM-NANTS--
CRACK

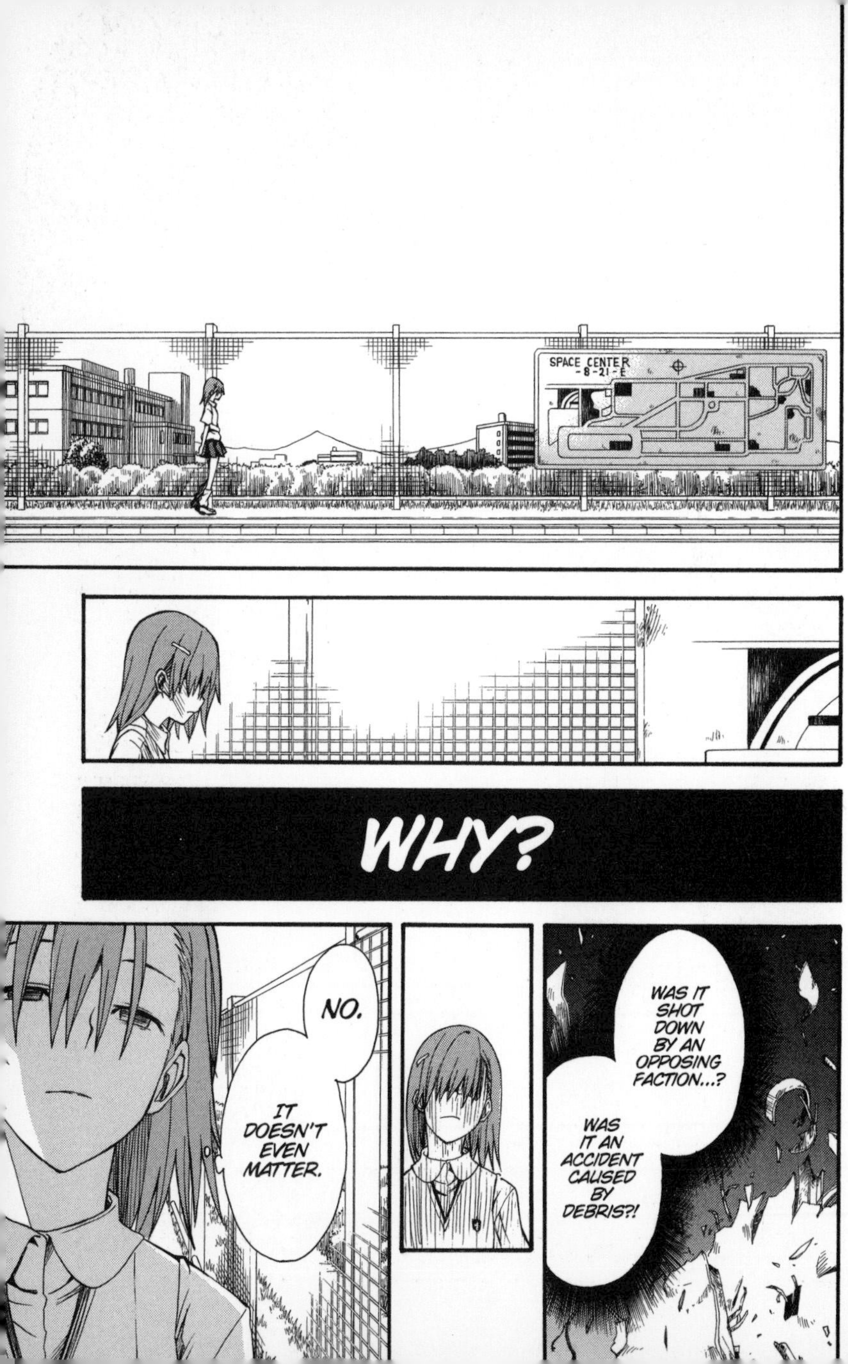
SPACE CENTER
-8-21-E
WHY?
WAS IT SHOT DOWN BY AN OPPOSING FACTION...?
WAS IT AN ACCIDENT CAUSED BY DEBRIS?!
NO.
IT DOESN'T EVEN MATTER.

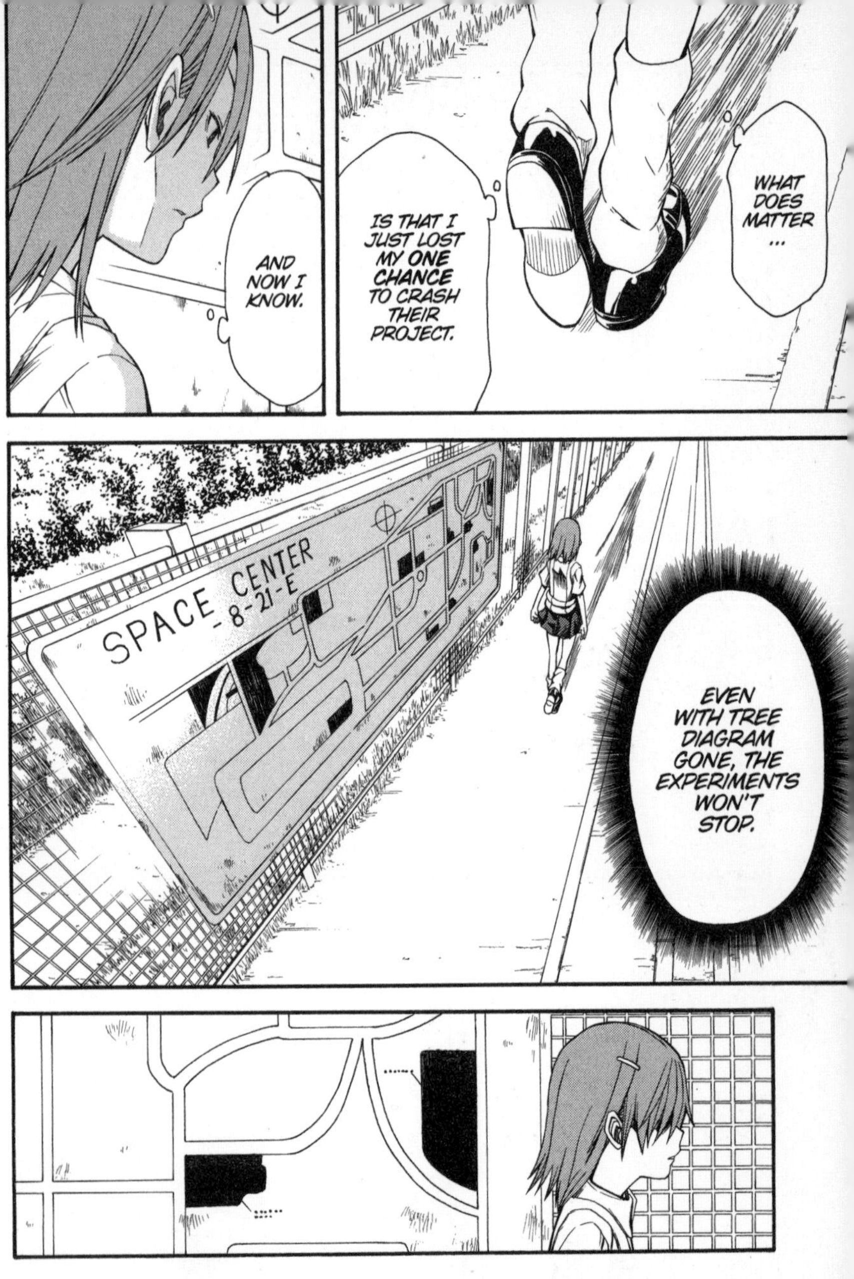
WHAT DOES MATTER ...
IS THAT I JUST LOST MY ONE CHANCE TO CRASH THEIR PROJECT.
AND NOW I KNOW.
EVEN WITH TREE DIAGRAM GONE, THE EXPERIMENTS WON'T STOP.
SPACE CENTER
-8-21-E

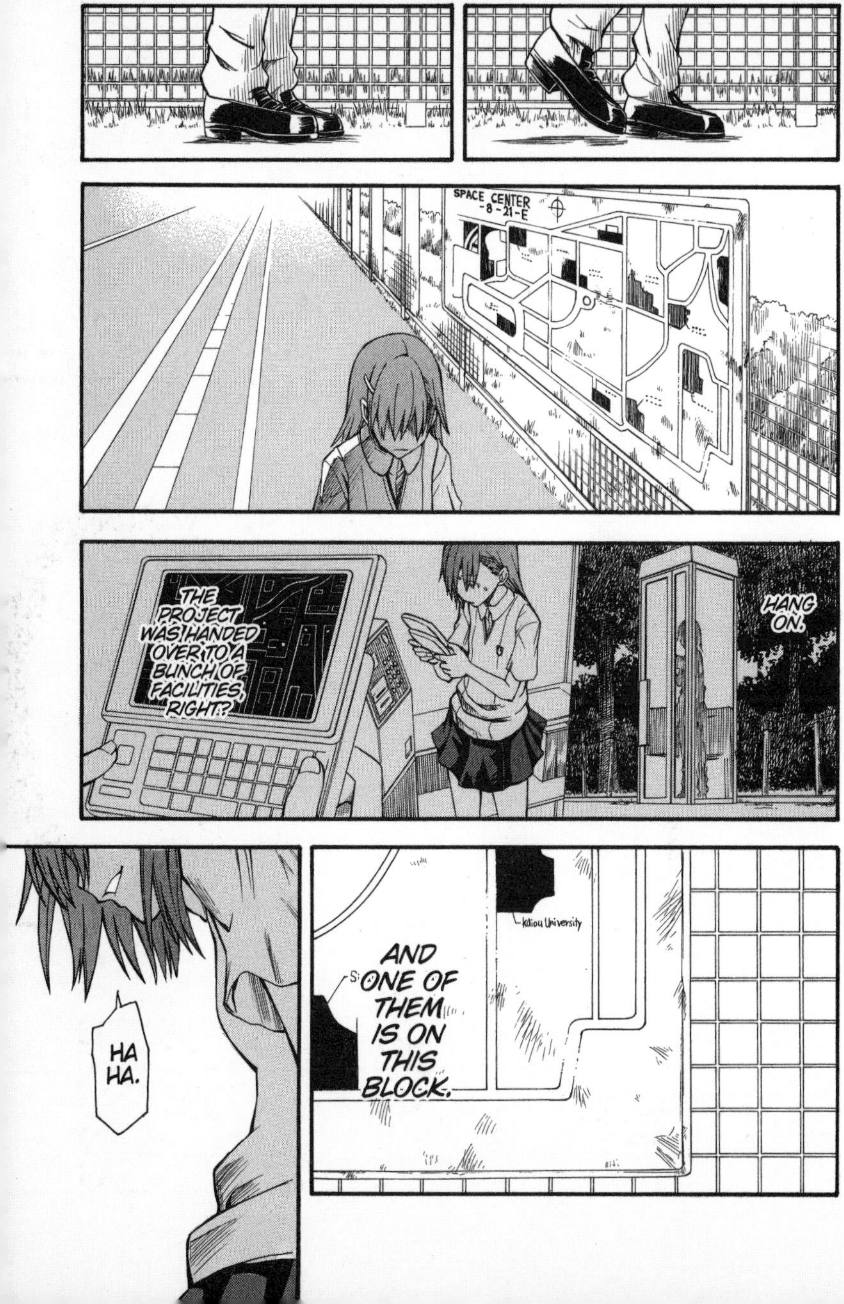
SPACE CENTER -8-21-E
HANG ON.
THE PROJECT WAS HANDED OVER TO A BUNCH OF FACILITIES, RIGHT?
Kdiou University
AND ONE OF THEM IS ON THIS BLOCK.
HA HA.

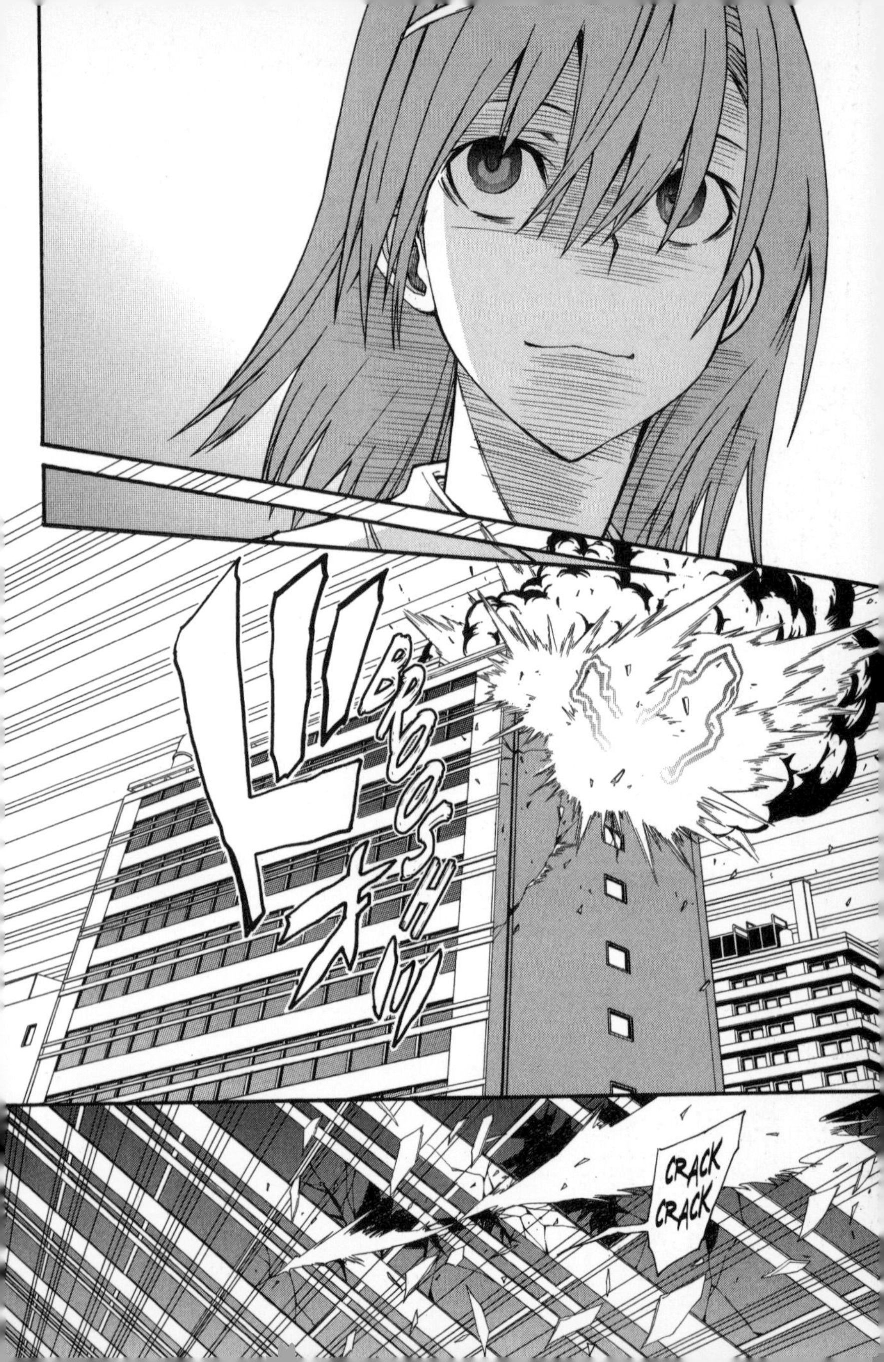
BROOSH
CRACK CRACK

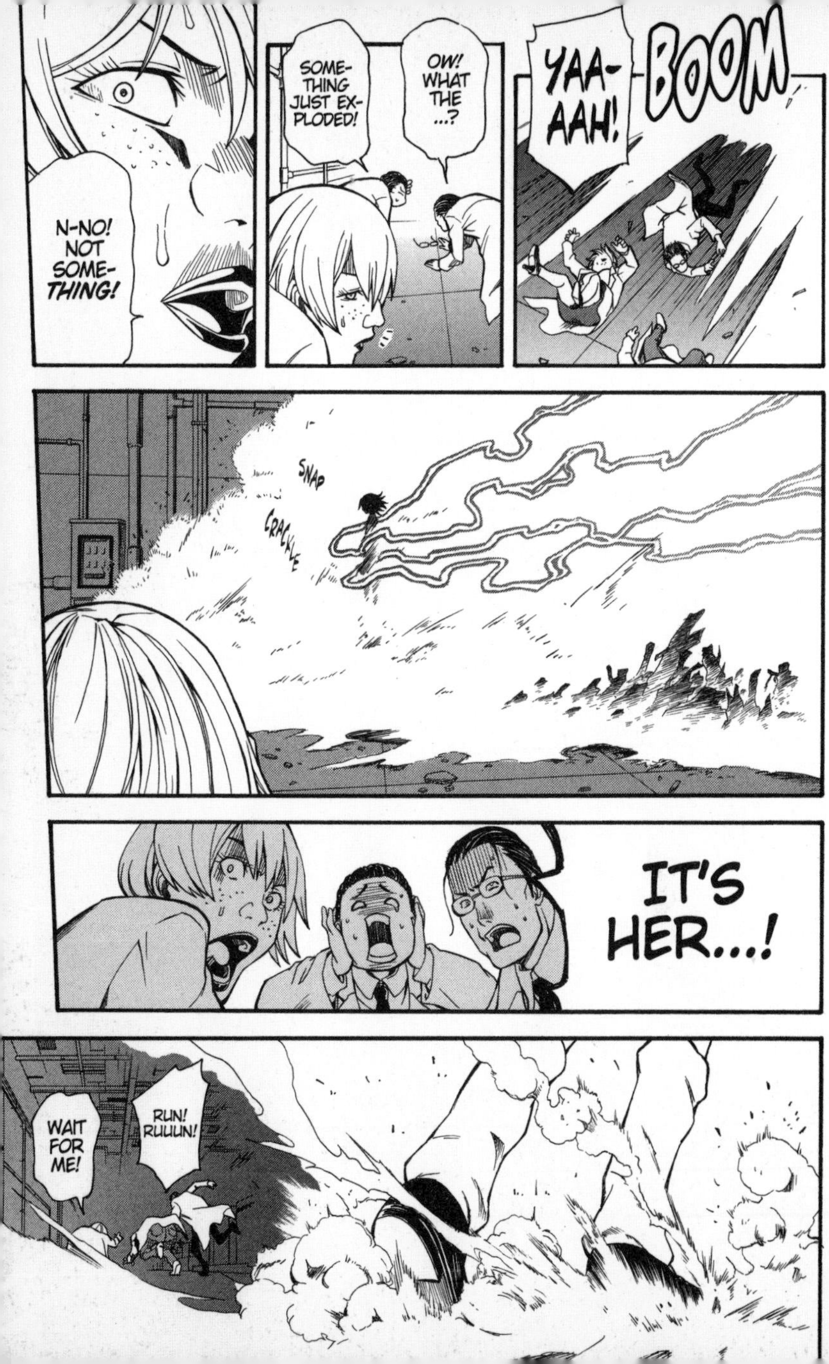
BOOM
YAAA-AAH!
OW! WHAT THE ...?
SOME-THING JUST EX-PLODED!
N-NO! NOT SOME-THING!
SNAP
CRACKLE
IT'S HER...!
RUN! RUUUN!
WAIT FOR ME!

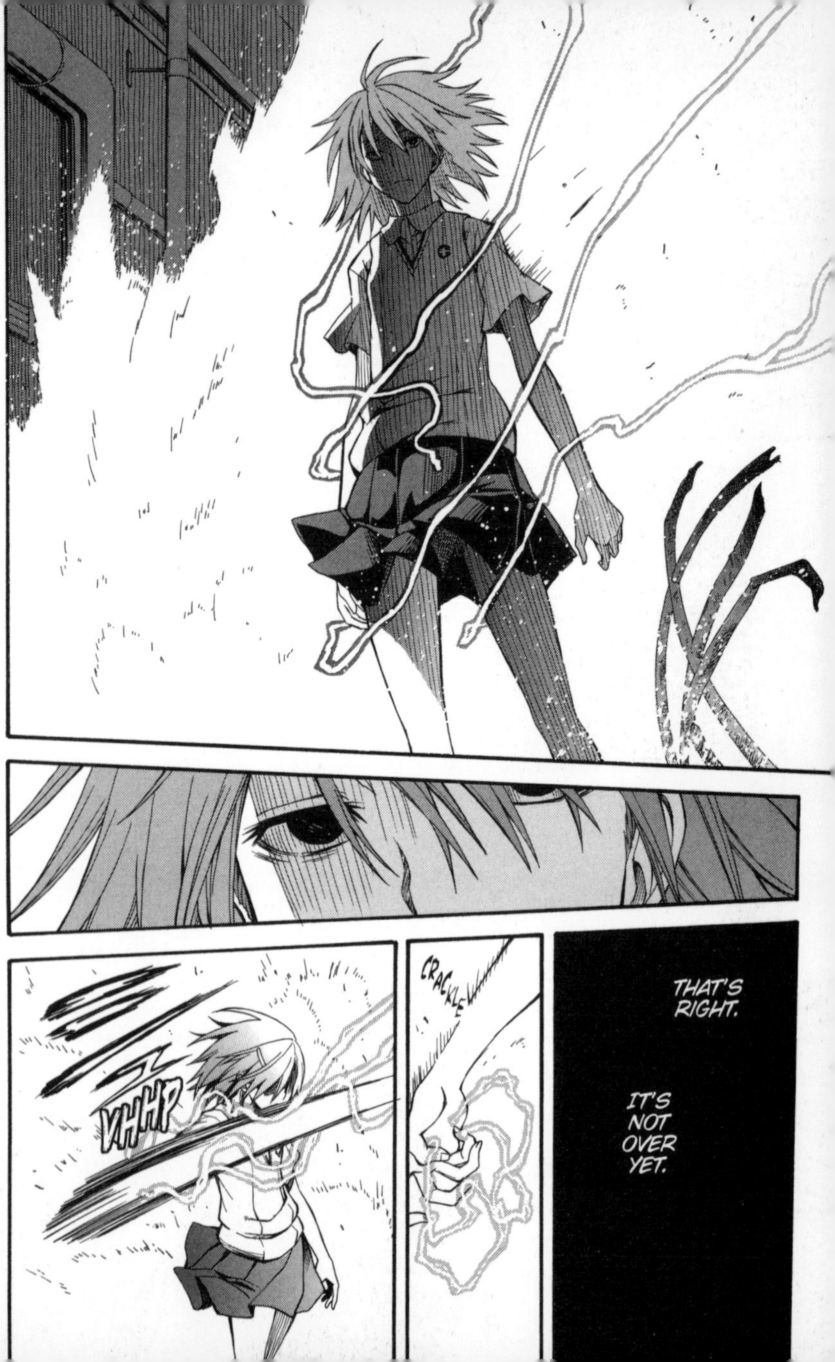
THAT'S RIGHT.
IT'S NOT OVER YET.
CRACKLE
VHHP

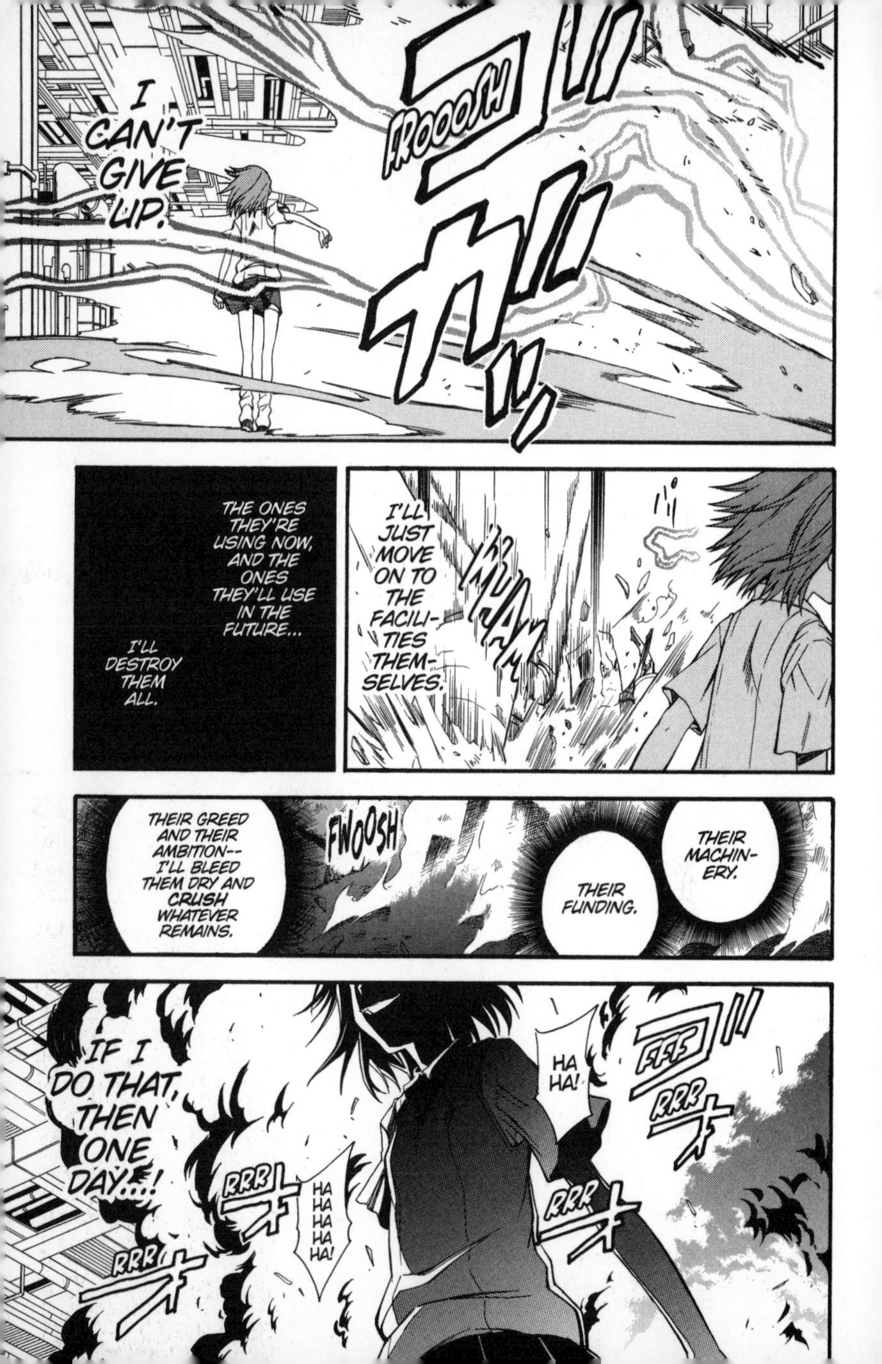
FROOOSH
I CAN'T GIVE UP.
I'LL JUST MOVE ON TO THE FACILITIES THEMSELVES.
WHAM
THE ONES THEY'RE USING NOW, AND THE ONES THEY'LL USE IN THE FUTURE...
I'LL DESTROY THEM ALL.
THEIR MACHINERY.
THEIR FUNDING.
FWOOSH
THEIR GREED AND THEIR AMBITION-- I'LL BLEED THEM DRY AND CRUSH WHATEVER REMAINS.
FFF
RRR
HA HA!
RRR
HA HA HA HA HA!
RRR
IF I DO THAT, THEN ONE DAY...!
RRR

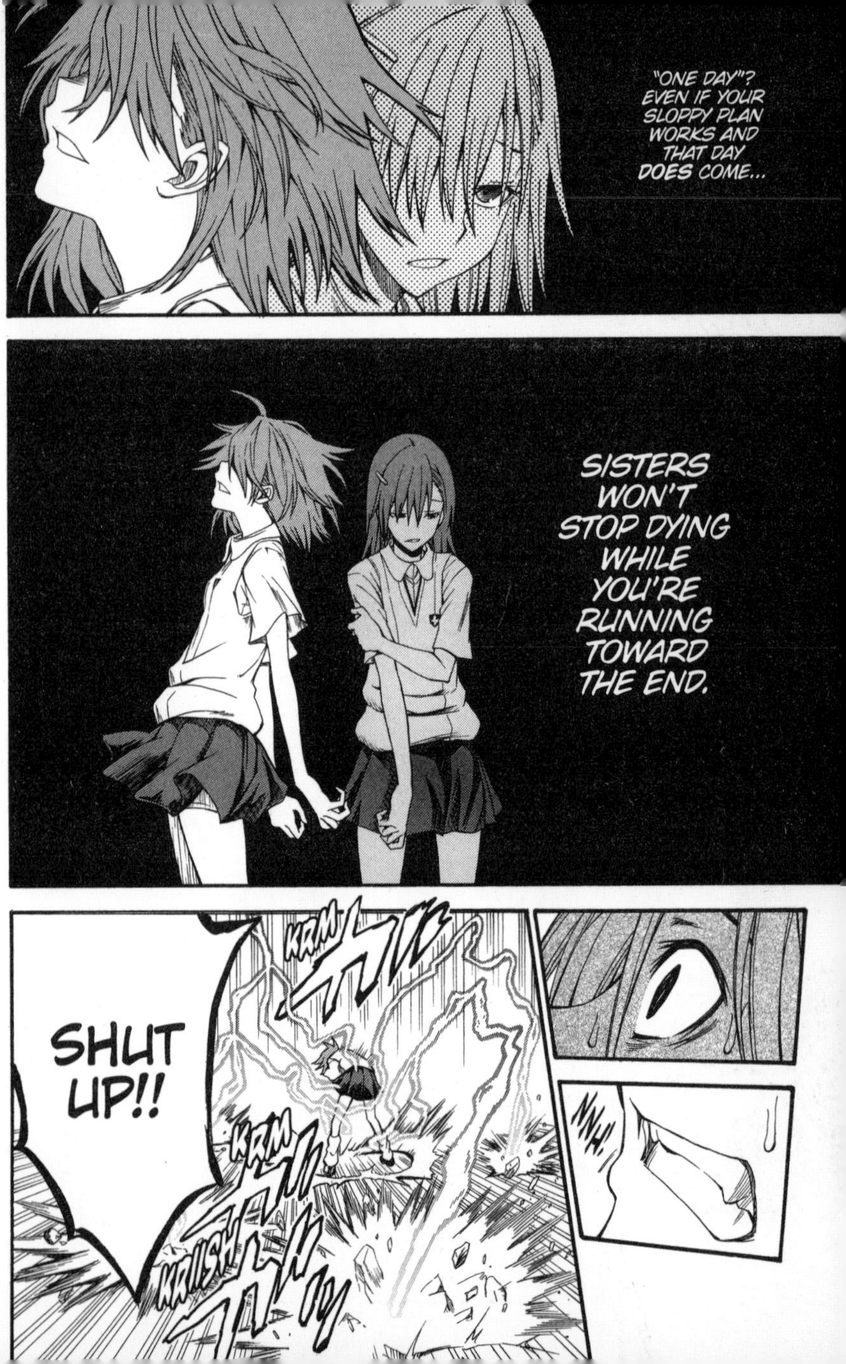
"ONE DAY"? EVEN IF YOUR SLOPPY PLAN WORKS AND THAT DAY DOES COME...
SISTERS WON'T STOP DYING WHILE YOU'RE RUNNING TOWARD THE END.
NNH
KRM
SHUT UP!!
KRM
KRUSH

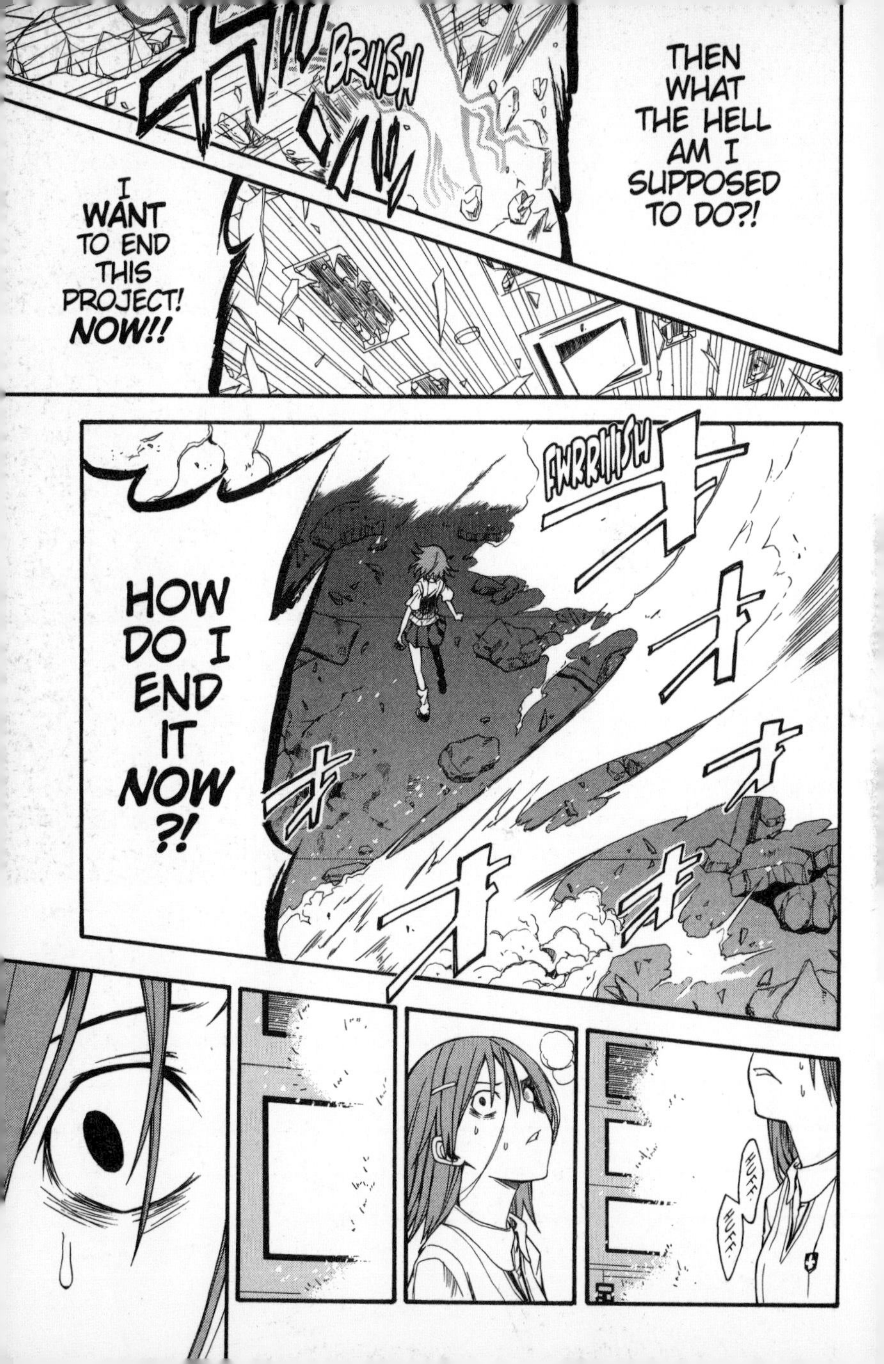
THEN WHAT THE HELL AM I SUPPOSED TO DO?!
BRIISH
I WANT TO END THIS PROJECT! NOW!!
FWRRIIISH
HOW DO I END IT NOW?!
HUFF HUFF

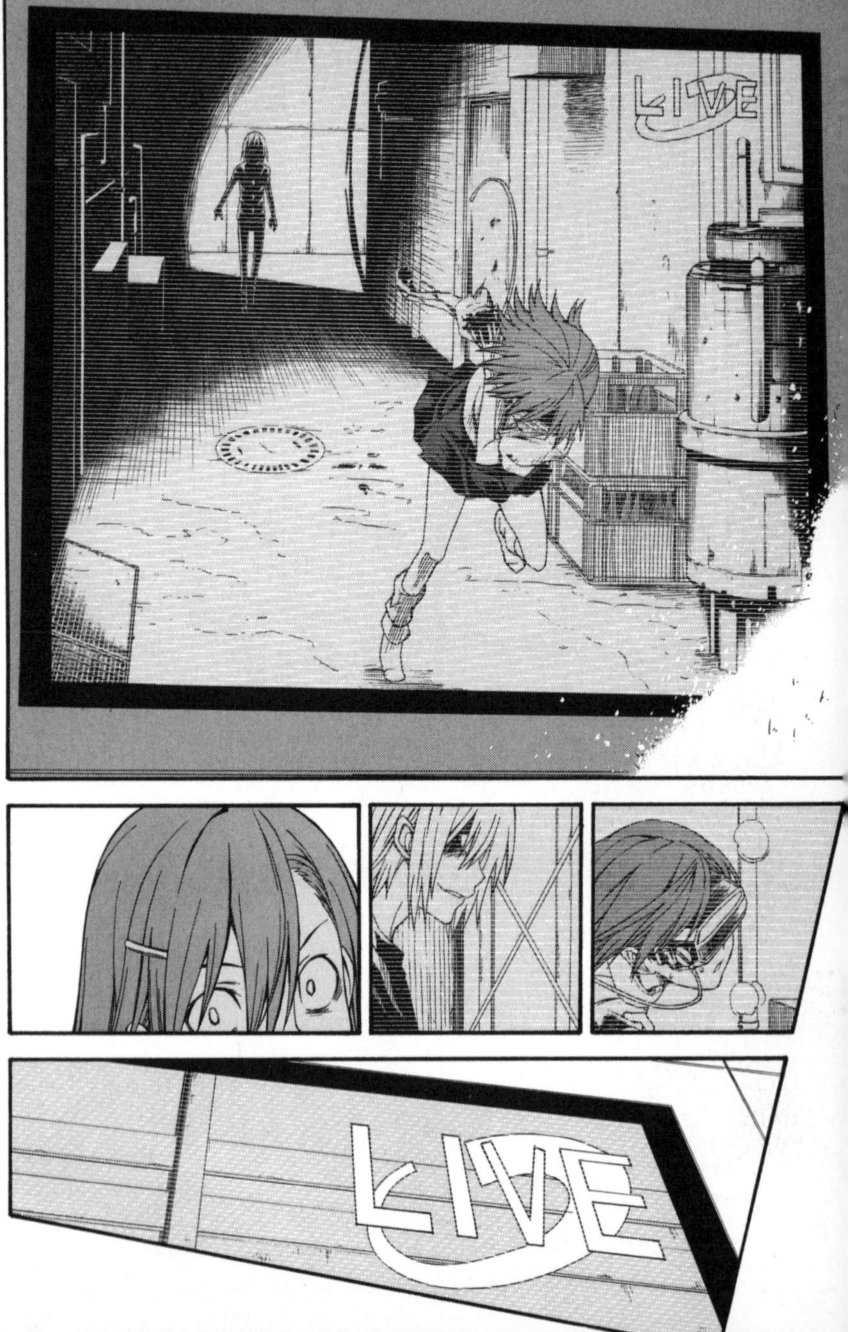
LIVE
LIVE

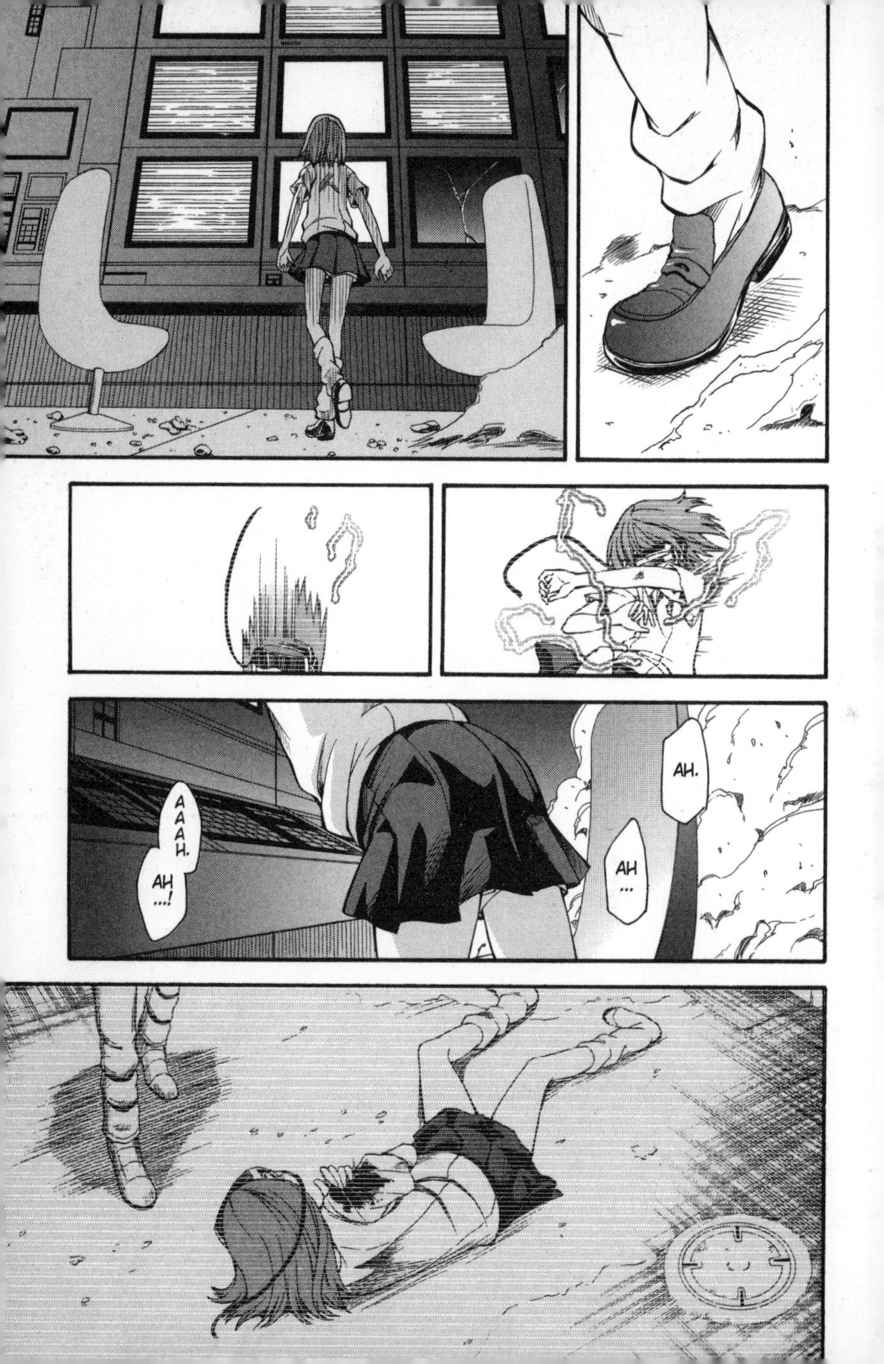
AH.
AH ...
AAAAH.
AH ...!

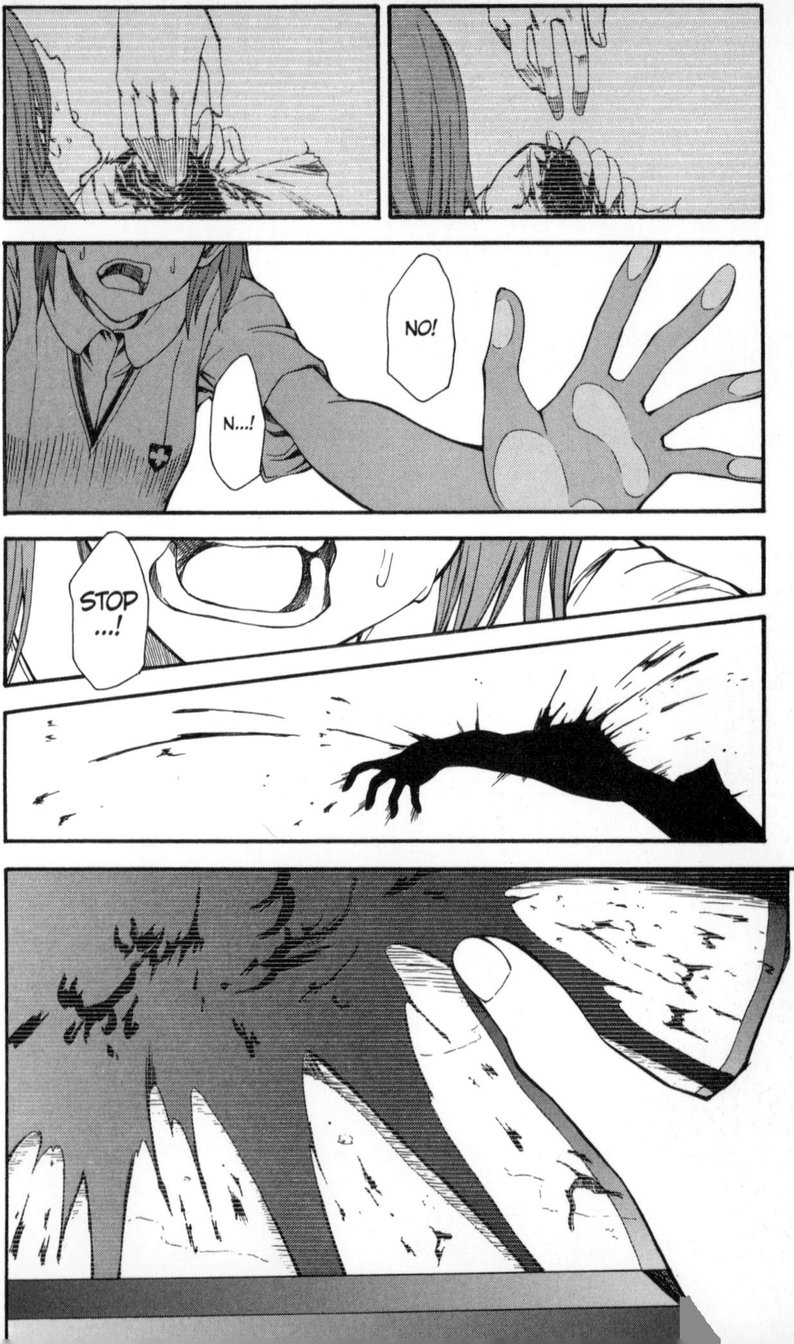
NO!
N...!
STOP ...!

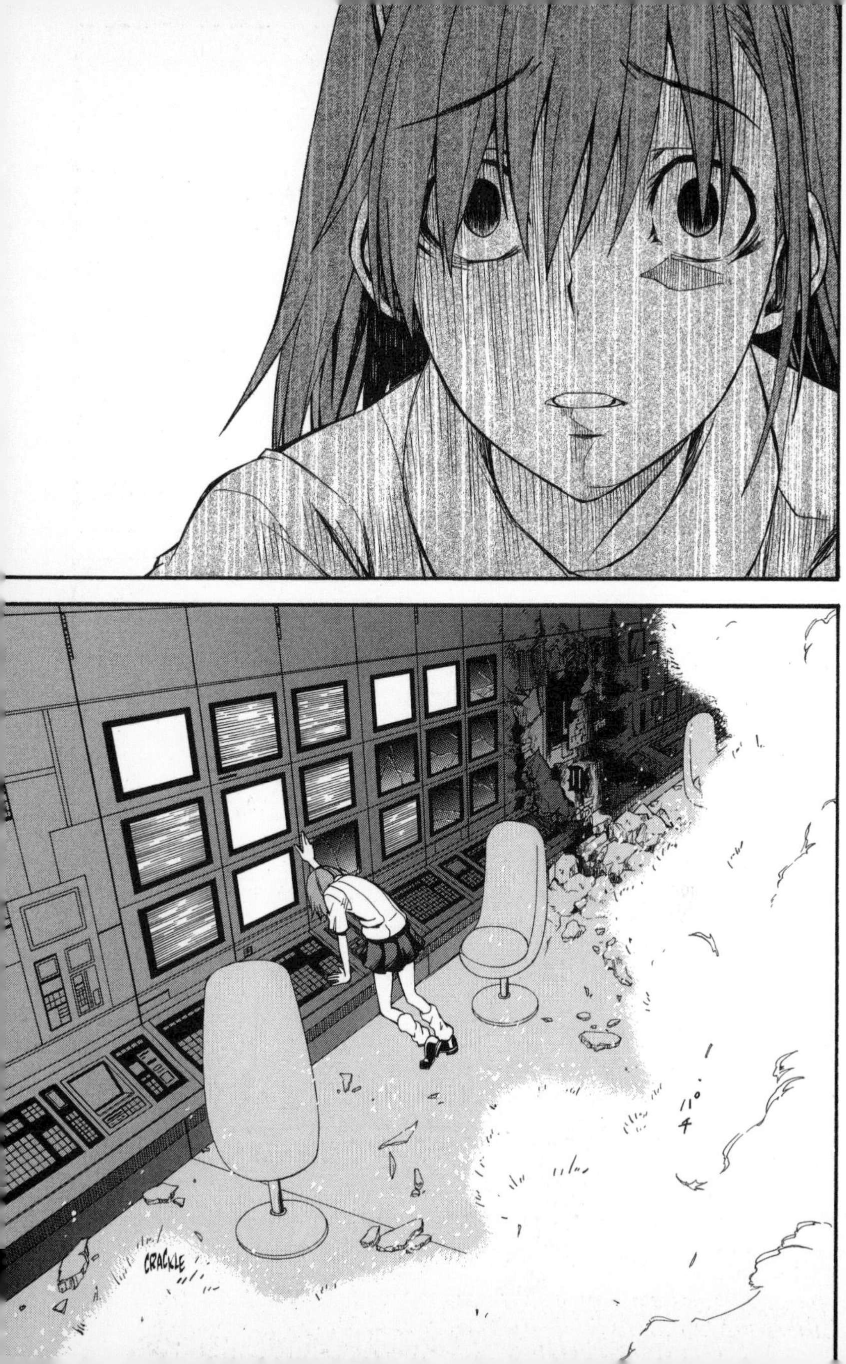
CRACKLE

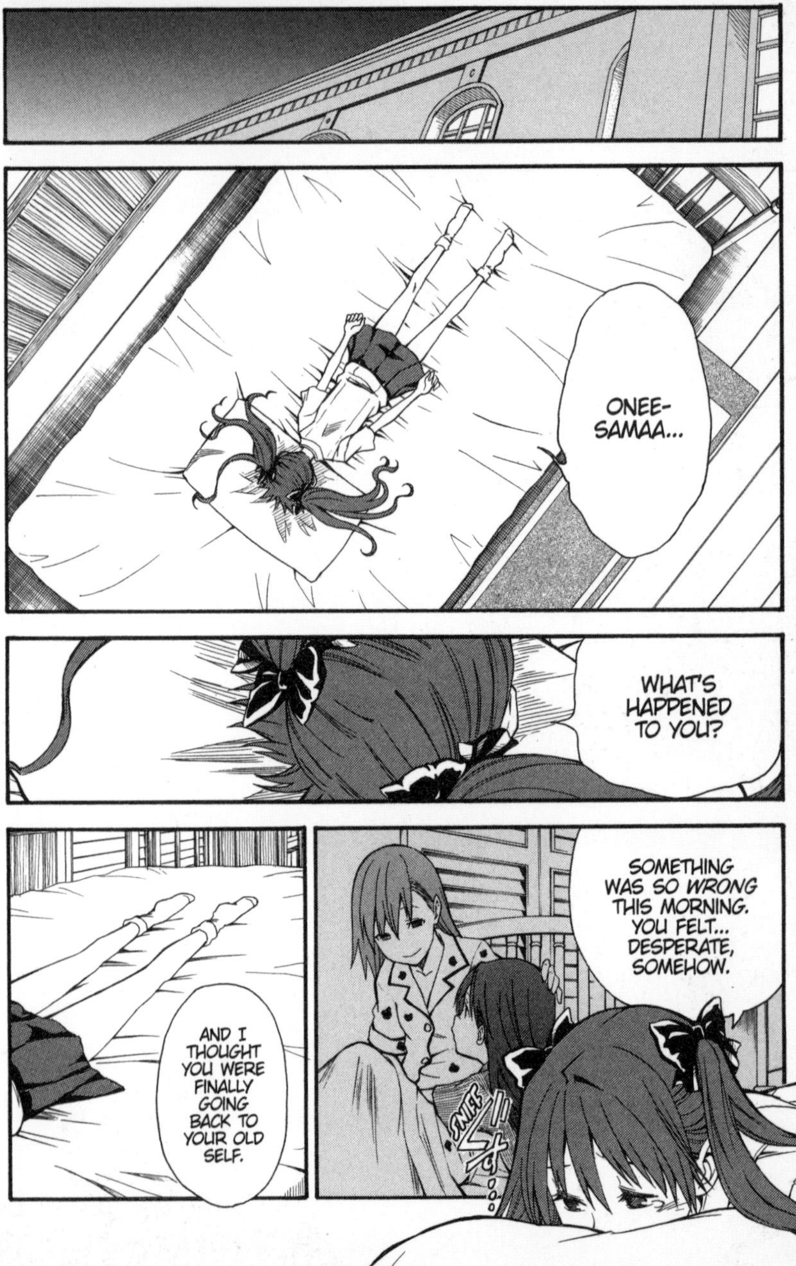
ONEE-SAMAA...
WHAT'S HAPPENED TO YOU?
SOMETHING WAS SO *WRONG* THIS MORNING. YOU FELT... DESPERATE, SOMEHOW.
SNIFF
AND I THOUGHT YOU WERE FINALLY GOING BACK TO YOUR OLD SELF.

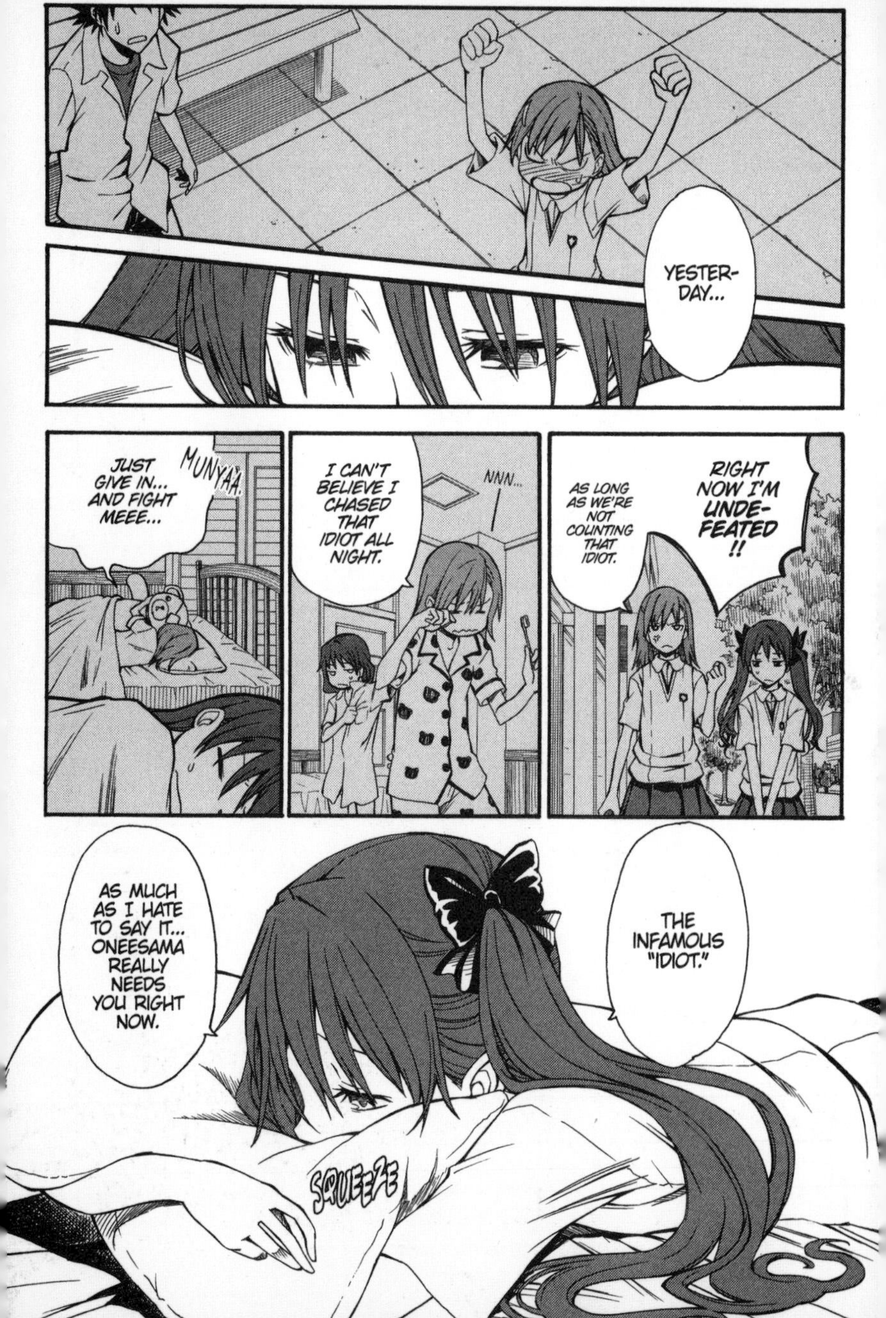
YESTER-DAY...
RIGHT NOW I'M UNDE-FEATED!!
AS LONG AS WE'RE NOT COUNTING THAT IDIOT.
NNN...
I CAN'T BELIEVE I CHASED THAT IDIOT ALL NIGHT.
MUNYAA.
JUST GIVE IN... AND FIGHT MEEE...
THE INFAMOUS "IDIOT."
AS MUCH AS I HATE TO SAY IT... ONEESAMA REALLY NEEDS YOU RIGHT NOW.
SQUEEZE

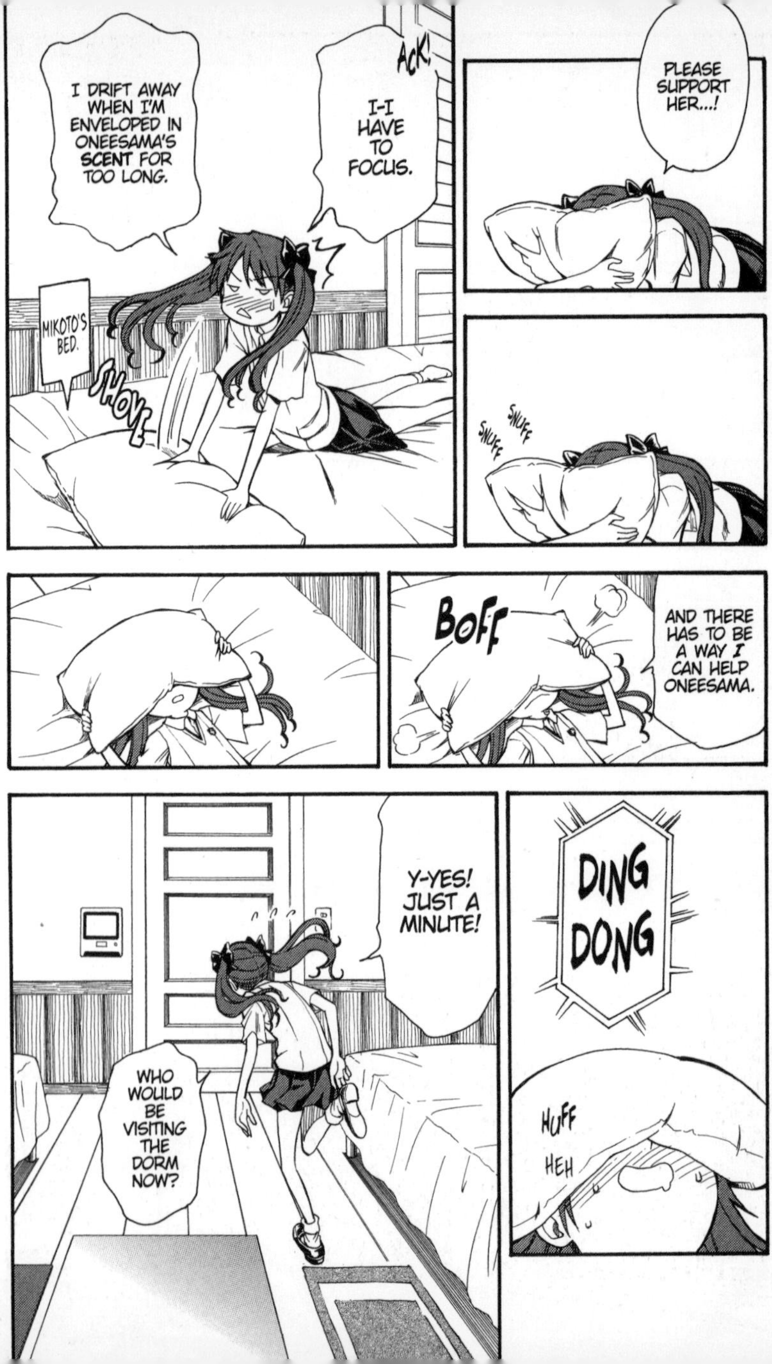
PLEASE SUPPORT HER...!
SNUFF SNUFF
ACK!
I-I HAVE TO FOCUS.
I DRIFT AWAY WHEN I'M ENVELOPED IN ONEESAMA'S SCENT FOR TOO LONG.
MIKOTO'S BED.
SHOVE
AND THERE HAS TO BE A WAY I CAN HELP ONEESAMA.
BOFF
DING DONG
HUFF HEH
Y-YES! JUST A MINUTE!
WHO WOULD BE VISITING THE DORM NOW?

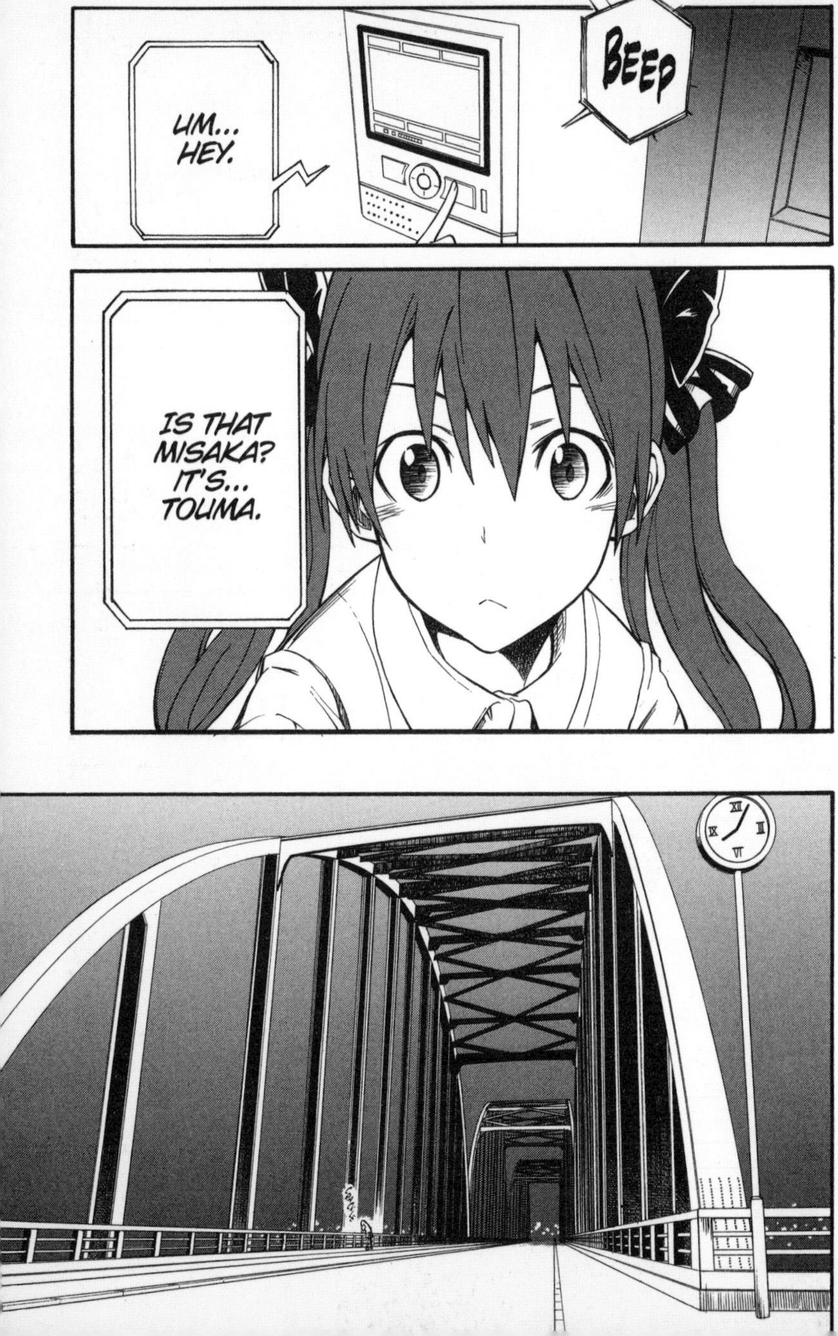
BEEP
UM... HEY.
IS THAT MISAKA? IT'S... TOUMA.

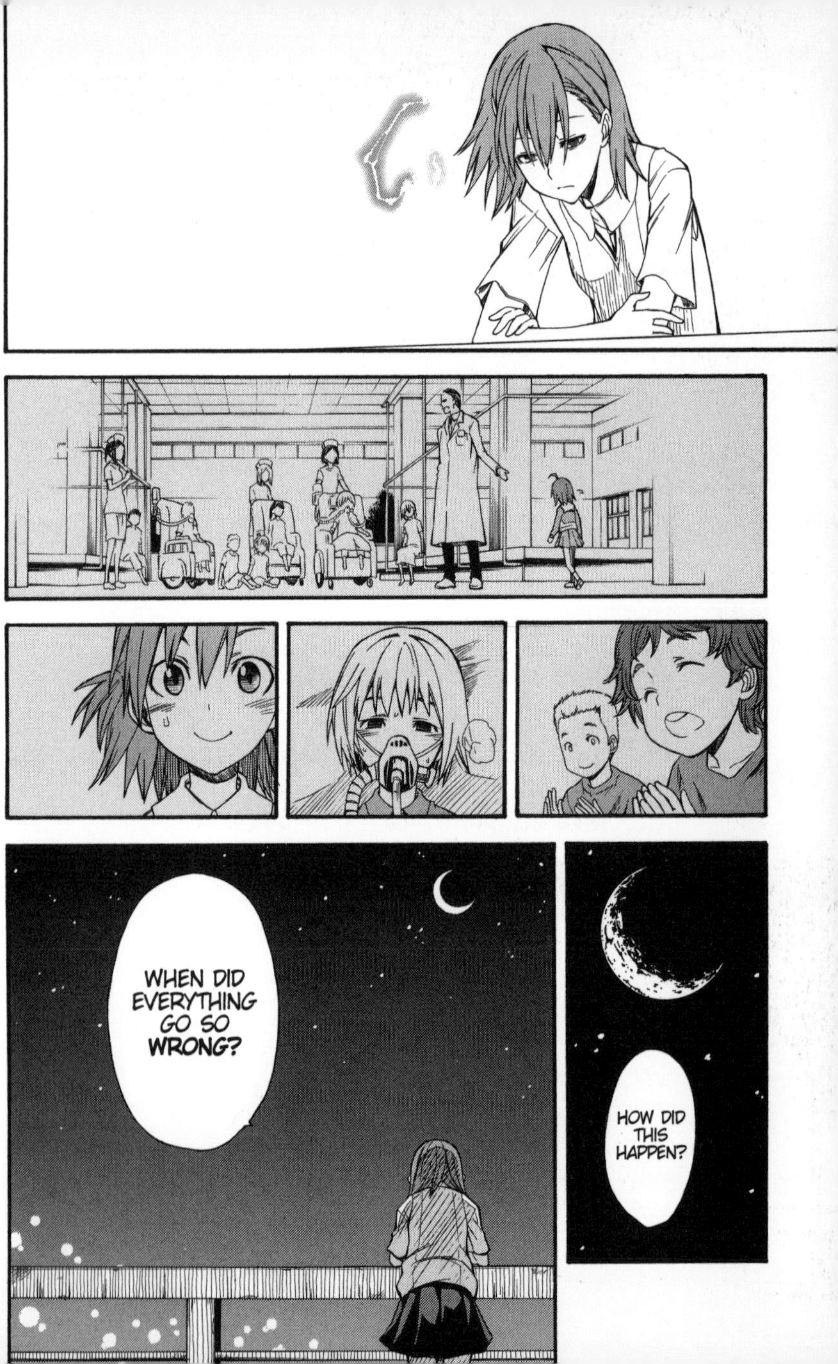
HOW DID THIS HAPPEN?
WHEN DID EVERYTHING GO SO WRONG?

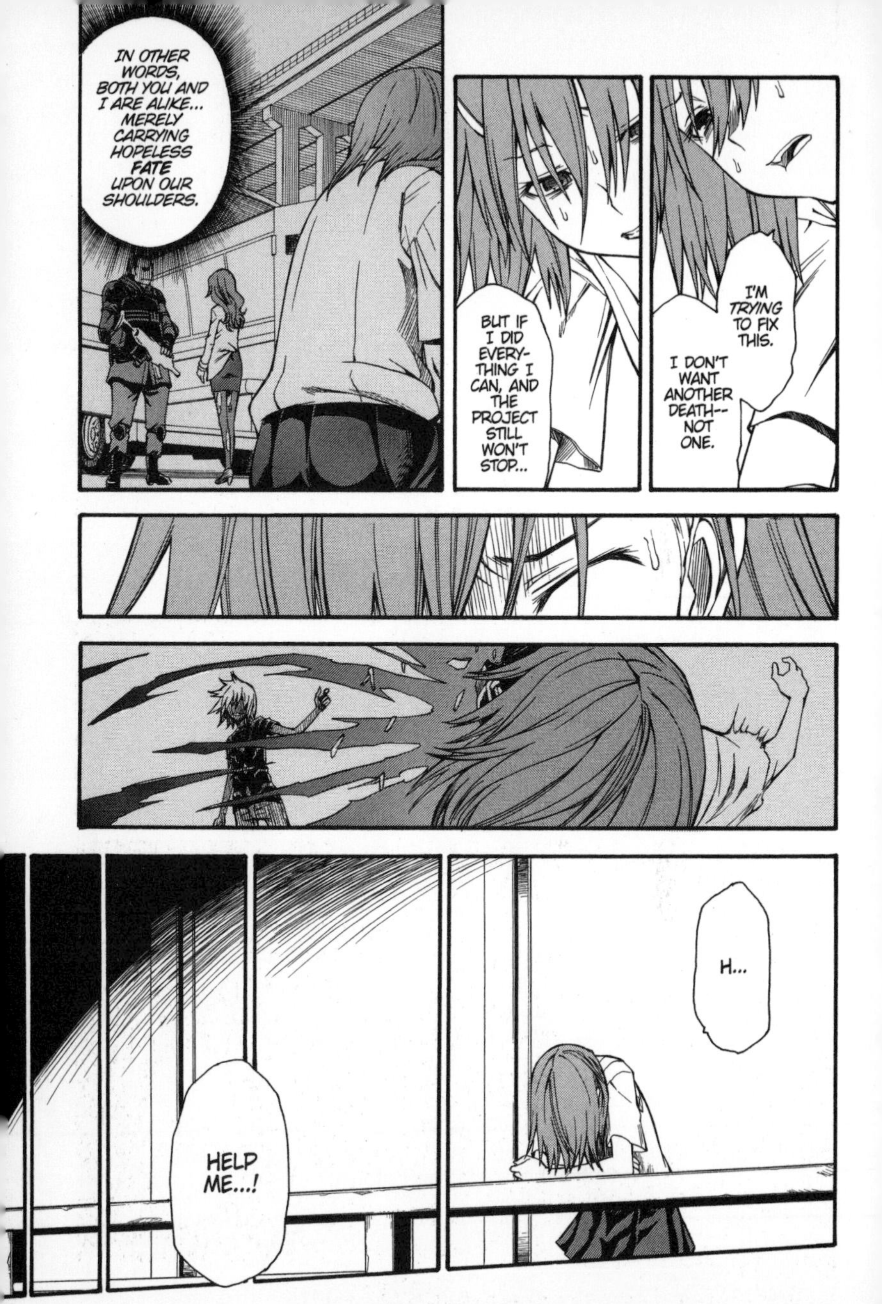
I'M *TRYING* TO FIX THIS.
I DON'T WANT ANOTHER DEATH-- NOT ONE.
BUT IF I DID EVERYTHING I CAN, AND THE PROJECT STILL WON'T STOP...
IN OTHER WORDS, BOTH YOU AND I ARE ALIKE... MERELY CARRYING HOPELESS **FATE** UPON OUR SHOULDERS.
H...
HELP ME...!

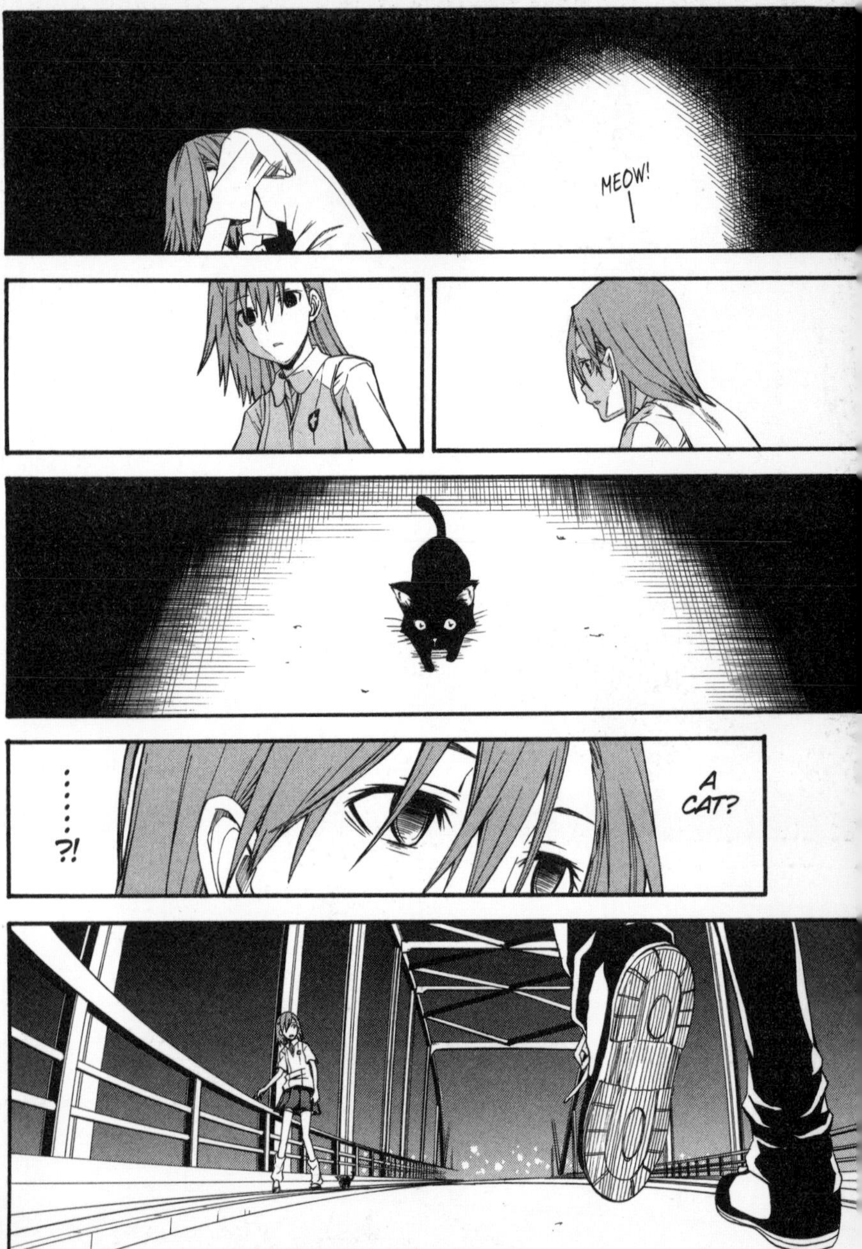
MEOW!
A CAT?
......
?!

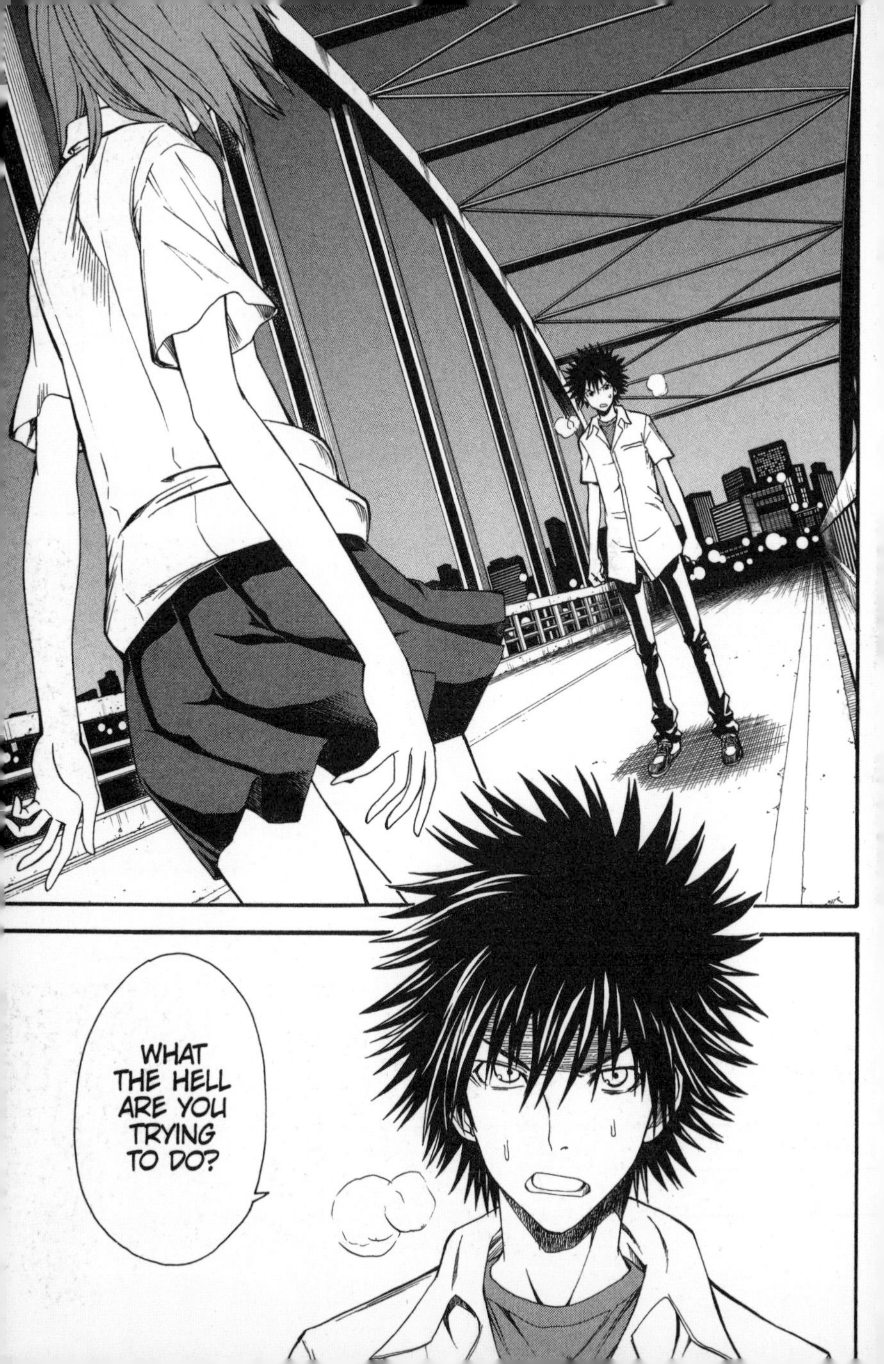
WHAT THE HELL ARE YOU TRYING TO DO?

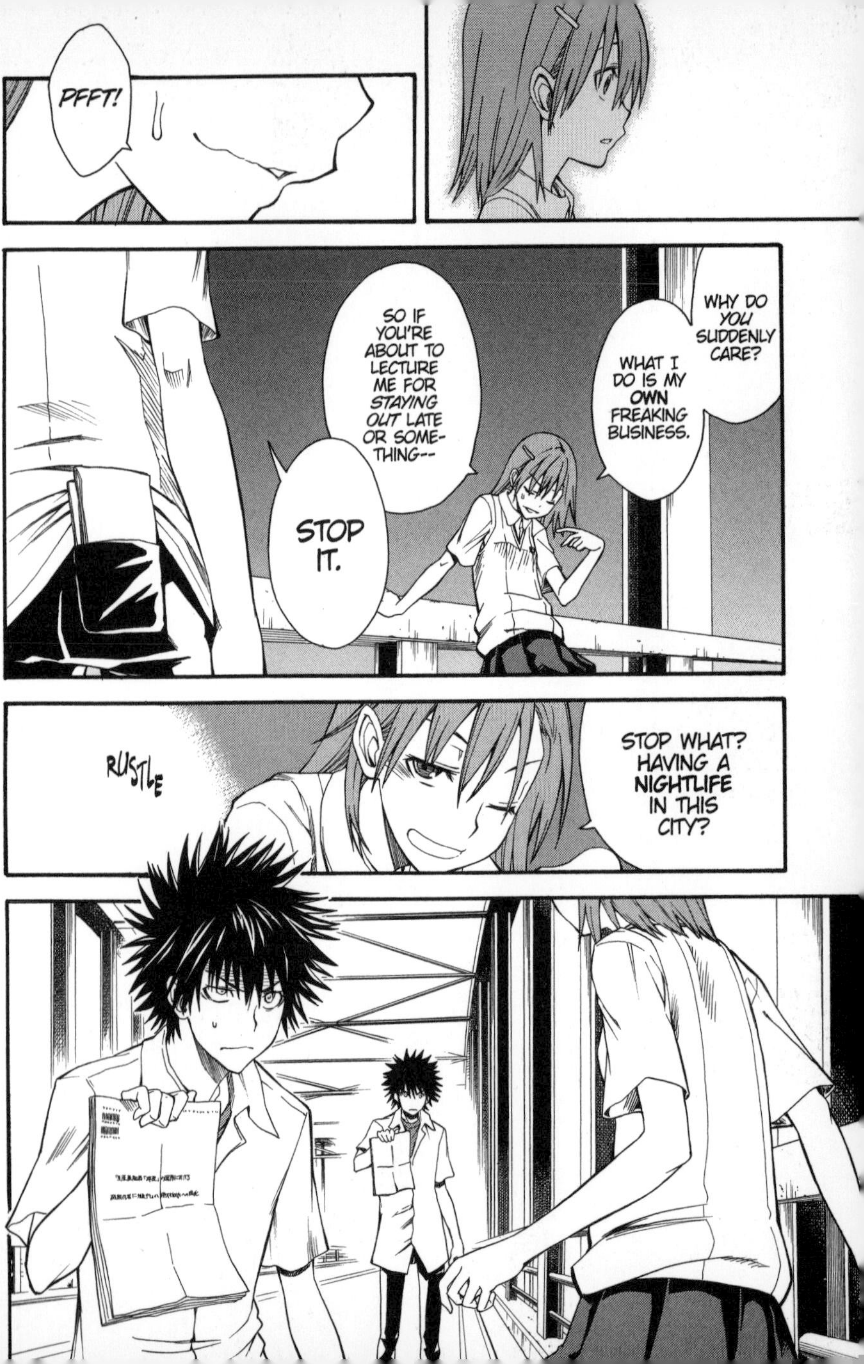
PFFT!
WHY DO YOU SUDDENLY CARE?
WHAT I DO IS MY OWN FREAKING BUSINESS.
SO IF YOU'RE ABOUT TO LECTURE ME FOR STAYING OUT LATE OR SOME-THING--
STOP IT.
STOP WHAT? HAVING A NIGHTLIFE IN THIS CITY?
RUSTLE

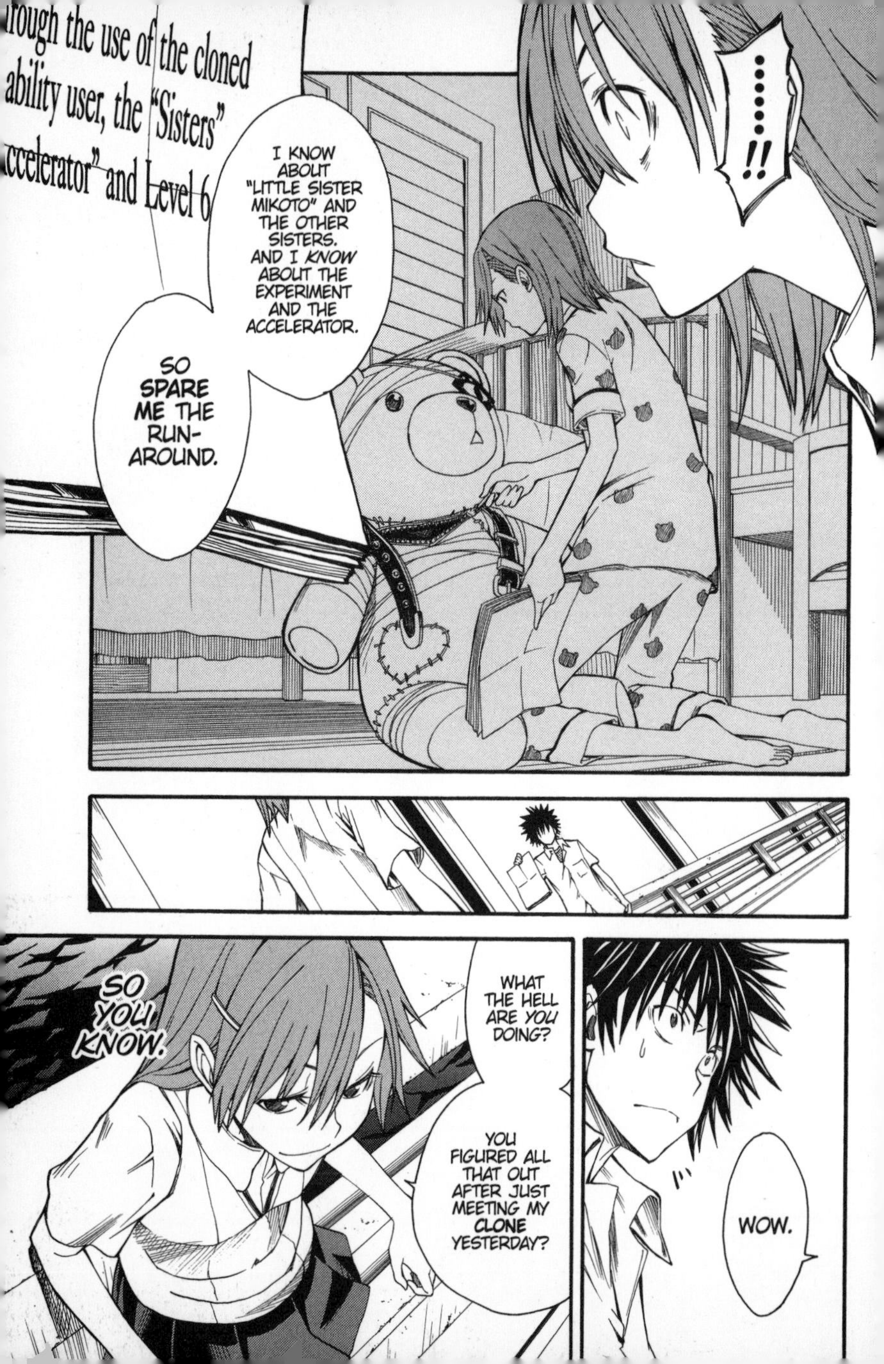
......!!
I KNOW ABOUT "LITTLE SISTER MIKOTO" AND THE OTHER SISTERS. AND I *KNOW* ABOUT THE EXPERIMENT AND THE ACCELERATOR.
SO SPARE ME THE RUN-AROUND.
rough the use of the cloned ability user, the "Sisters" ccelerator" and Level 6
WOW.
WHAT THE HELL ARE *YOU* DOING?
YOU FIGURED ALL THAT OUT AFTER JUST MEETING MY CLONE YESTERDAY?
SO YOU KNOW.

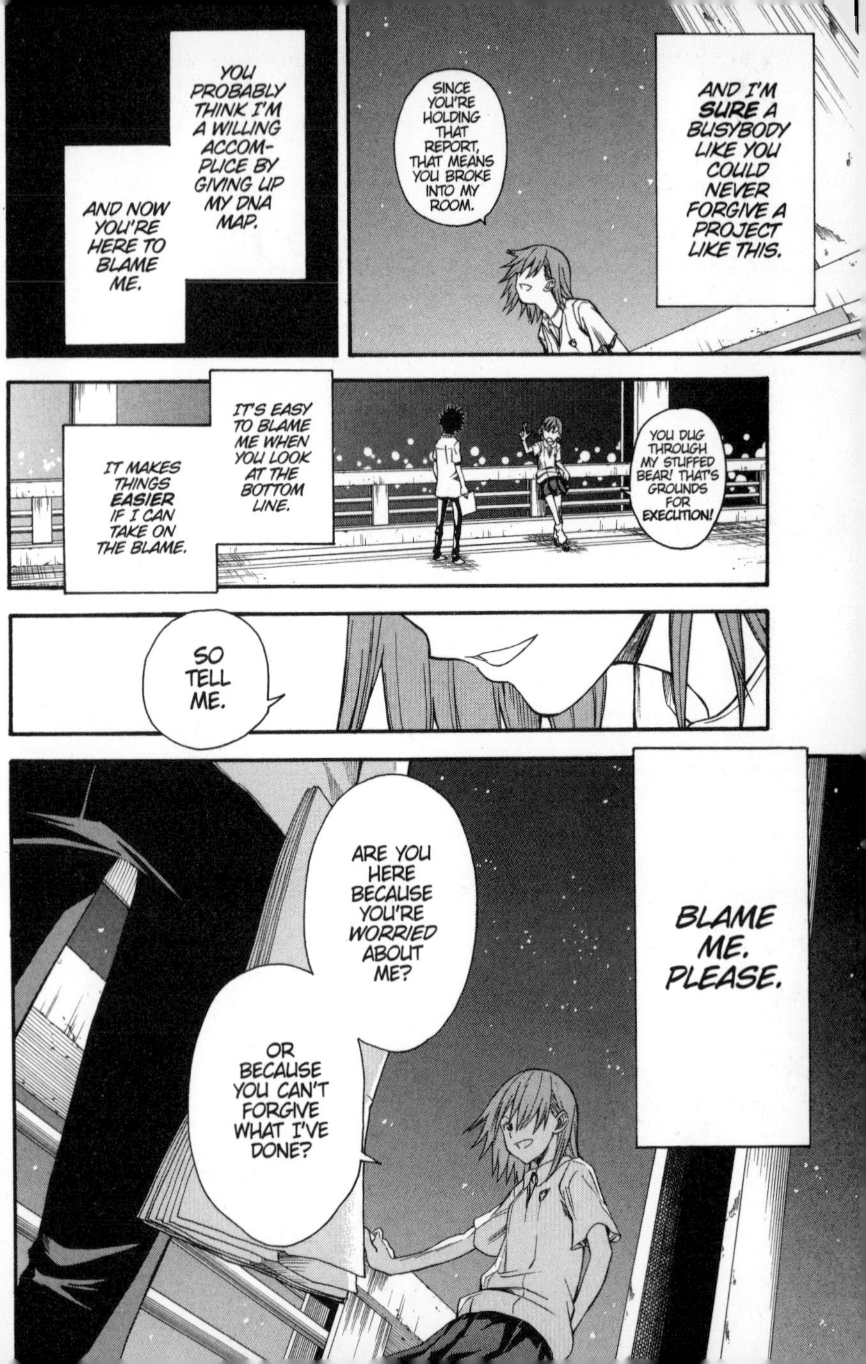
AND I'M SURE A BUSYBODY LIKE YOU COULD NEVER FORGIVE A PROJECT LIKE THIS.
SINCE YOU'RE HOLDING THAT REPORT, THAT MEANS YOU BROKE INTO MY ROOM.
YOU PROBABLY THINK I'M A WILLING ACCOMPLICE BY GIVING UP MY DNA MAP.
AND NOW YOU'RE HERE TO BLAME ME.
YOU DUG THROUGH MY STUFFED BEAR! THAT'S GROUNDS FOR EXECUTION!
IT'S EASY TO BLAME ME WHEN YOU LOOK AT THE BOTTOM LINE.
IT MAKES THINGS EASIER IF I CAN TAKE ON THE BLAME.
SO TELL ME.
BLAME ME. PLEASE.
ARE YOU HERE BECAUSE YOU'RE WORRIED ABOUT ME?
OR BECAUSE YOU CAN'T FORGIVE WHAT I'VE DONE?

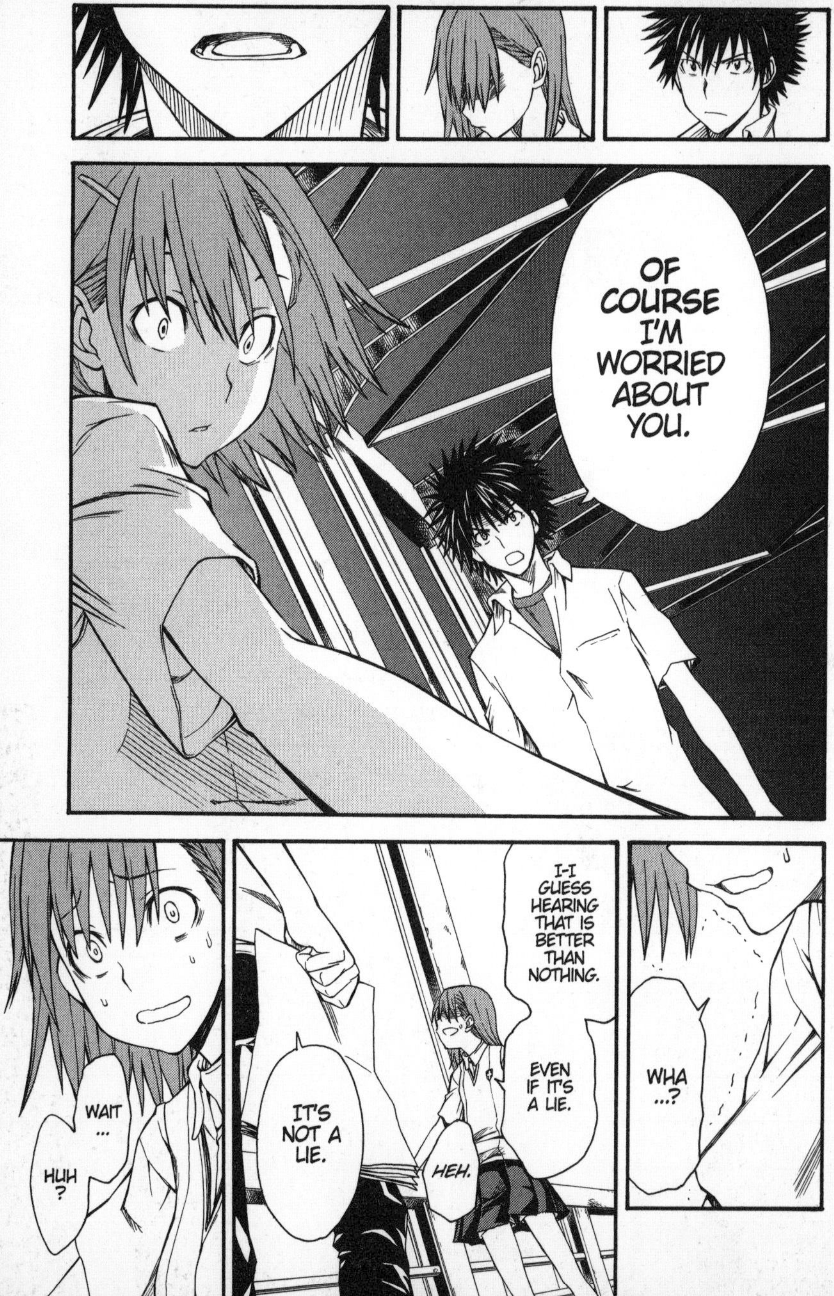
OF COURSE I'M WORRIED ABOUT YOU.
WHA ...?
I-I GUESS HEARING THAT IS BETTER THAN NOTHING.
EVEN IF IT'S A LIE.
IT'S NOT A LIE.
HEH.
WAIT ...
HUH ?

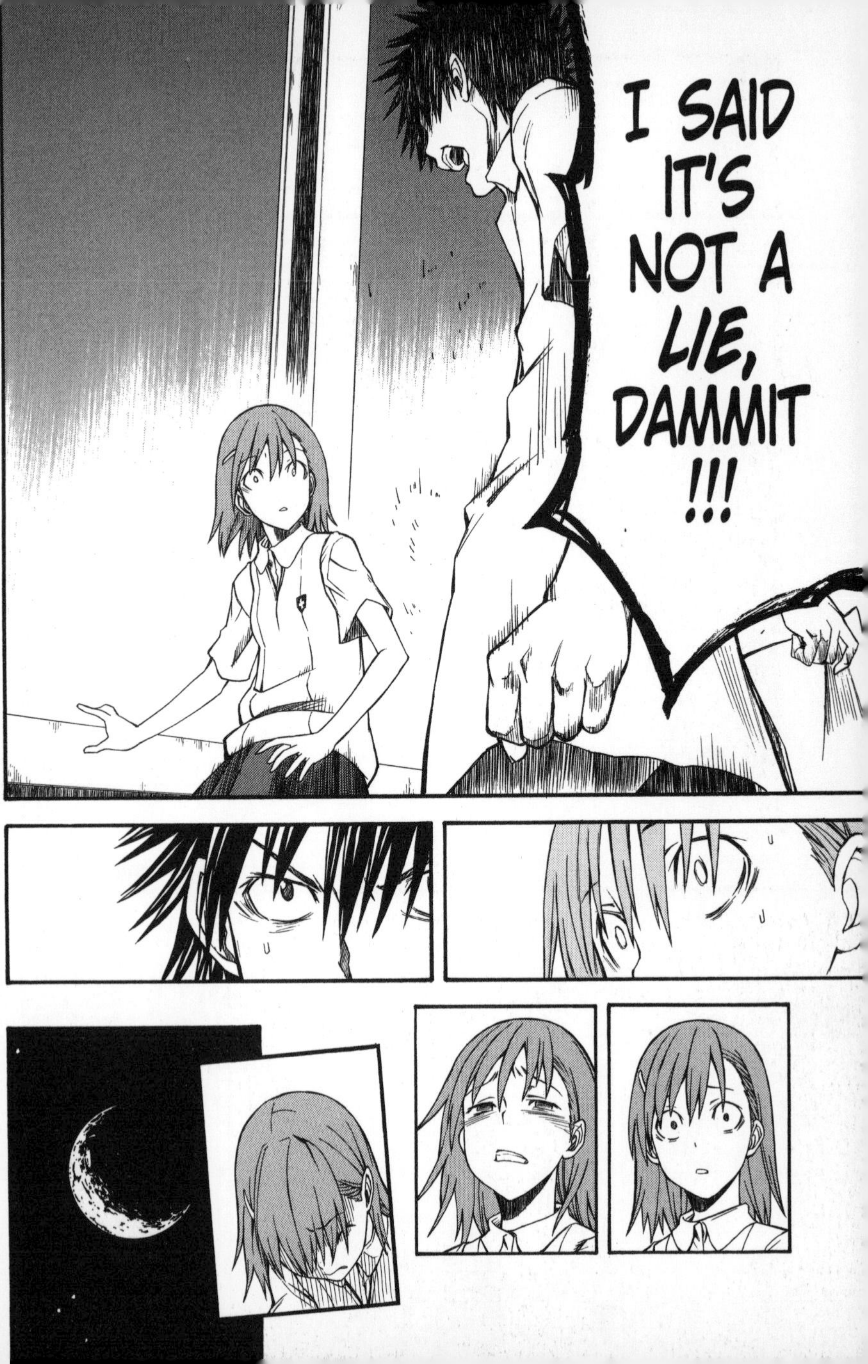
I SAID IT'S NOT A LIE, DAMMIT!!!

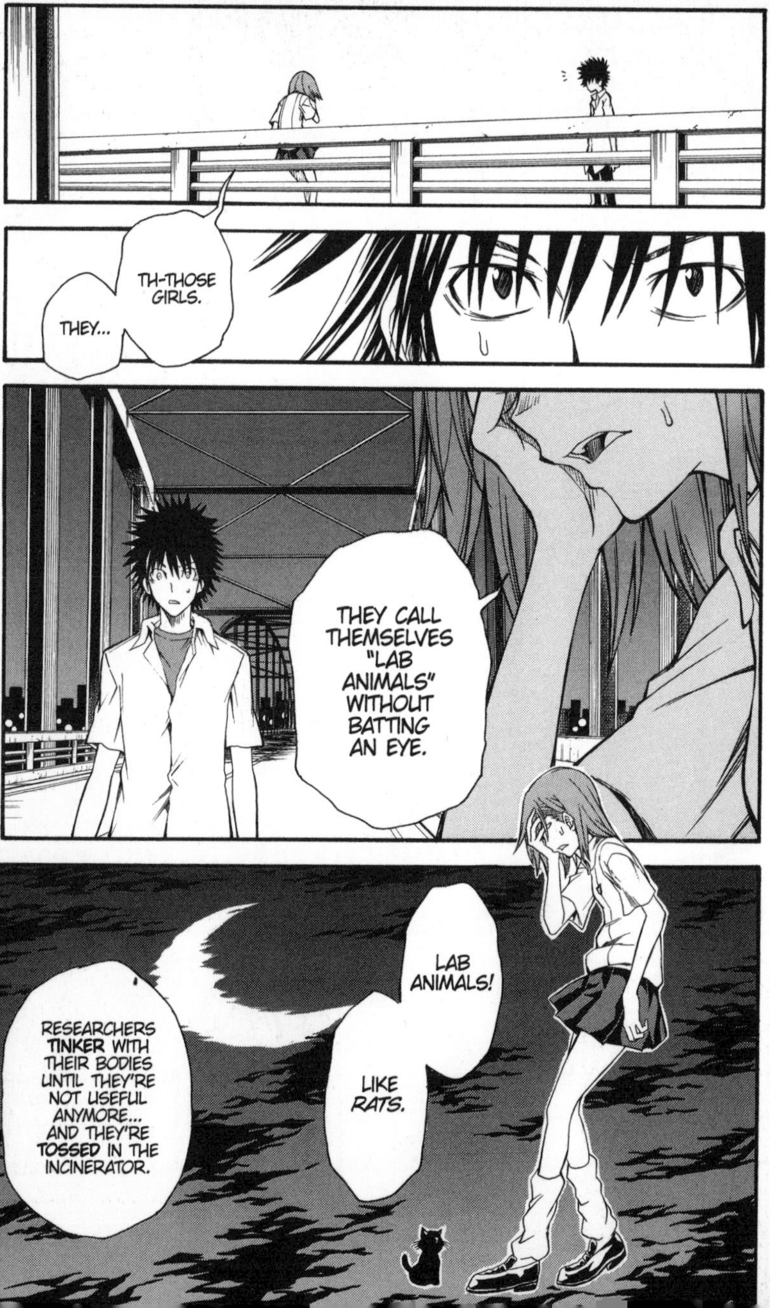
TH-THOSE GIRLS.
THEY...
THEY CALL THEMSELVES "LAB ANIMALS" WITHOUT BATTING AN EYE.
LAB ANIMALS!
LIKE RATS.
RESEARCHERS TINKER WITH THEIR BODIES UNTIL THEY'RE NOT USEFUL ANYMORE... AND THEY'RE TOSSED IN THE INCINERATOR.

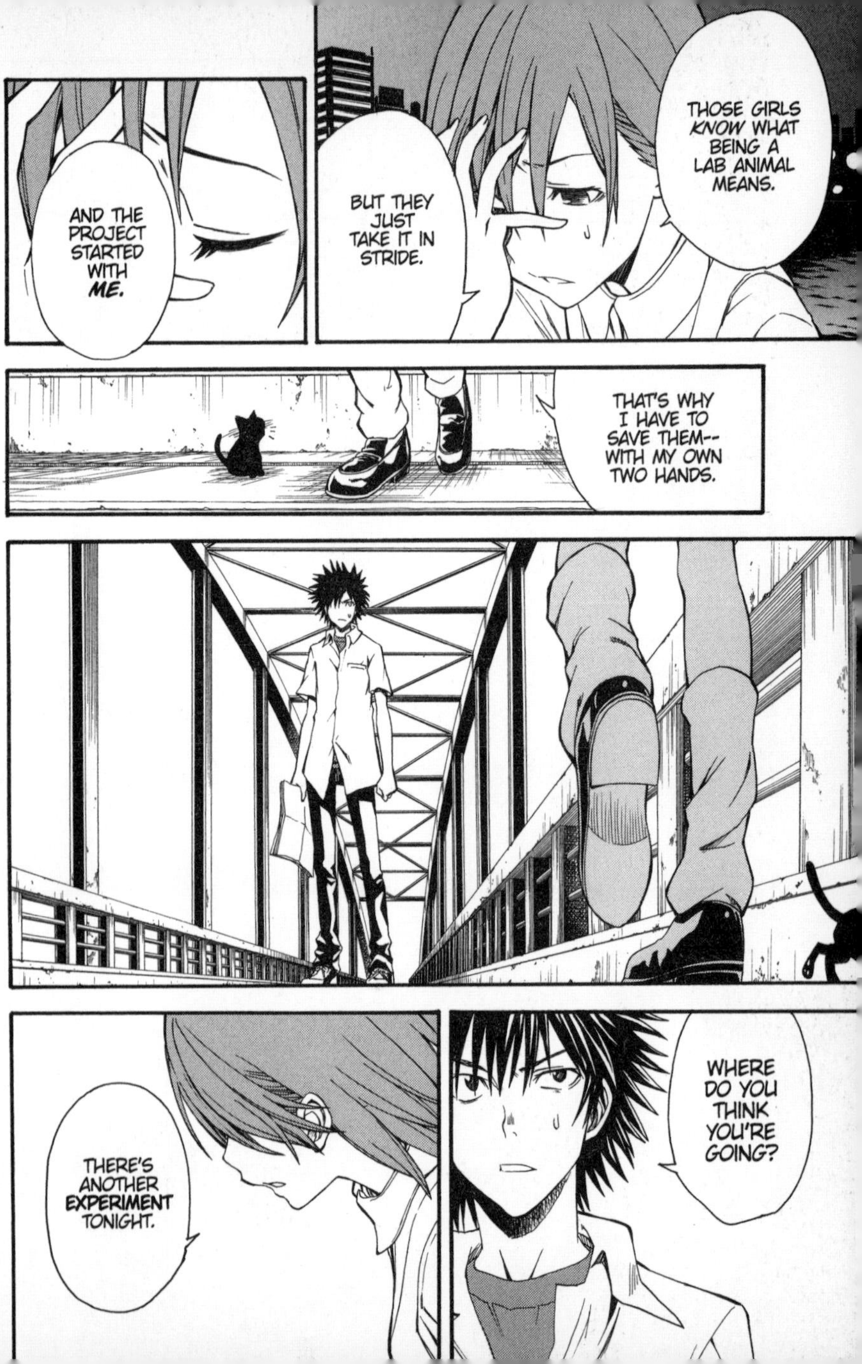
THOSE GIRLS *KNOW* WHAT BEING A LAB ANIMAL MEANS.
BUT THEY JUST TAKE IT IN STRIDE.
AND THE PROJECT STARTED WITH ***ME.***
THAT'S WHY I HAVE TO SAVE THEM-- WITH MY OWN TWO HANDS.
WHERE DO YOU THINK YOU'RE GOING?
THERE'S ANOTHER **EXPERIMENT** TONIGHT.

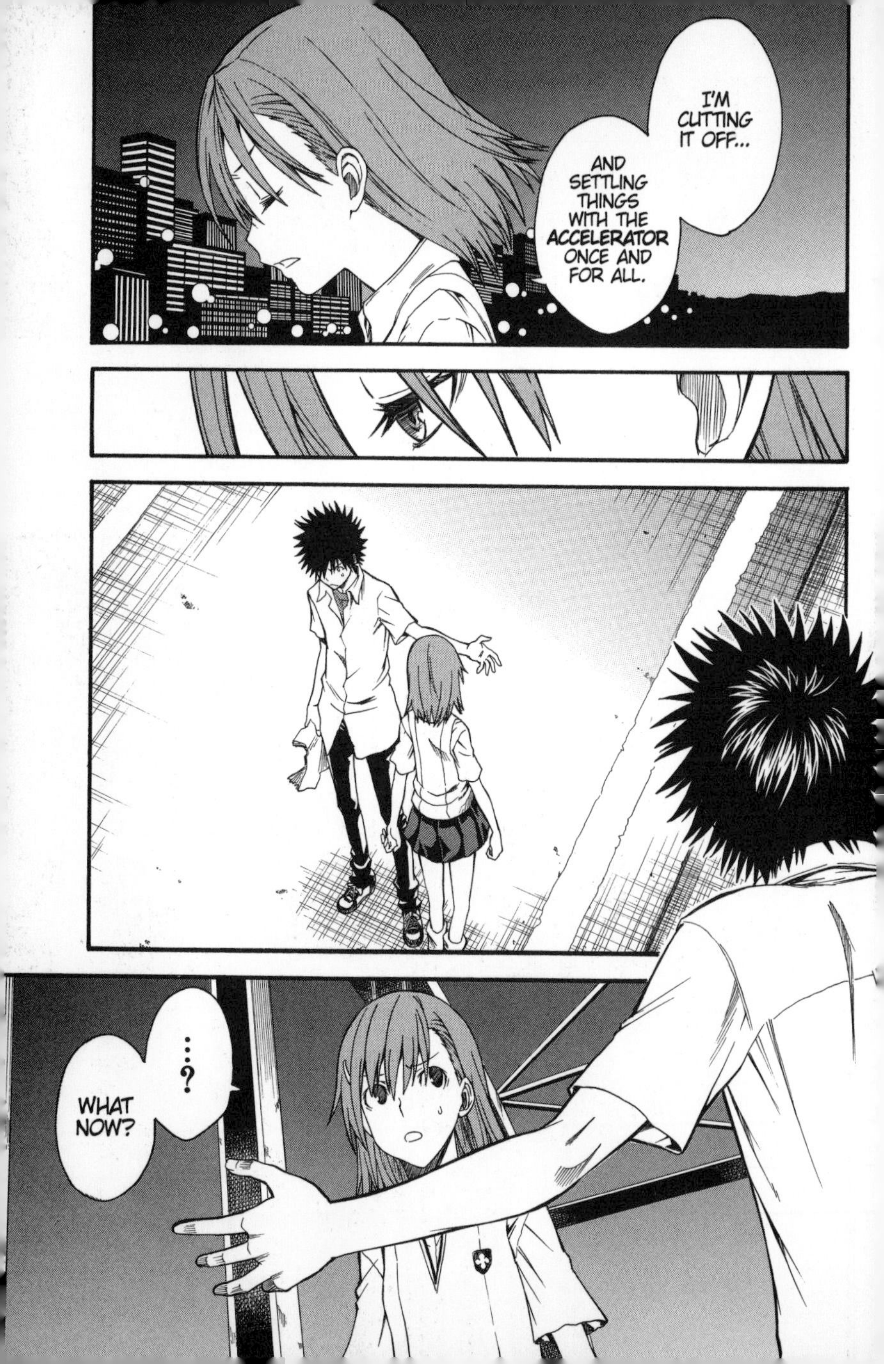
I'M CUTTING IT OFF...
AND SETTLING THINGS WITH THE ACCELERATOR ONCE AND FOR ALL.
...?
WHAT NOW?

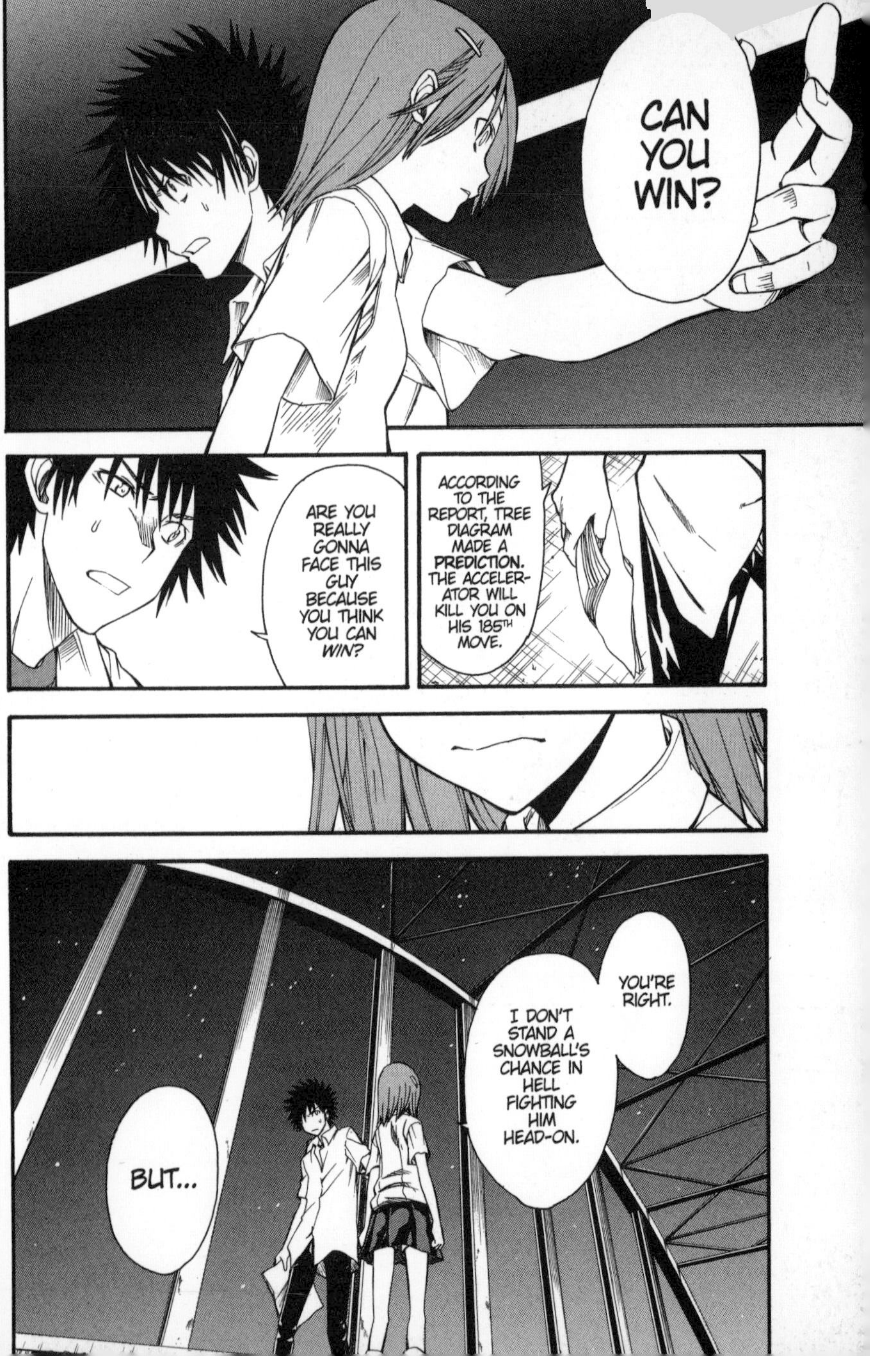
CAN YOU WIN?
ACCORDING TO THE REPORT, TREE DIAGRAM MADE A PREDICTION. THE ACCELERATOR WILL KILL YOU ON HIS 185TH MOVE.
ARE YOU REALLY GONNA FACE THIS GUY BECAUSE YOU THINK YOU CAN *WIN*?
YOU'RE RIGHT.
I DON'T STAND A SNOWBALL'S CHANCE IN HELL FIGHTING HIM HEAD-ON.
BUT...

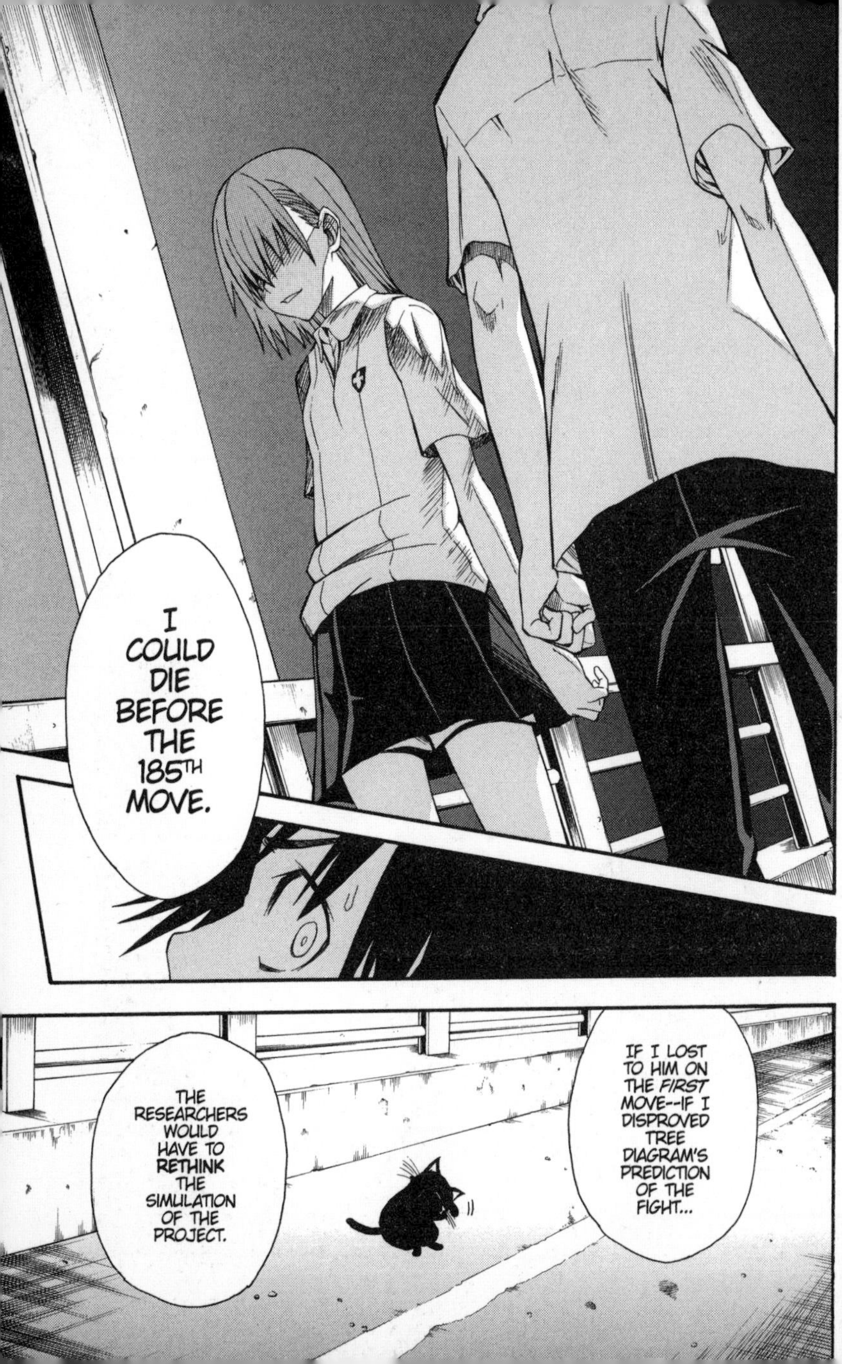
I COULD DIE BEFORE THE 185TH MOVE.
IF I LOST TO HIM ON THE *FIRST* MOVE--IF I DISPROVED TREE DIAGRAM'S PREDICTION OF THE FIGHT...
THE RESEARCHERS WOULD HAVE TO RETHINK THE SIMULATION OF THE PROJECT.

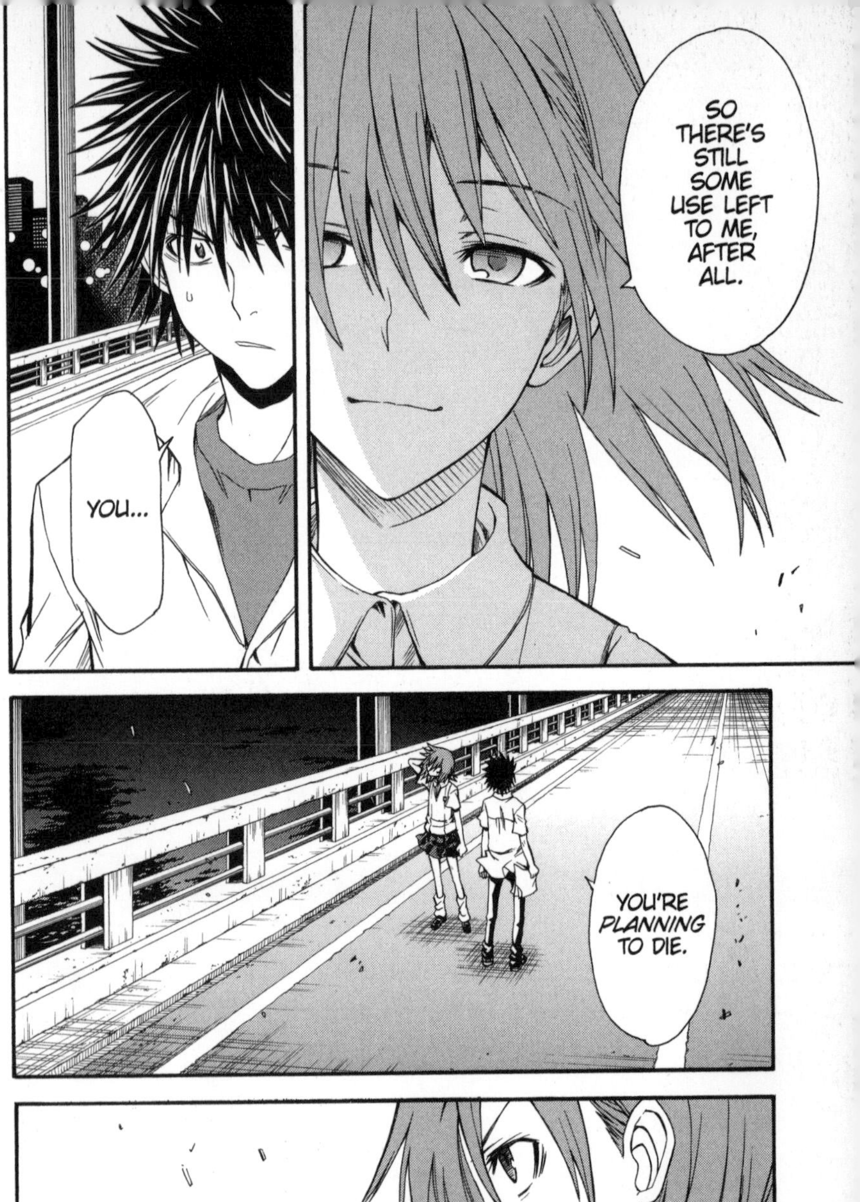
SO THERE'S STILL SOME USE LEFT TO ME, AFTER ALL.
YOU...
YOU'RE *PLANNING* TO DIE.

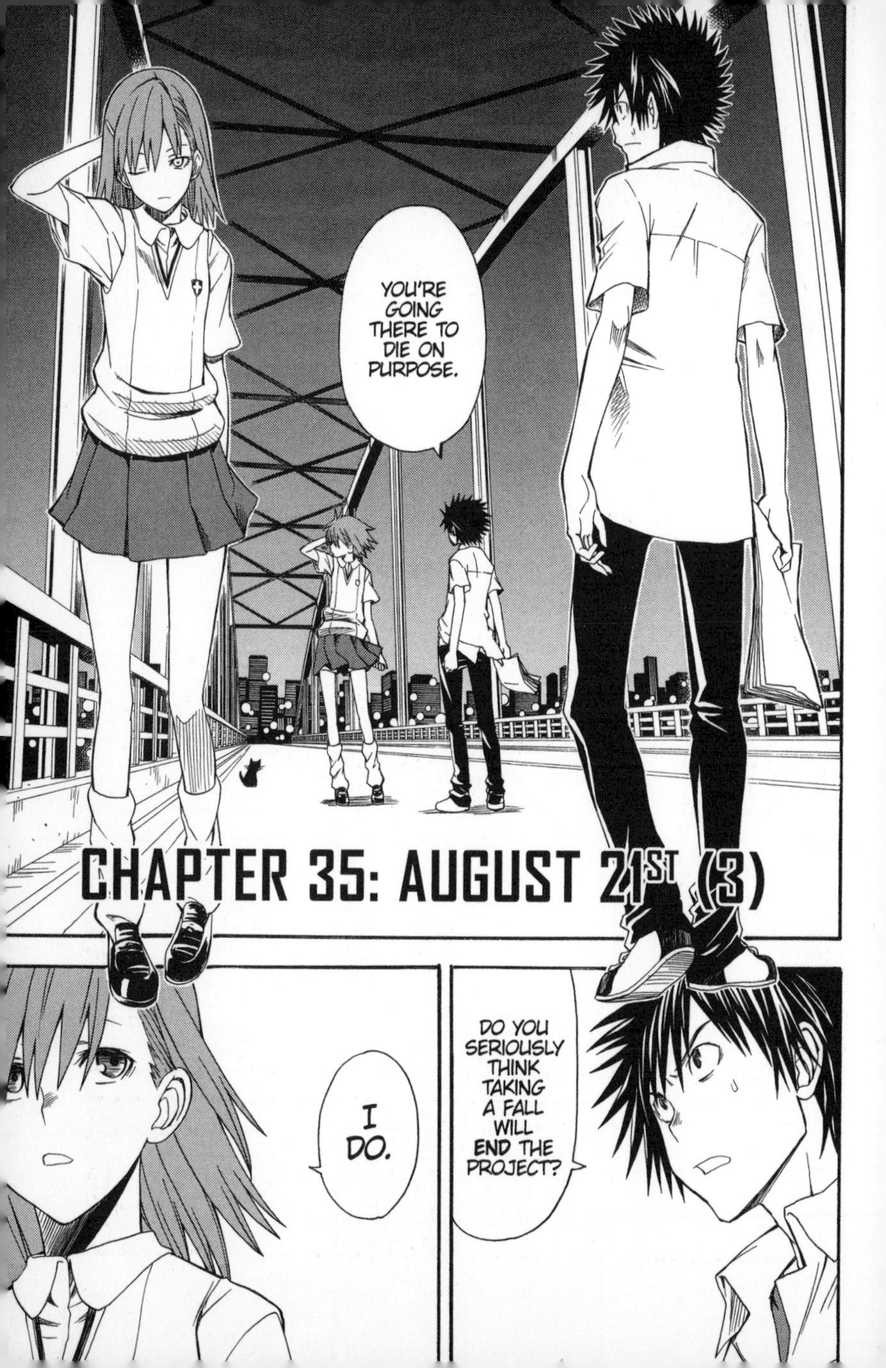
YOU'RE GOING THERE TO DIE ON PURPOSE.
CHAPTER 35: AUGUST 21ST (3)
DO YOU SERIOUSLY THINK TAKING A FALL WILL END THE PROJECT?
I DO.

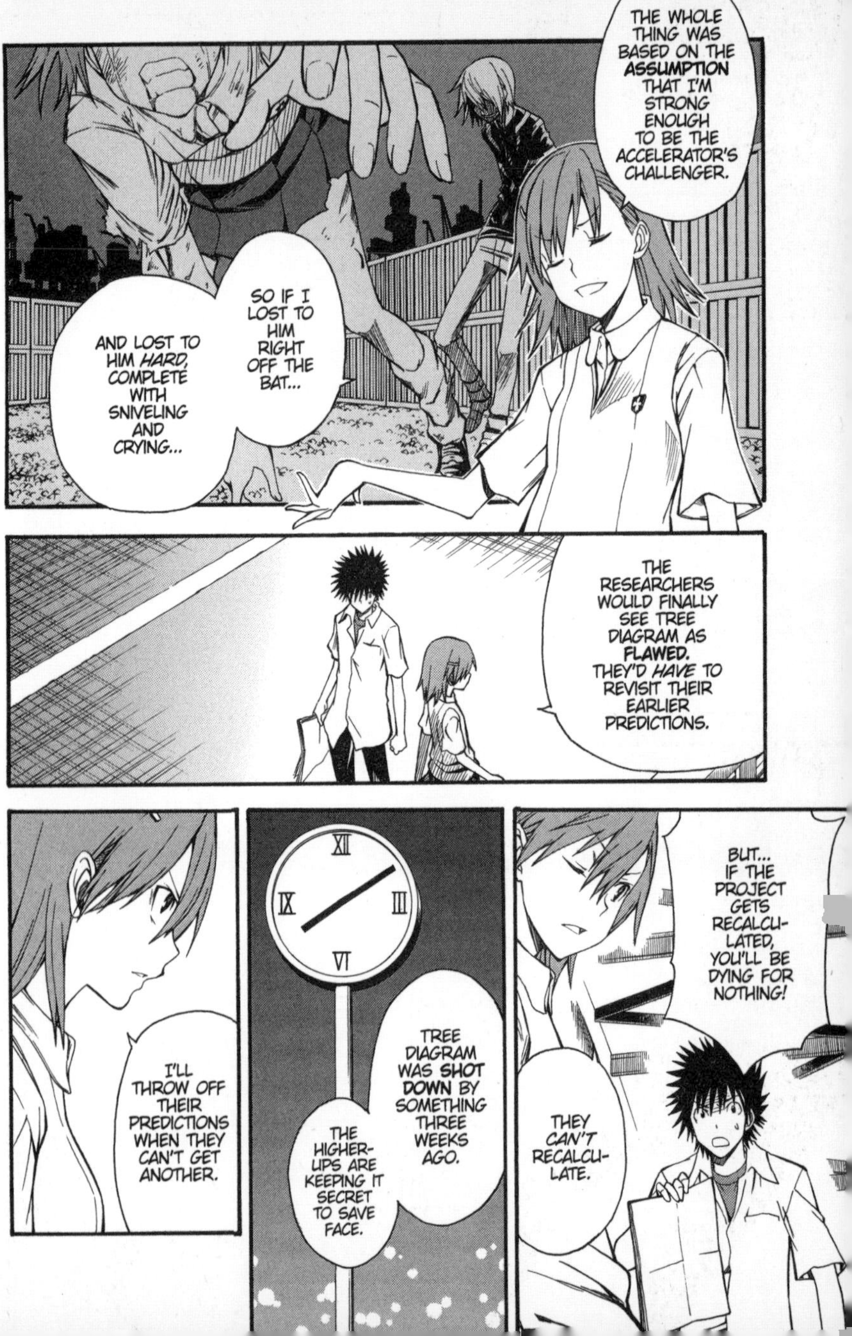
THE WHOLE THING WAS BASED ON THE **ASSUMPTION** THAT I'M STRONG ENOUGH TO BE THE ACCELERATOR'S CHALLENGER.
SO IF I LOST TO HIM RIGHT OFF THE BAT...
AND LOST TO HIM *HARD*, COMPLETE WITH SNIVELING AND CRYING...
THE RESEARCHERS WOULD FINALLY SEE TREE DIAGRAM AS **FLAWED.** THEY'D *HAVE* TO REVISIT THEIR EARLIER PREDICTIONS.
BUT... IF THE PROJECT GETS RECALCU-LATED, YOU'LL BE DYING FOR NOTHING!
THEY *CAN'T* RECALCU-LATE.
TREE DIAGRAM WAS **SHOT DOWN** BY SOMETHING THREE WEEKS AGO.
THE HIGHER-UPS ARE KEEPING IT SECRET TO SAVE FACE.
I'LL THROW OFF THEIR PREDICTIONS WHEN THEY CAN'T GET ANOTHER.

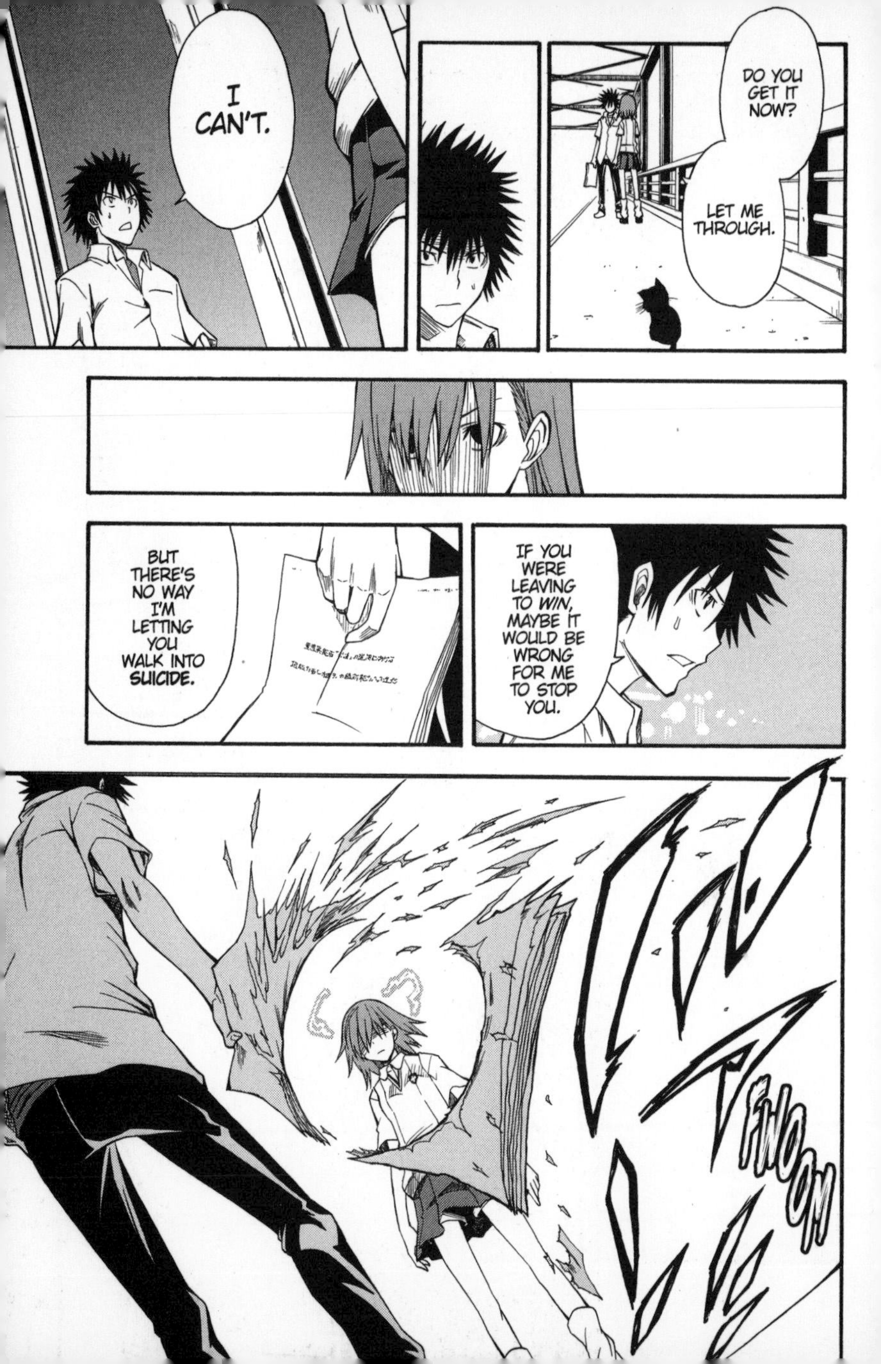
DO YOU GET IT NOW?
LET ME THROUGH.
I CAN'T.
IF YOU WERE LEAVING TO *WIN*, MAYBE IT WOULD BE WRONG FOR ME TO STOP YOU.
BUT THERE'S NO WAY I'M LETTING YOU WALK INTO SUICIDE.
FWOOM

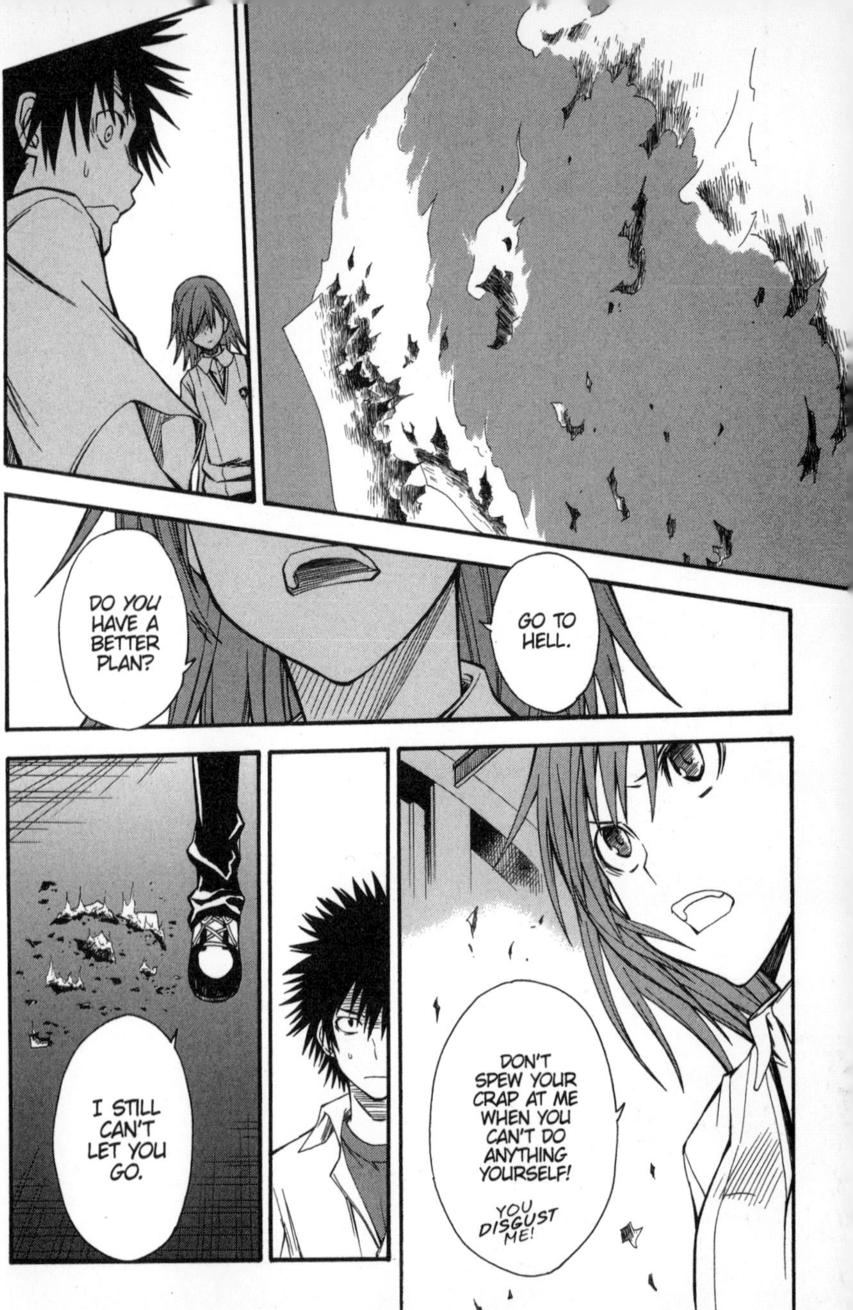
GO TO HELL.
DO YOU HAVE A BETTER PLAN?
DON'T SPEW YOUR CRAP AT ME WHEN YOU CAN'T DO ANYTHING YOURSELF!
YOU DISGUST ME!
I STILL CAN'T LET YOU GO.

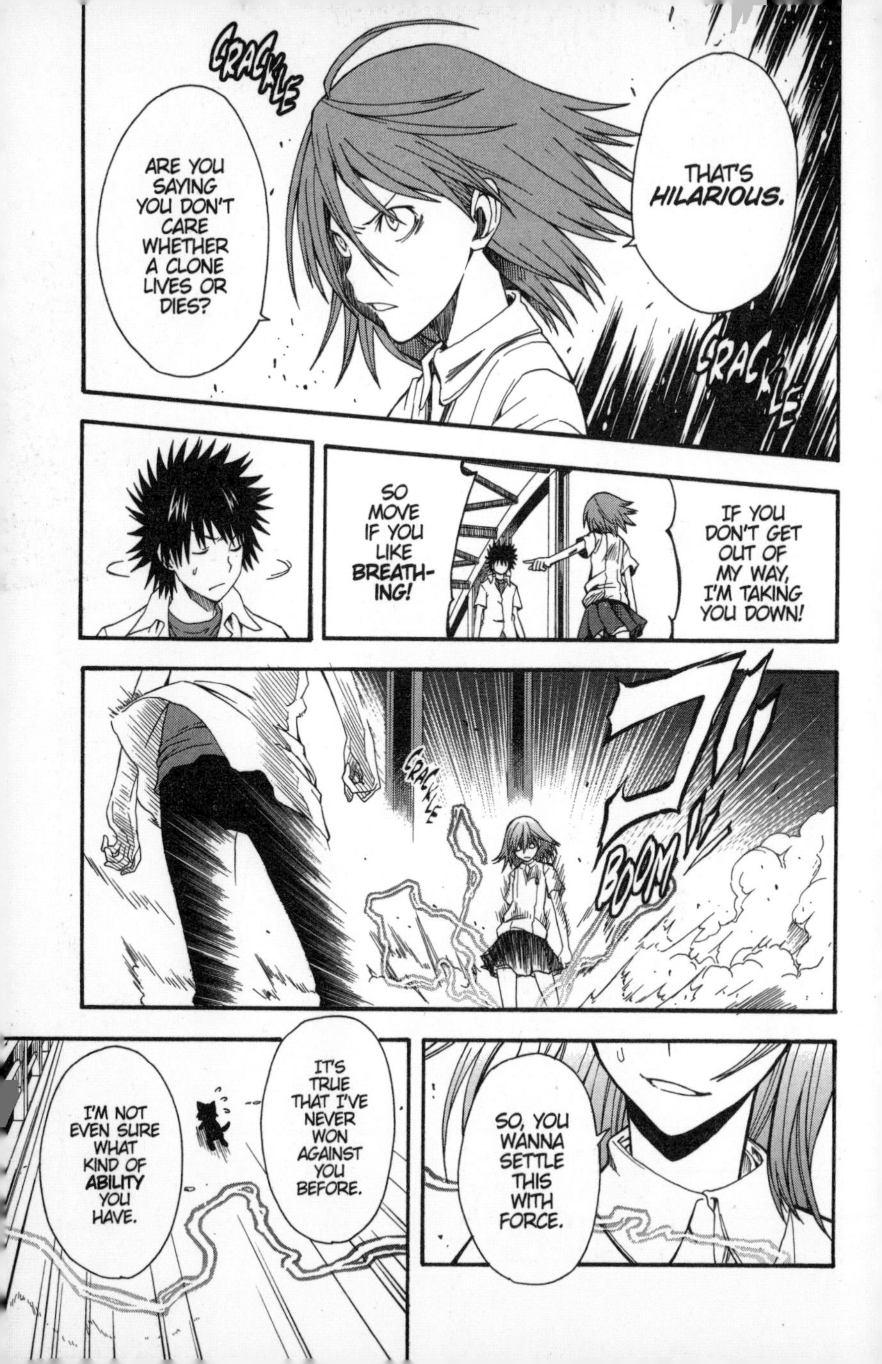
THAT'S HILARIOUS.
CRACKLE
CRACKLE
ARE YOU SAYING YOU DON'T CARE WHETHER A CLONE LIVES OR DIES?
IF YOU DON'T GET OUT OF MY WAY, I'M TAKING YOU DOWN!
SO MOVE IF YOU LIKE BREATH-ING!
BOOM!!
CRACKLE
SO, YOU WANNA SETTLE THIS WITH FORCE.
IT'S TRUE THAT I'VE NEVER WON AGAINST YOU BEFORE.
I'M NOT EVEN SURE WHAT KIND OF ABILITY YOU HAVE.

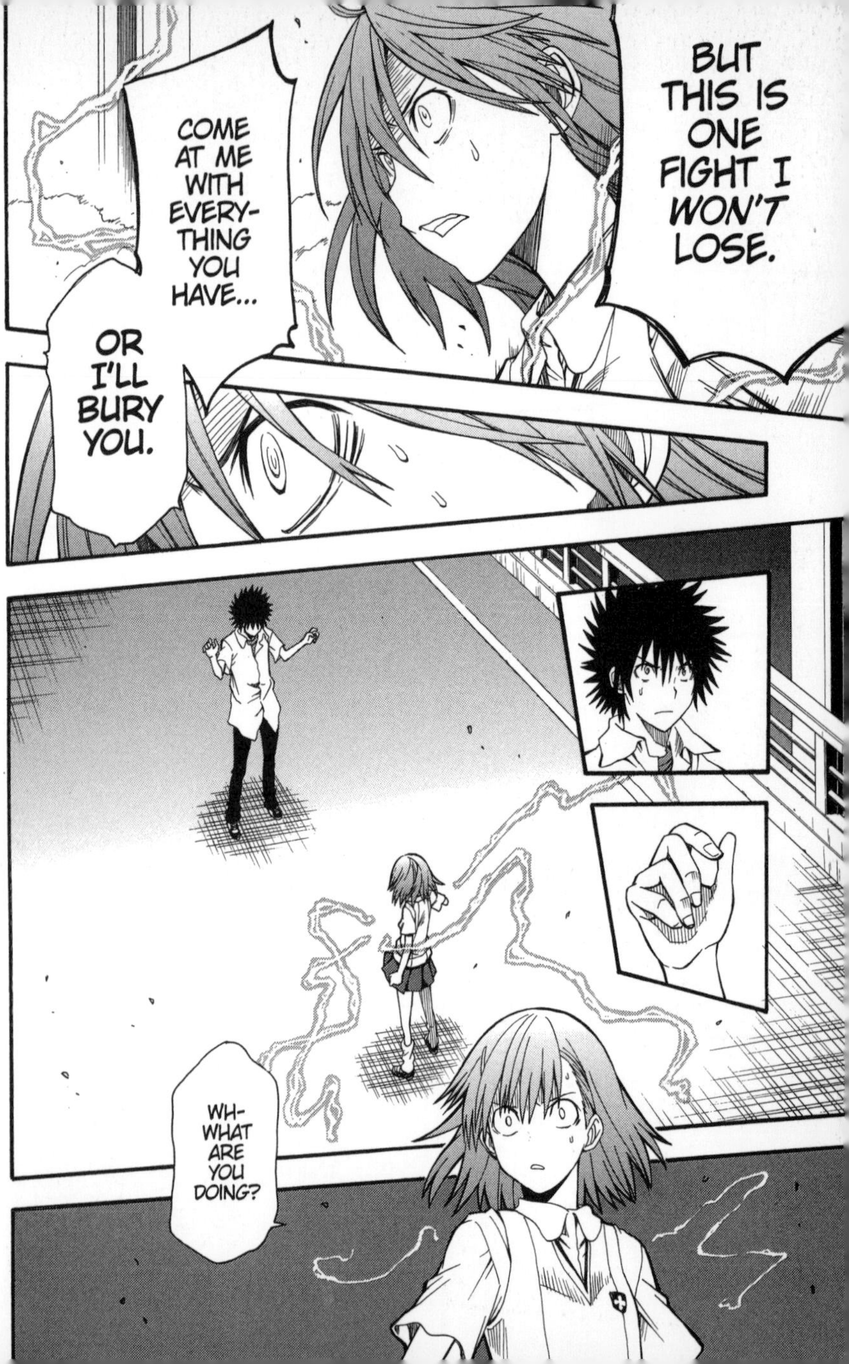
BUT THIS IS ONE FIGHT I WON'T LOSE.
COME AT ME WITH EVERYTHING YOU HAVE...
OR I'LL BURY YOU.
WH-WHAT ARE YOU DOING?

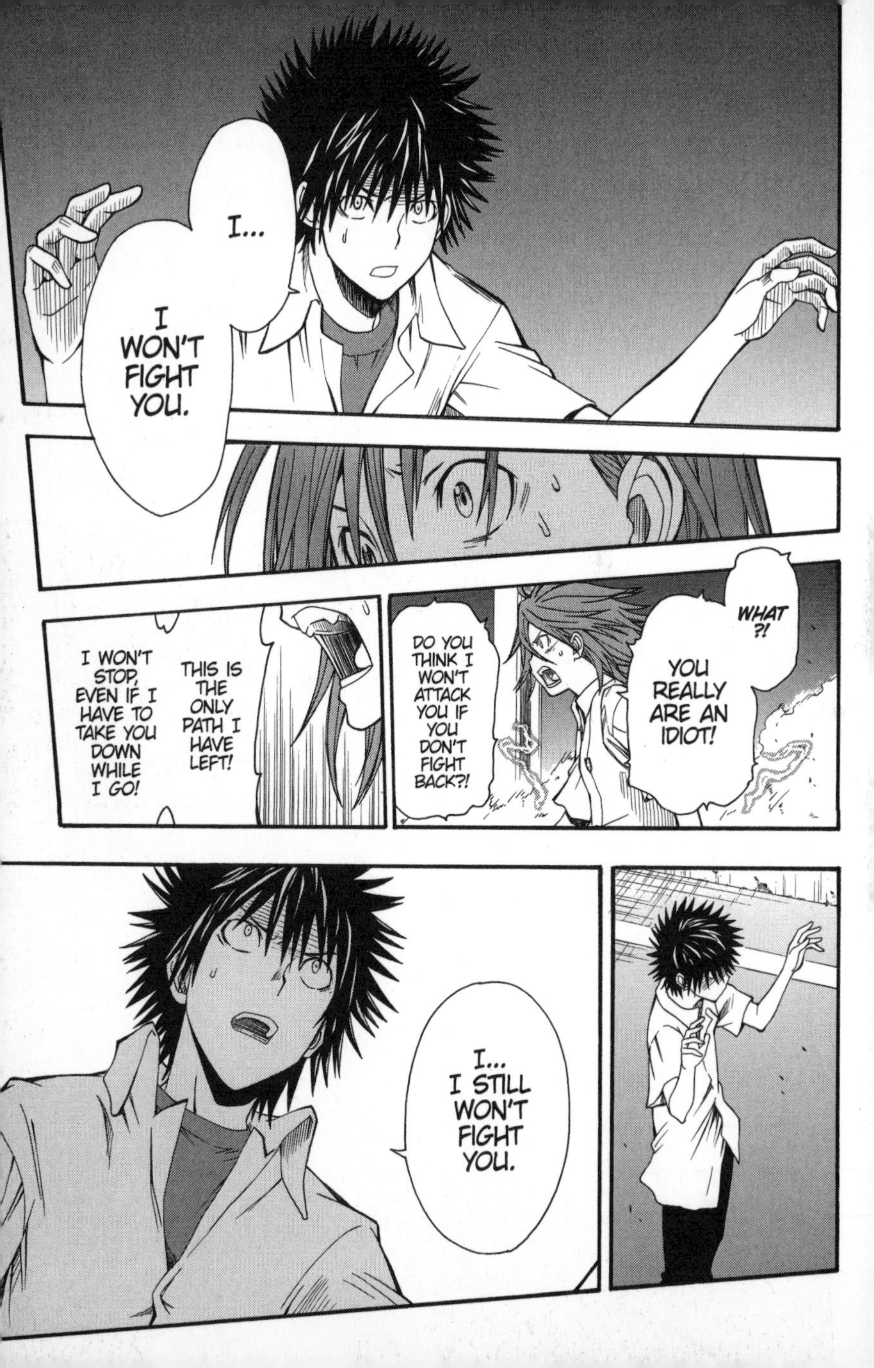
I...
I WON'T FIGHT YOU.
WHAT?!
YOU REALLY ARE AN IDIOT!
DO YOU THINK I WON'T ATTACK YOU IF YOU DON'T FIGHT BACK?!
THIS IS THE ONLY PATH I HAVE LEFT!
I WON'T STOP, EVEN IF I HAVE TO TAKE YOU DOWN WHILE I GO!
I... I STILL WON'T FIGHT YOU.

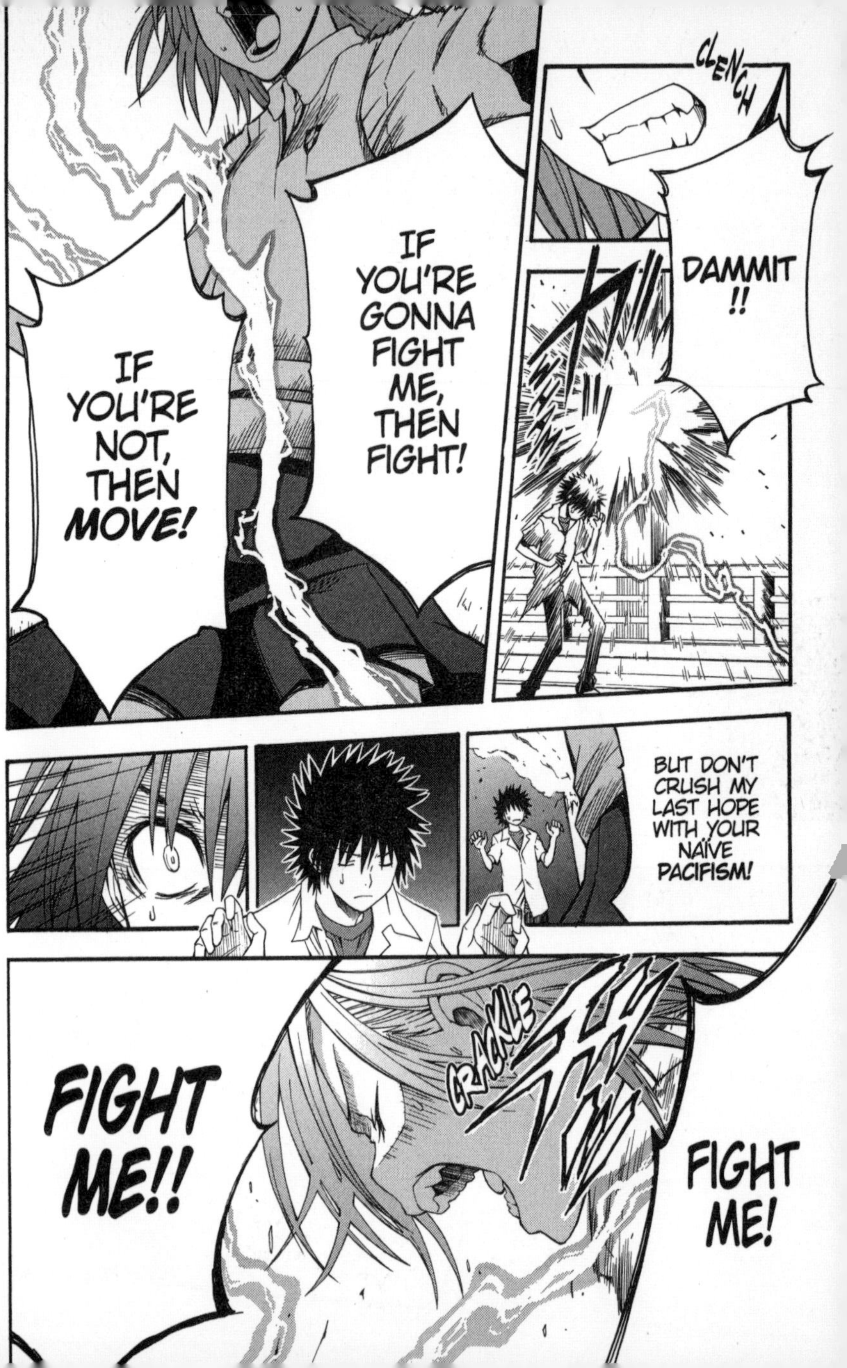
CLENCH
DAMMIT!!
WHAM
IF YOU'RE GONNA FIGHT ME, THEN FIGHT!
IF YOU'RE NOT, THEN MOVE!
BUT DON'T CRUSH MY LAST HOPE WITH YOUR NAÏVE PACIFISM!
FIGHT ME!
CRACKLE
FIGHT ME!!

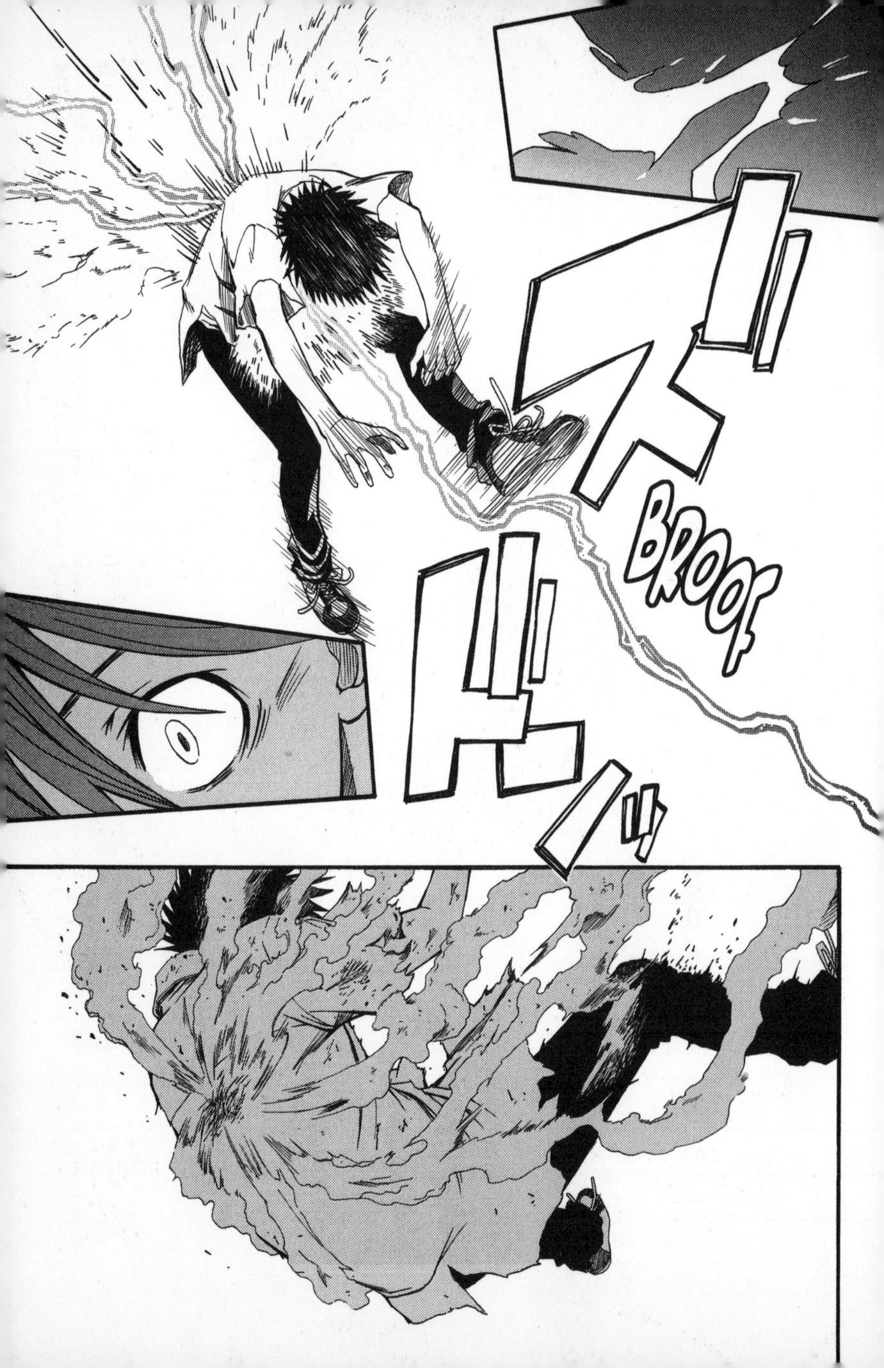
BROOF

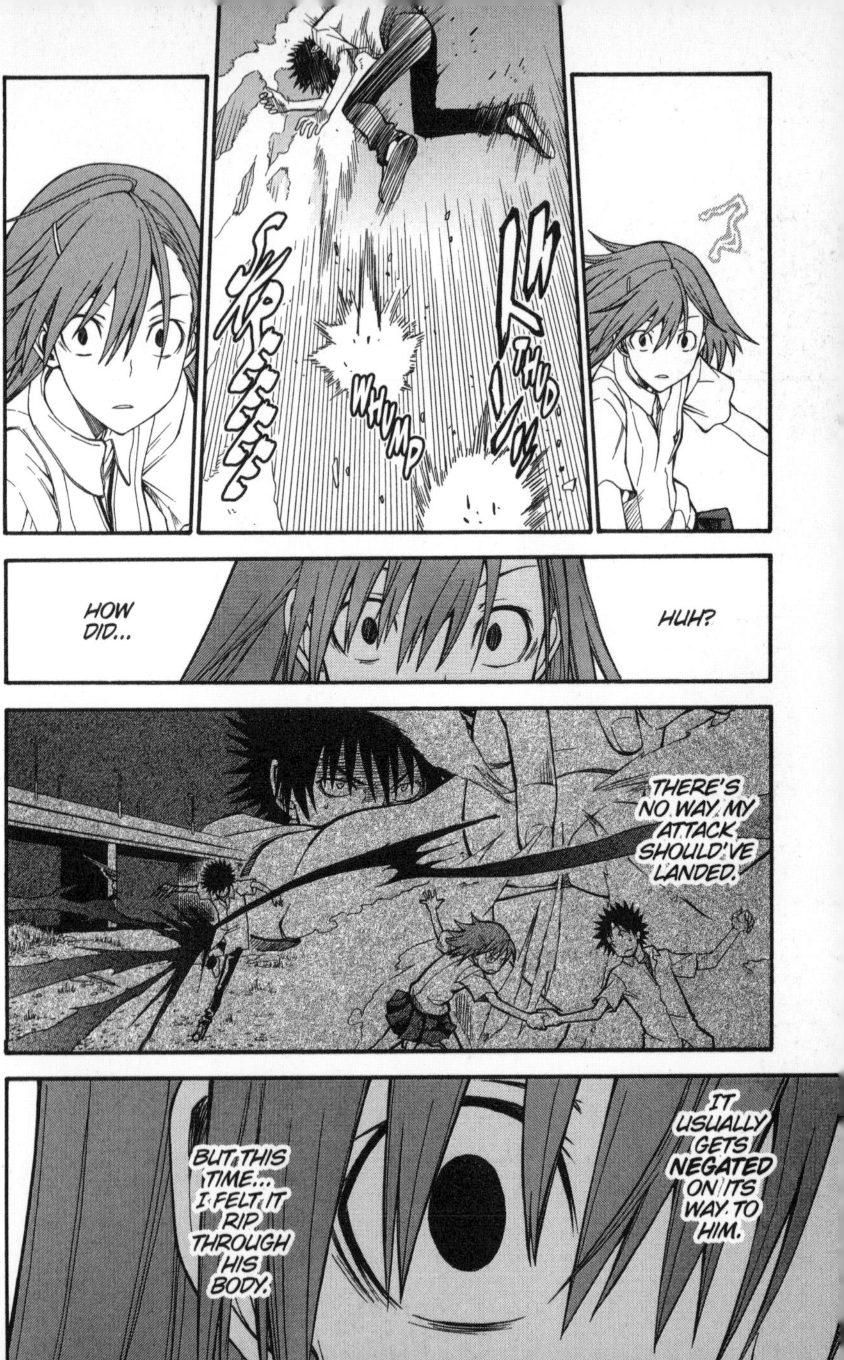
THUD
WHUMP
HUH?
HOW DID...
THERE'S NO WAY MY ATTACK SHOULD'VE LANDED.
IT USUALLY GETS NEGATED ON ITS WAY TO HIM.
BUT THIS TIME... I FELT IT RIP THROUGH HIS BODY.

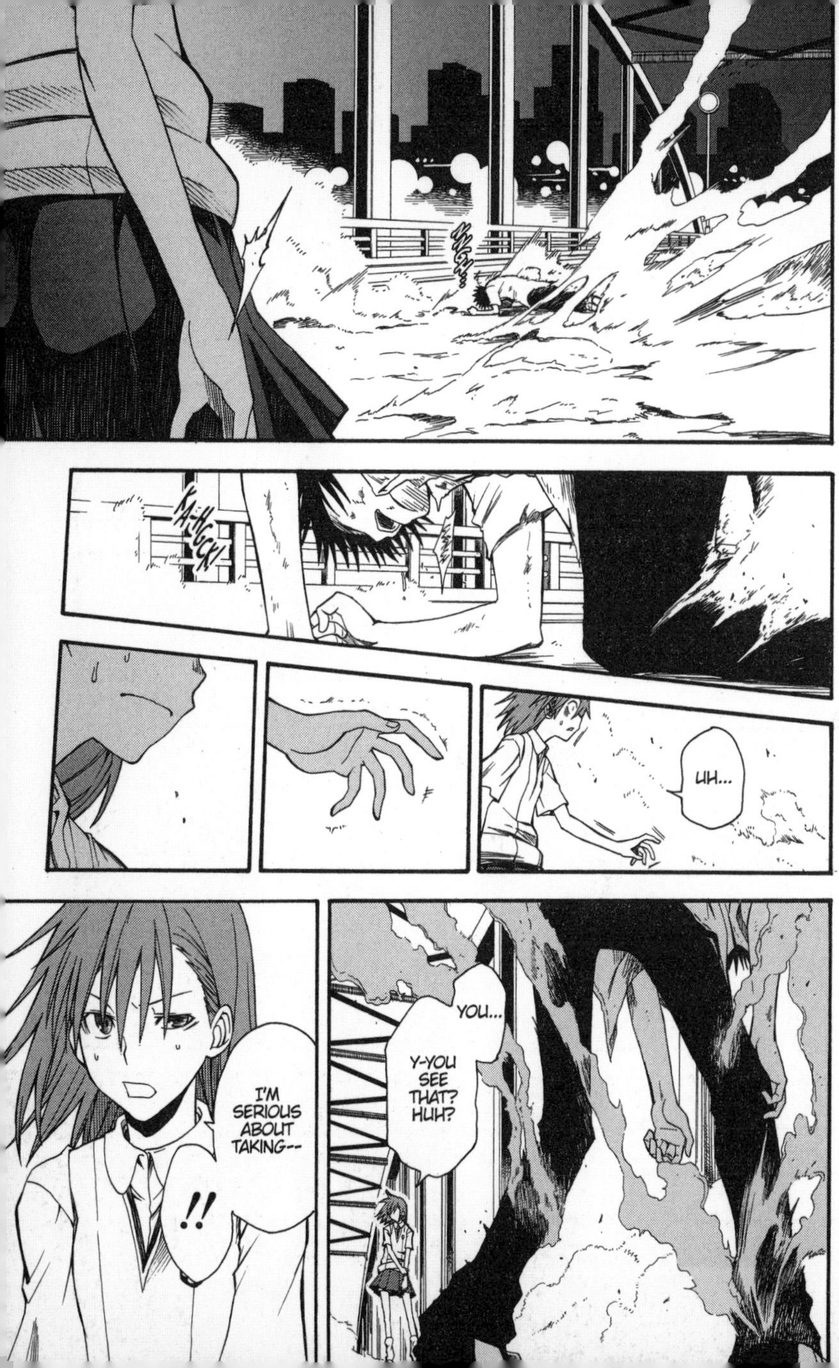
KNGH...
KA-HGCK!
UH...
YOU...
Y-YOU SEE THAT? HUH?
I'M SERIOUS ABOUT TAKING--
!!

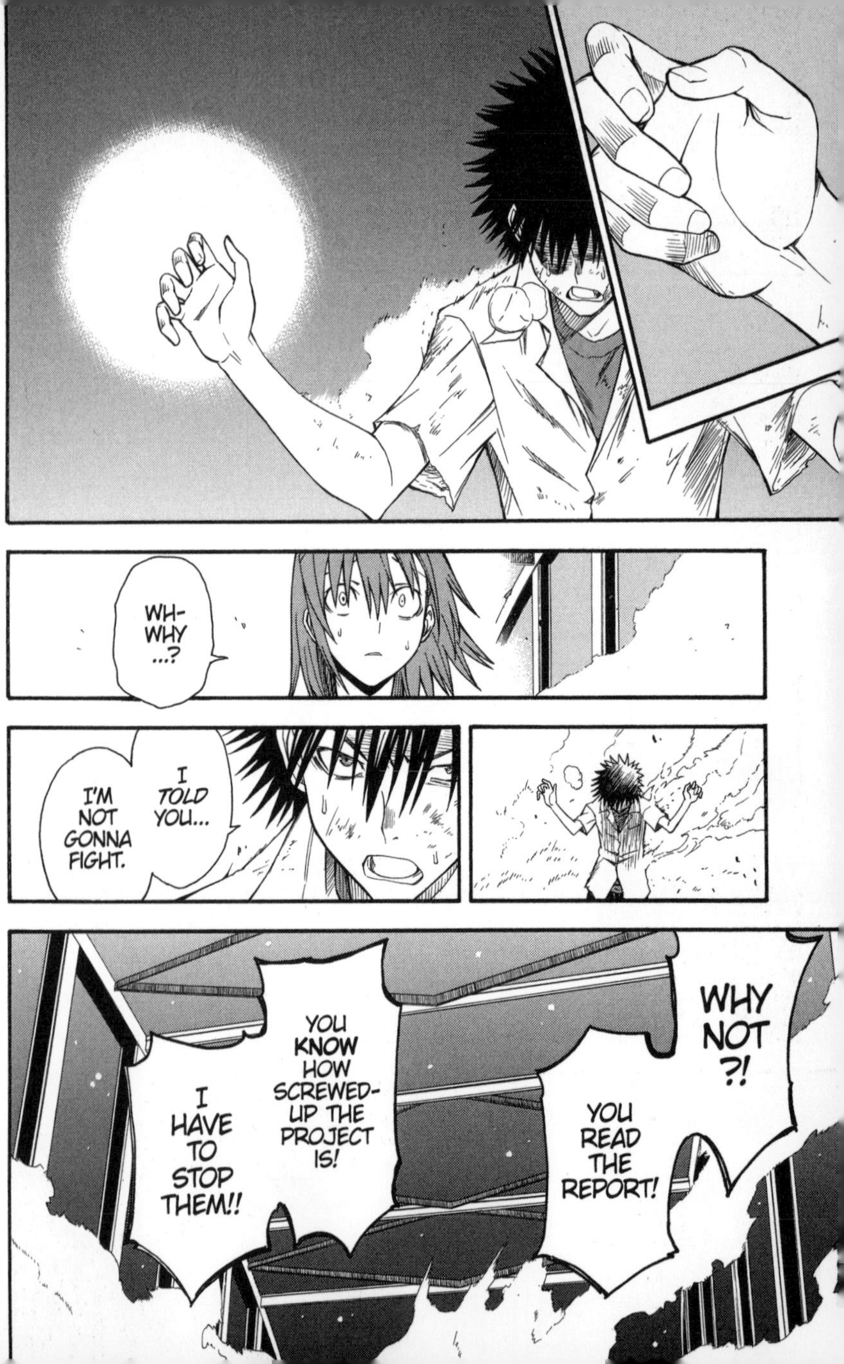
WH- WHY ...?
I TOLD YOU...
I'M NOT GONNA FIGHT.
WHY NOT ?!
YOU READ THE REPORT!
YOU KNOW HOW SCREWED-UP THE PROJECT IS!
I HAVE TO STOP THEM!!

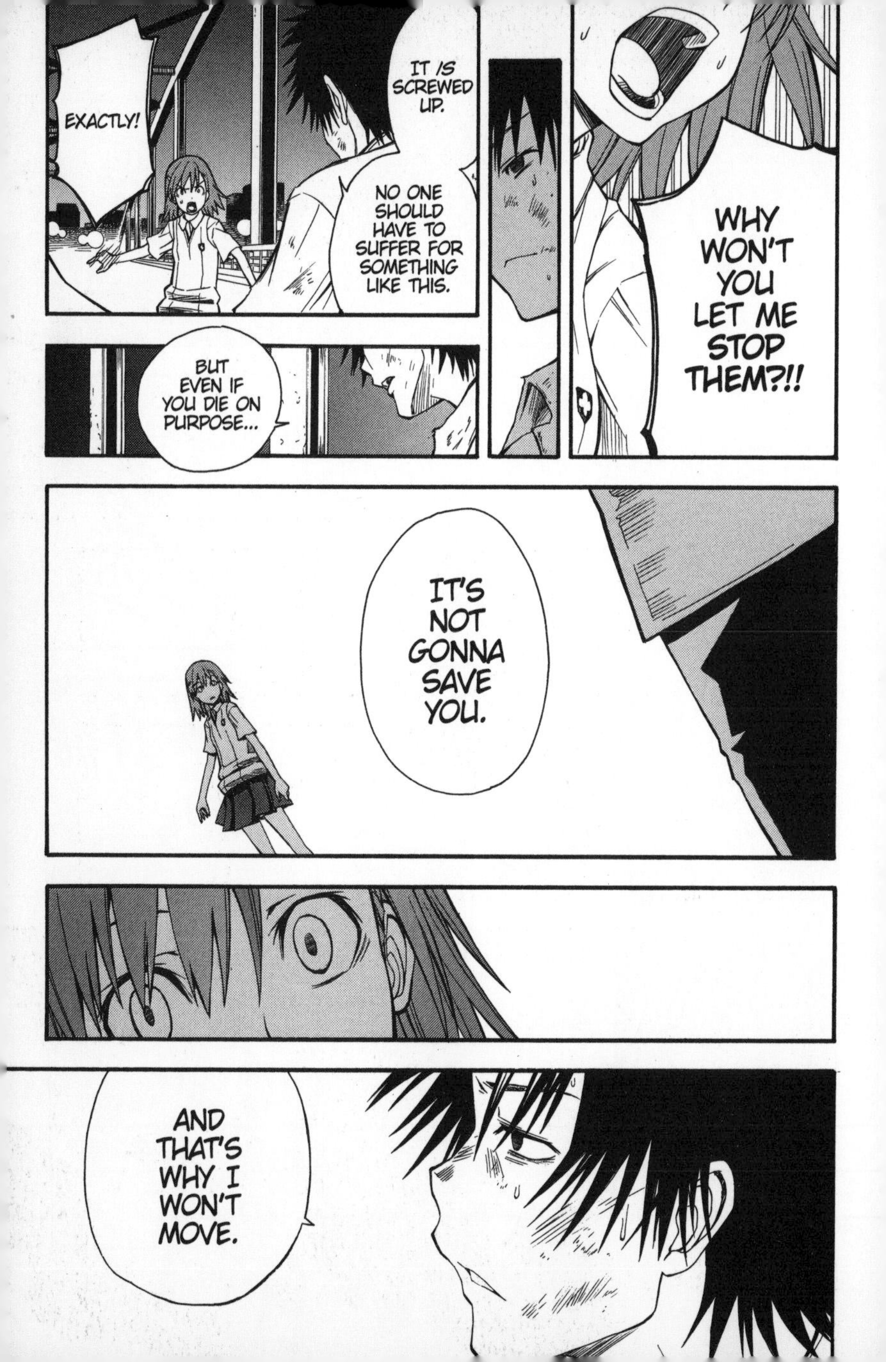

WHY WON'T YOU LET ME STOP THEM?!!
IT IS SCREWED UP.
NO ONE SHOULD HAVE TO SUFFER FOR SOMETHING LIKE THIS.
EXACTLY!
BUT EVEN IF YOU DIE ON PURPOSE...
IT'S NOT GONNA SAVE YOU.
AND THAT'S WHY I WON'T MOVE.

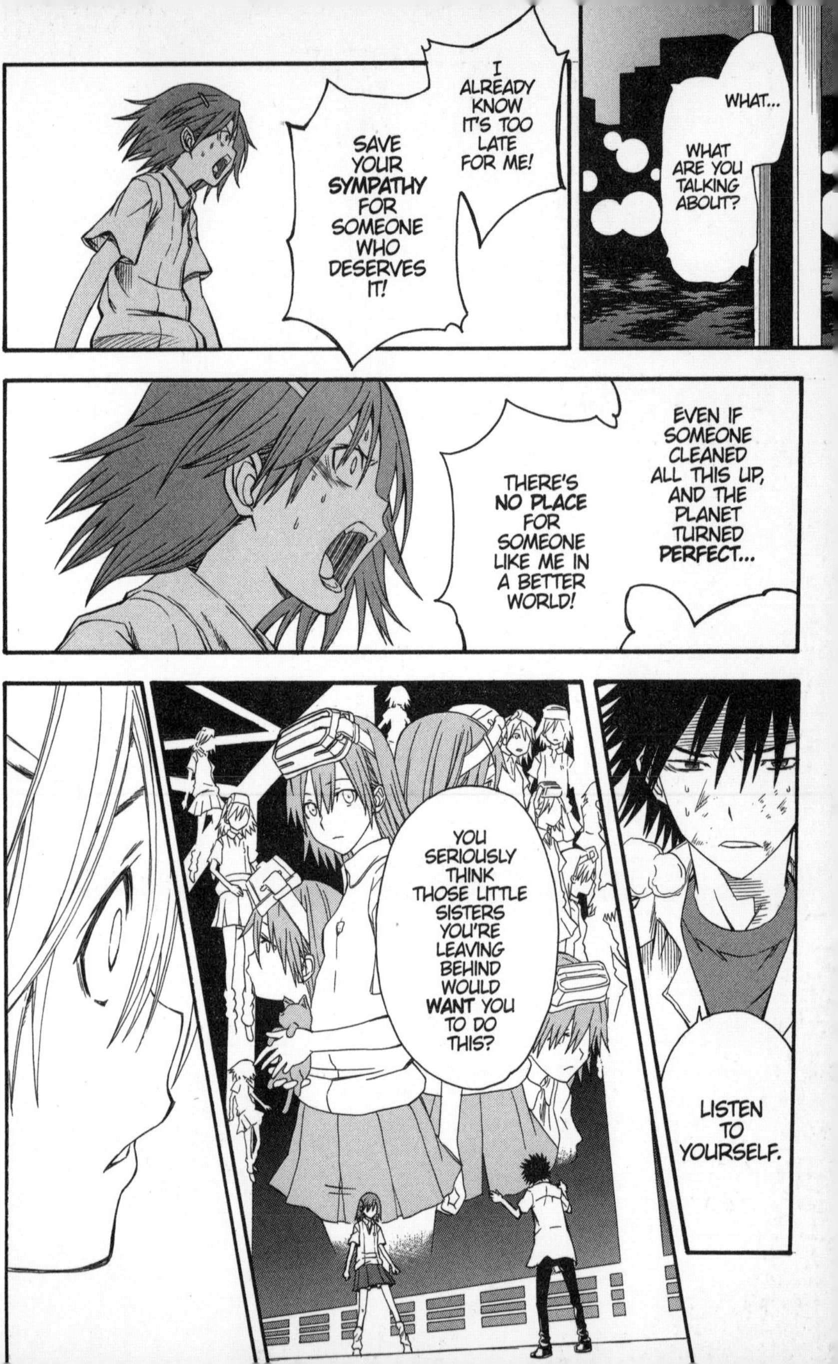
WHAT...
WHAT ARE YOU TALKING ABOUT?
I ALREADY KNOW IT'S TOO LATE FOR ME!
SAVE YOUR **SYMPATHY** FOR SOMEONE WHO DESERVES IT!
EVEN IF SOMEONE CLEANED ALL THIS UP, AND THE PLANET TURNED **PERFECT...**
THERE'S **NO PLACE** FOR SOMEONE LIKE ME IN A BETTER WORLD!
LISTEN TO YOURSELF.
YOU SERIOUSLY THINK THOSE LITTLE SISTERS YOU'RE LEAVING BEHIND WOULD **WANT** YOU TO DO THIS?

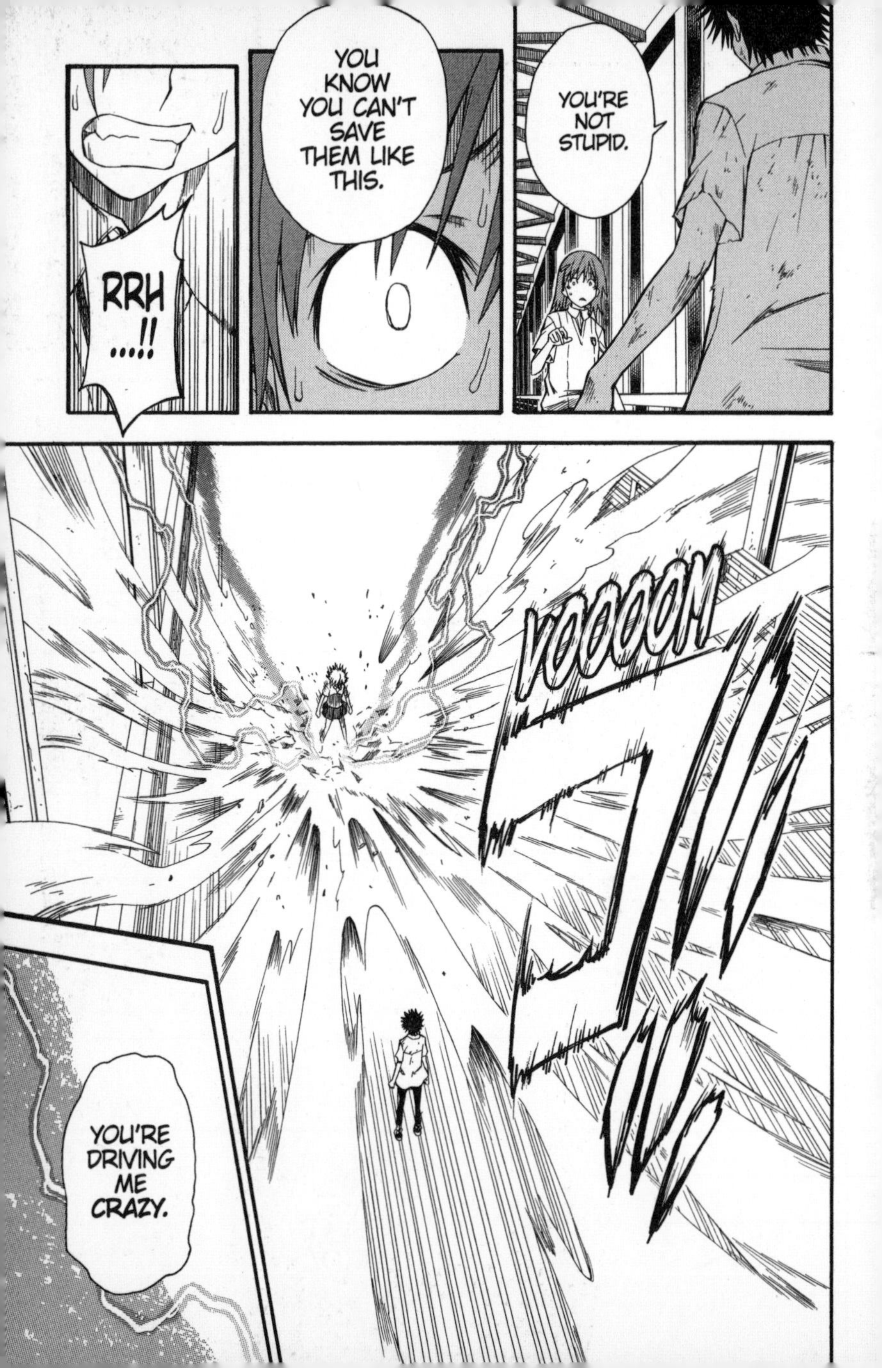
YOU'RE NOT STUPID.
YOU KNOW YOU CAN'T SAVE THEM LIKE THIS.
RRH ....!!
VOOOOM
YOU'RE DRIVING ME CRAZY.

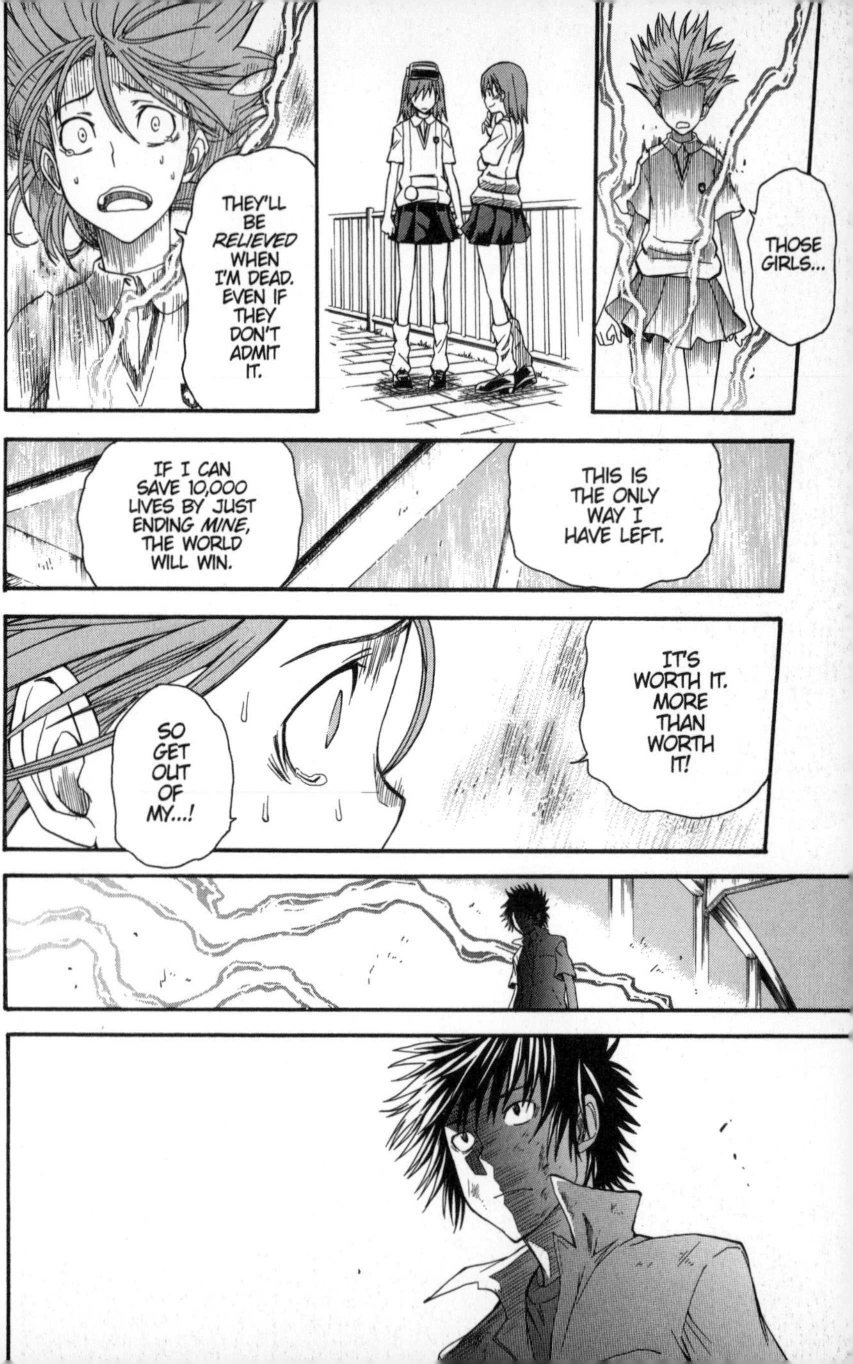
THOSE GIRLS...
THEY'LL BE *RELIEVED* WHEN I'M DEAD. EVEN IF THEY DON'T ADMIT IT.
THIS IS THE ONLY WAY I HAVE LEFT.
IF I CAN SAVE 10,000 LIVES BY JUST ENDING *MINE*, THE WORLD WILL WIN.
IT'S WORTH IT. MORE THAN WORTH IT!
SO GET OUT OF MY...!

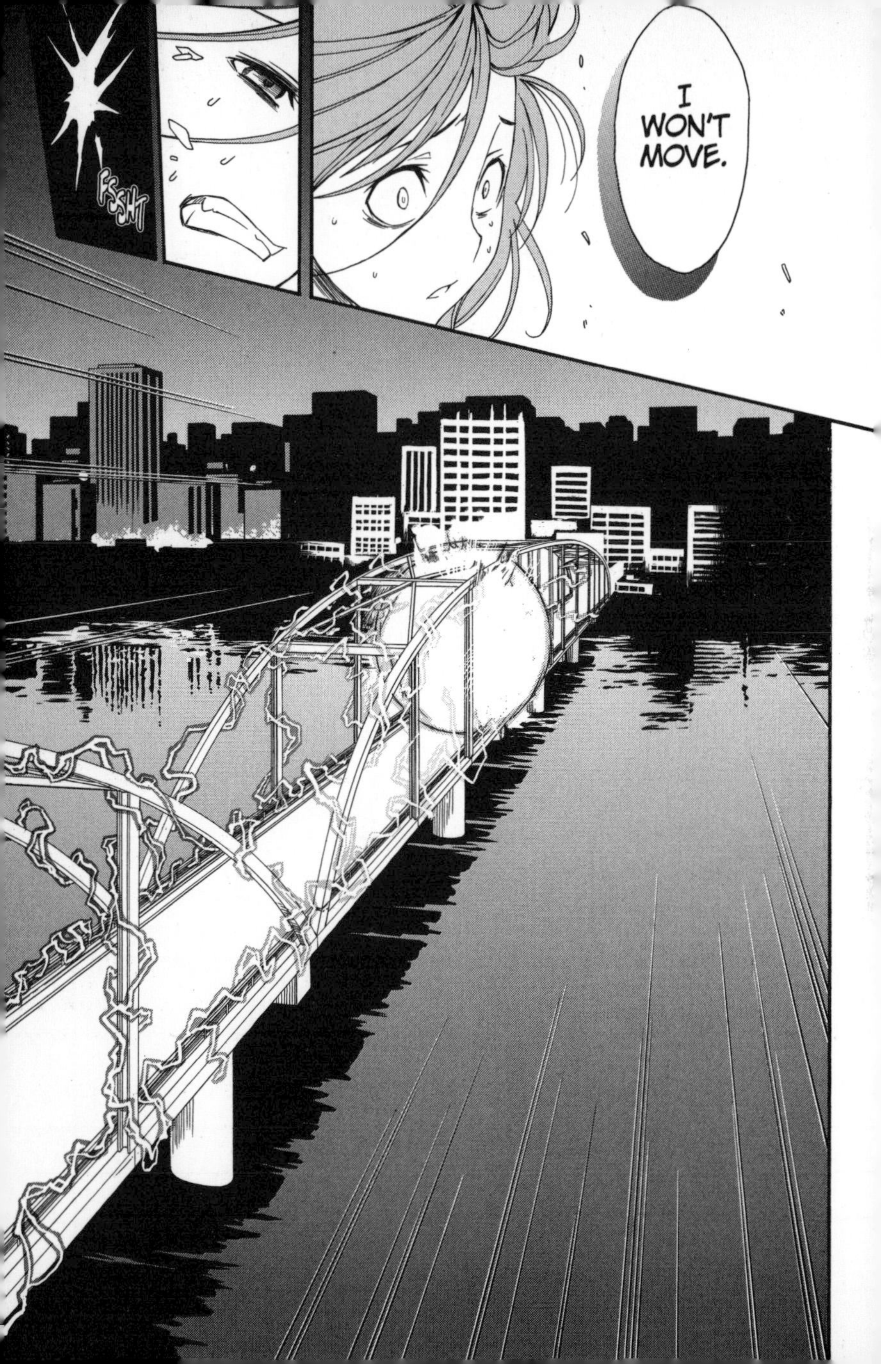
I WON'T MOVE.
FSSHT

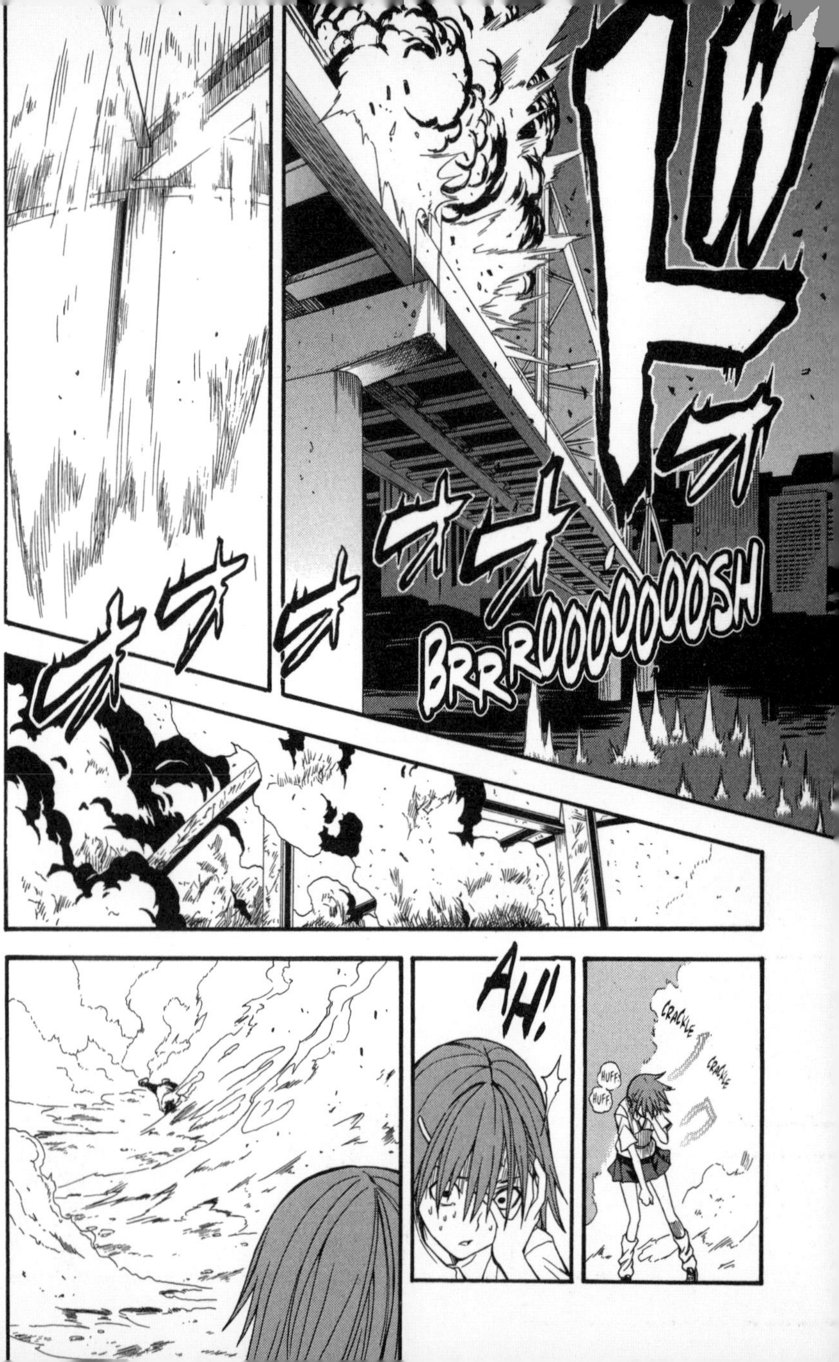
BRRROOOOOOOOSH
AH!
CRACKLE
CRACKLE
HUFF
HUFF

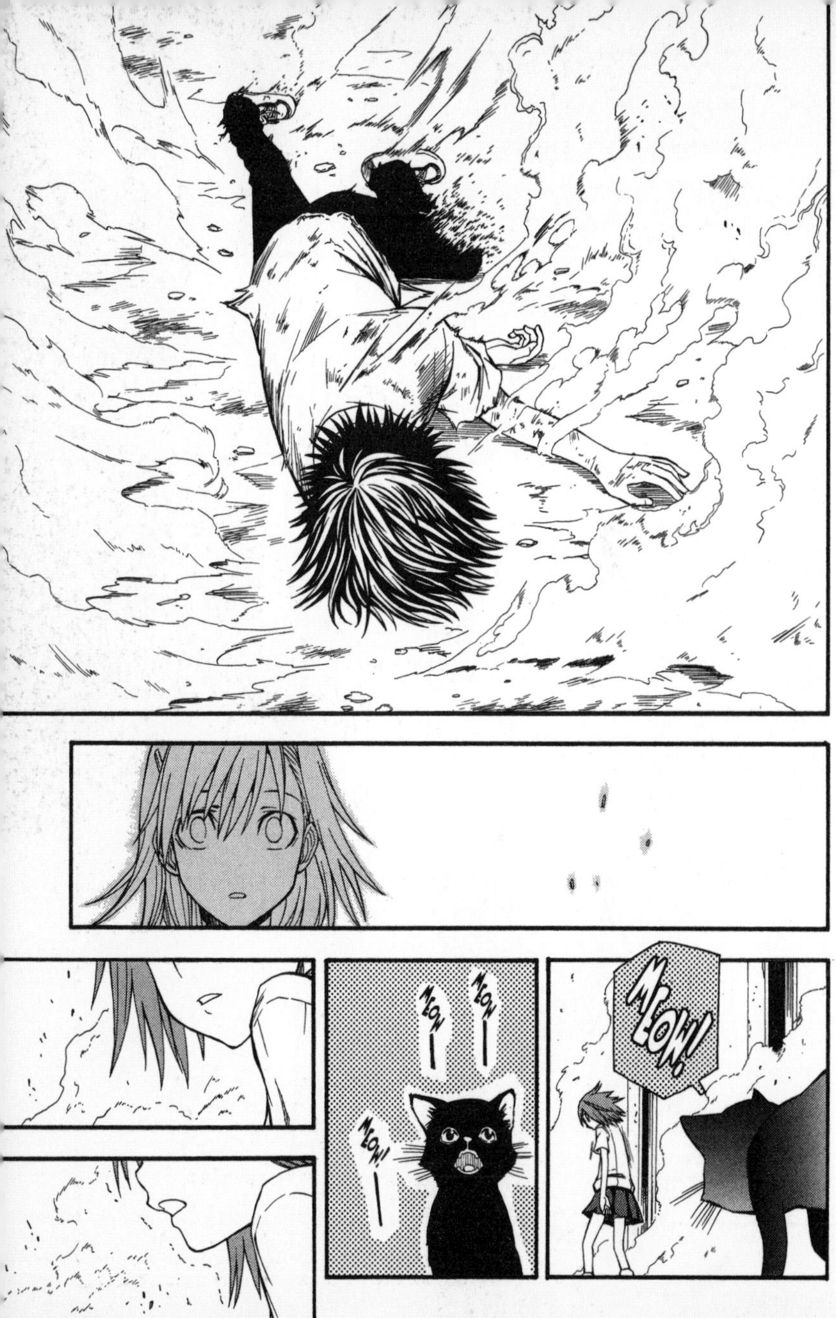
MEOW!
MEOW—
MEOW—
MEOW!—

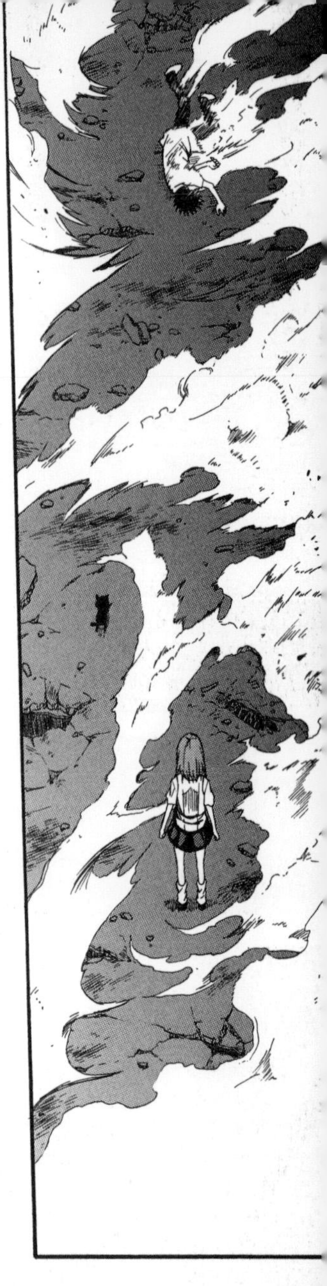

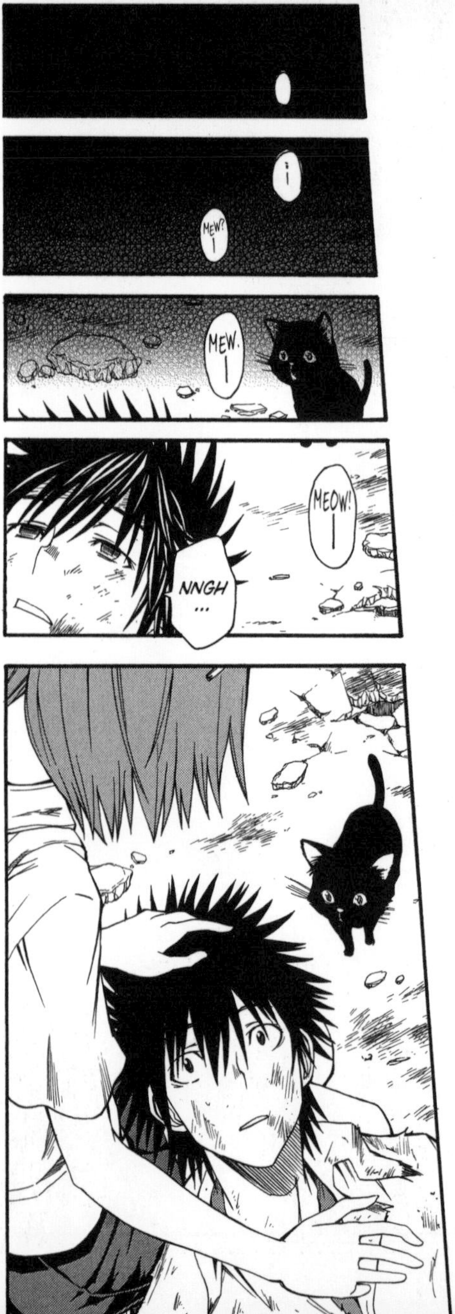

!
!?
MEW?
MEW.
MEOW!
NNGH ...

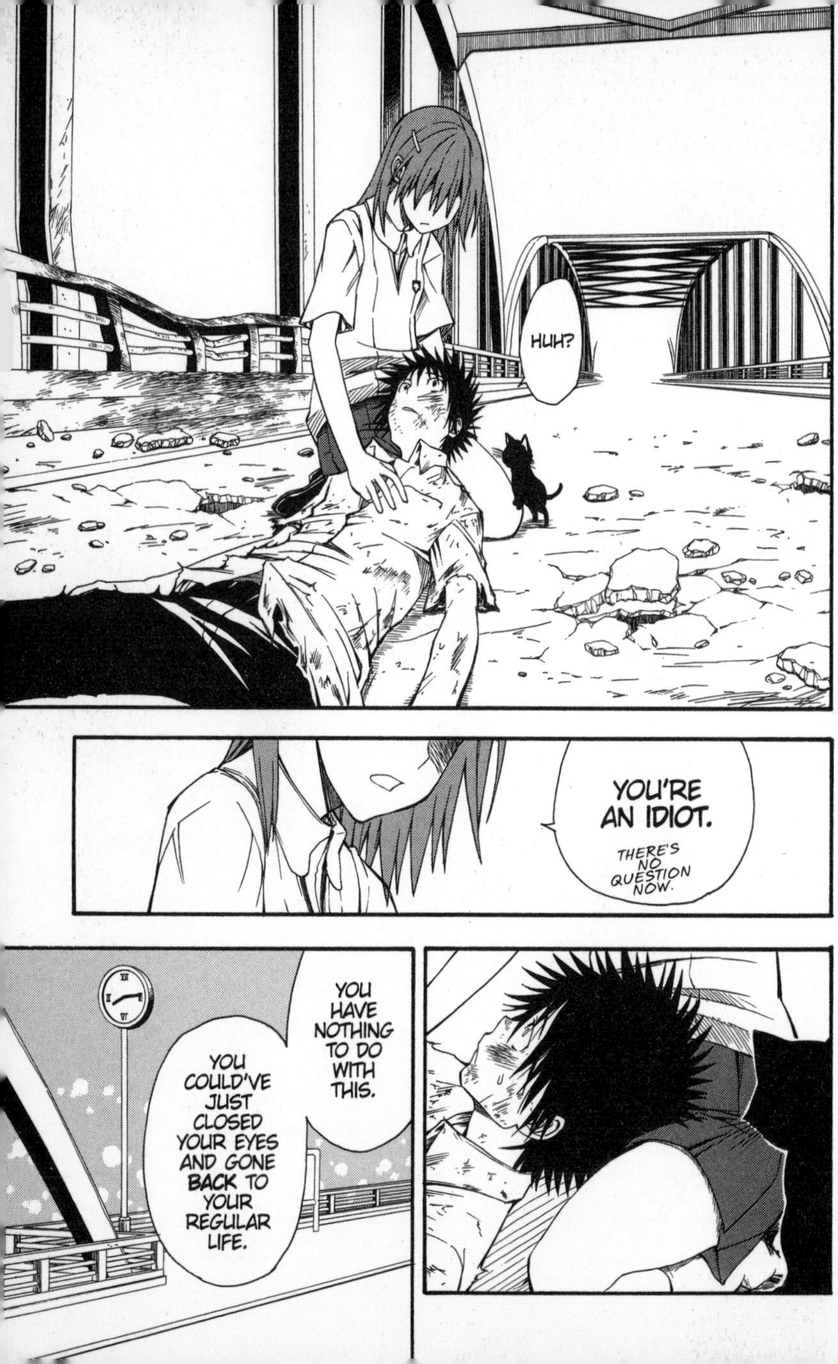
HUH?
YOU'RE AN IDIOT.
THERE'S NO QUESTION NOW.
YOU HAVE NOTHING TO DO WITH THIS.
YOU COULD'VE JUST CLOSED YOUR EYES AND GONE BACK TO YOUR REGULAR LIFE.

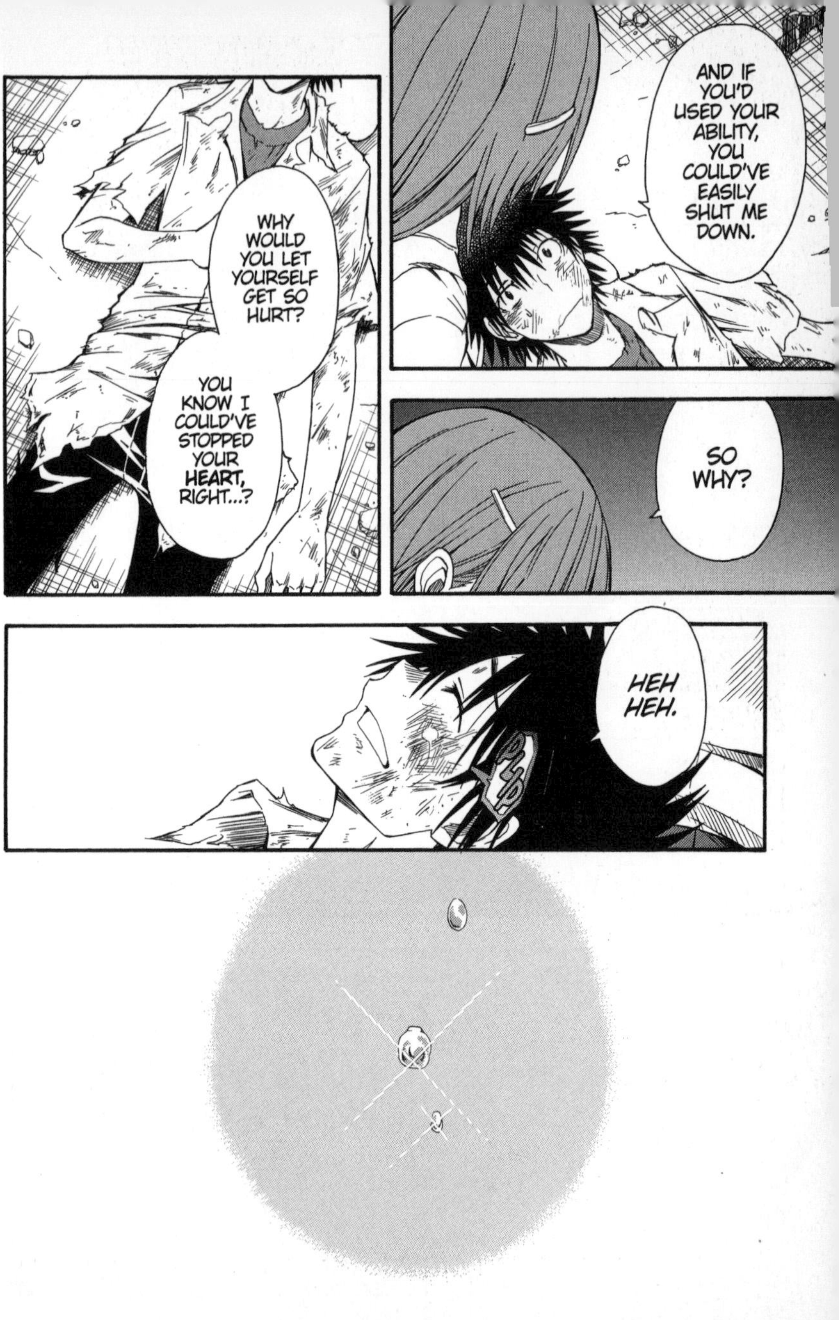
AND IF YOU'D USED YOUR ABILITY, YOU COULD'VE EASILY SHUT ME DOWN.
SO WHY?
WHY WOULD YOU LET YOURSELF GET SO HURT?
YOU KNOW I COULD'VE STOPPED YOUR HEART, RIGHT...?
HEH HEH.

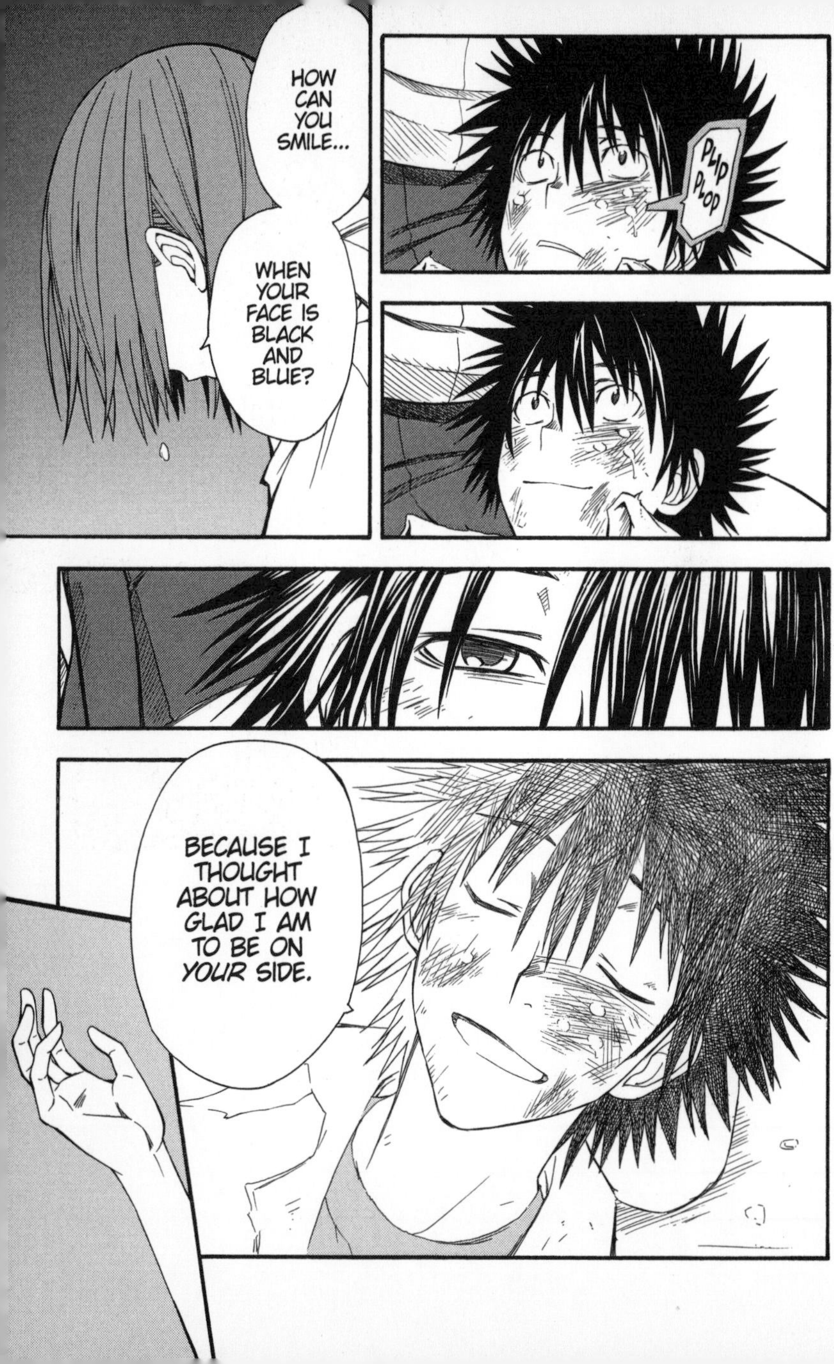
PLIP PLOP
HOW CAN YOU SMILE...
WHEN YOUR FACE IS BLACK AND BLUE?
BECAUSE I THOUGHT ABOUT HOW GLAD I AM TO BE ON *YOUR* SIDE.

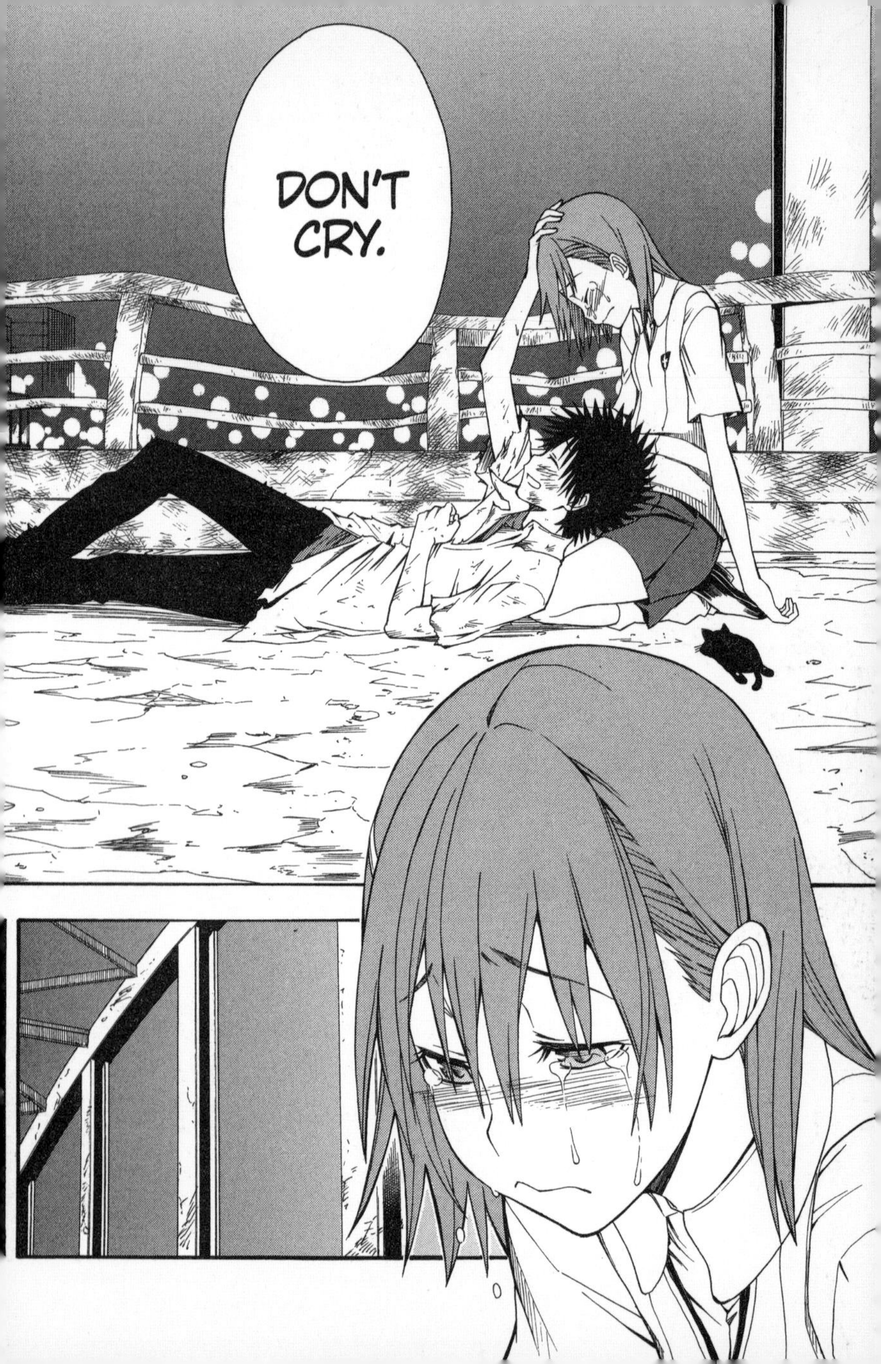
DON'T CRY.

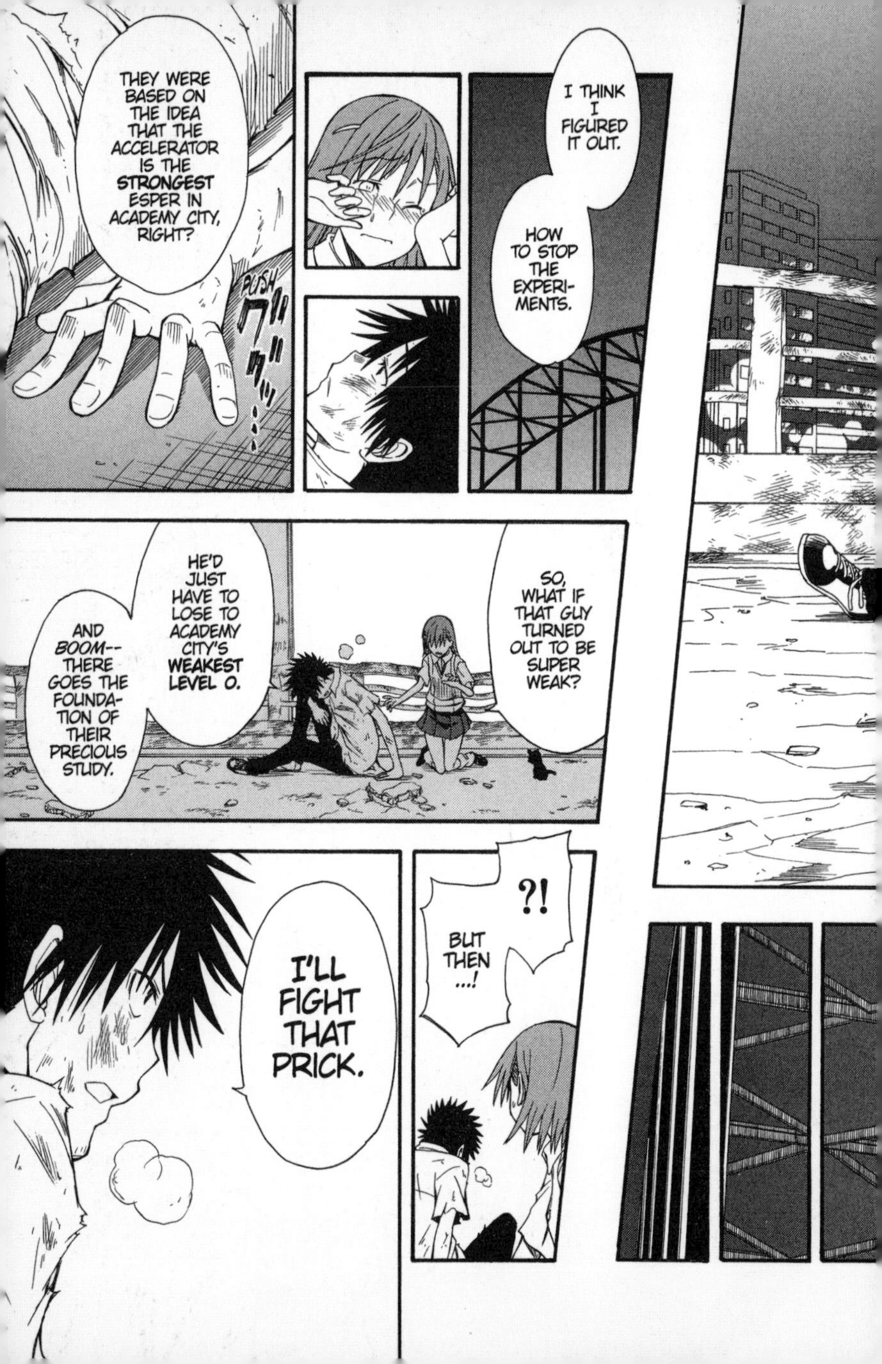
I THINK I FIGURED IT OUT.
HOW TO STOP THE EXPERIMENTS.
THEY WERE BASED ON THE IDEA THAT THE ACCELERATOR IS THE **STRONGEST** ESPER IN ACADEMY CITY, RIGHT?
PUSH
SO, WHAT IF THAT GUY TURNED OUT TO BE SUPER WEAK?
HE'D JUST HAVE TO LOSE TO ACADEMY CITY'S **WEAKEST** LEVEL 0.
AND *BOOM*-- THERE GOES THE FOUNDATION OF THEIR PRECIOUS STUDY.
?!
BUT THEN ...!
I'LL FIGHT THAT PRICK.

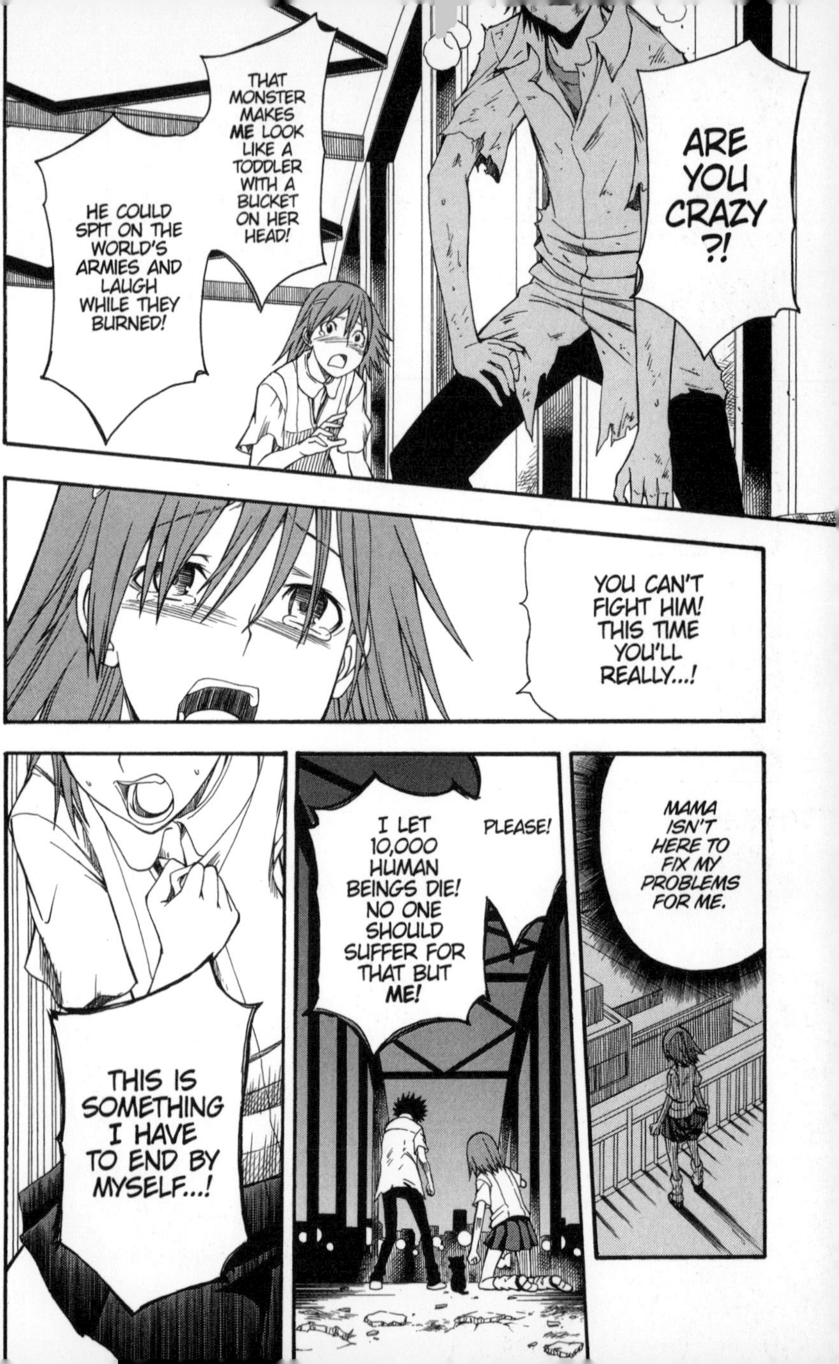
ARE YOU CRAZY?!
THAT MONSTER MAKES ME LOOK LIKE A TODDLER WITH A BUCKET ON HER HEAD!
HE COULD SPIT ON THE WORLD'S ARMIES AND LAUGH WHILE THEY BURNED!
YOU CAN'T FIGHT HIM! THIS TIME YOU'LL REALLY...!
MAMA ISN'T HERE TO FIX MY PROBLEMS FOR ME.
PLEASE!
I LET 10,000 HUMAN BEINGS DIE! NO ONE SHOULD SUFFER FOR THAT BUT ME!
THIS IS SOMETHING I HAVE TO END BY MYSELF...!

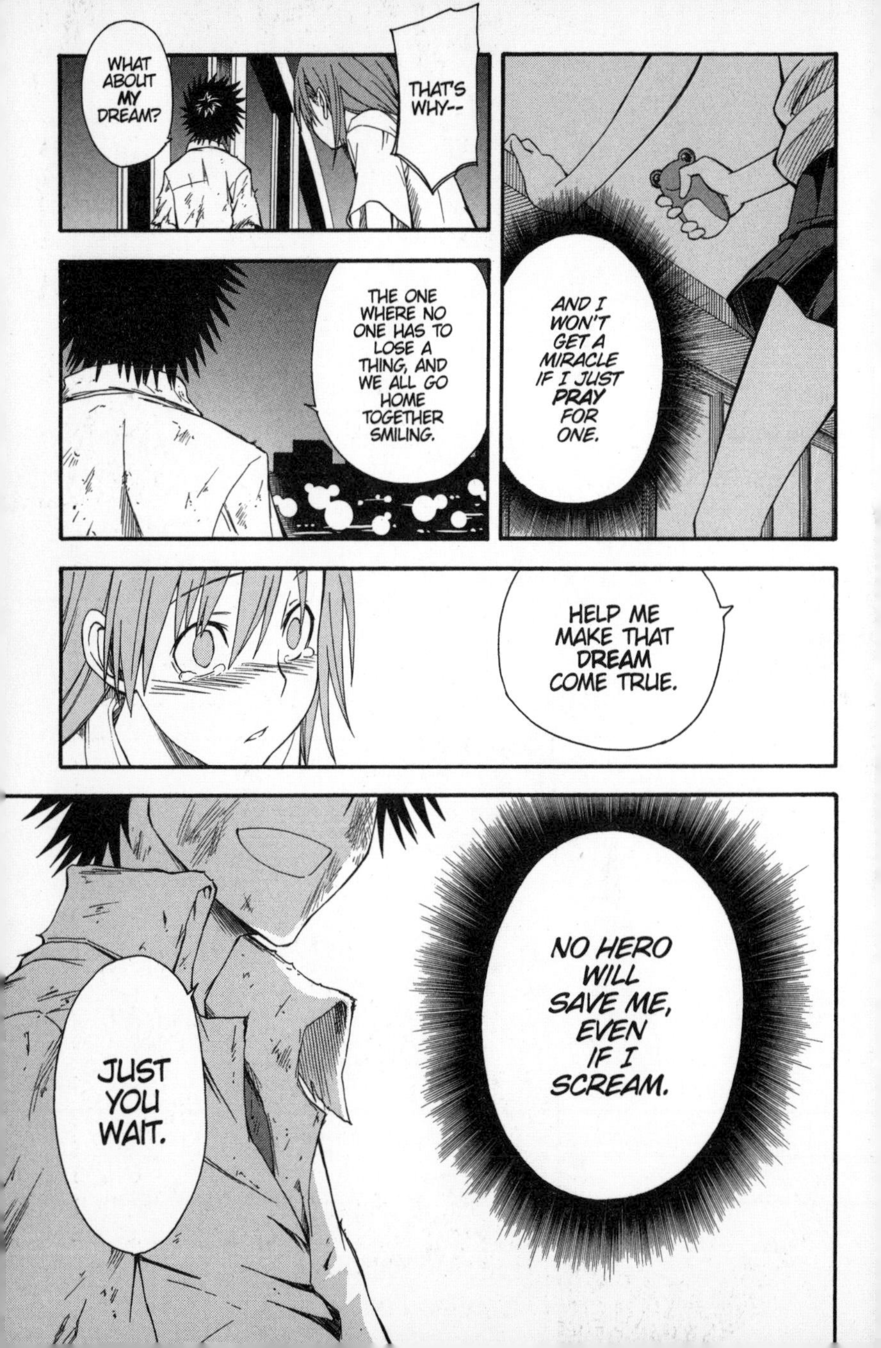
AND I WON'T GET A MIRACLE IF I JUST PRAY FOR ONE.
THAT'S WHY--
WHAT ABOUT MY DREAM?
THE ONE WHERE NO ONE HAS TO LOSE A THING, AND WE ALL GO HOME TOGETHER SMILING.
HELP ME MAKE THAT DREAM COME TRUE.
NO HERO WILL SAVE ME, EVEN IF I SCREAM.
JUST YOU WAIT.

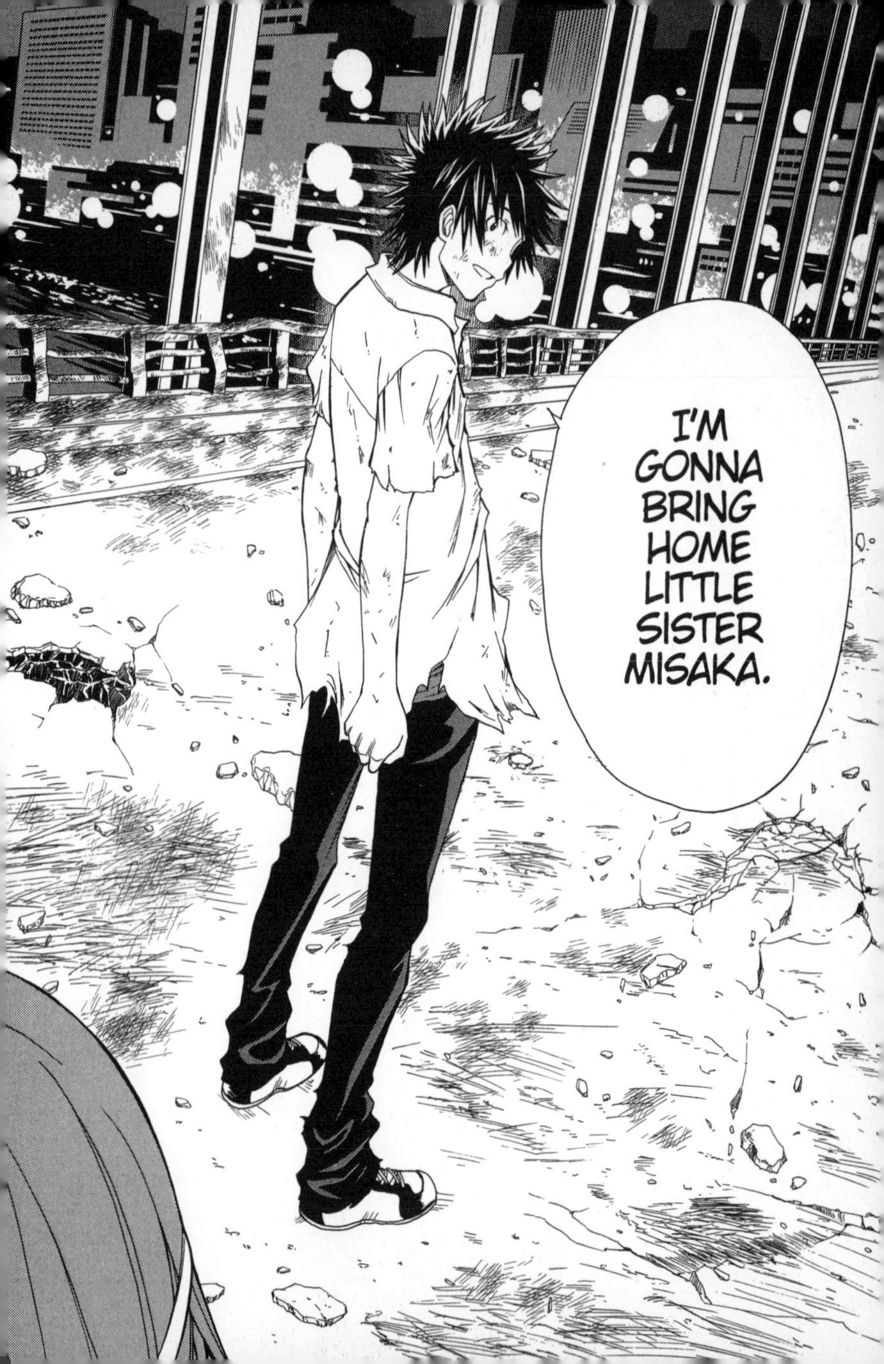
I'M GONNA BRING HOME LITTLE SISTER MISAKA.

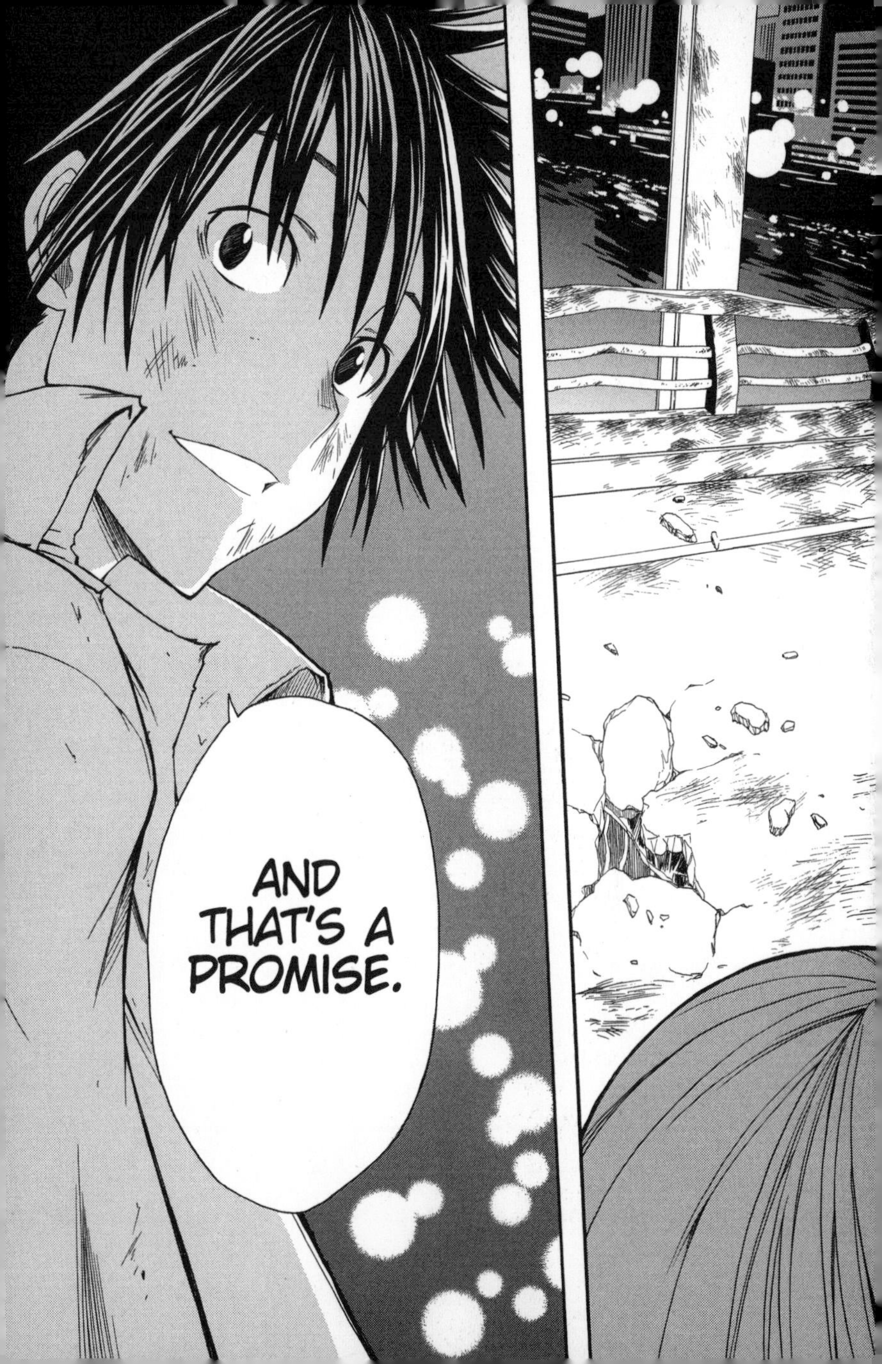
AND THAT'S A PROMISE.

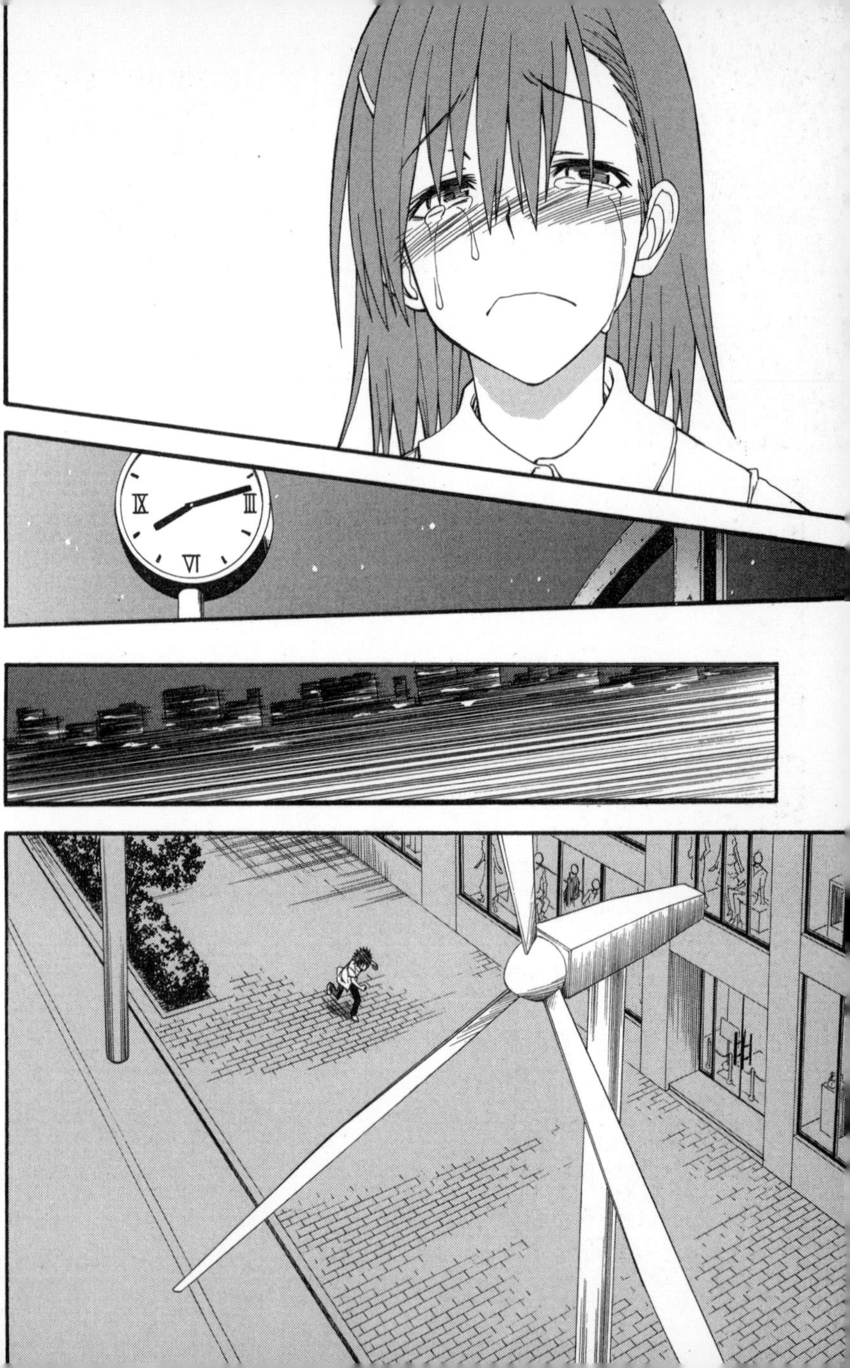

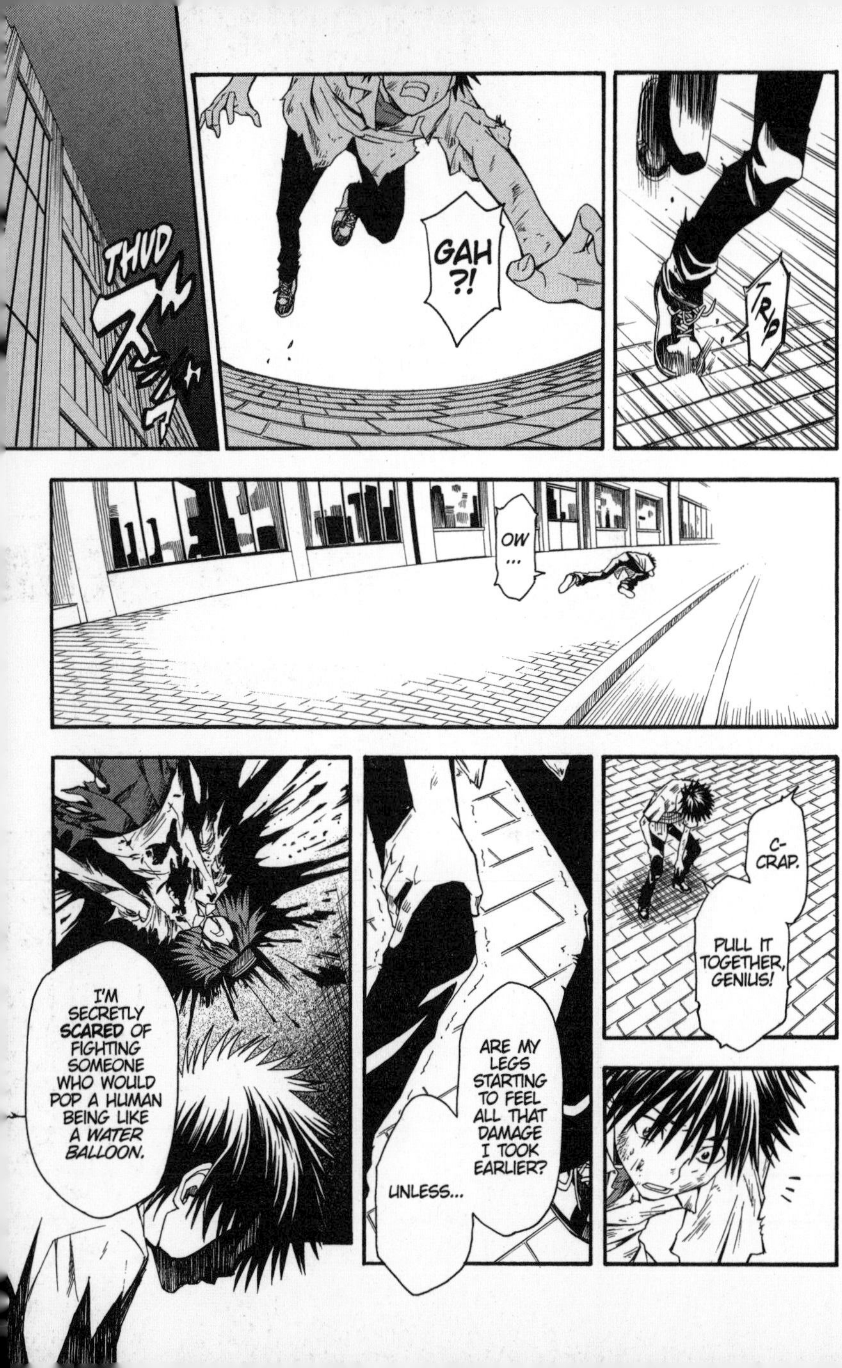

TRIP
GAH?!
THUD
OW...
C-CRAP.
PULL IT TOGETHER, GENIUS!
ARE MY LEGS STARTING TO FEEL ALL THAT DAMAGE I TOOK EARLIER?
UNLESS...
I'M SECRETLY SCARED OF FIGHTING SOMEONE WHO WOULD POP A HUMAN BEING LIKE A WATER BALLOON.

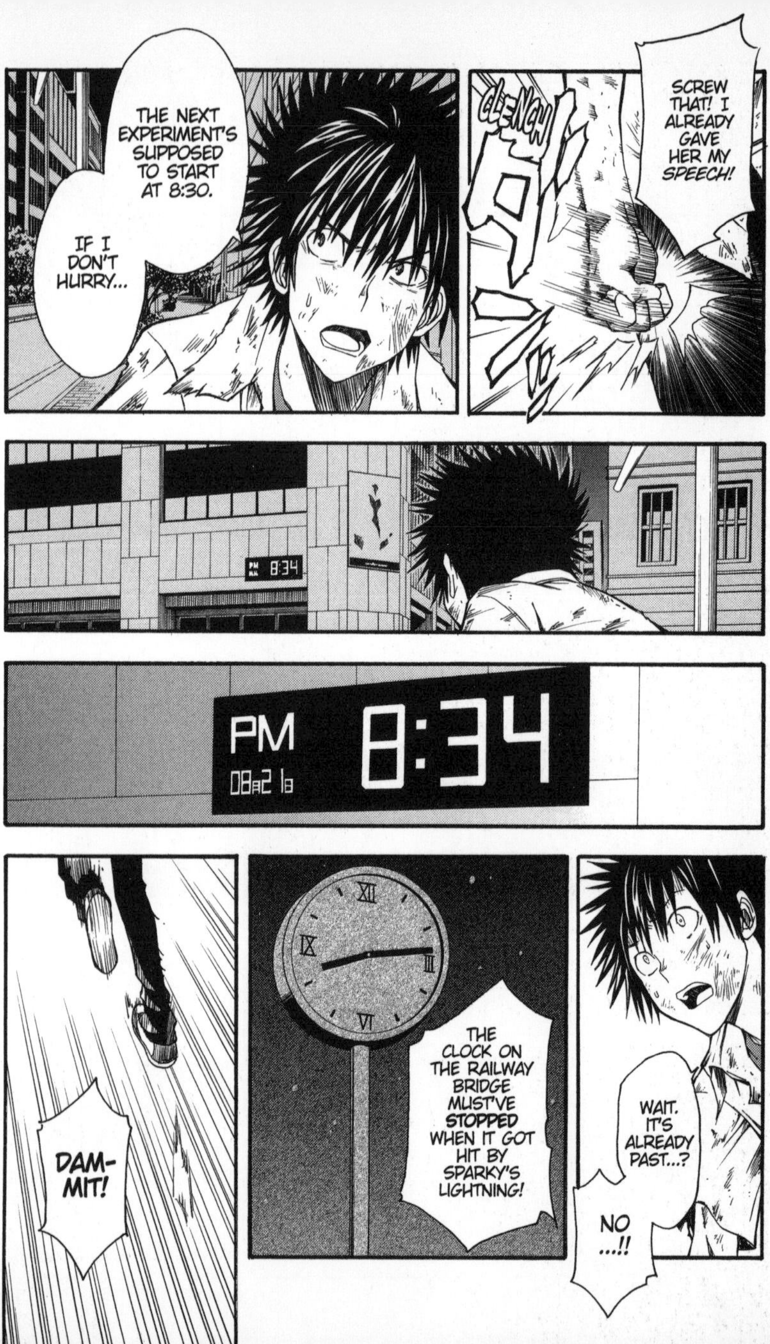
CLENCH
SCREW THAT! I ALREADY GAVE HER MY SPEECH!
THE NEXT EXPERIMENT'S SUPPOSED TO START AT 8:30.
IF I DON'T HURRY...
PM 8:34
PM 8:34
08月21日
WAIT. IT'S ALREADY PAST...?
NO ...!!
THE CLOCK ON THE RAILWAY BRIDGE MUST'VE STOPPED WHEN IT GOT HIT BY SPARKY'S LIGHTNING!
DAM-MIT!

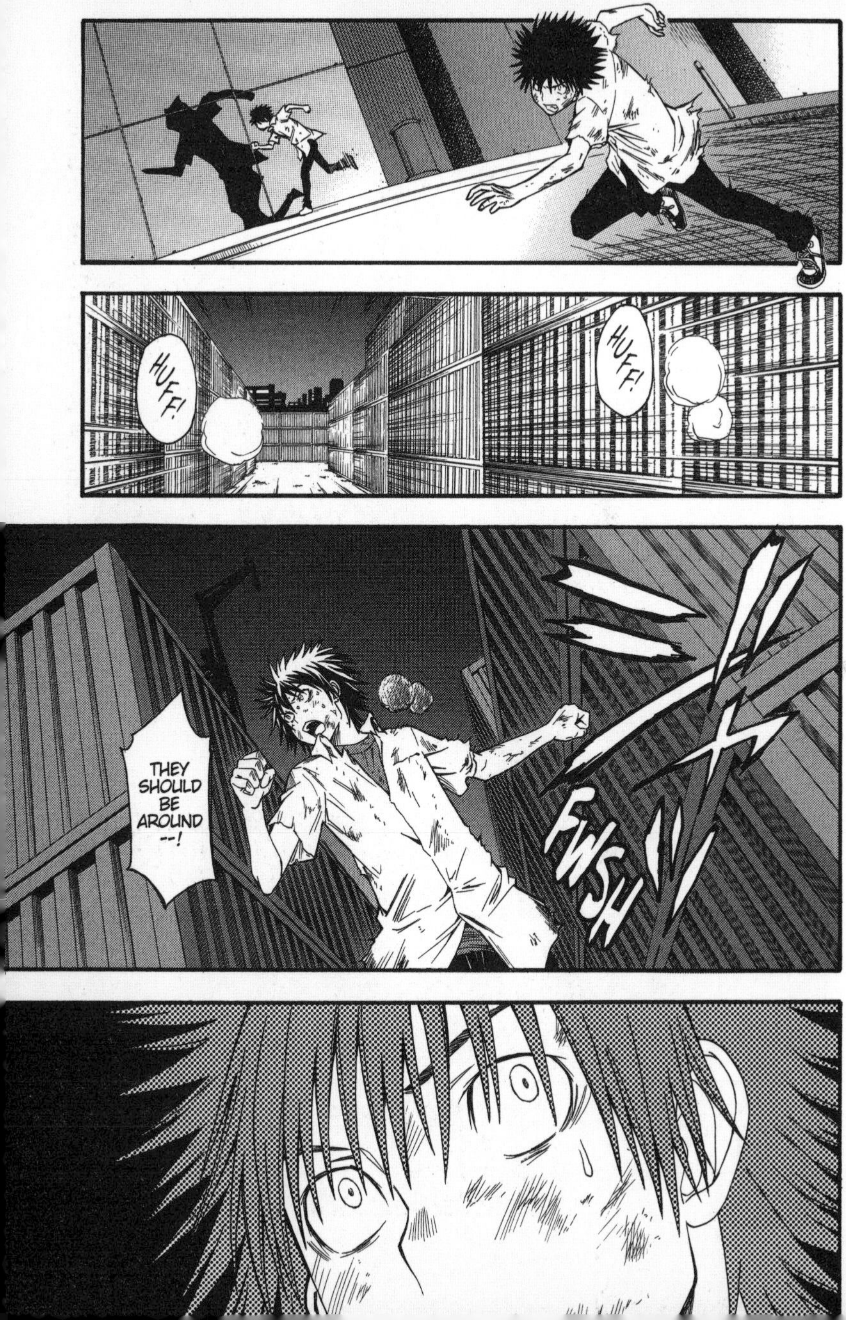
HUFF!
HUFF!
FWSH
THEY SHOULD BE AROUND --!

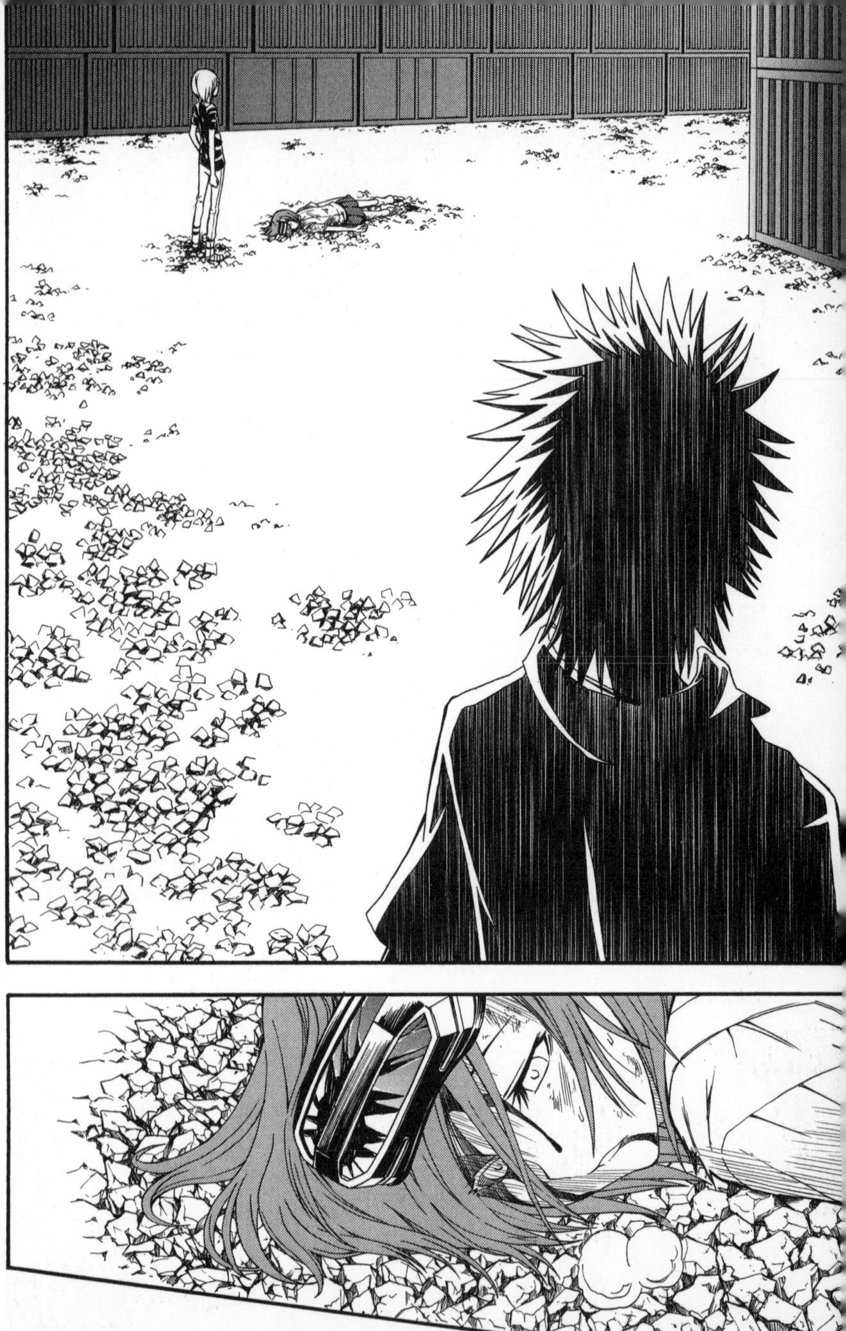

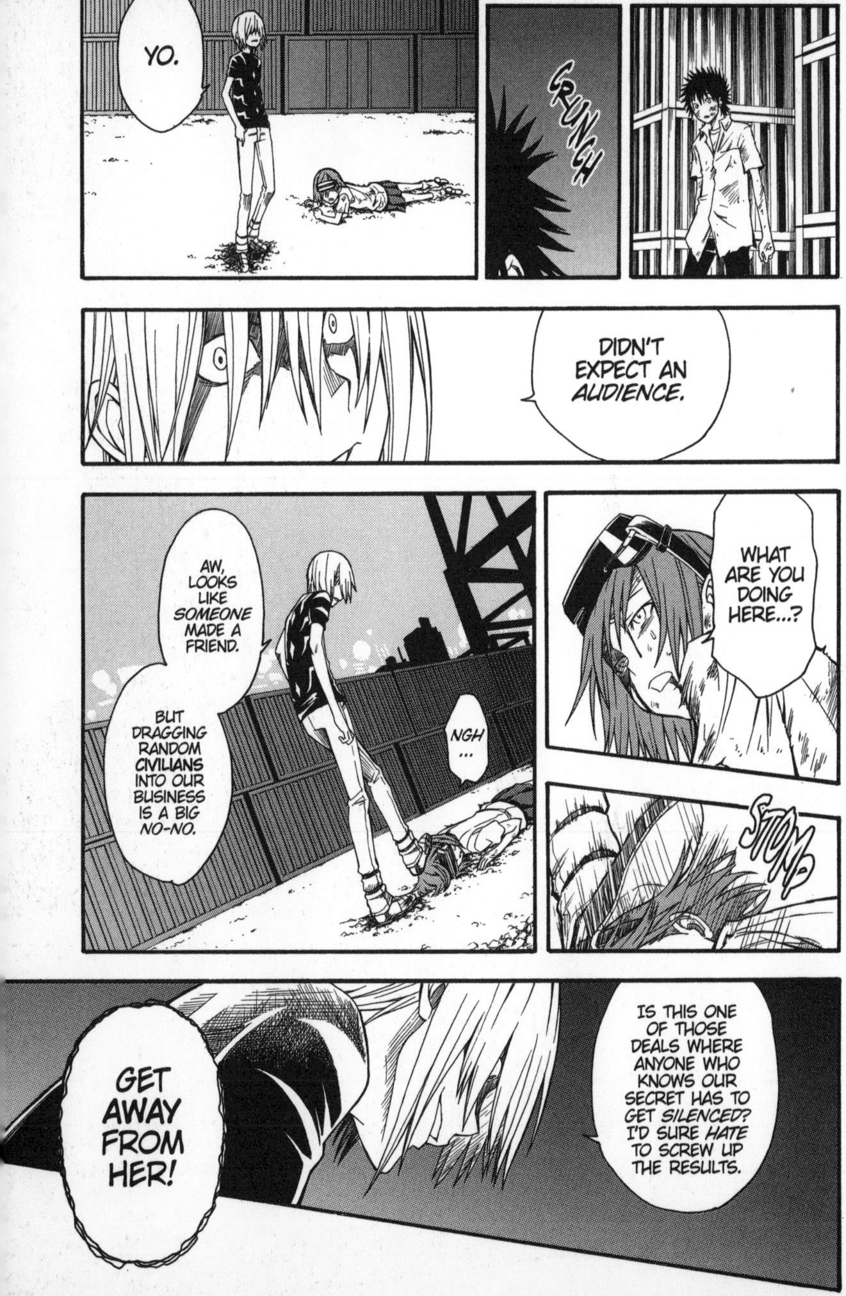
CRUNCH
YO.
DIDN'T EXPECT AN *AUDIENCE.*
WHAT ARE YOU DOING HERE...?
STOMP
AW, LOOKS LIKE *SOMEONE* MADE A FRIEND.
BUT DRAGGING RANDOM CIVILIANS INTO OUR BUSINESS IS A BIG *NO-NO.*
NGH...
IS THIS ONE OF THOSE DEALS WHERE ANYONE WHO KNOWS OUR SECRET HAS TO GET *SILENCED?* I'D SURE *HATE* TO SCREW UP THE RESULTS.
GET AWAY FROM HER!

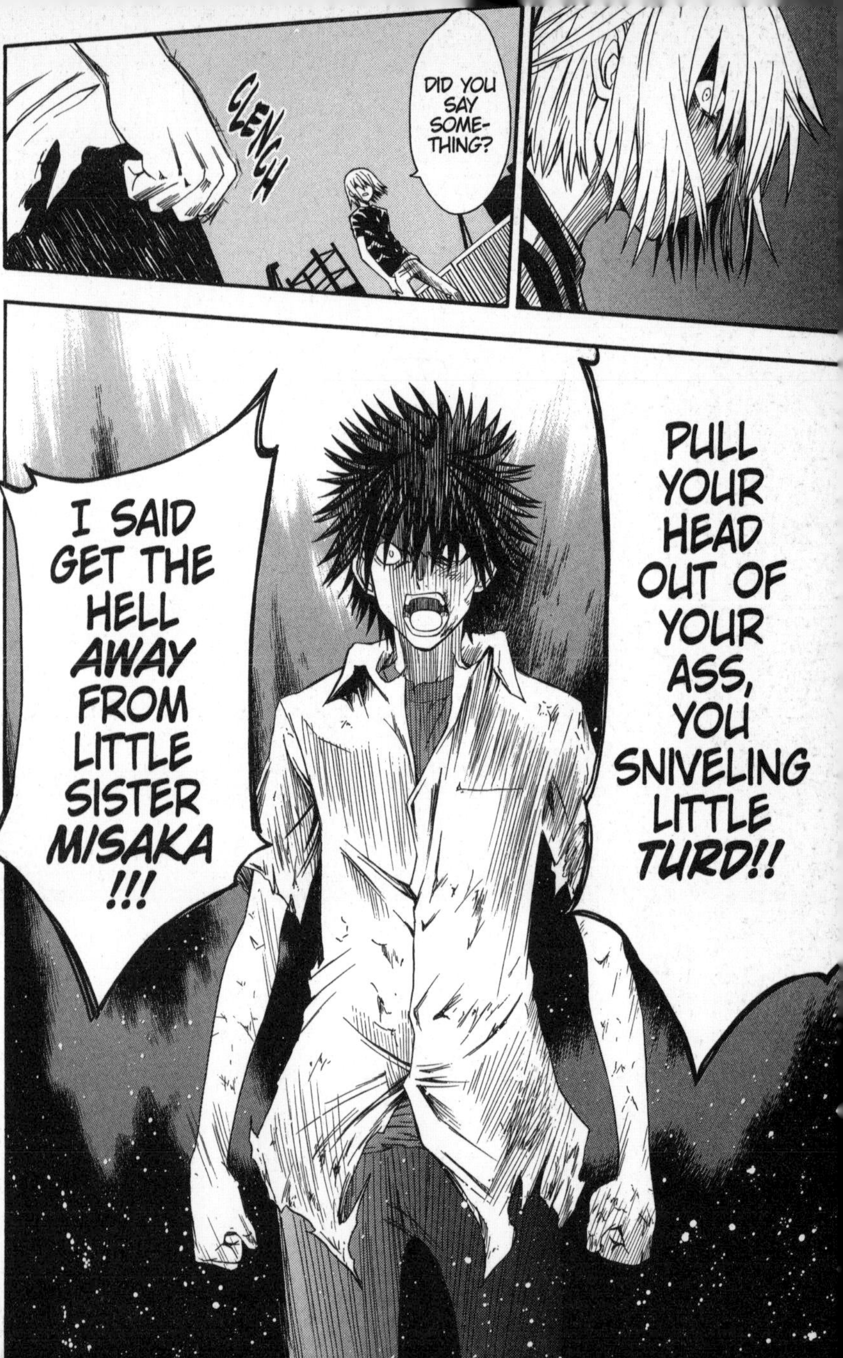
DID YOU SAY SOME-THING?
CLENCH
PULL YOUR HEAD OUT OF YOUR ASS, YOU SNIVELING LITTLE TURD!!
I SAID GET THE HELL AWAY FROM LITTLE SISTER MISAKA !!!

A Certain
SCIENTIFIC
Railgun

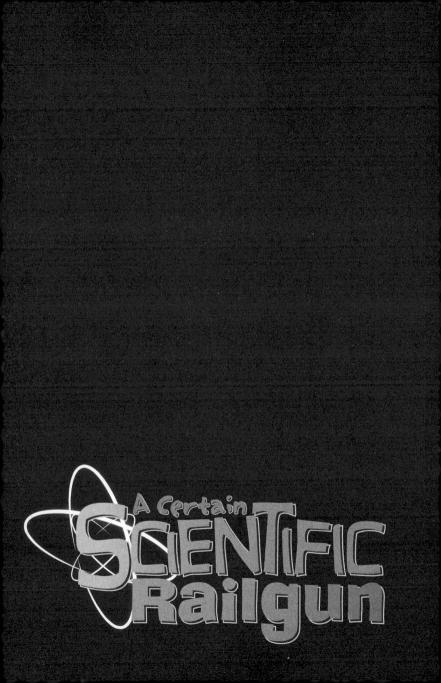

A Certain Hero's Image Change

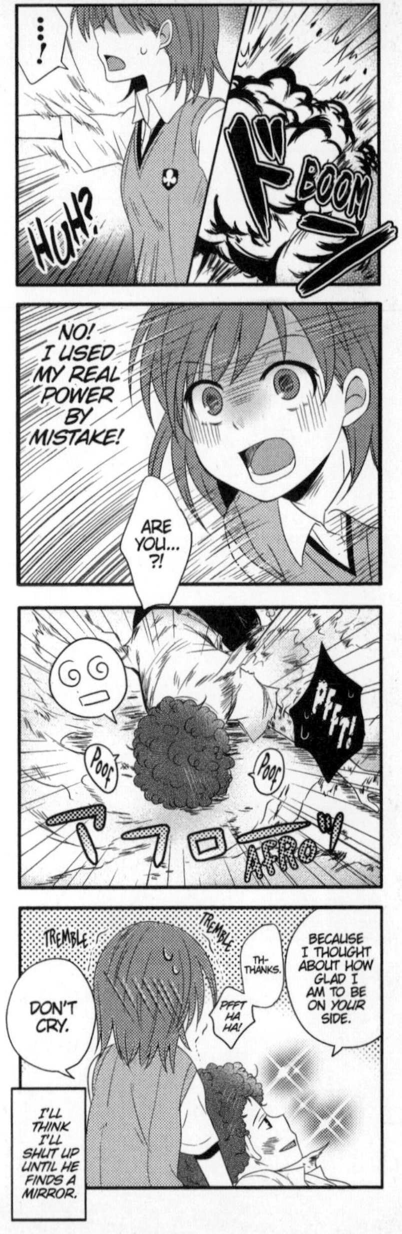

ド BOOM
...!
HUH?
NO! I USED MY REAL POWER BY MISTAKE!
ARE YOU...?!
PFFT!
Poof
Poof
アフロ AFRO!
BECAUSE I THOUGHT ABOUT HOW GLAD I AM TO BE ON YOUR SIDE.
TH-THANKS.
TREMBLE
PFFT HA HA!
TREMBLE
DON'T CRY.
I'LL THINK I'LL SHUT UP UNTIL HE FINDS A MIRROR.

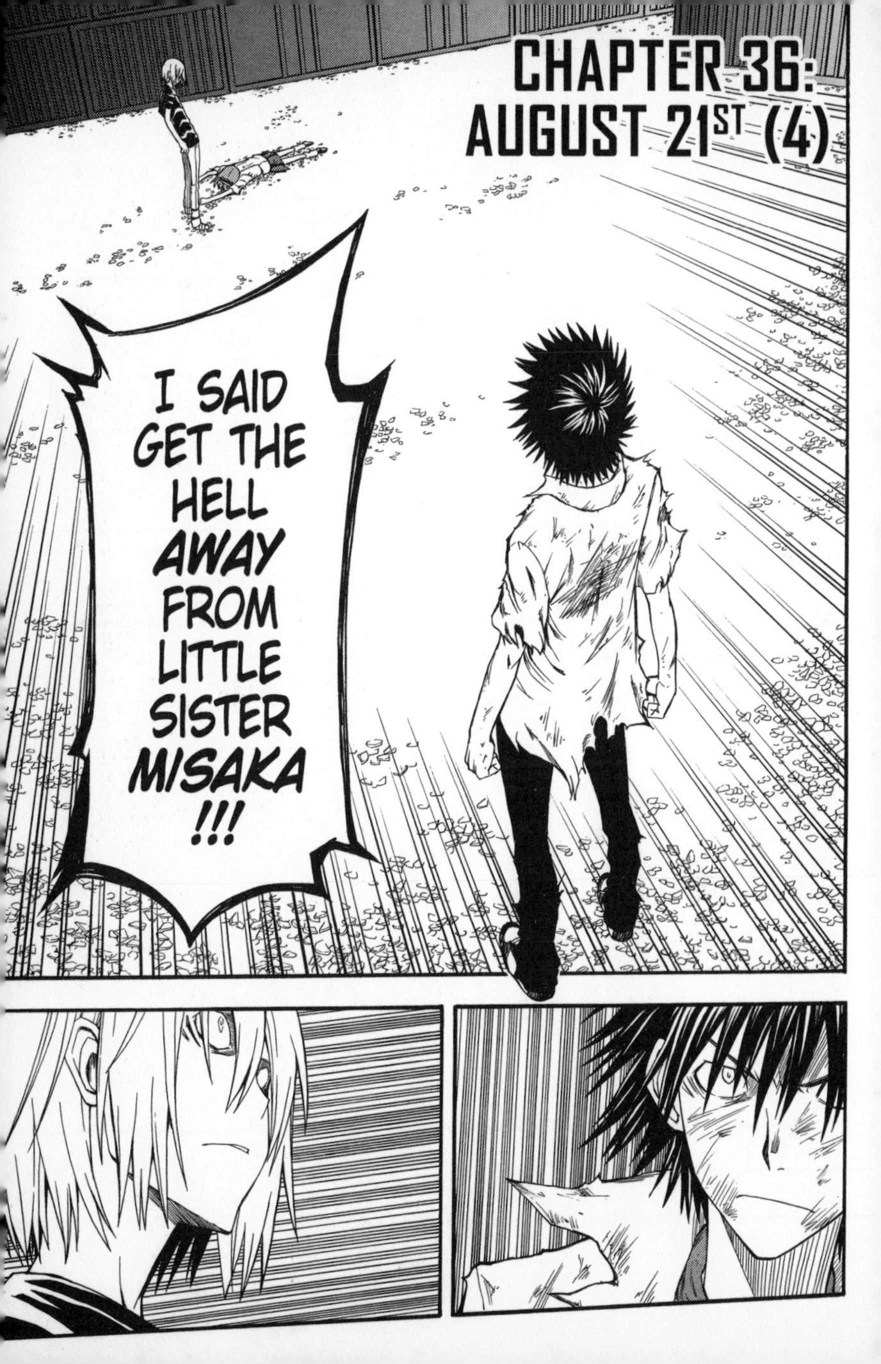
CHAPTER 36: AUGUST 21ST (4)
I SAID GET THE HELL AWAY FROM LITTLE SISTER MISAKA !!!

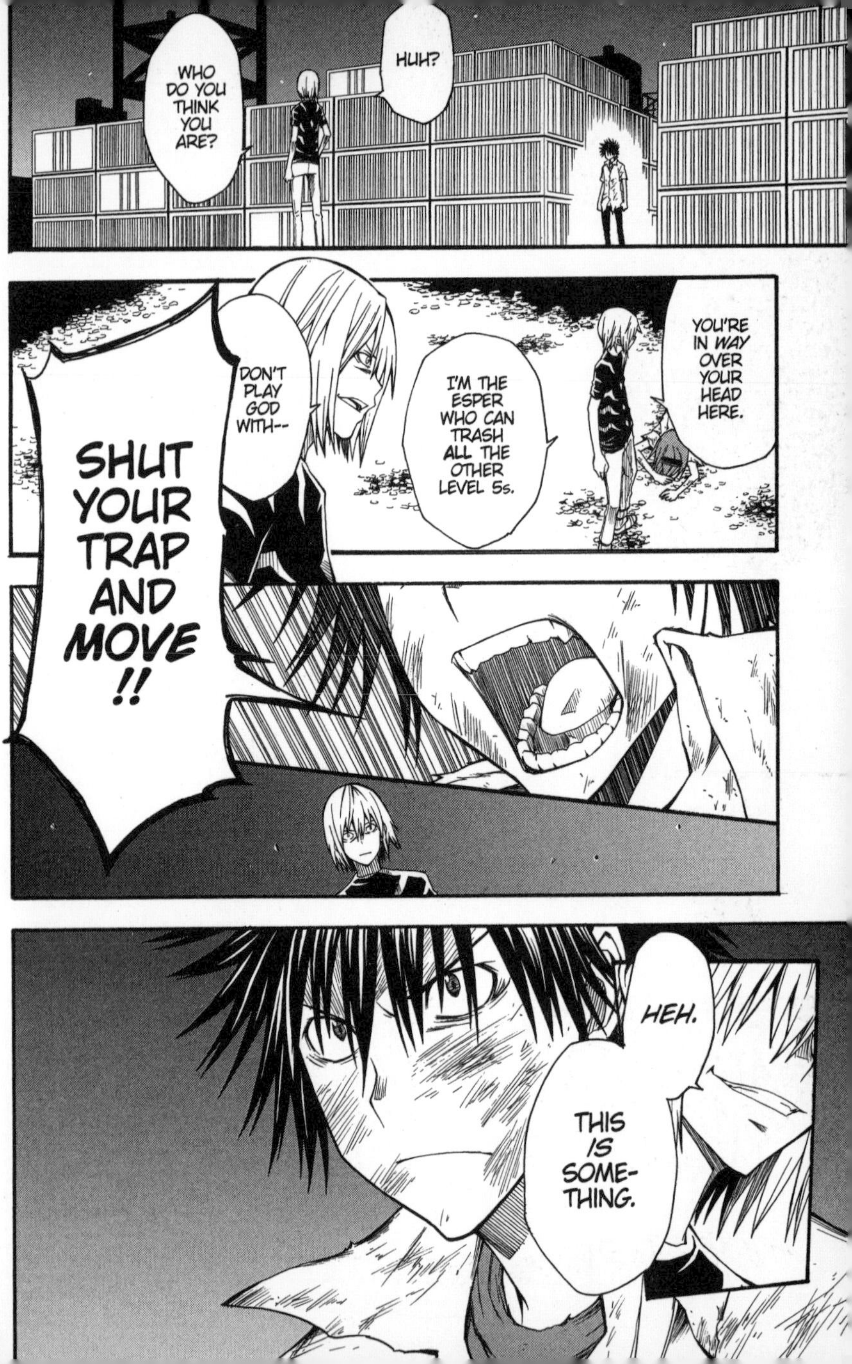
HUH?
WHO DO YOU THINK YOU ARE?
YOU'RE IN *WAY* OVER YOUR HEAD HERE.
I'M THE ESPER WHO CAN TRASH ALL THE OTHER LEVEL 5s.
DON'T PLAY GOD WITH--
SHUT YOUR TRAP AND *MOVE*!!
HEH.
THIS *IS* SOME-THING.

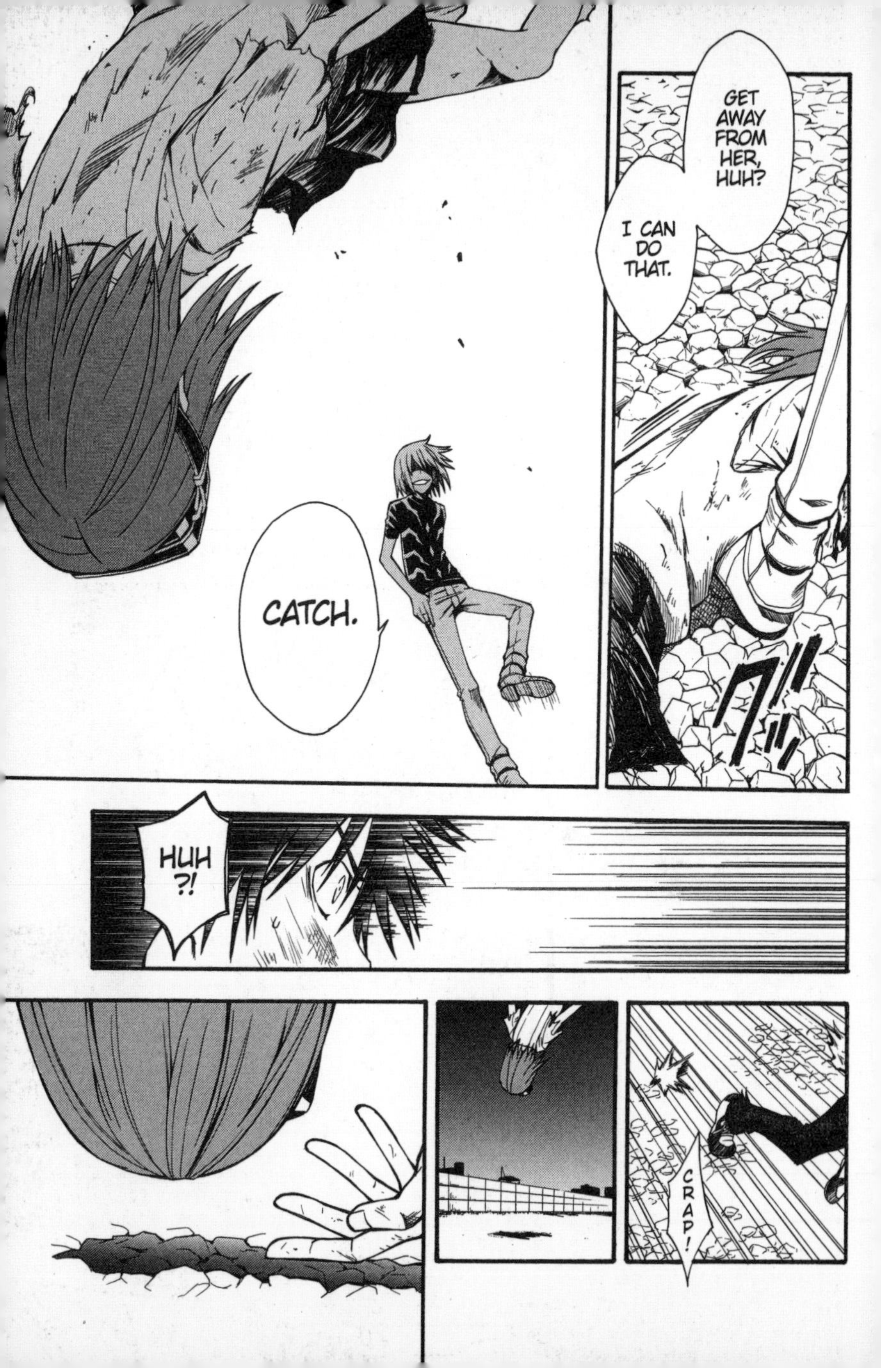
GET AWAY FROM HER, HUH?
I CAN DO THAT.
CATCH.
HUH ?!
CRAP!

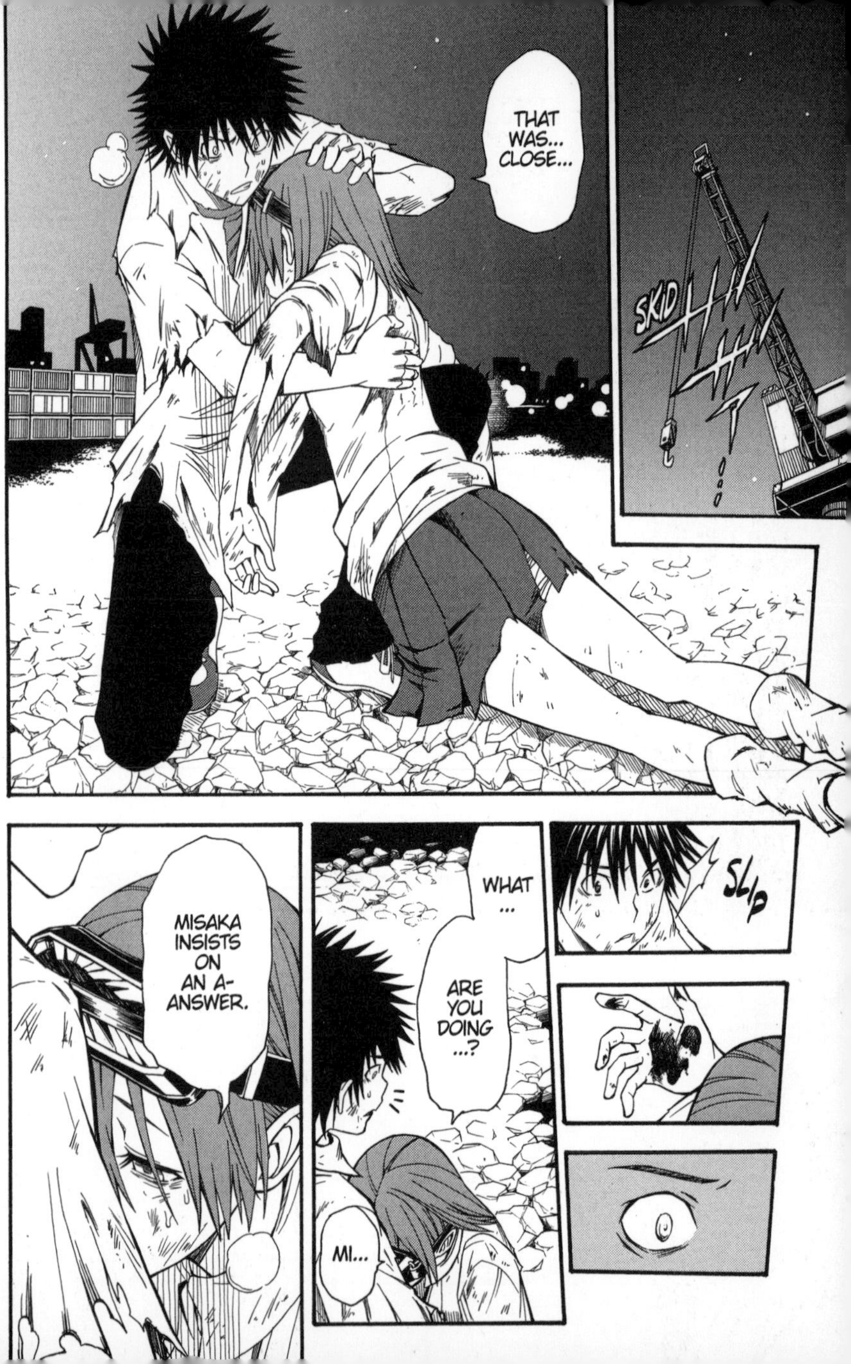
SKID
THAT WAS... CLOSE...
SLIP
WHAT ...
ARE YOU DOING ...?
MI...
MISAKA INSISTS ON AN A-ANSWER.

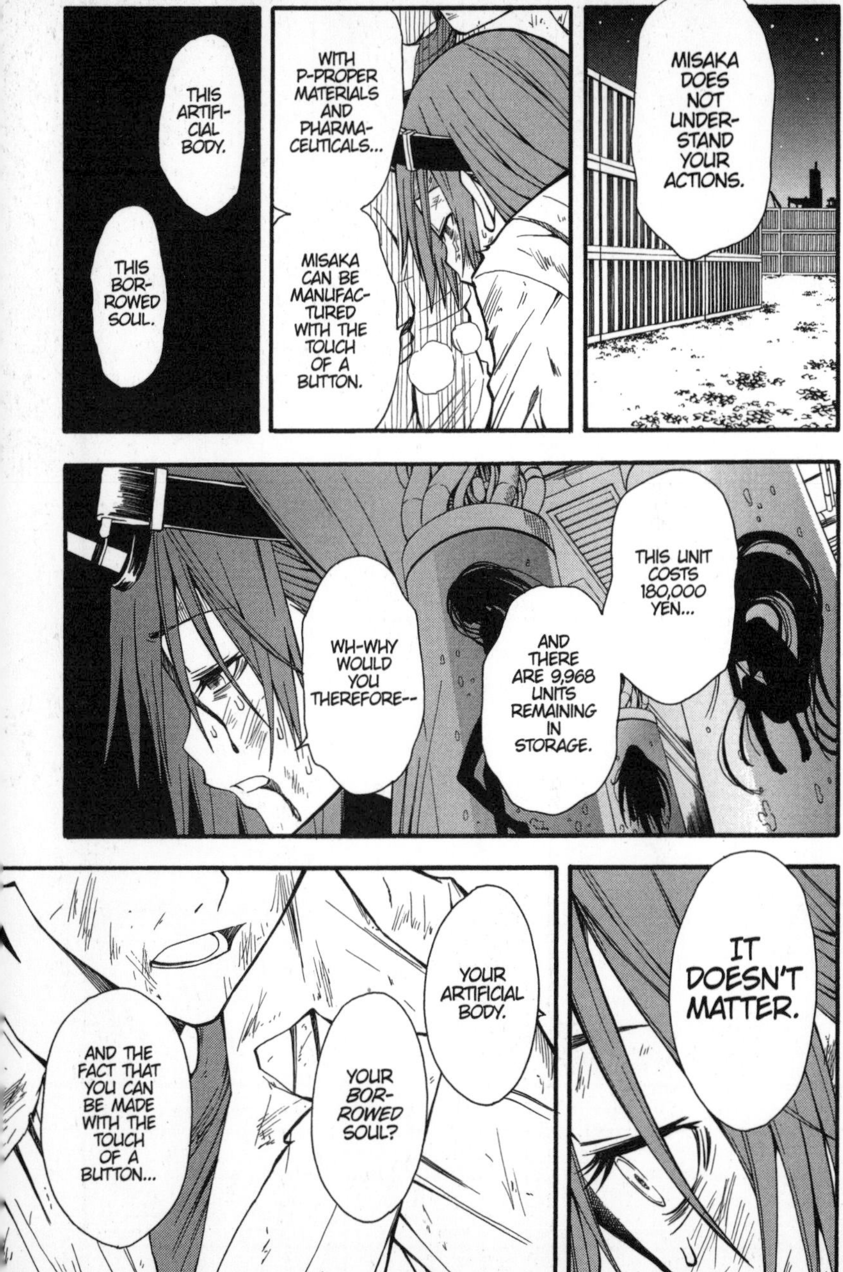
MISAKA DOES NOT UNDERSTAND YOUR ACTIONS.
WITH P-PROPER MATERIALS AND PHARMACEUTICALS...
MISAKA CAN BE MANUFACTURED WITH THE TOUCH OF A BUTTON.
THIS ARTIFICIAL BODY.
THIS BORROWED SOUL.
THIS UNIT COSTS 180,000 YEN...
AND THERE ARE 9,968 UNITS REMAINING IN STORAGE.
WH-WHY WOULD YOU THEREFORE--
IT DOESN'T MATTER.
YOUR ARTIFICIAL BODY.
YOUR BORROWED SOUL?
AND THE FACT THAT YOU CAN BE MADE WITH THE TOUCH OF A BUTTON...

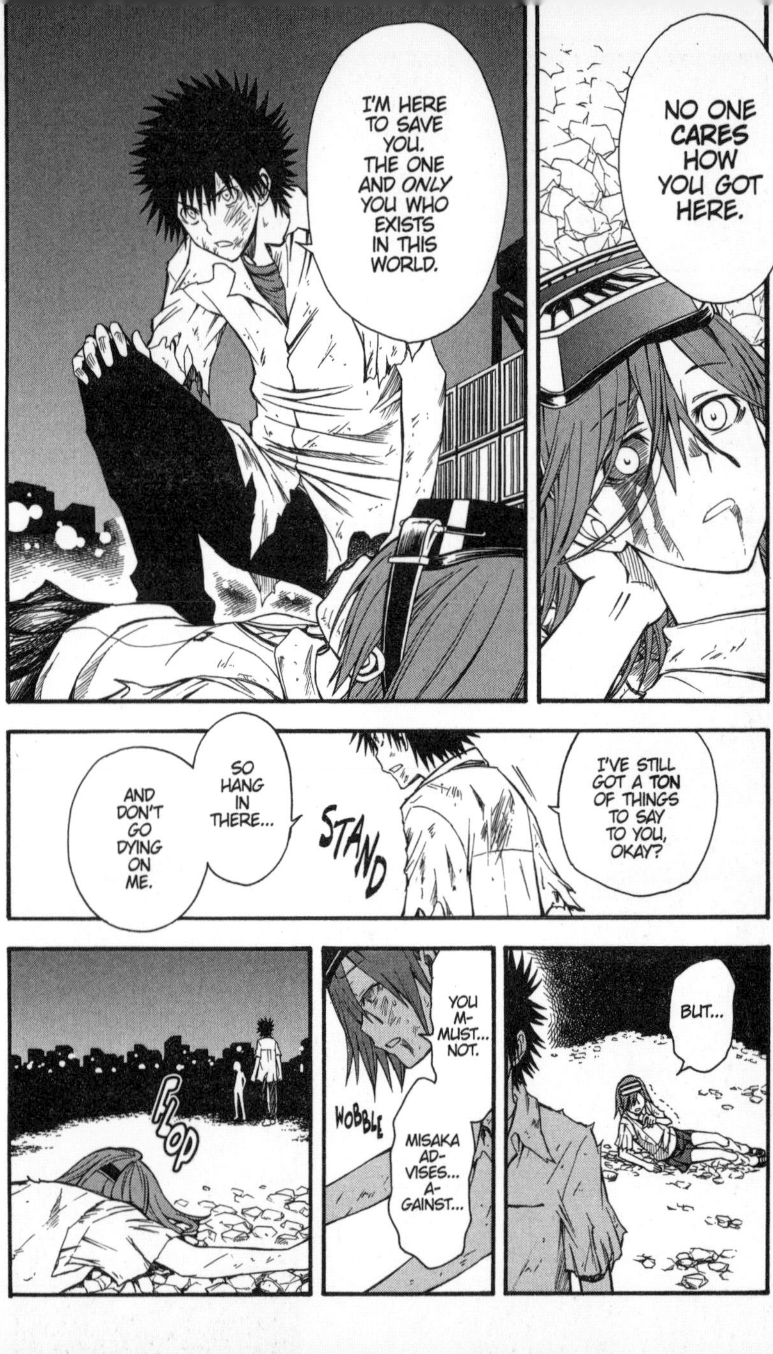
NO ONE CARES HOW YOU GOT HERE.
I'M HERE TO SAVE YOU. THE ONE AND *ONLY* YOU WHO EXISTS IN THIS WORLD.
I'VE STILL GOT A TON OF THINGS TO SAY TO YOU, OKAY?
STAND
SO HANG IN THERE...
AND DON'T GO DYING ON ME.
BUT...
YOU M-MUST... NOT.
WOBBLE
MISAKA AD-VISES... A-GAINST...
FLOP

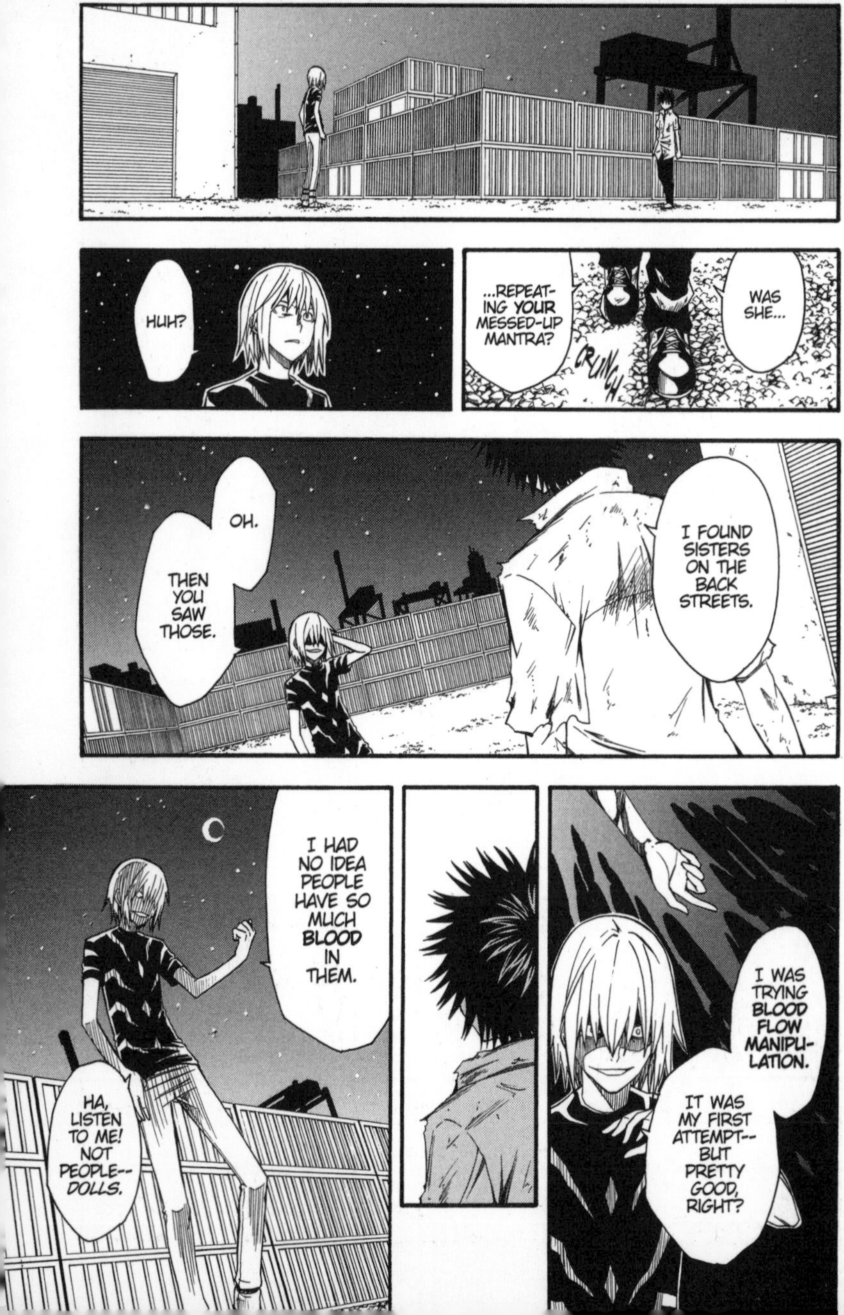
WAS SHE...
...REPEATING YOUR MESSED-UP MANTRA?
CRUNCH
HUH?
I FOUND SISTERS ON THE BACK STREETS.
OH.
THEN YOU SAW THOSE.
I WAS TRYING BLOOD FLOW MANIPULATION.
IT WAS MY FIRST ATTEMPT--BUT PRETTY GOOD, RIGHT?
I HAD NO IDEA PEOPLE HAVE SO MUCH BLOOD IN THEM.
HA, LISTEN TO ME! NOT PEOPLE--DOLLS.

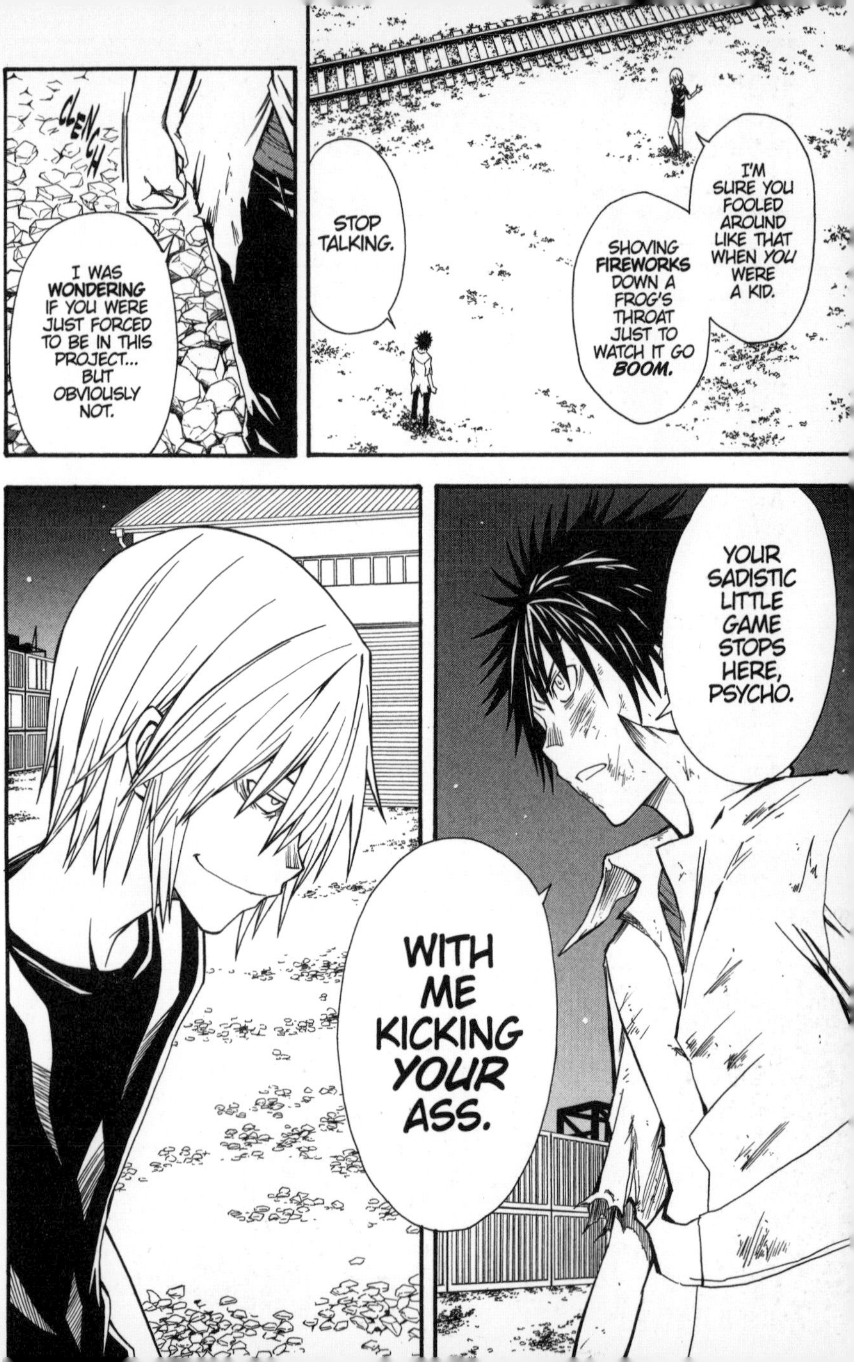
I'M SURE YOU FOOLED AROUND LIKE THAT WHEN *YOU* WERE A KID.
SHOVING **FIREWORKS** DOWN A FROG'S THROAT JUST TO WATCH IT GO ***BOOM.***
STOP TALKING.
CLENCH
I WAS **WONDERING** IF YOU WERE JUST FORCED TO BE IN THIS PROJECT... BUT OBVIOUSLY NOT.
YOUR SADISTIC LITTLE GAME STOPS HERE, PSYCHO.
WITH ME KICKING *YOUR* ASS.

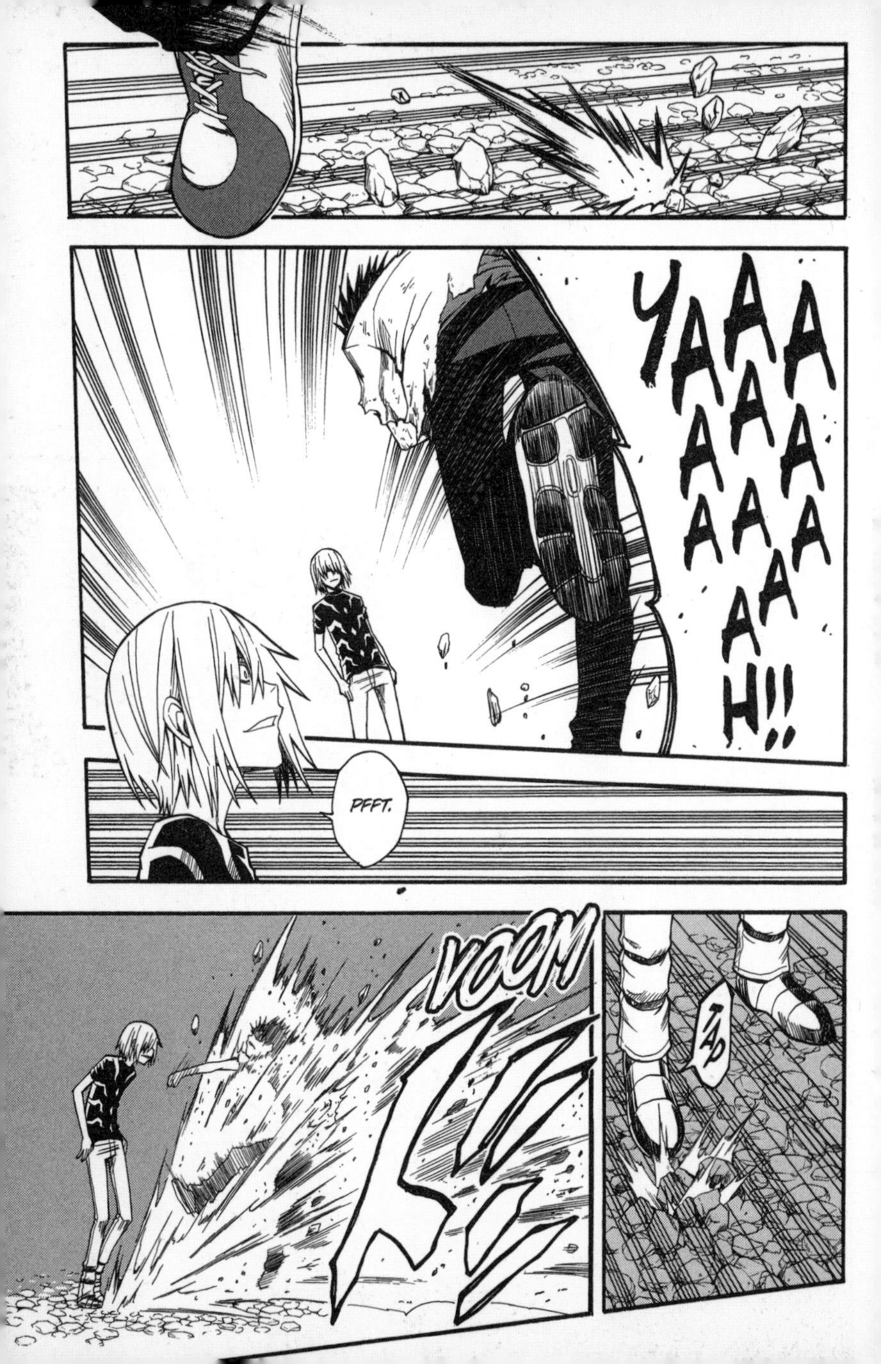
YAAAAAAAAAAAAAAAH!!
PFFT.
TAP
VOOM

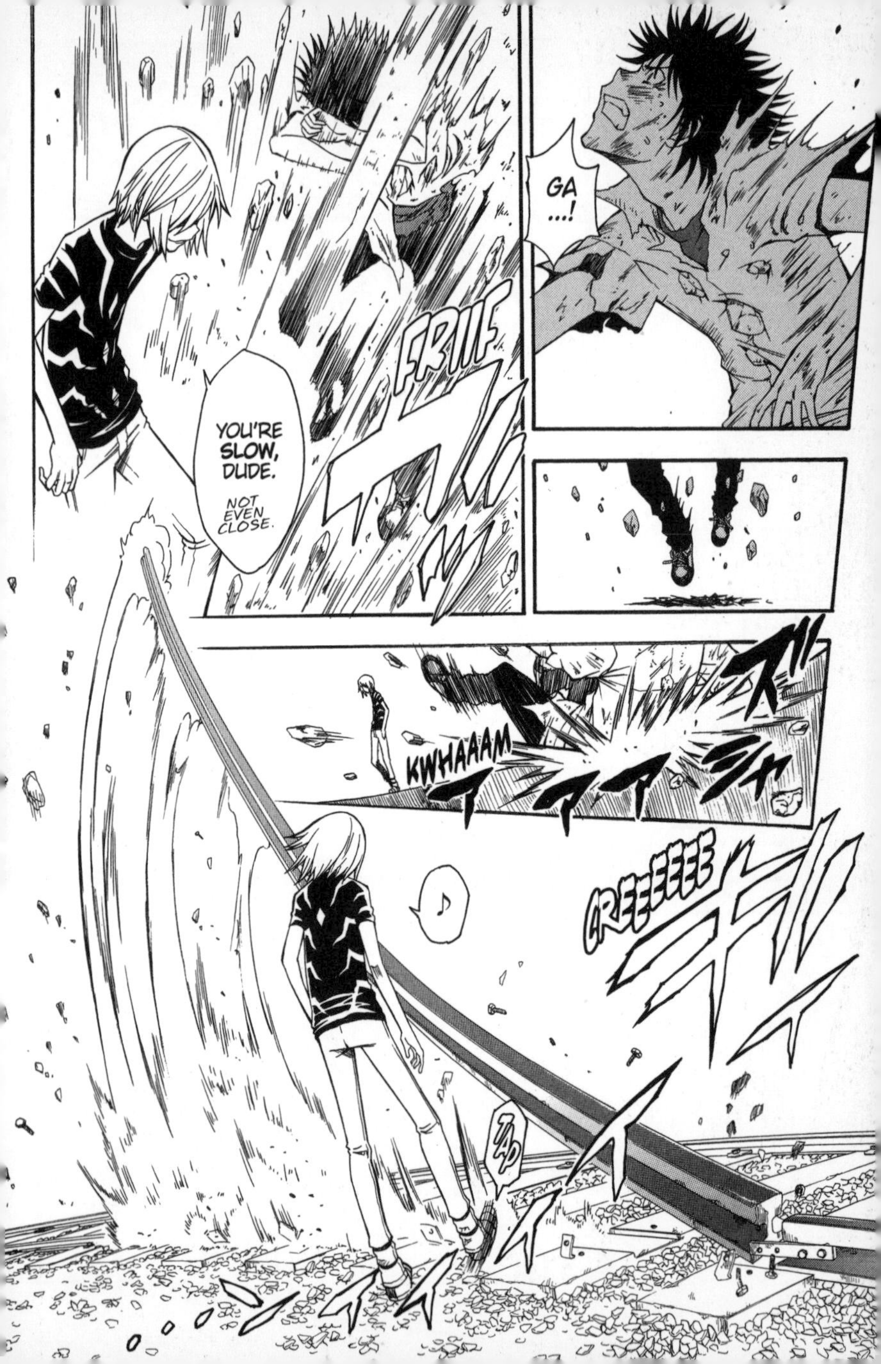
GA ...!
FRIIF
YOU'RE SLOW, DUDE.
NOT EVEN CLOSE.
KWHAAAM
CREEEEEEE
♪
TAP

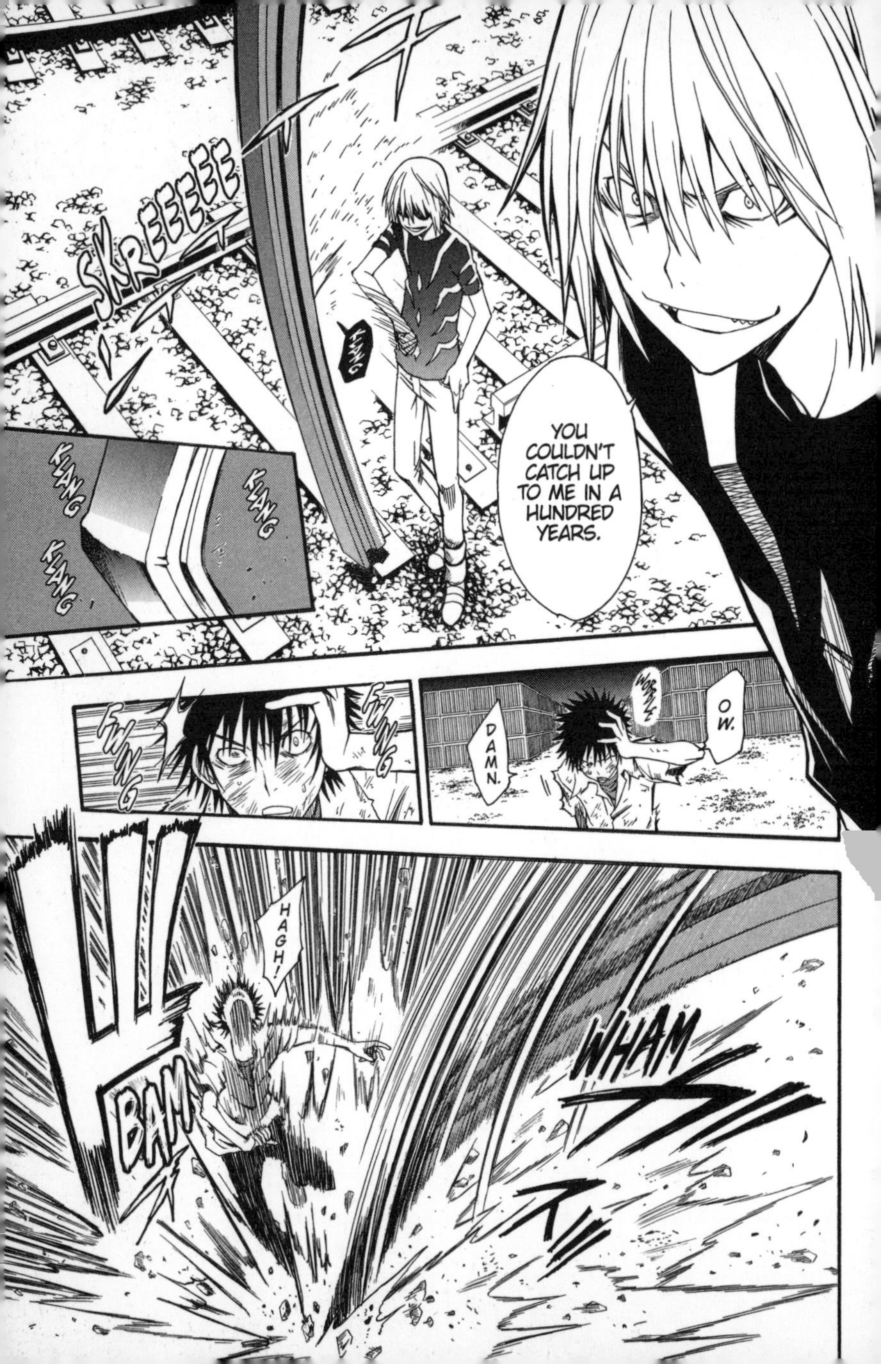
YOU COULDN'T CATCH UP TO ME IN A HUNDRED YEARS.
KLANG
SKREEEEE
KLANG
KLANG
KLANG
OW.
WOBBLE
DAMN.
FWING
FWING
WHAM
HAGH!
BAM

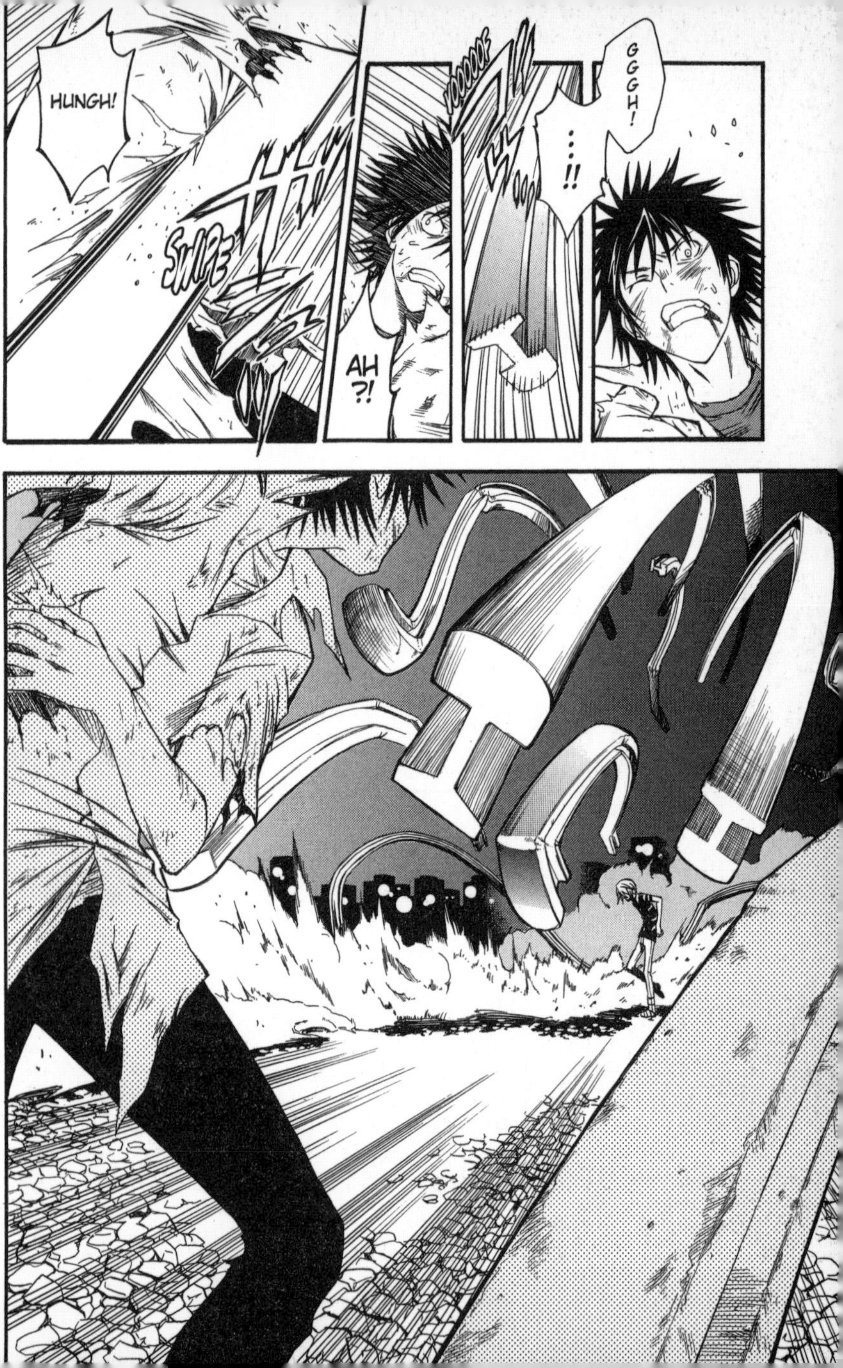
GGGH!
...!!
VOOOOOF
AH?!
HUNGH!
SWIPE

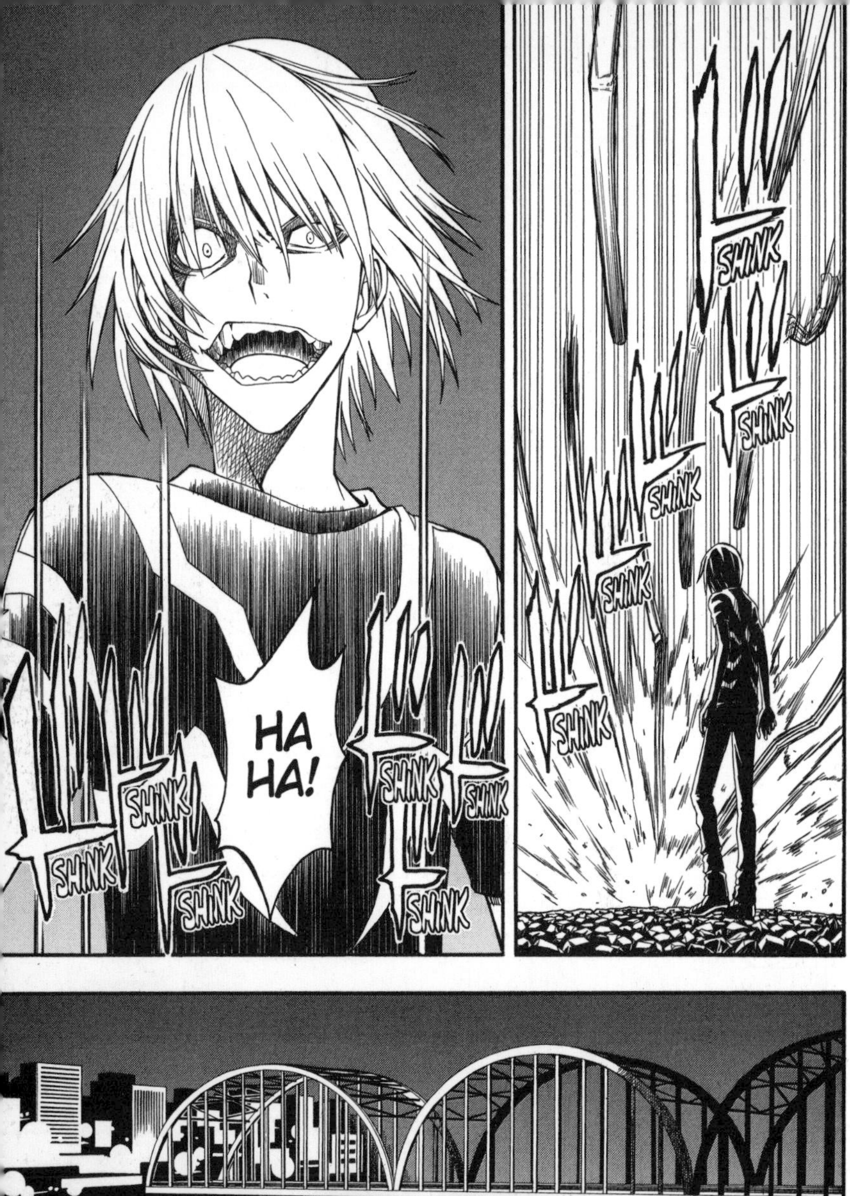

SHINK
SHINK
SHINK
SHINK
SHINK
SHINK
SHINK
HA HA!
SHINK
SHINK
SHINK
SHINK
SHINK

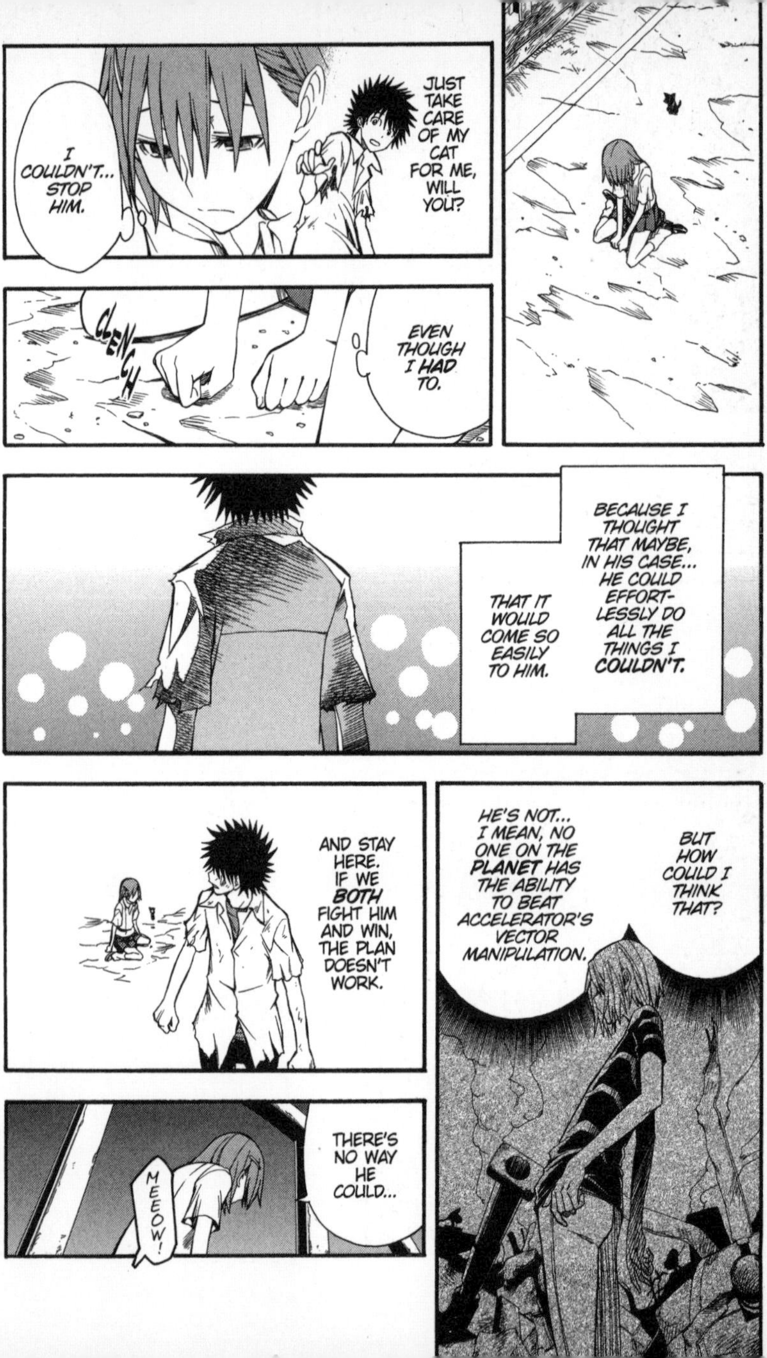
JUST TAKE CARE OF MY CAT FOR ME, WILL YOU?
I COULDN'T... STOP HIM.
CLENCH
EVEN THOUGH I HAD TO.
BECAUSE I THOUGHT THAT MAYBE, IN HIS CASE... HE COULD EFFORTLESSLY DO ALL THE THINGS I COULDN'T.
THAT IT WOULD COME SO EASILY TO HIM.
BUT HOW COULD I THINK THAT?
HE'S NOT... I MEAN, NO ONE ON THE PLANET HAS THE ABILITY TO BEAT ACCELERATOR'S VECTOR MANIPULATION.
AND STAY HERE. IF WE BOTH FIGHT HIM AND WIN, THE PLAN DOESN'T WORK.
THERE'S NO WAY HE COULD...
MEEEOW!

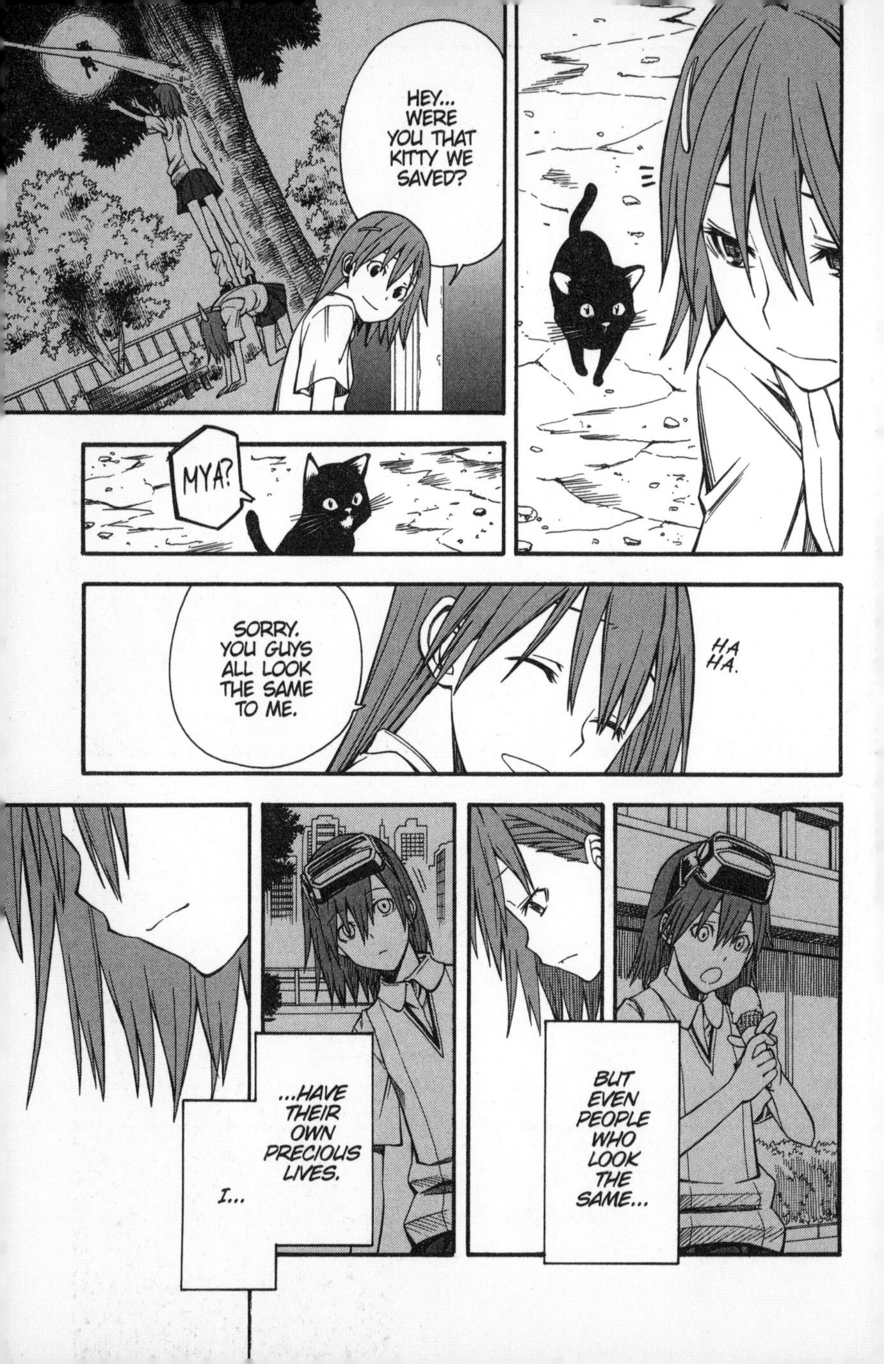
HEY... WERE YOU THAT KITTY WE SAVED?
MYA?
SORRY. YOU GUYS ALL LOOK THE SAME TO ME.
HA HA.
BUT EVEN PEOPLE WHO LOOK THE SAME...
...HAVE THEIR OWN PRECIOUS LIVES.
I...

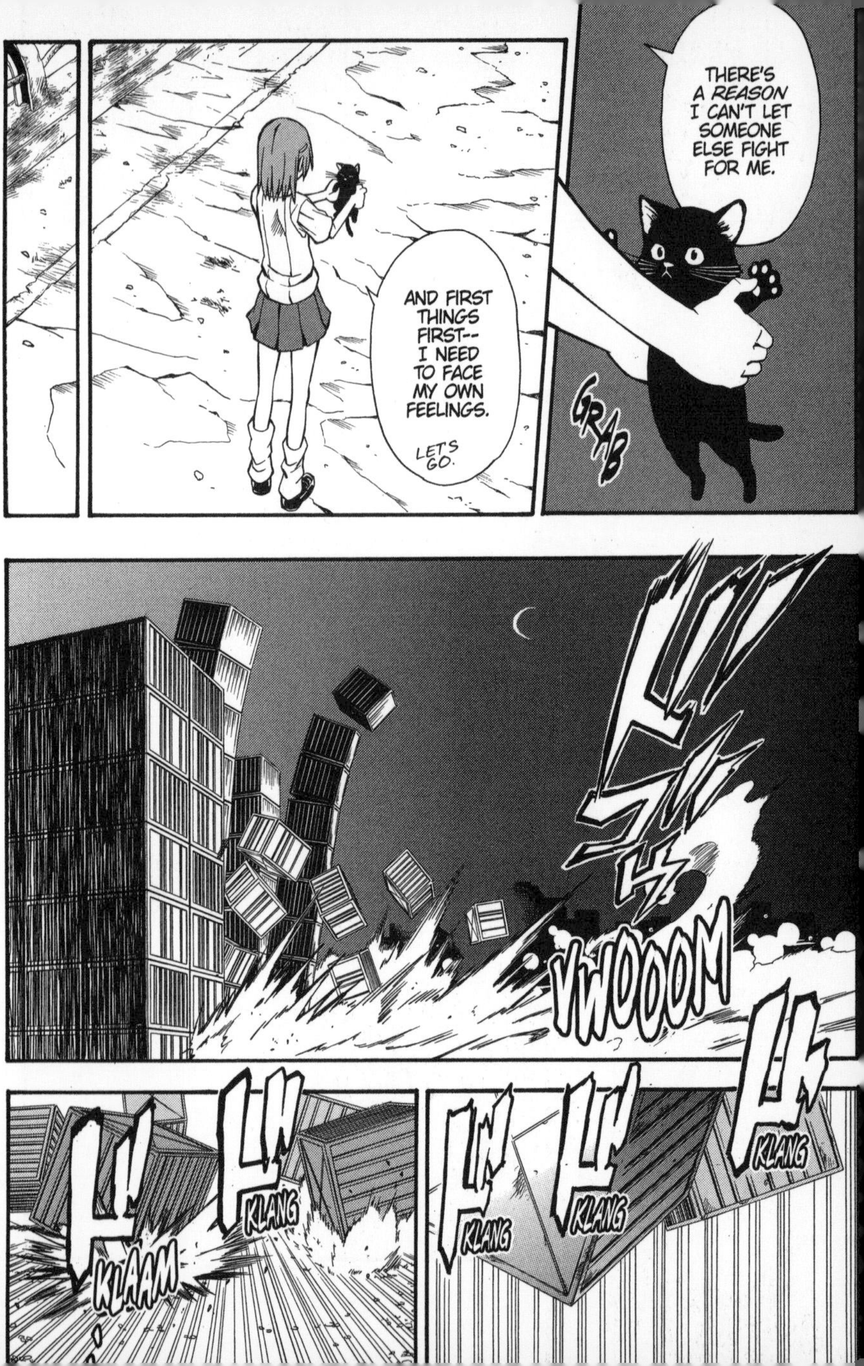
THERE'S A *REASON* I CAN'T LET SOMEONE ELSE FIGHT FOR ME.
GRAB
AND FIRST THINGS FIRST-- I NEED TO FACE MY OWN FEELINGS.
LET'S GO.
VWOOOM
KLANG
KLANG
KLANG
KLANG
KLAAM

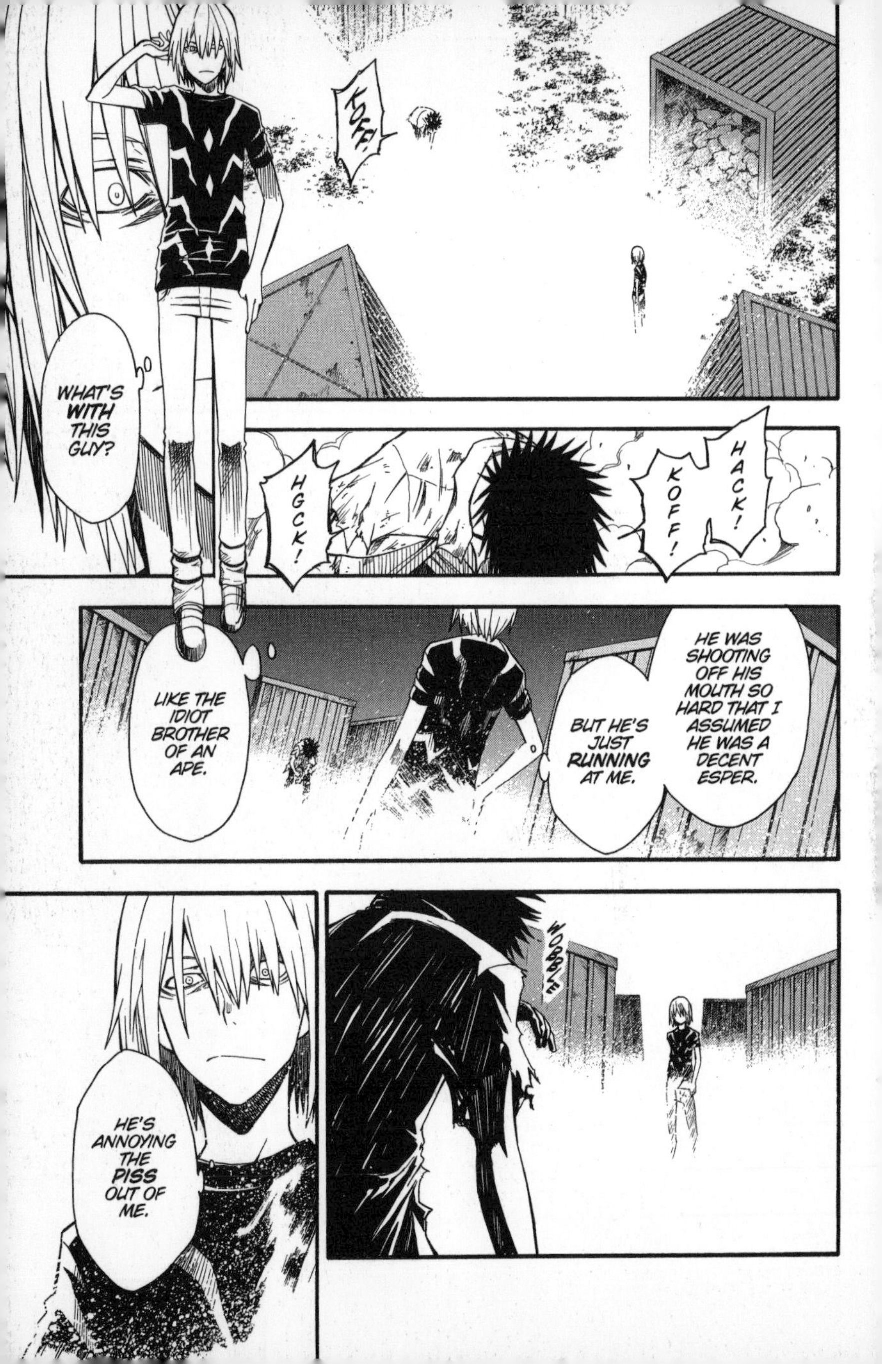
KOFF!
HACK! KOFF!
HGCK!
WHAT'S WITH THIS GUY?
HE WAS SHOOTING OFF HIS MOUTH SO HARD THAT I ASSUMED HE WAS A DECENT ESPER.
BUT HE'S JUST RUNNING AT ME.
LIKE THE IDIOT BROTHER OF AN APE.
WOBBLE
HE'S ANNOYING THE PISS OUT OF ME.

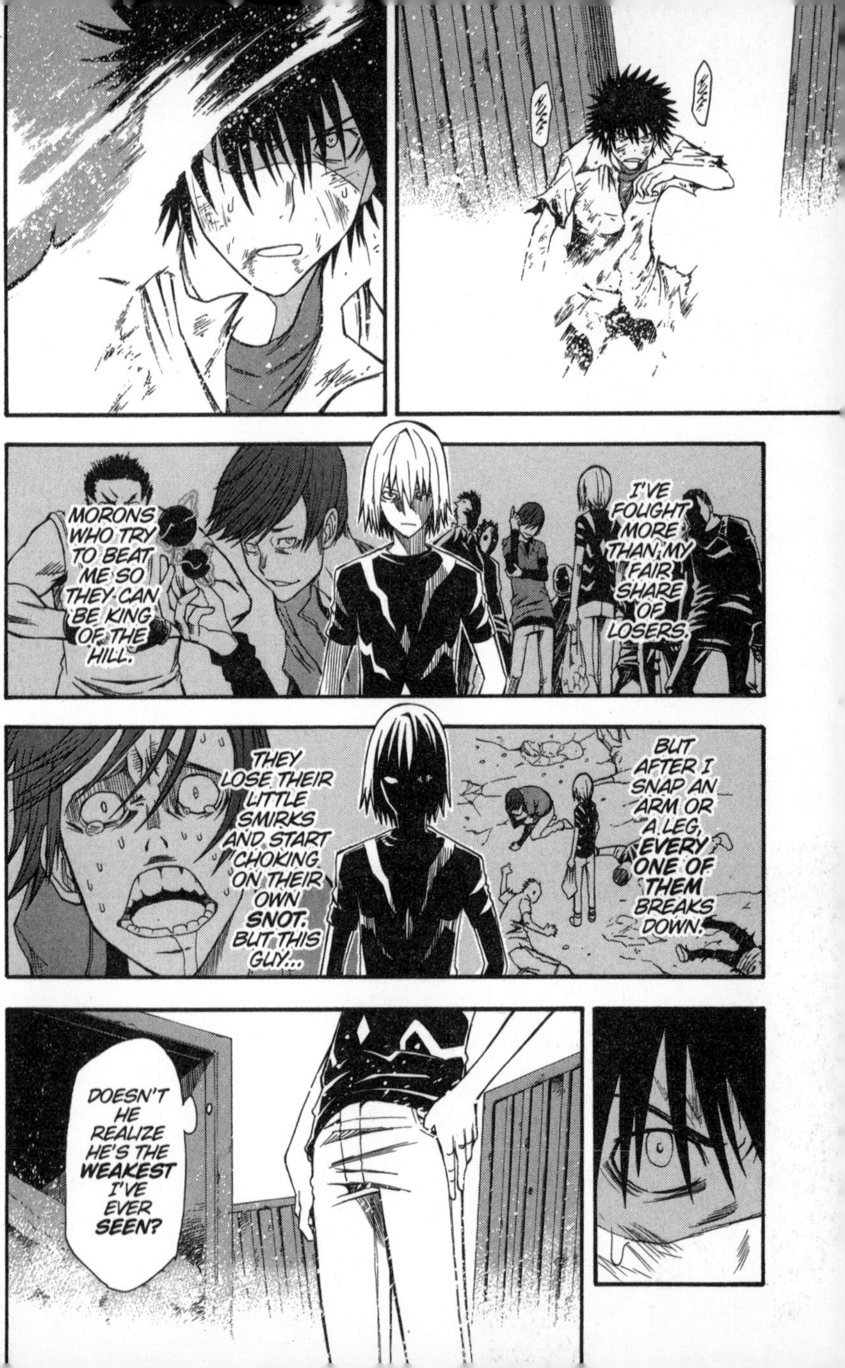
HUFF
HUFF
I'VE FOUGHT MORE THAN MY FAIR SHARE OF LOSERS.
MORONS WHO TRY TO BEAT ME SO THEY CAN BE KING OF THE HILL.
BUT AFTER I SNAP AN ARM OR A LEG, **EVERY ONE OF THEM** BREAKS DOWN.
THEY LOSE THEIR LITTLE SMIRKS AND START CHOKING ON THEIR OWN **SNOT.** BUT THIS GUY...
DOESN'T HE REALIZE HE'S THE **WEAKEST** I'VE EVER **SEEN?**

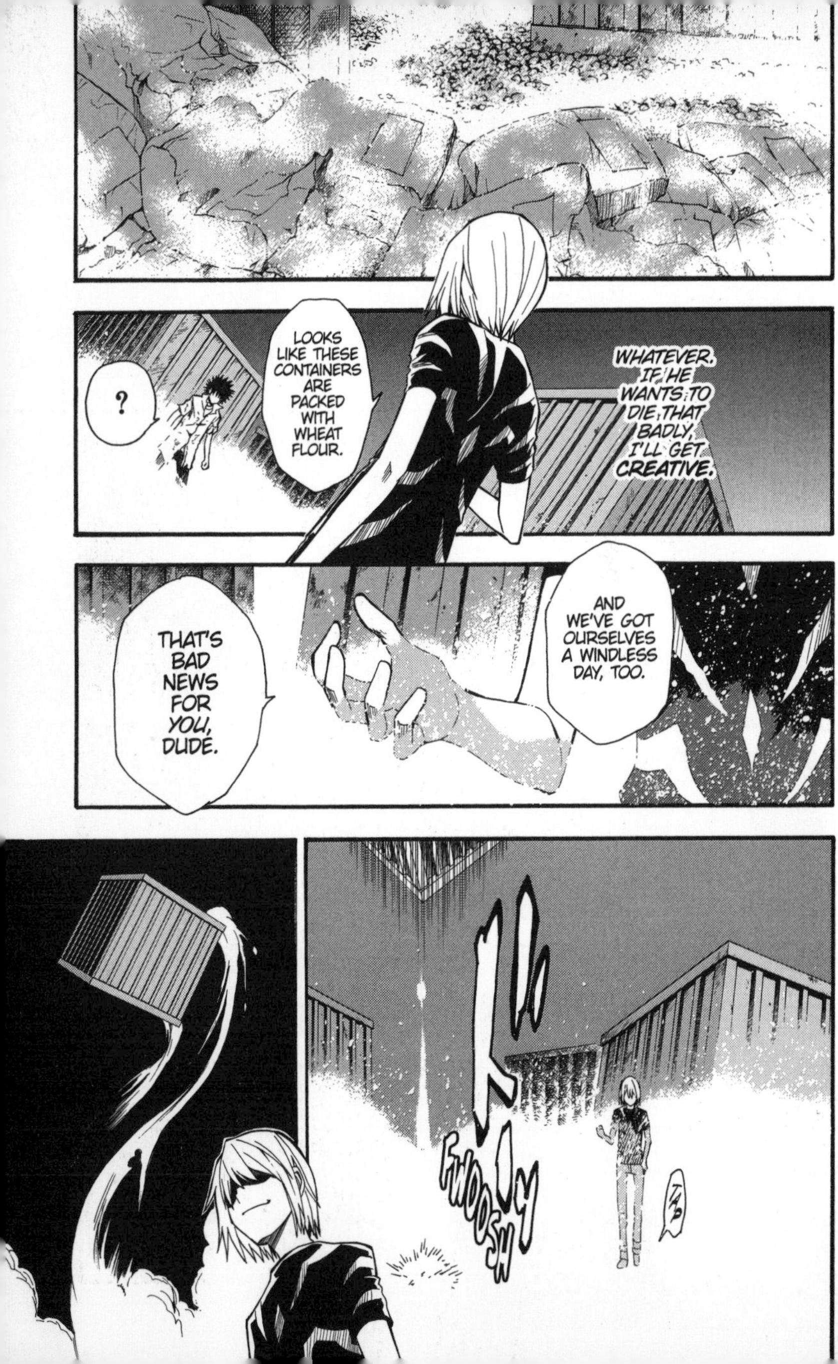
WHATEVER. IF HE WANTS TO DIE THAT BADLY, I'LL GET CREATIVE.
LOOKS LIKE THESE CONTAINERS ARE PACKED WITH WHEAT FLOUR.
?
AND WE'VE GOT OURSELVES A WINDLESS DAY, TOO.
THAT'S BAD NEWS FOR YOU, DUDE.
TAP
FWOOSH

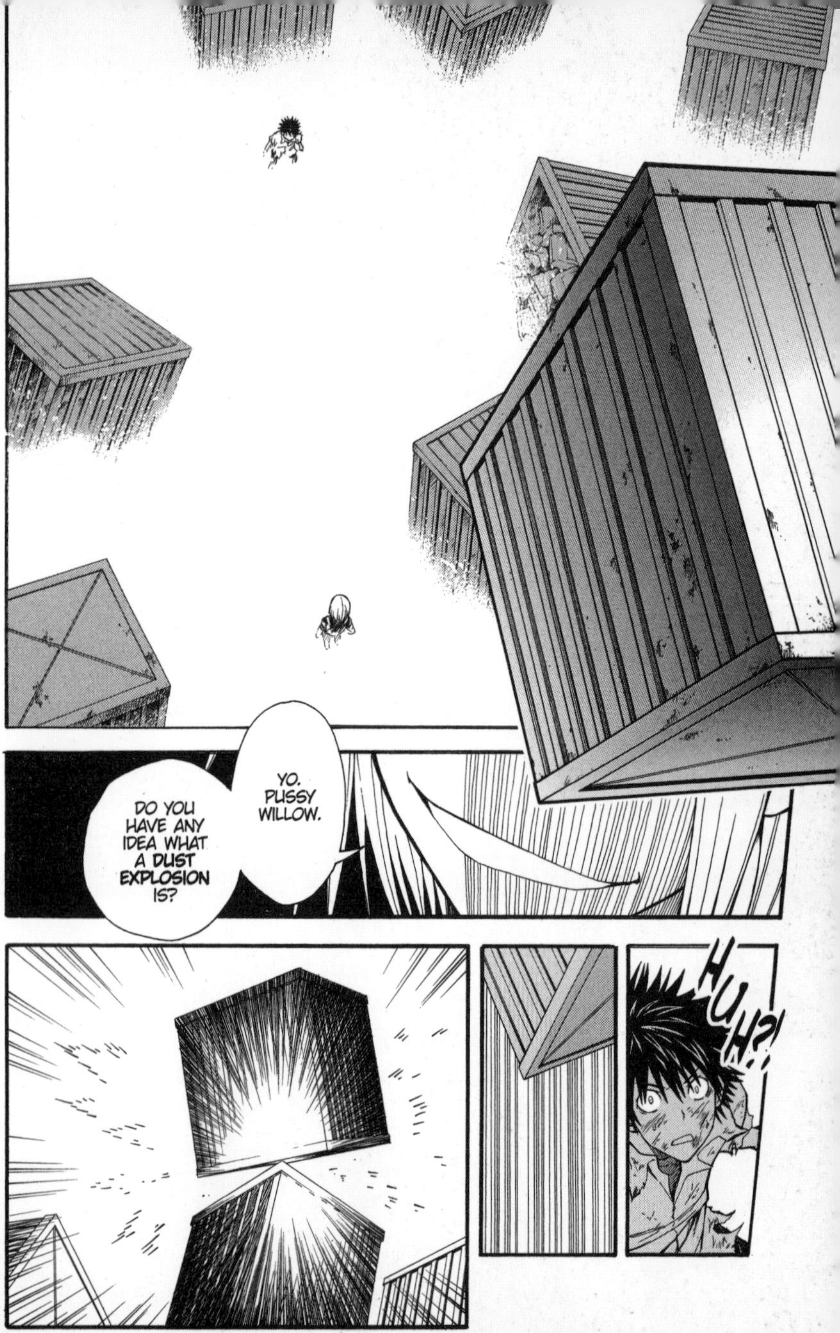
YO. PUSSY WILLOW.
DO YOU HAVE ANY IDEA WHAT A DUST EXPLOSION IS?
HUH?!

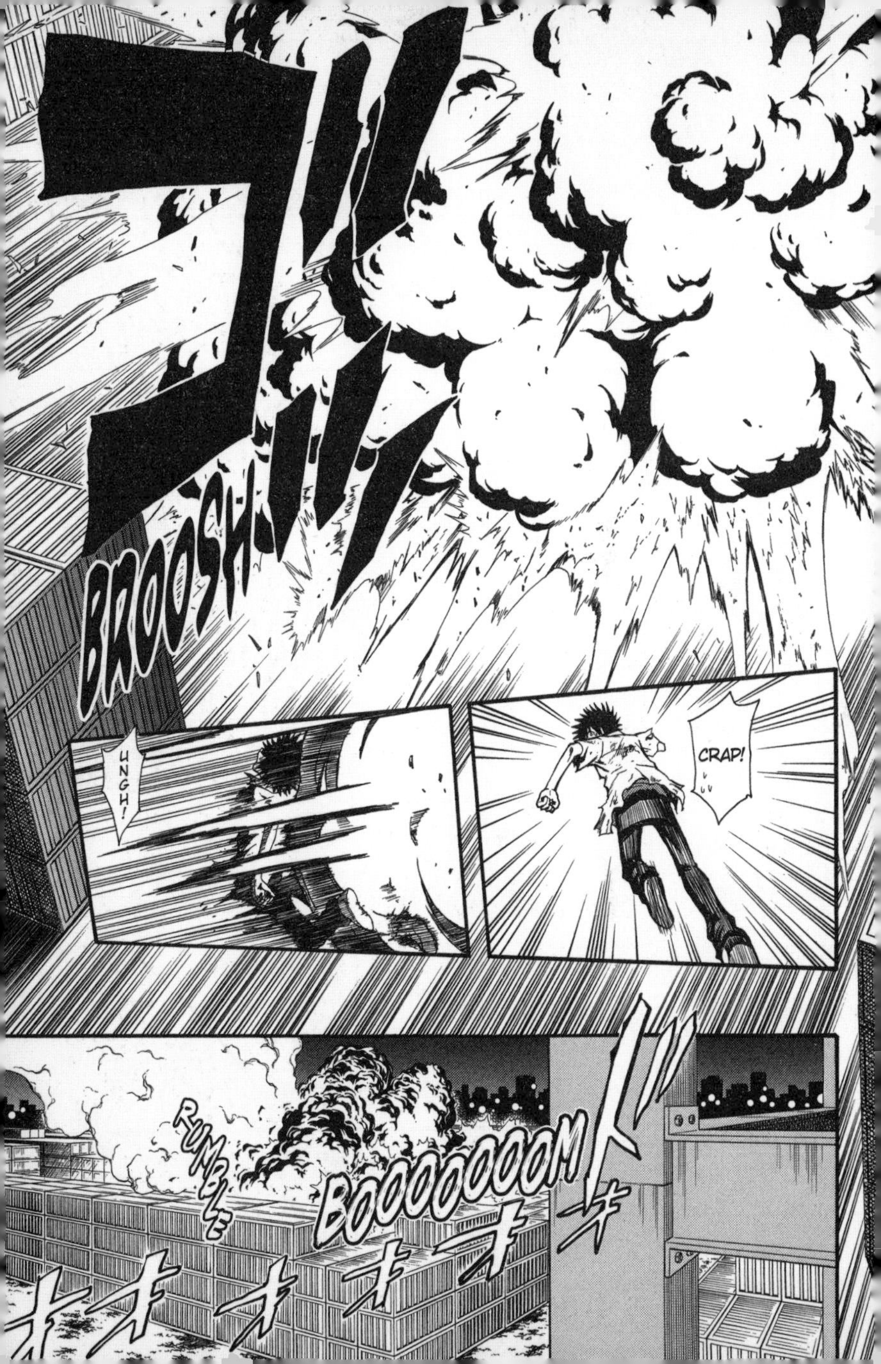
BROOSH
CRAP!
UNGH!
RUMBLE
BOOOOOOOM

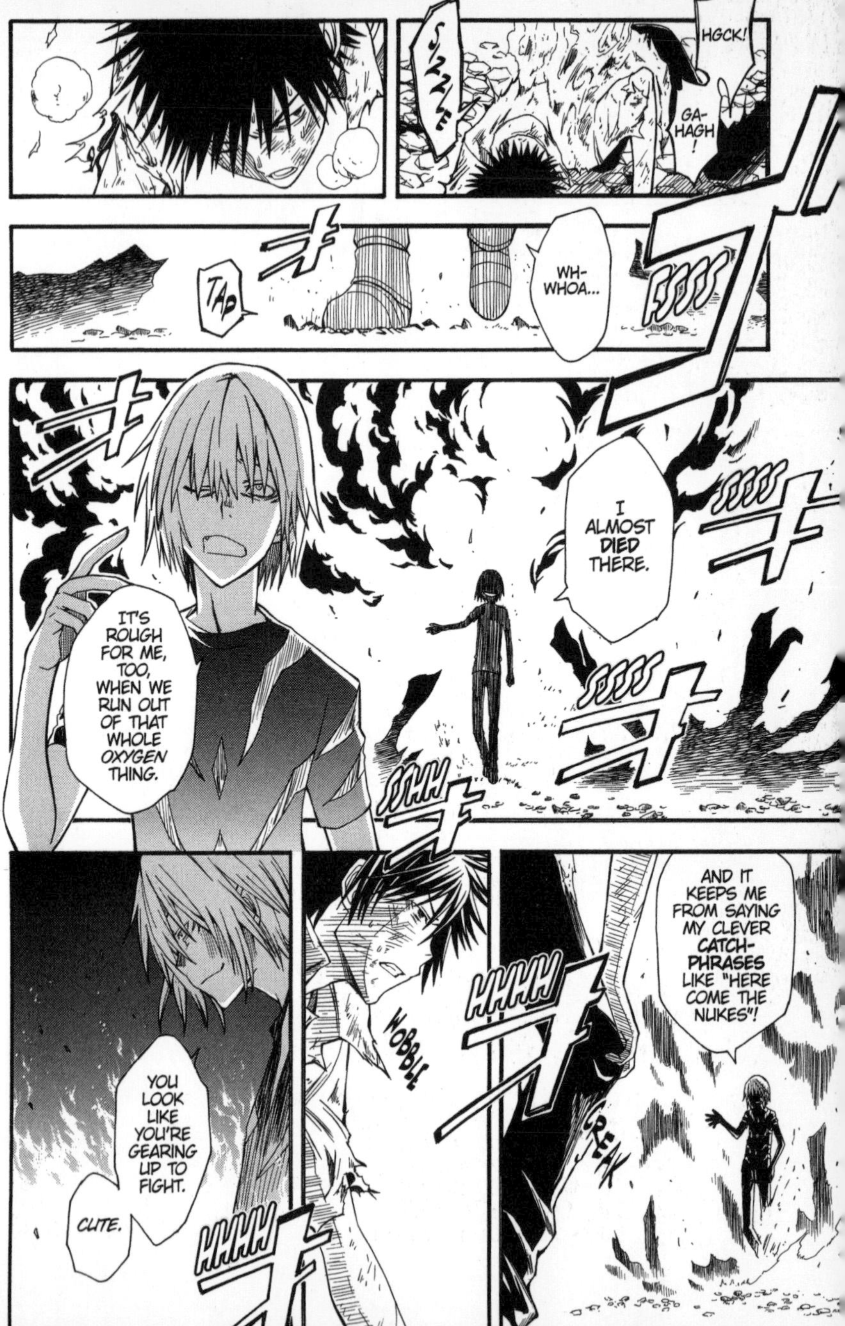
HGCK!
GA-HAGH!
SIZZLE
WH-WHOA...
TAP
I ALMOST DIED THERE.
IT'S ROUGH FOR ME, TOO, WHEN WE RUN OUT OF THAT WHOLE OXYGEN THING.
AND IT KEEPS ME FROM SAYING MY CLEVER CATCH-PHRASES LIKE "HERE COME THE NUKES"!
HHHH
CREAK
WOBBLE
YOU LOOK LIKE YOU'RE GEARING UP TO FIGHT.
CUTE.
HHHH

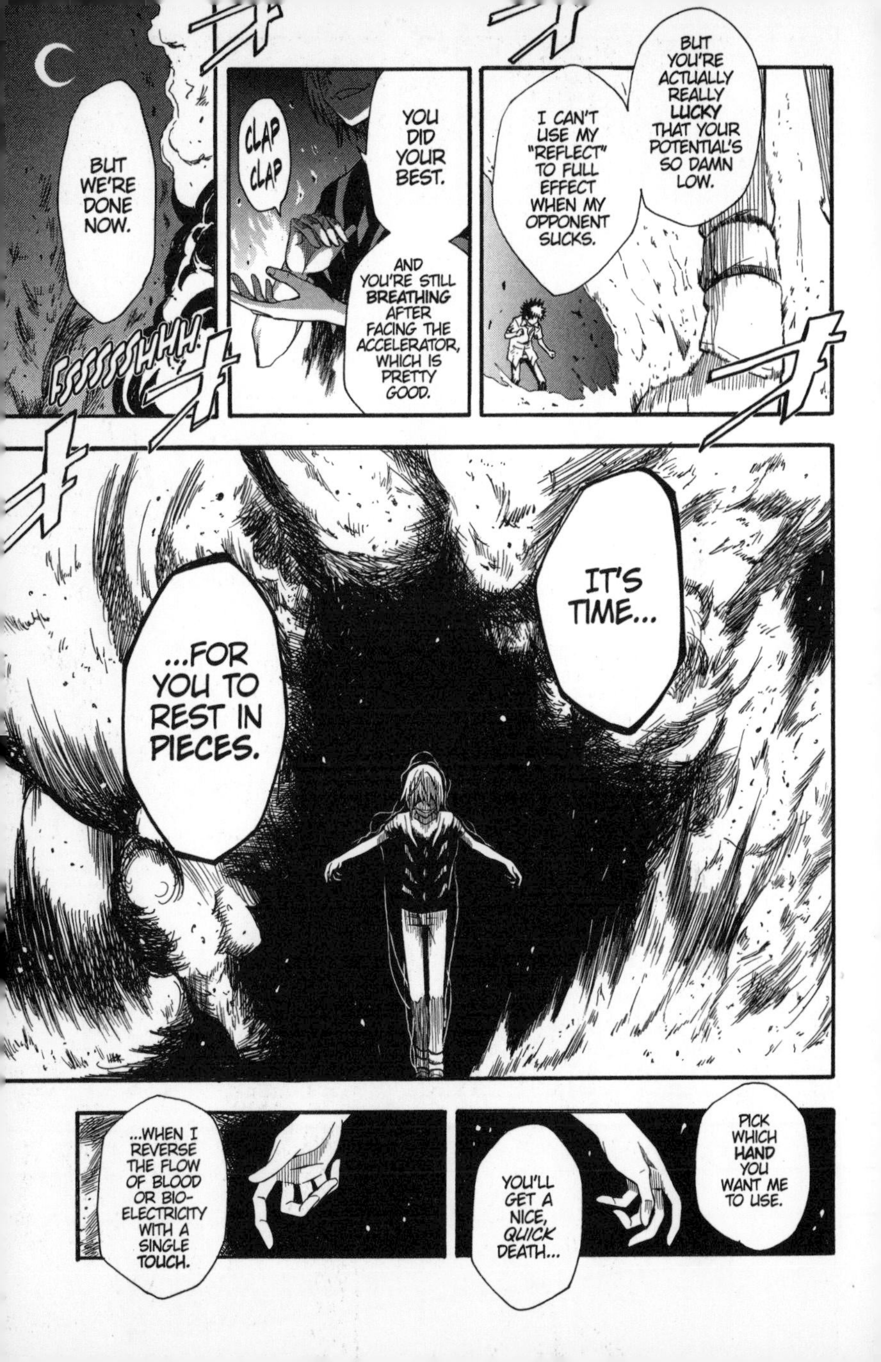
BUT YOU'RE ACTUALLY REALLY **LUCKY** THAT YOUR POTENTIAL'S SO DAMN LOW.
I CAN'T USE MY "REFLECT" TO FULL EFFECT WHEN MY OPPONENT SUCKS.
YOU DID YOUR BEST.
CLAP CLAP
AND YOU'RE STILL **BREATHING** AFTER FACING THE ACCELERATOR, WHICH IS PRETTY GOOD.
BUT WE'RE DONE NOW.
FSSSSSHHH
IT'S TIME...
...FOR YOU TO REST IN PIECES.
PICK WHICH **HAND** YOU WANT ME TO USE.
YOU'LL GET A NICE, *QUICK* DEATH...
...WHEN I REVERSE THE FLOW OF BLOOD OR BIO-ELECTRICITY WITH A SINGLE TOUCH.

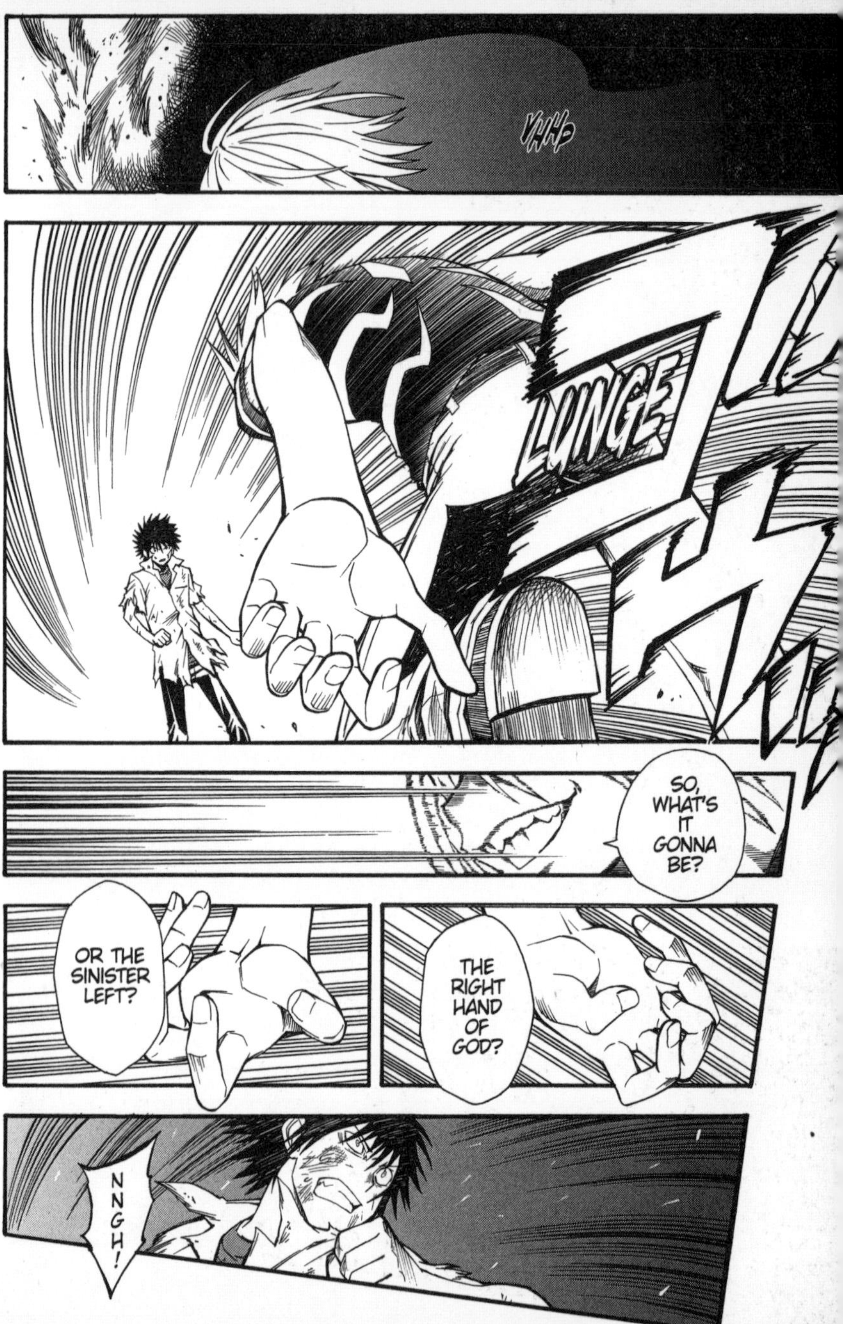
LUNGE
SO, WHAT'S IT GONNA BE?
THE RIGHT HAND OF GOD?
OR THE SINISTER LEFT?
NNGH!

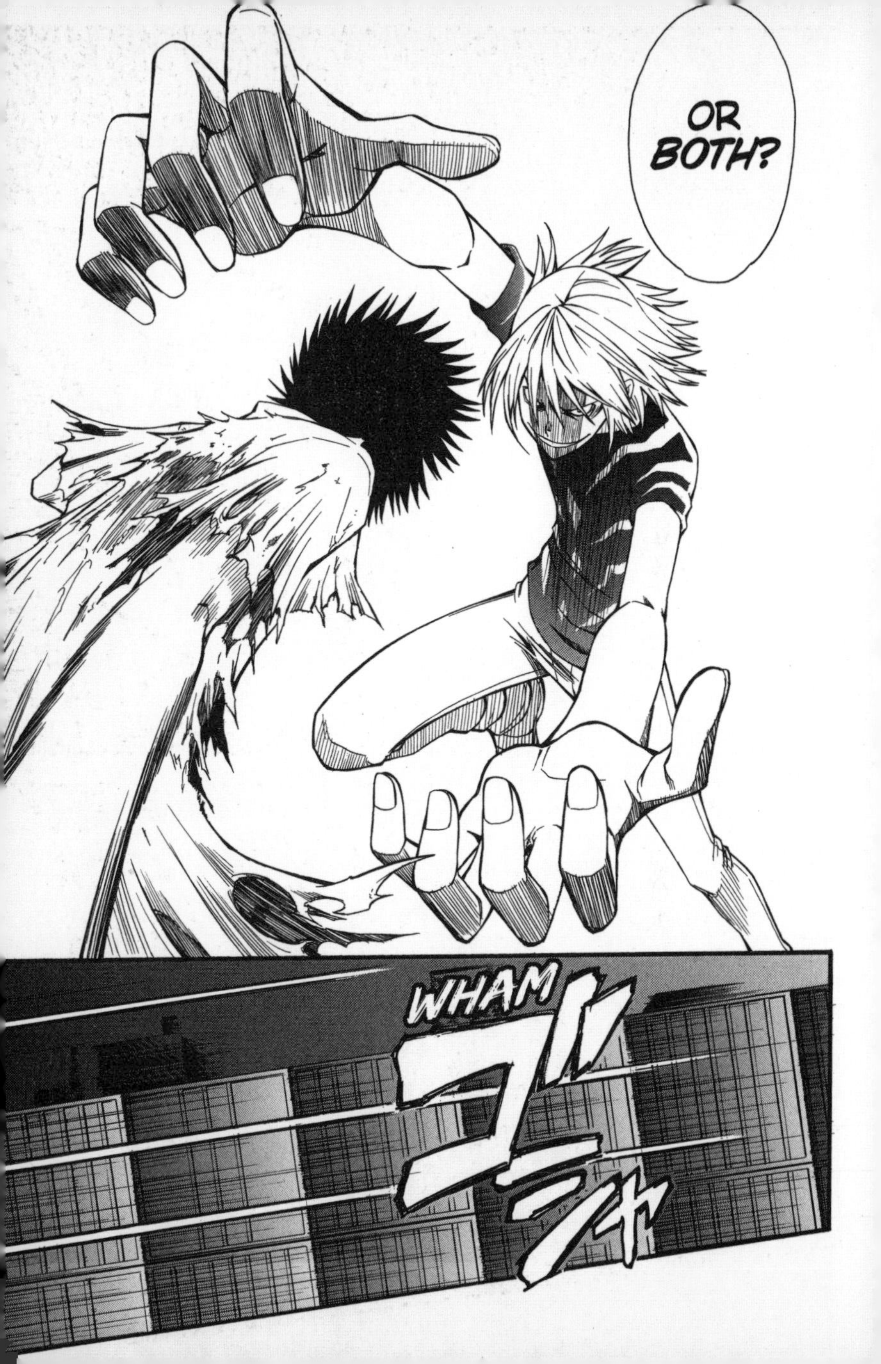
OR BOTH?
WHAM
ゴシャ

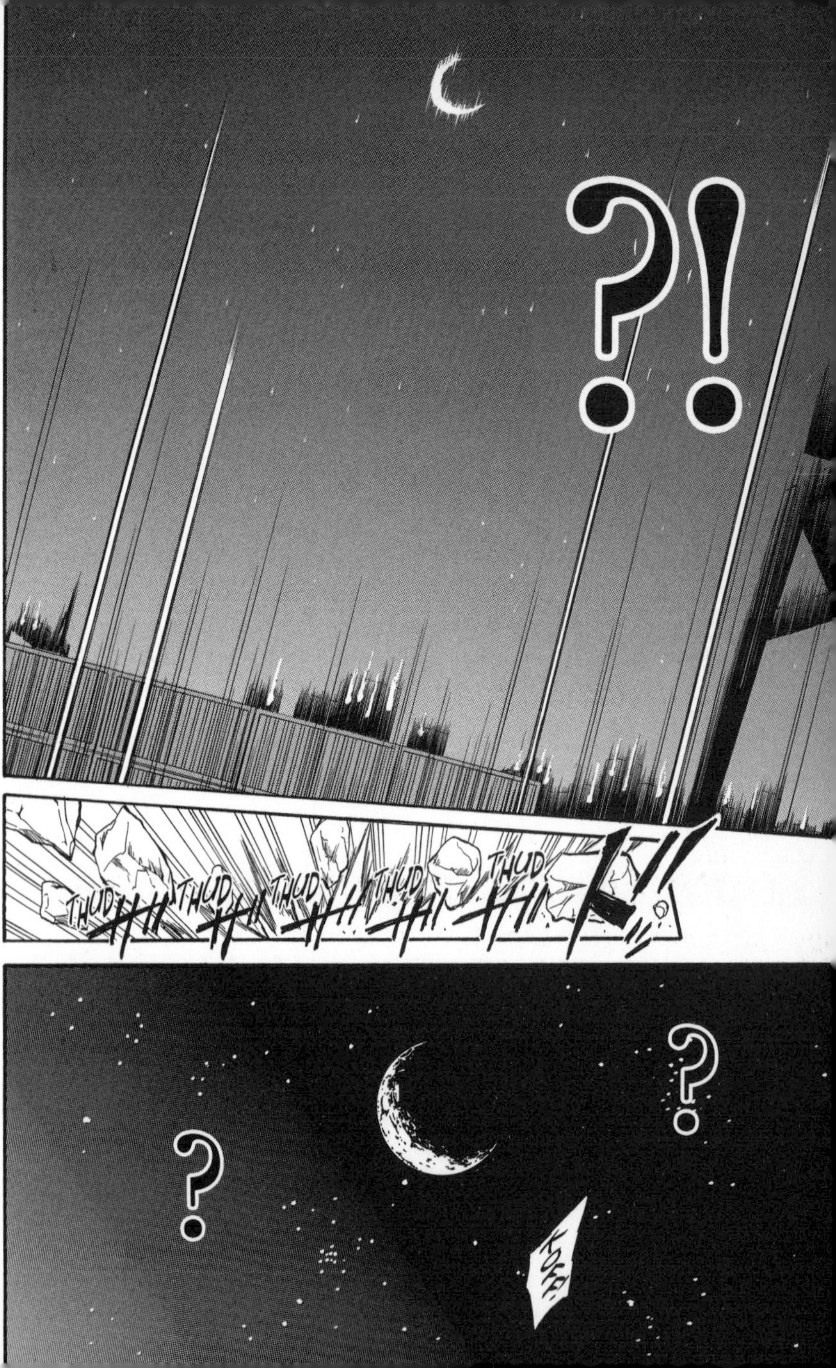
?!
THUD
THUD
THUD
THUD
THUD
?
?
KOFF!

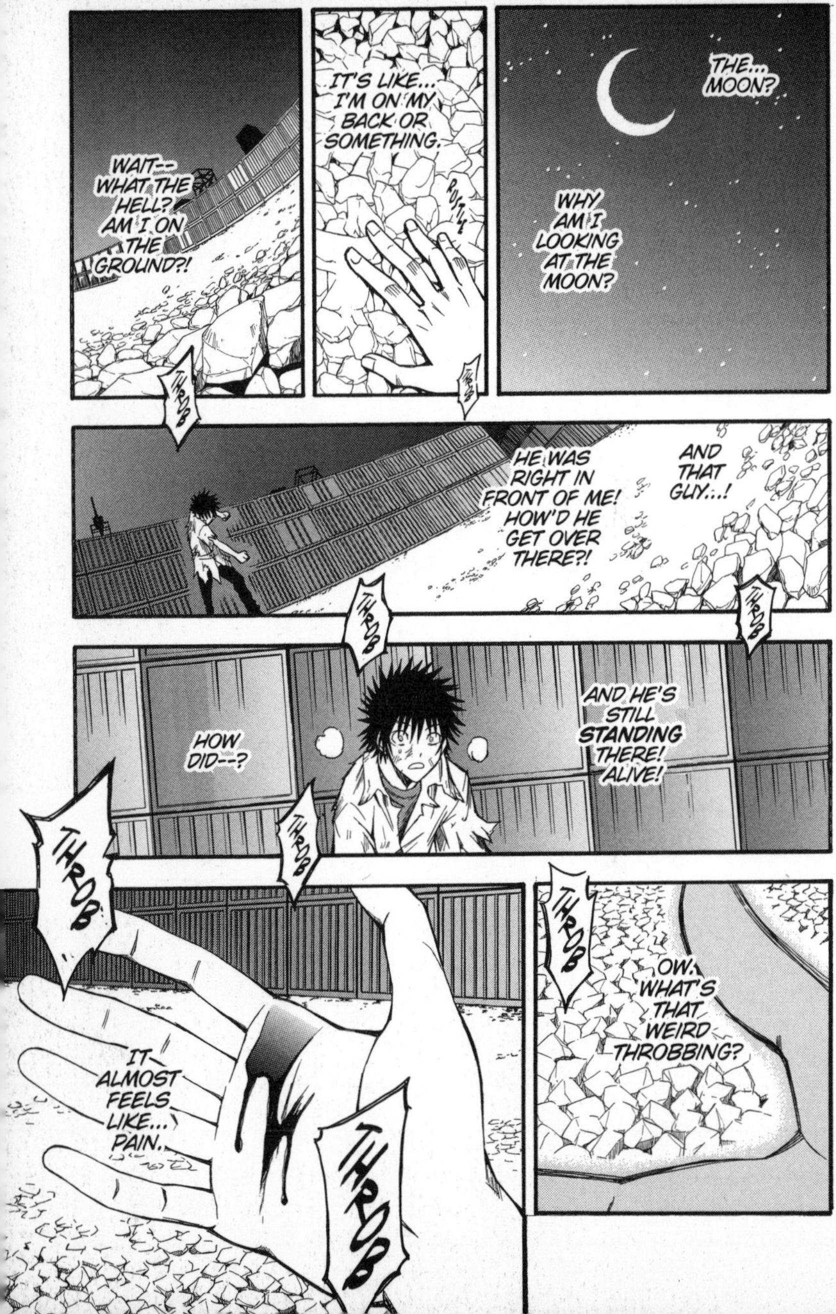
THE... MOON?
WHY AM I LOOKING AT THE MOON?
IT'S LIKE... I'M ON MY BACK OR SOMETHING.
RUSTLE
WAIT-- WHAT THE HELL? AM I ON THE GROUND?!
THROB
AND THAT GUY...!
HE WAS RIGHT IN FRONT OF ME! HOW'D HE GET OVER THERE?!
THROB
THROB
AND HE'S STILL STANDING THERE! ALIVE!
HOW DID--?
THROB
THROB
OW. WHAT'S THAT WEIRD THROBBING?
THROB
IT ALMOST FEELS LIKE... PAIN.
THROB

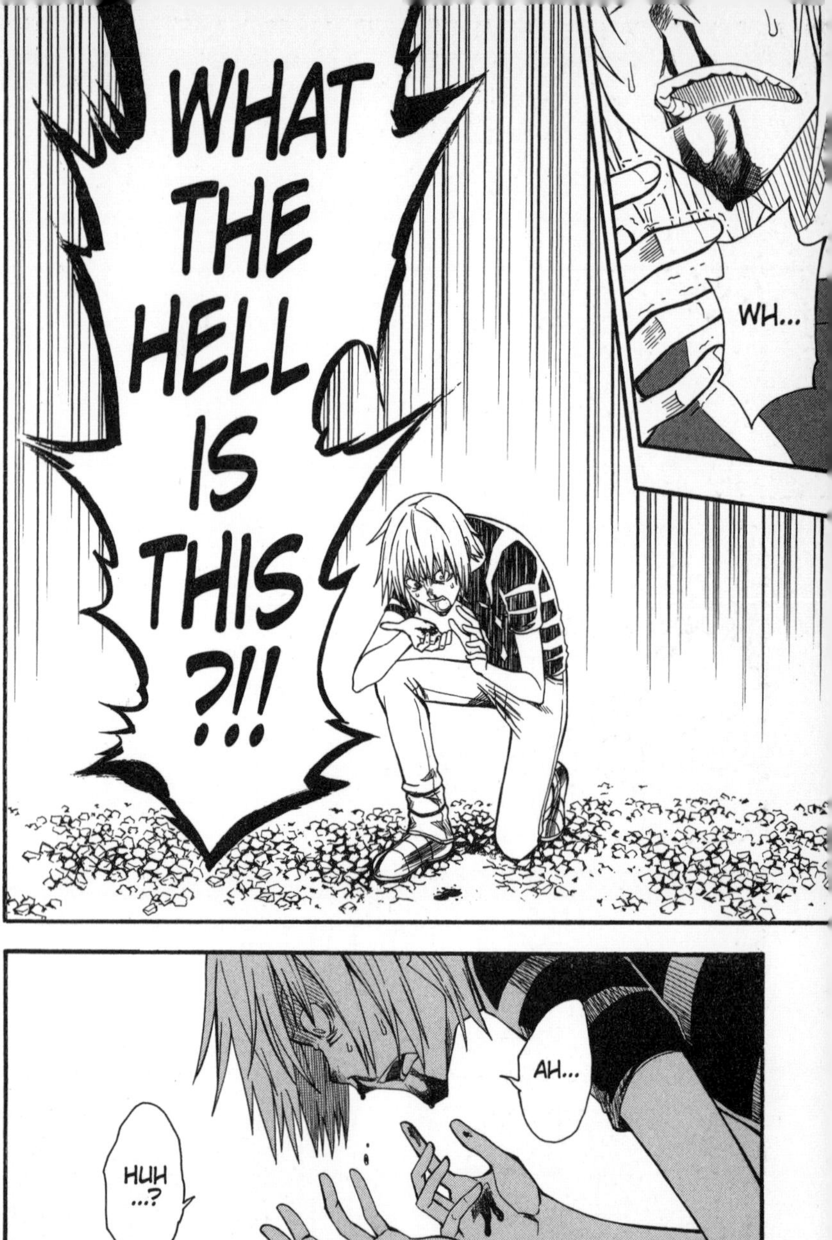
WH...
WHAT THE HELL IS THIS ?!!
AH...
HUH ...?

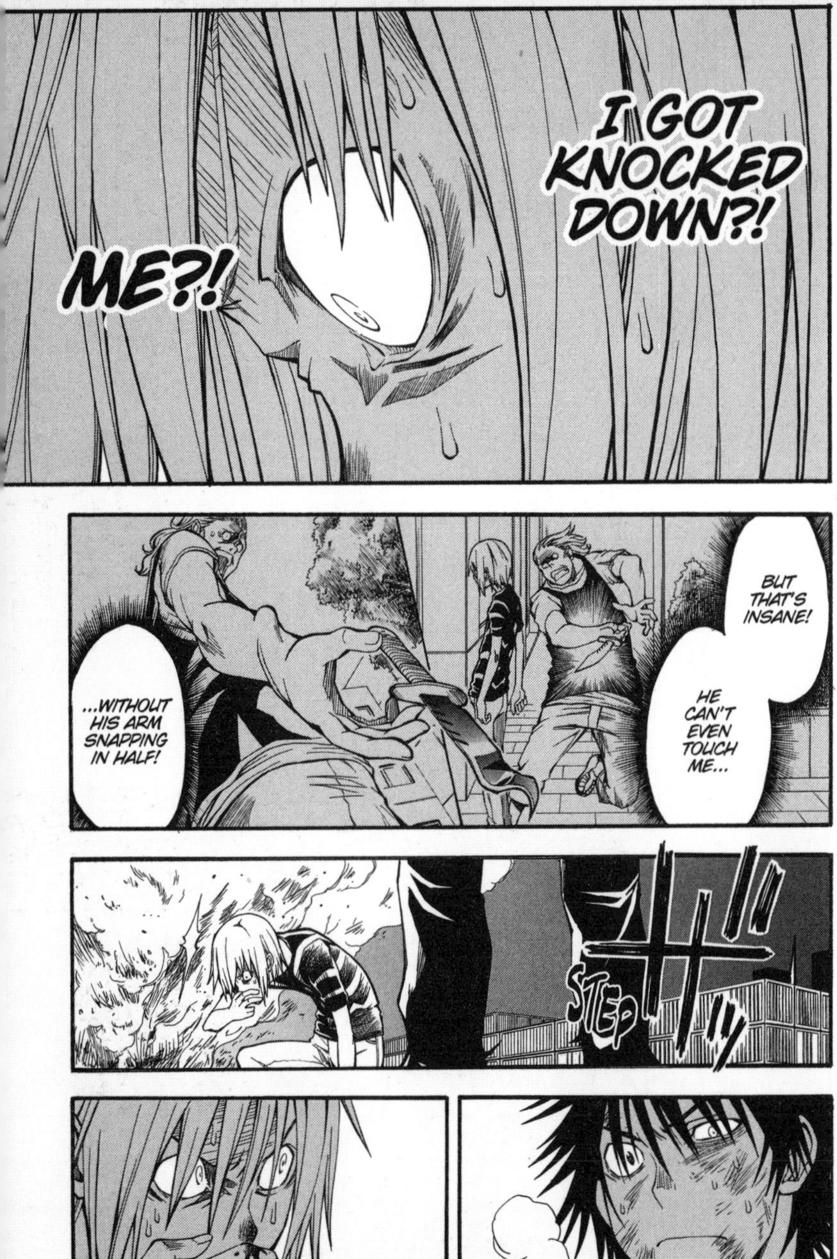
I GOT KNOCKED DOWN?!
ME?!
BUT THAT'S INSANE!
HE CAN'T EVEN TOUCH ME...
...WITHOUT HIS ARM SNAPPING IN HALF!
STEP

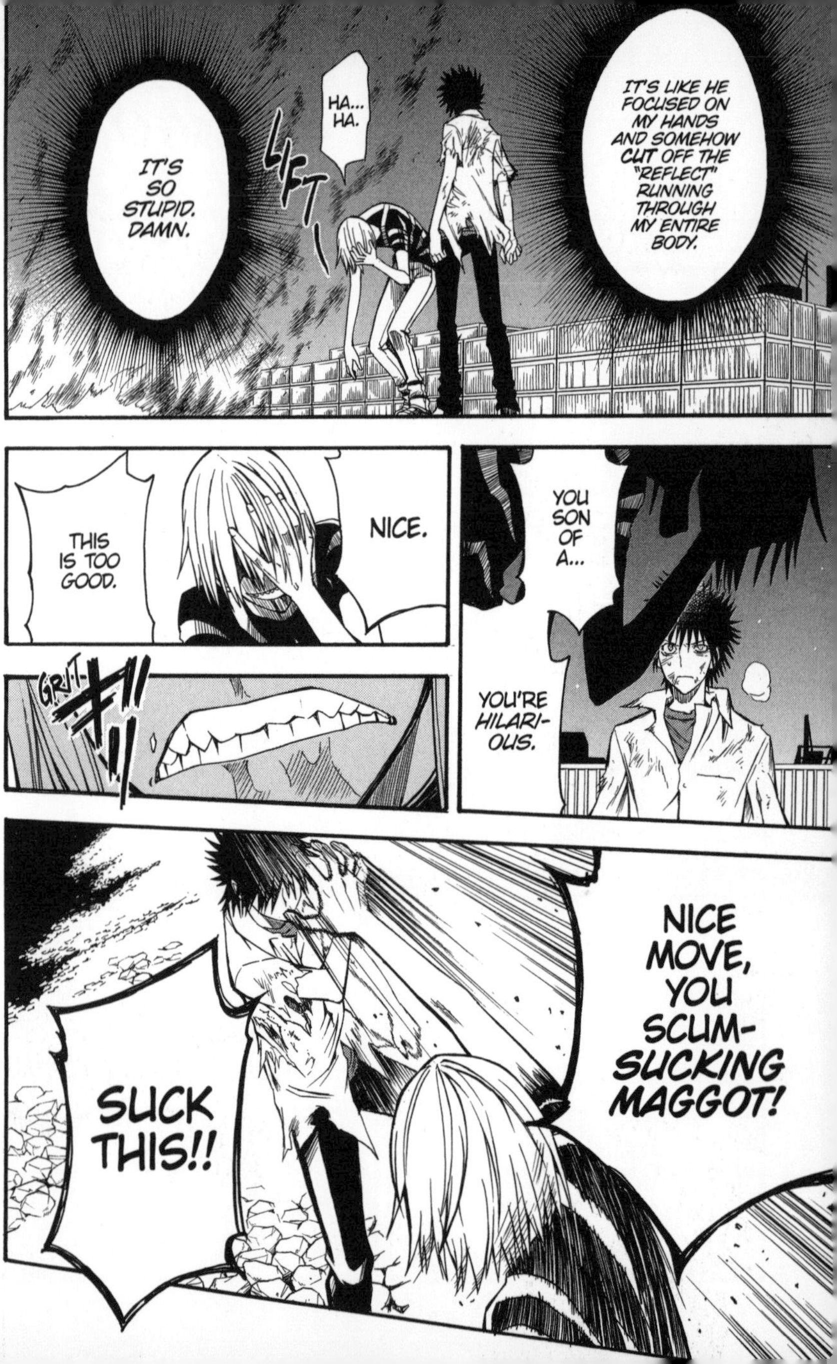
IT'S LIKE HE FOCUSED ON MY HANDS AND SOMEHOW CUT OFF THE "REFLECT" RUNNING THROUGH MY ENTIRE BODY.
HA... HA.
LIFT
IT'S SO STUPID. DAMN.
YOU SON OF A...
YOU'RE HILARI-OUS.
NICE.
THIS IS TOO GOOD.
GRIT
NICE MOVE, YOU SCUM-SUCKING MAGGOT!
SUCK THIS!!

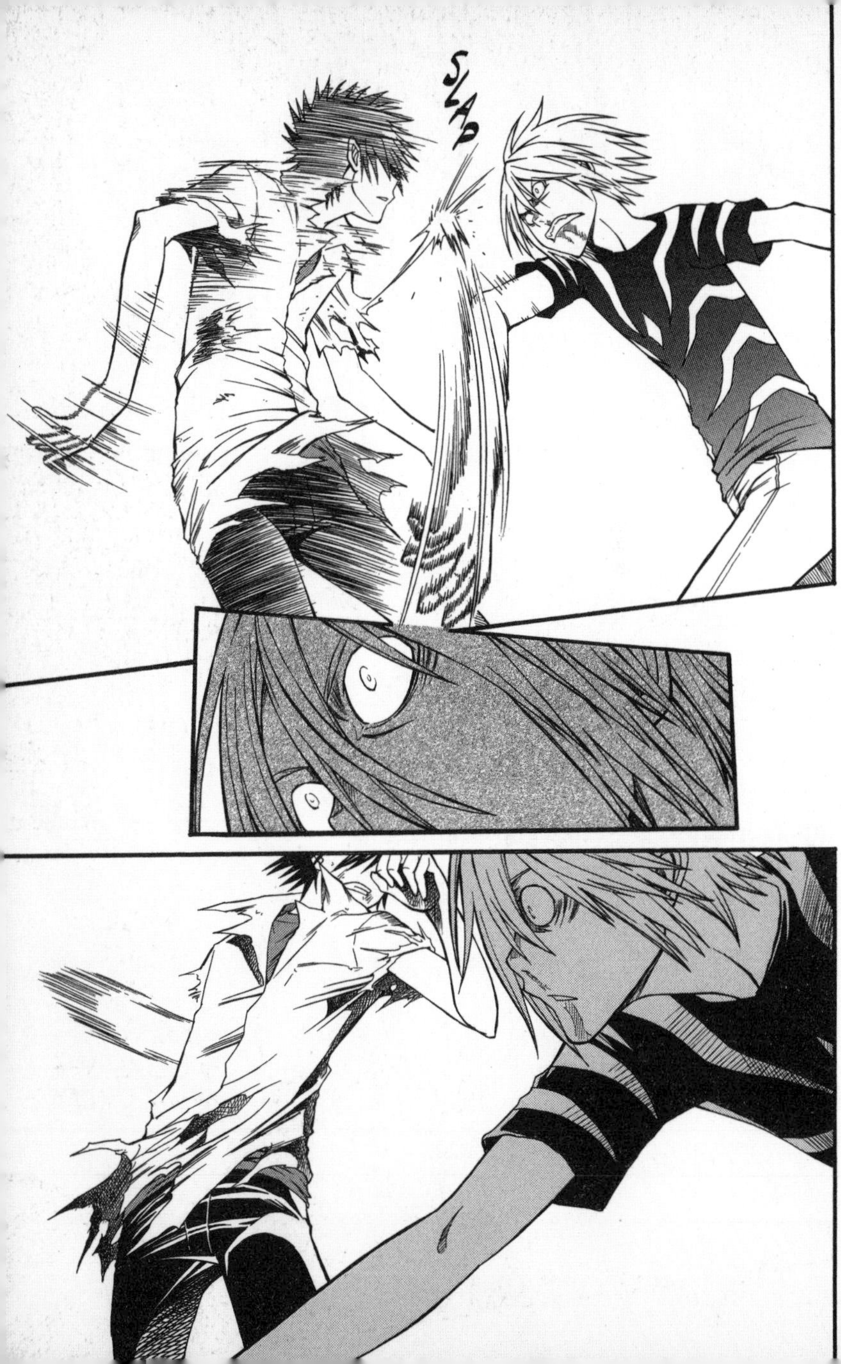
SLAP

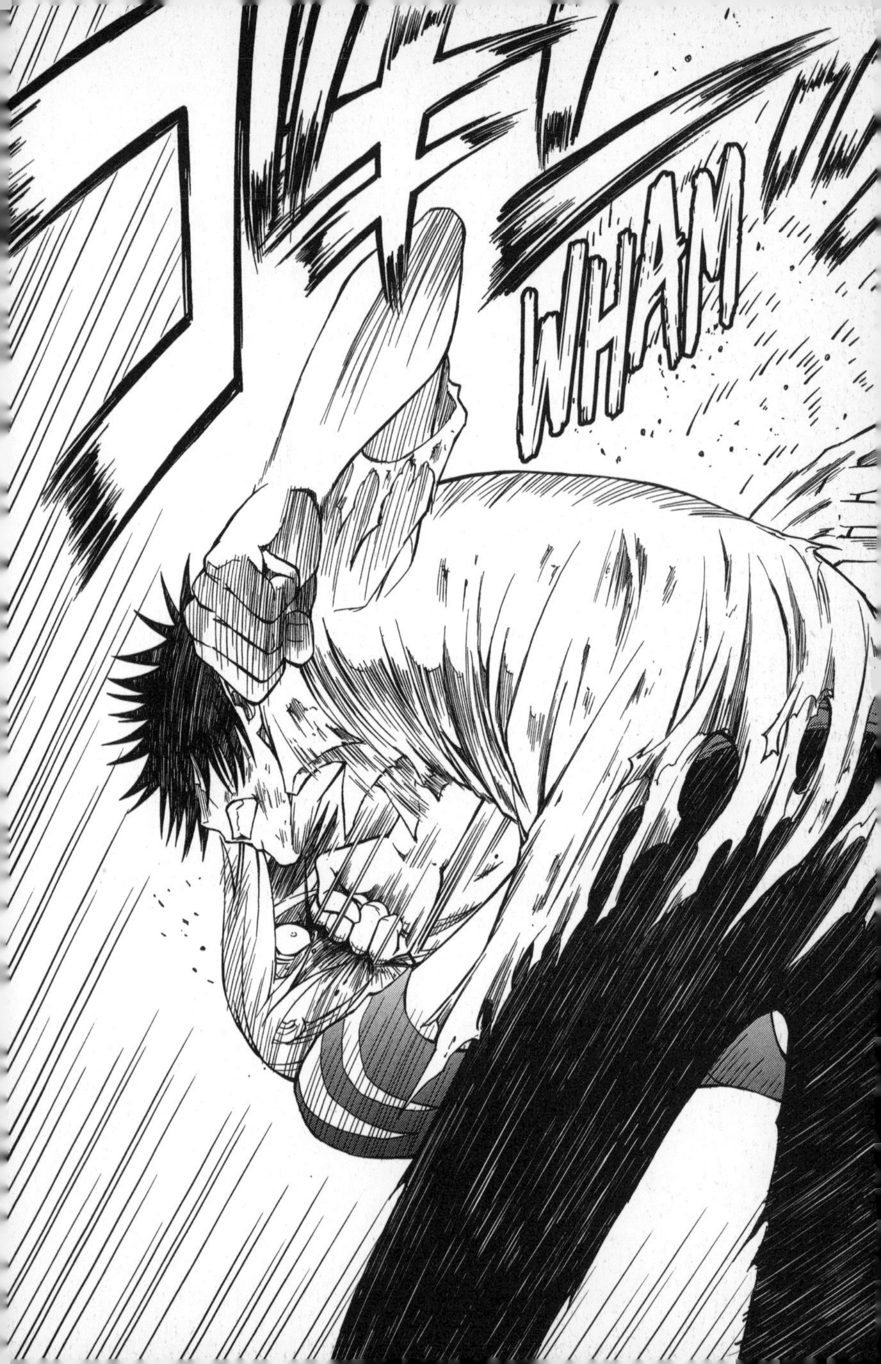
WHAM

A Certain
SCIENTIFIC
Railgun

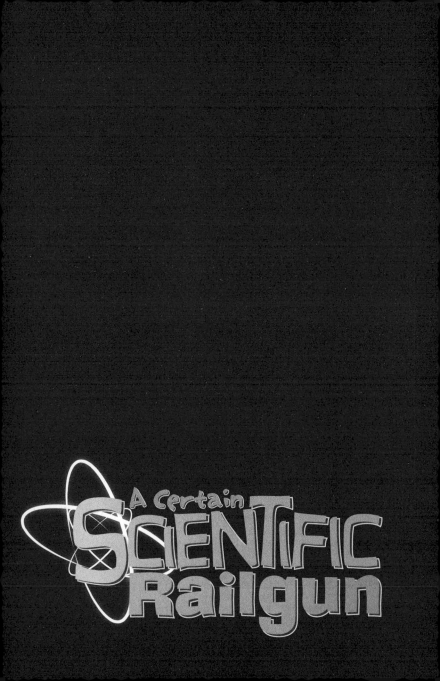

A Certain Playful Accelerator

SO.
WHAT'S IT GONNA BE?
STEP
THE RIGHT HAND OF GOD?
OR THE SINISTER LEFT?
OR ME?!
BUT I WANNA START AS FRIENDS BEFORE WE GET TO THE FREAKY STUFF!
NONE OF THE ABOVE, THANKS!
WHAM

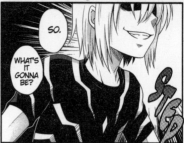

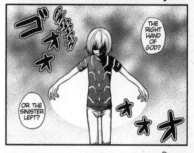

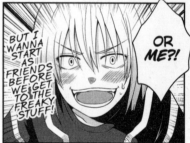

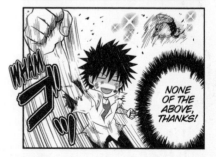

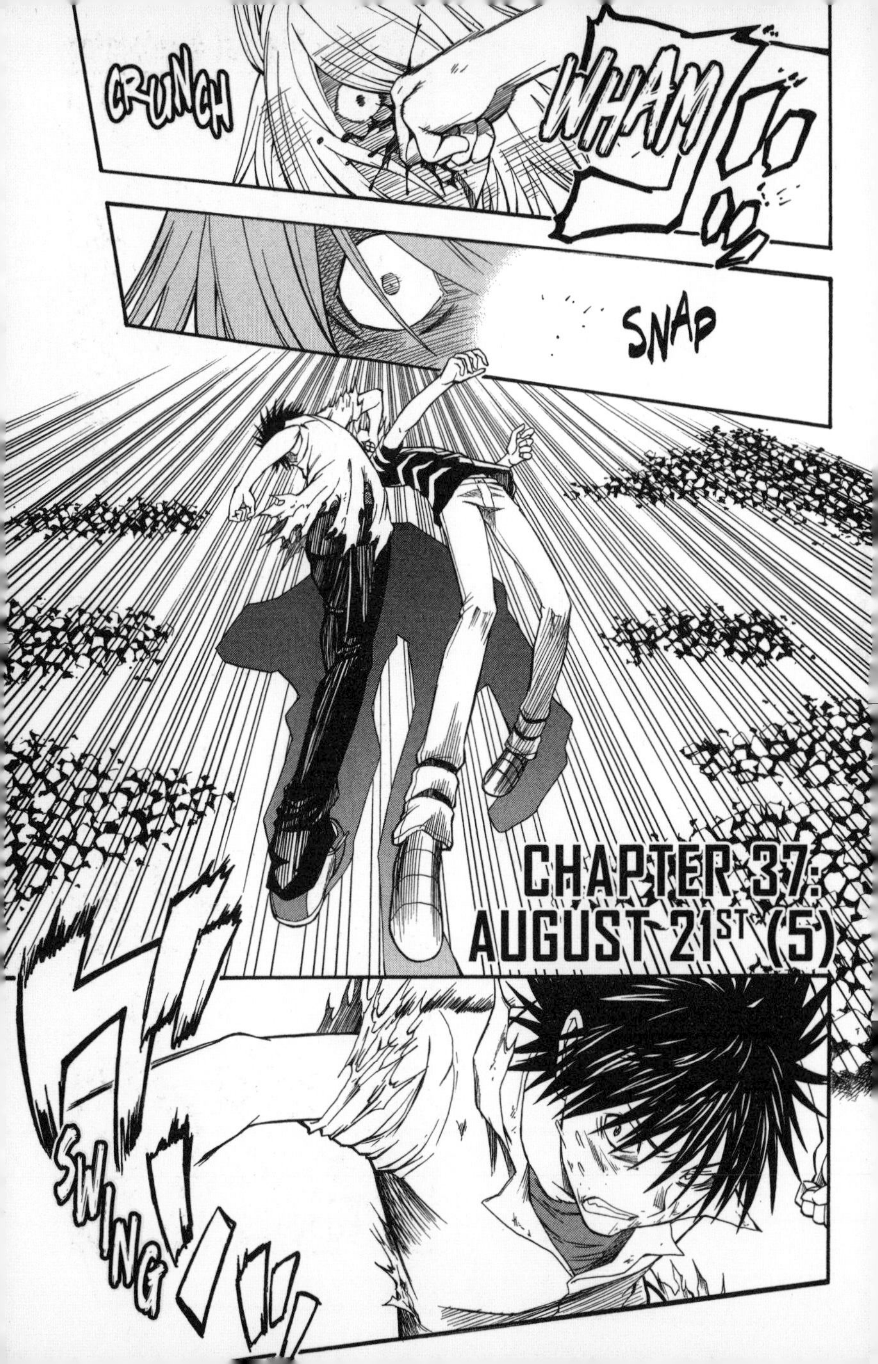
WHAM
CRUNCH
SNAP
CHAPTER 37: AUGUST 21ST (5)
SWING

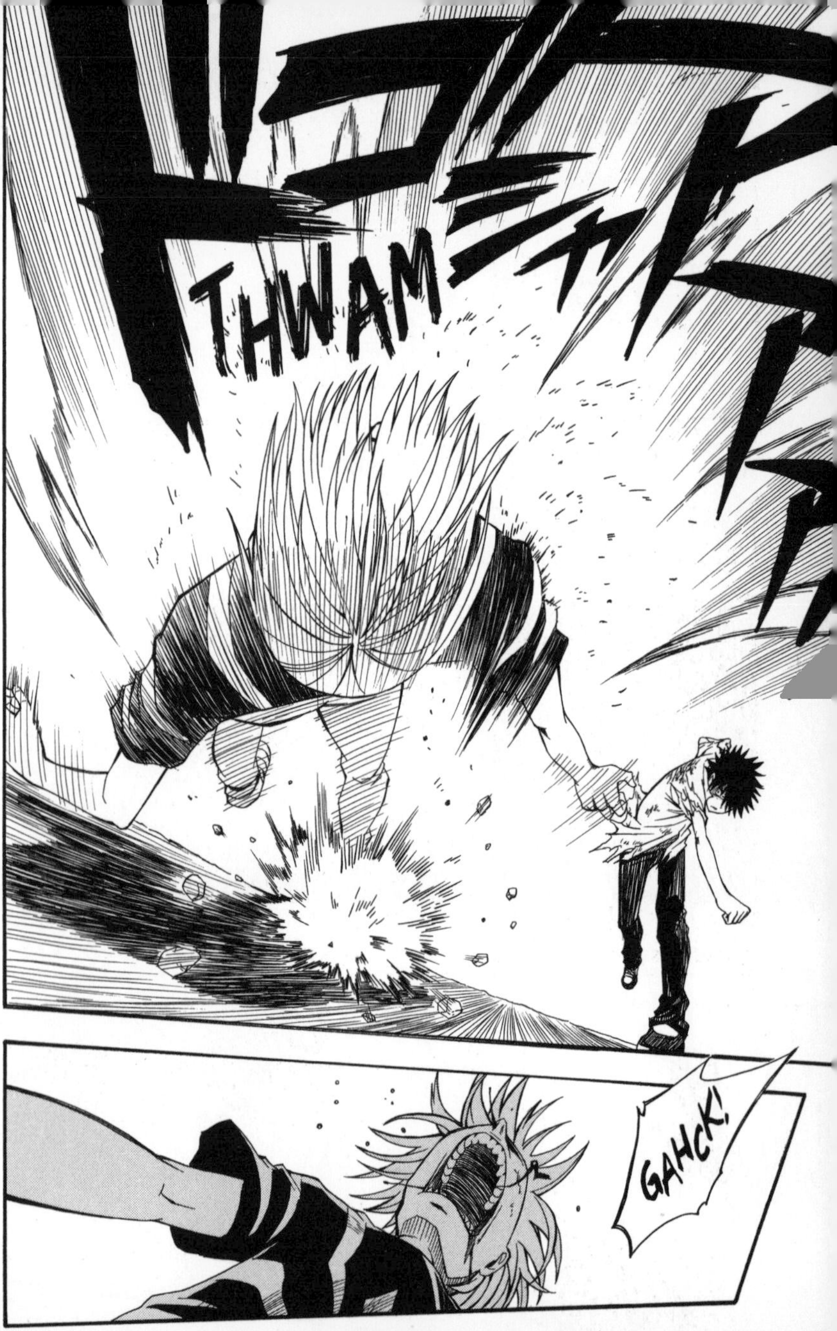
THWAM
GAHCK!

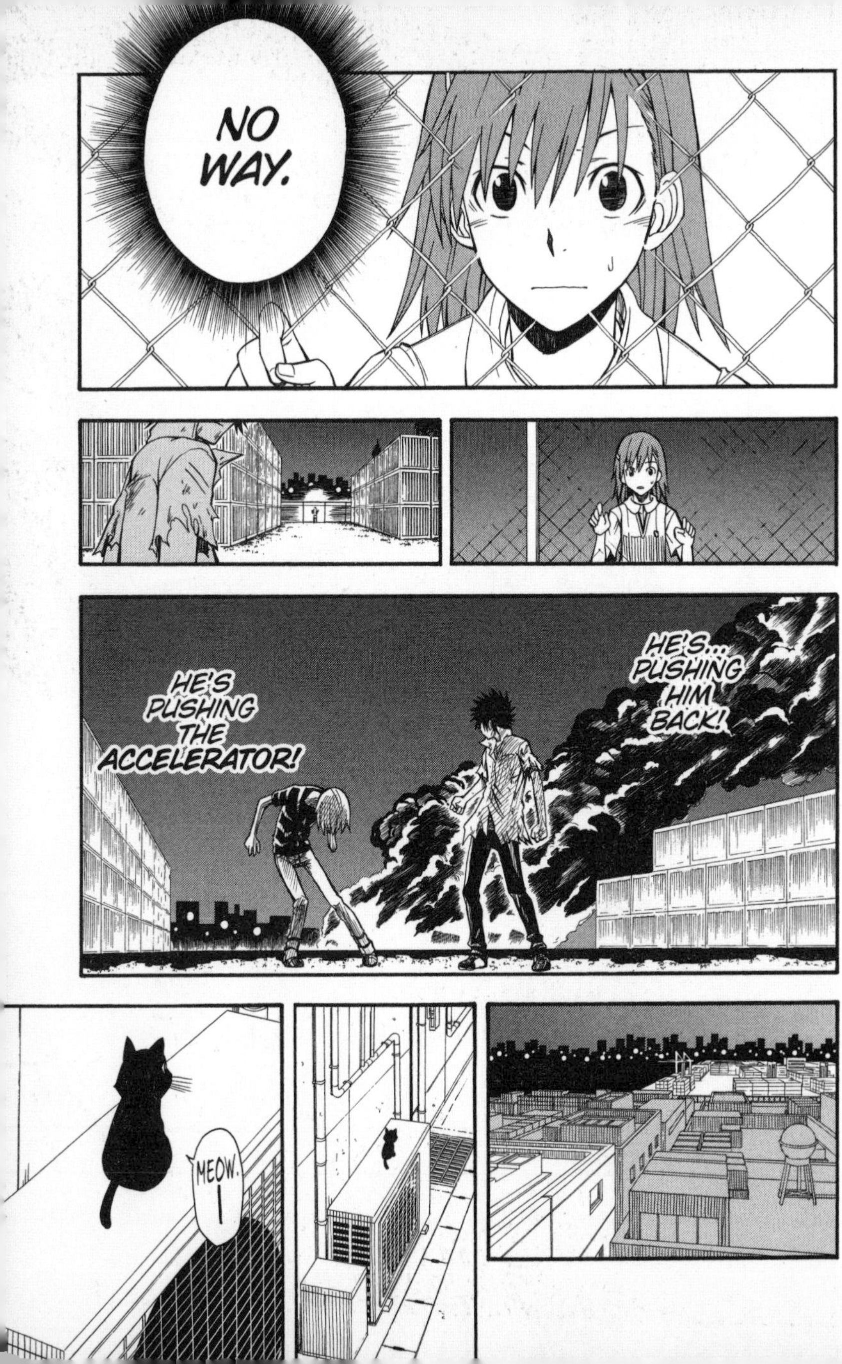
NO WAY.
HE'S... PUSHING HIM BACK!
HE'S PUSHING THE ACCELERATOR!
MEOW.

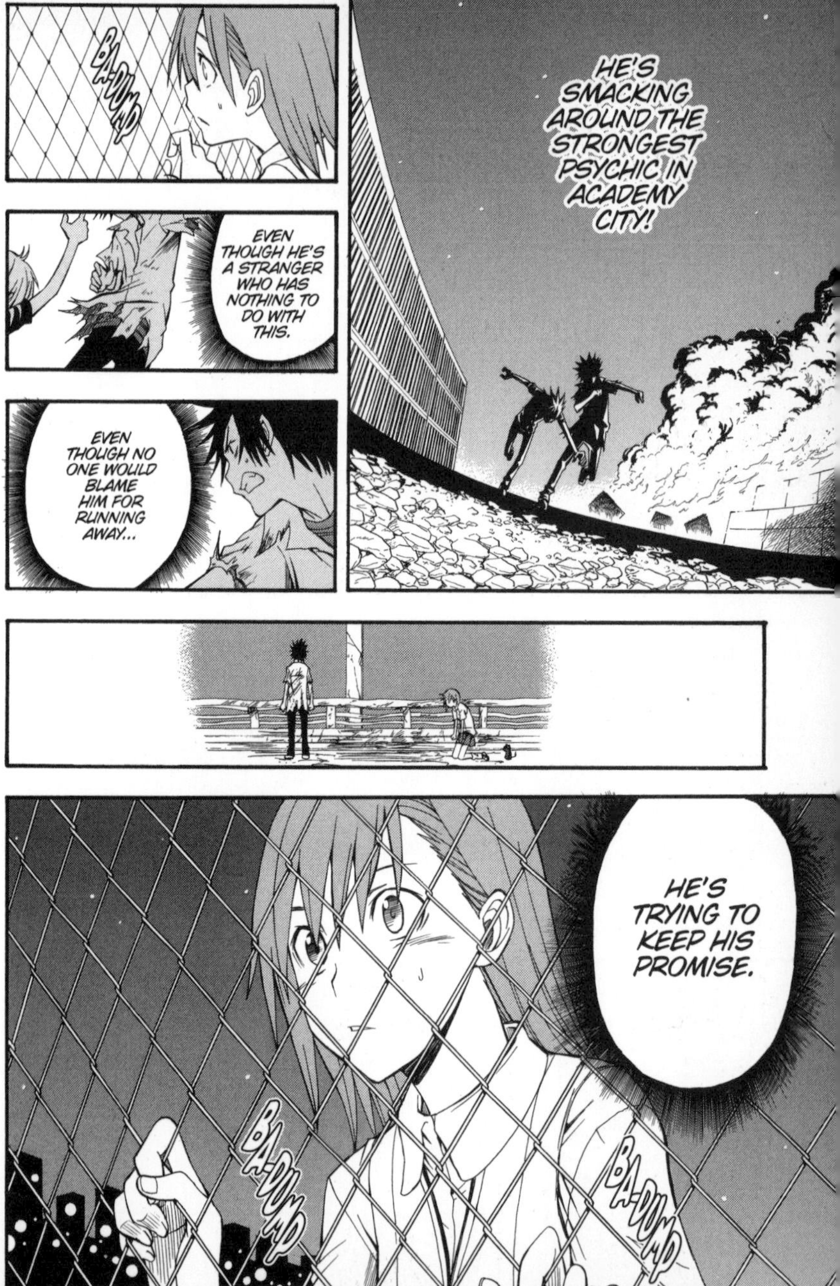
HE'S SMACKING AROUND THE STRONGEST PSYCHIC IN ACADEMY CITY!
BADUMP
EVEN THOUGH HE'S A STRANGER WHO HAS NOTHING TO DO WITH THIS.
EVEN THOUGH NO ONE WOULD BLAME HIM FOR RUNNING AWAY...
HE'S TRYING TO KEEP HIS PROMISE.
BA-DUMP
BADUMP

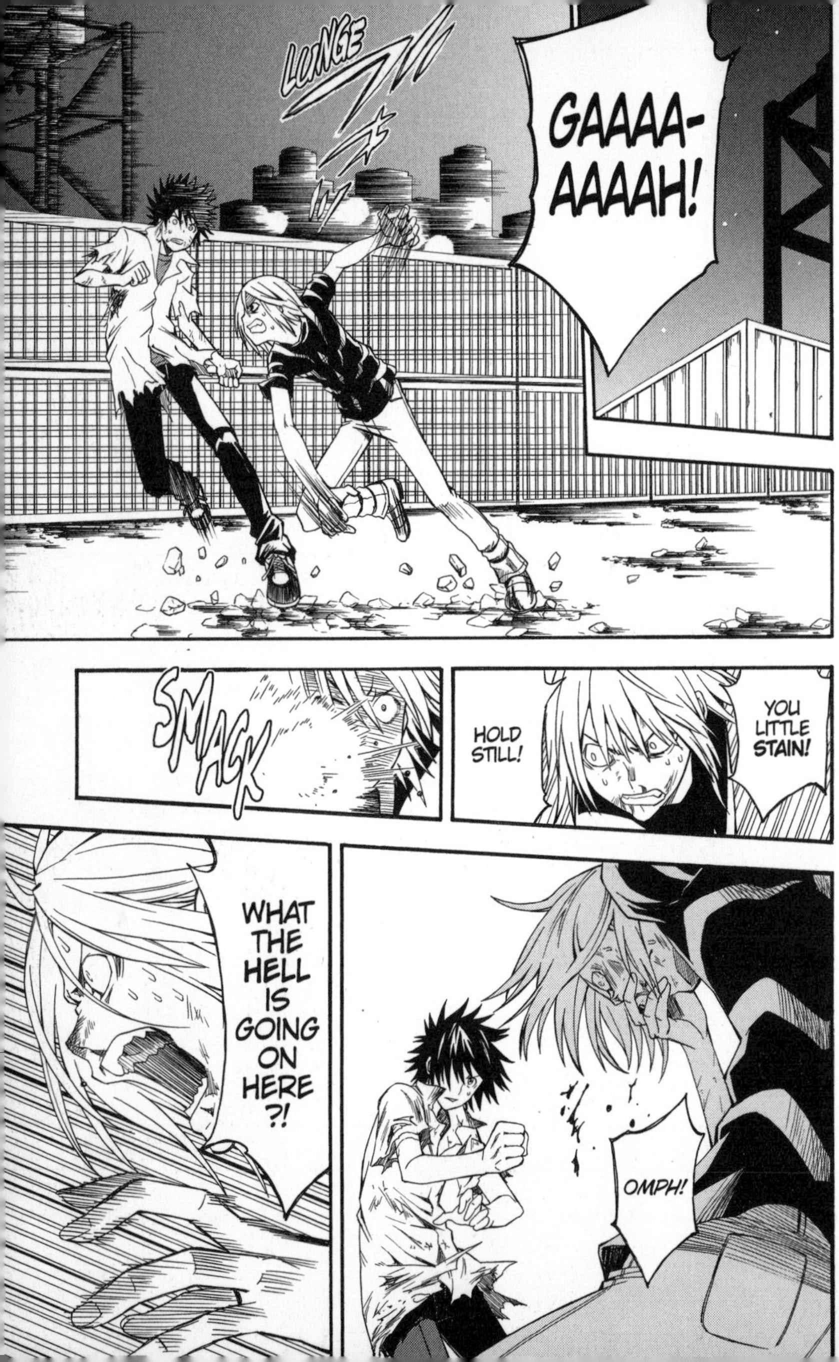
GAAAA-AAAAH!
LUNGE
YOU LITTLE STAIN!
HOLD STILL!
SMACK
OMPH!
WHAT THE HELL IS GOING ON HERE?!

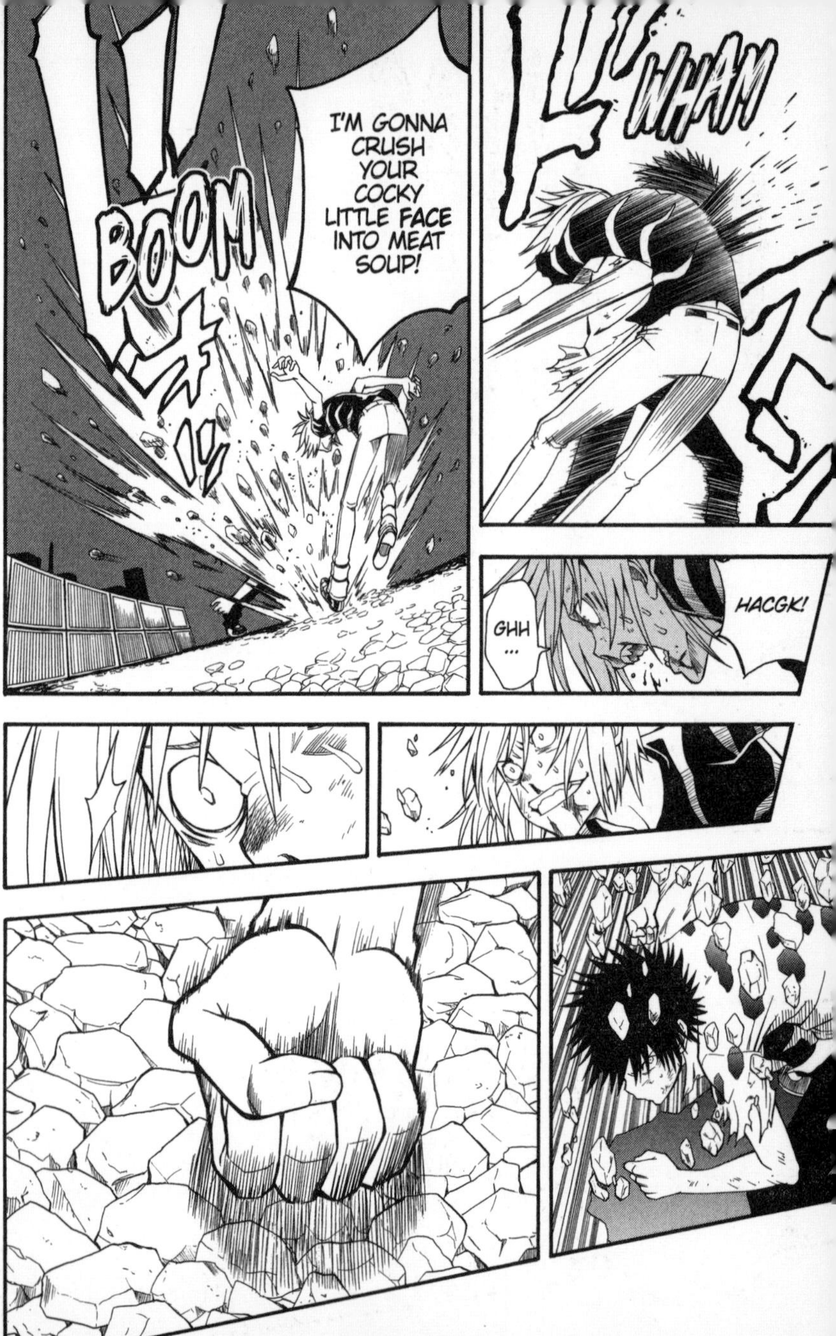
WHAM
HACGK!
GHH ...
BOOM
I'M GONNA CRUSH YOUR COCKY LITTLE FACE INTO MEAT SOUP!

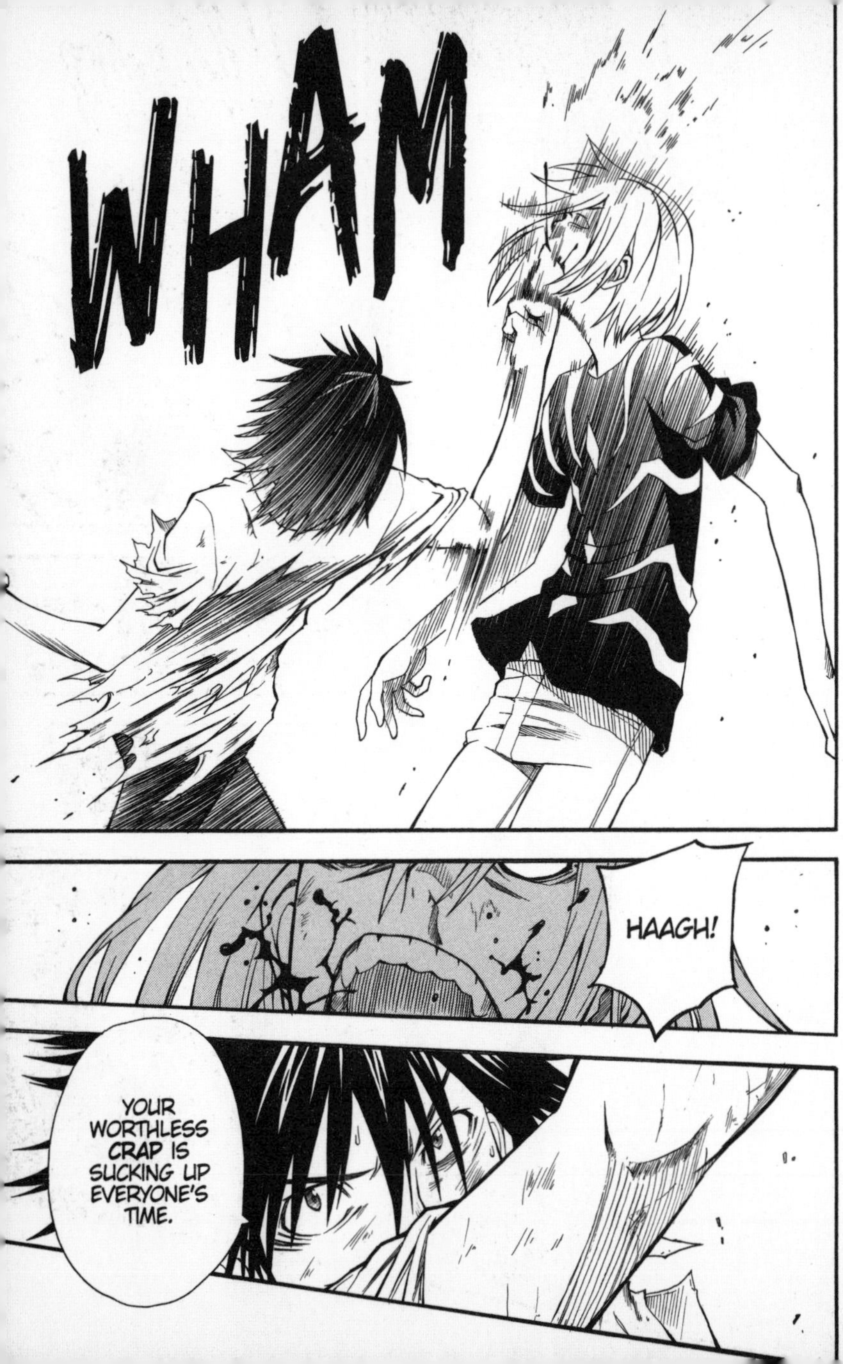
WHAM
HAAGH!
YOUR WORTHLESS CRAP IS SUCKING UP EVERYONE'S TIME.

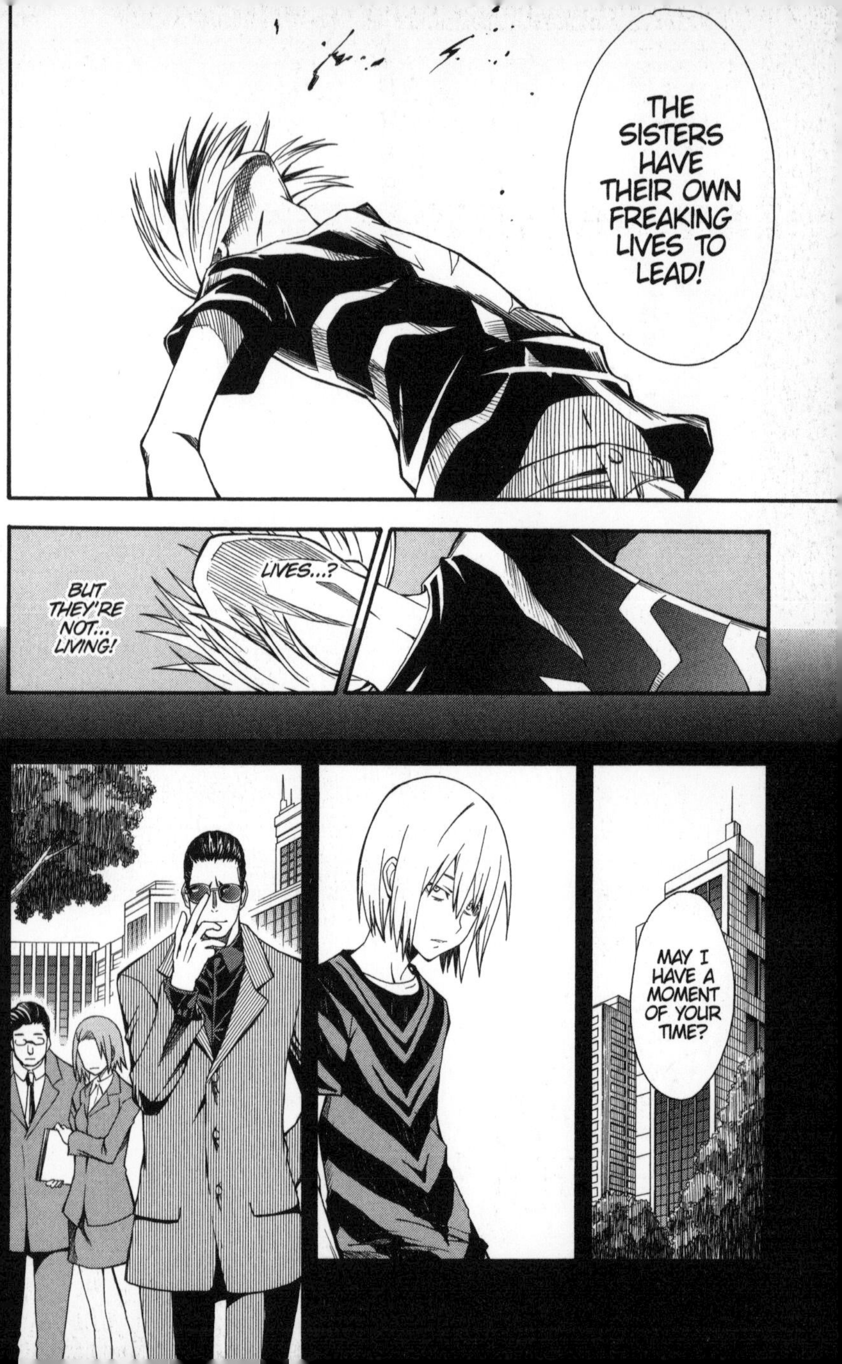
THE SISTERS HAVE THEIR OWN FREAKING LIVES TO LEAD!
LIVES...?
BUT THEY'RE NOT... LIVING!
MAY I HAVE A MOMENT OF YOUR TIME?

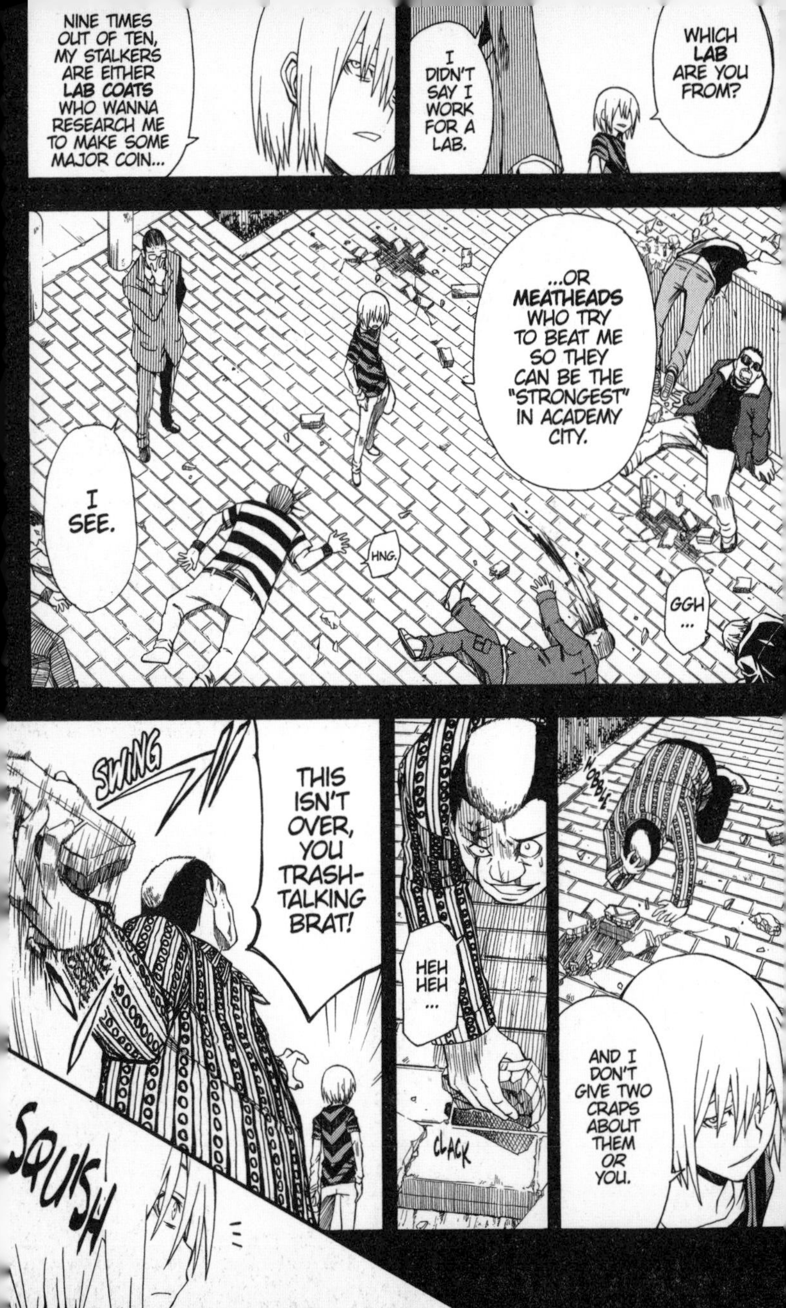
WHICH LAB ARE YOU FROM?
I DIDN'T SAY I WORK FOR A LAB.
NINE TIMES OUT OF TEN, MY STALKERS ARE EITHER LAB COATS WHO WANNA RESEARCH ME TO MAKE SOME MAJOR COIN...
...OR MEATHEADS WHO TRY TO BEAT ME SO THEY CAN BE THE "STRONGEST" IN ACADEMY CITY.
GGH...
HNG.
I SEE.
WOBBLE
AND I DON'T GIVE TWO CRAPS ABOUT THEM OR YOU.
HEH HEH...
CLACK
SWING
THIS ISN'T OVER, YOU TRASH-TALKING BRAT!
SQUISH

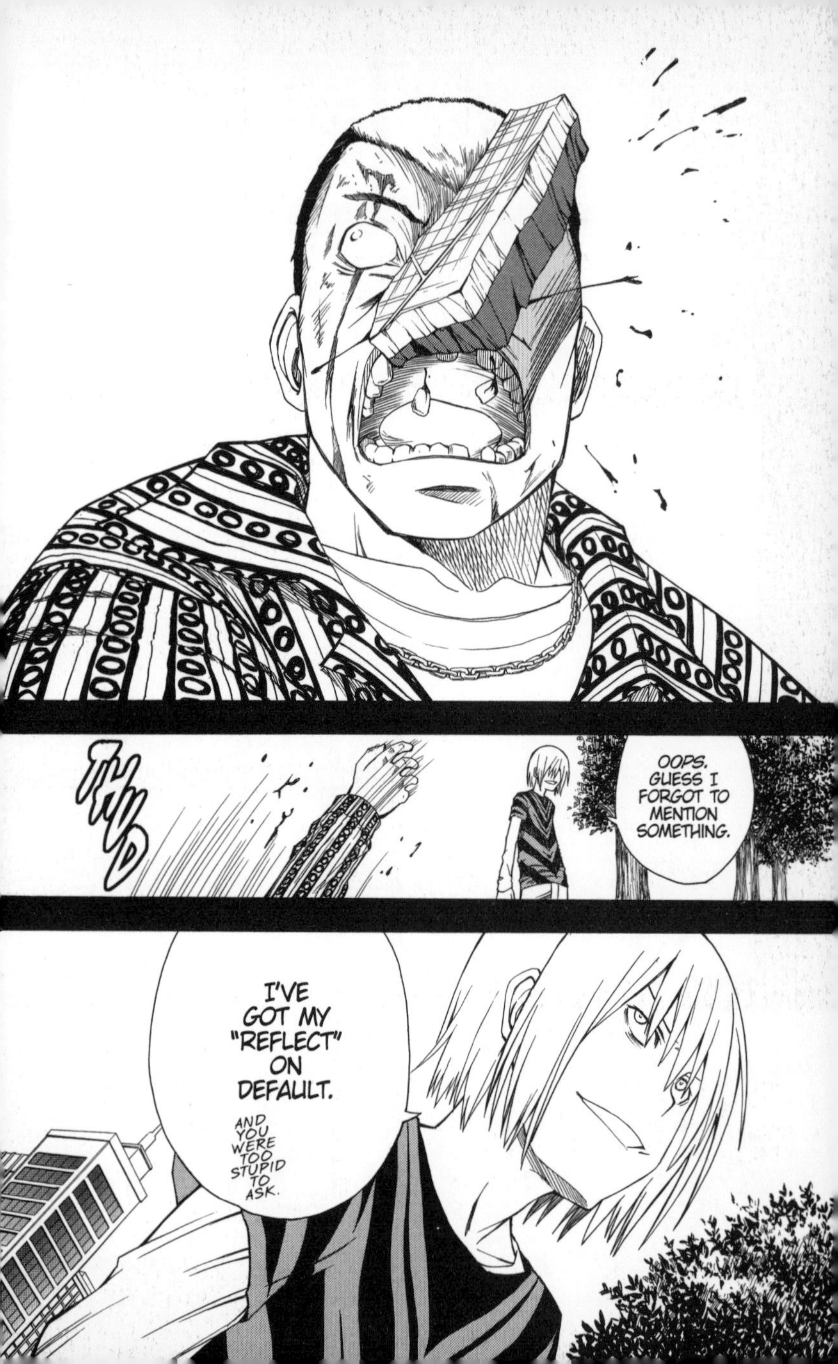
OOPS. GUESS I FORGOT TO MENTION SOMETHING.
I'VE GOT MY "REFLECT" ON DEFAULT.
AND YOU WERE TOO STUPID TO ASK.

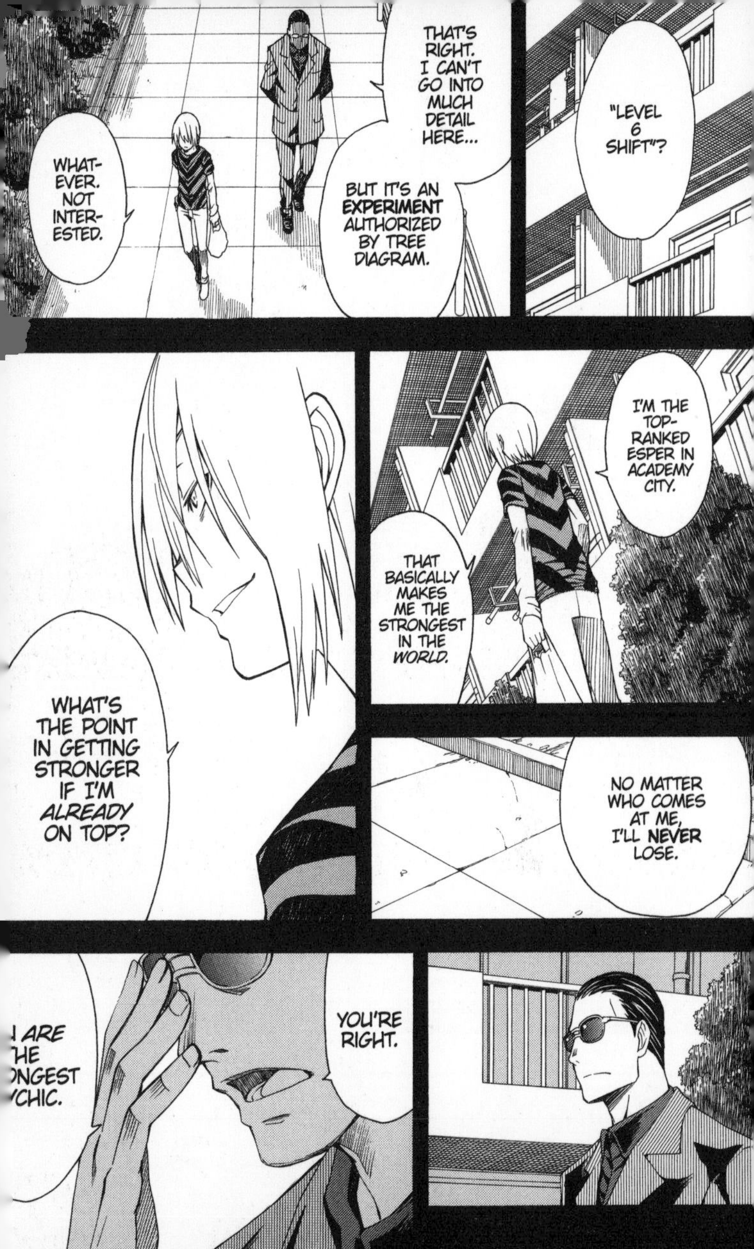
"LEVEL 6 SHIFT"?
THAT'S RIGHT. I CAN'T GO INTO MUCH DETAIL HERE...
BUT IT'S AN **EXPERIMENT** AUTHORIZED BY TREE DIAGRAM.
WHAT-EVER. NOT INTER-ESTED.
I'M THE TOP-RANKED ESPER IN ACADEMY CITY.
THAT BASICALLY MAKES ME THE STRONGEST IN THE *WORLD.*
NO MATTER WHO COMES AT ME, I'LL **NEVER** LOSE.
WHAT'S THE POINT IN GETTING STRONGER IF I'M *ALREADY* ON TOP?
YOU'RE RIGHT.
ARE HE ONGEST YCHIC.

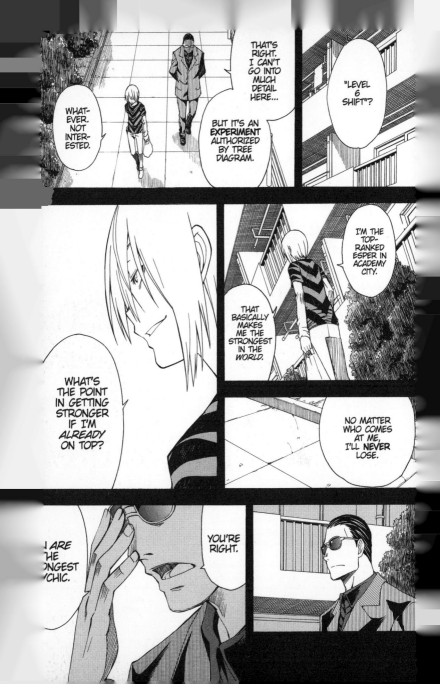

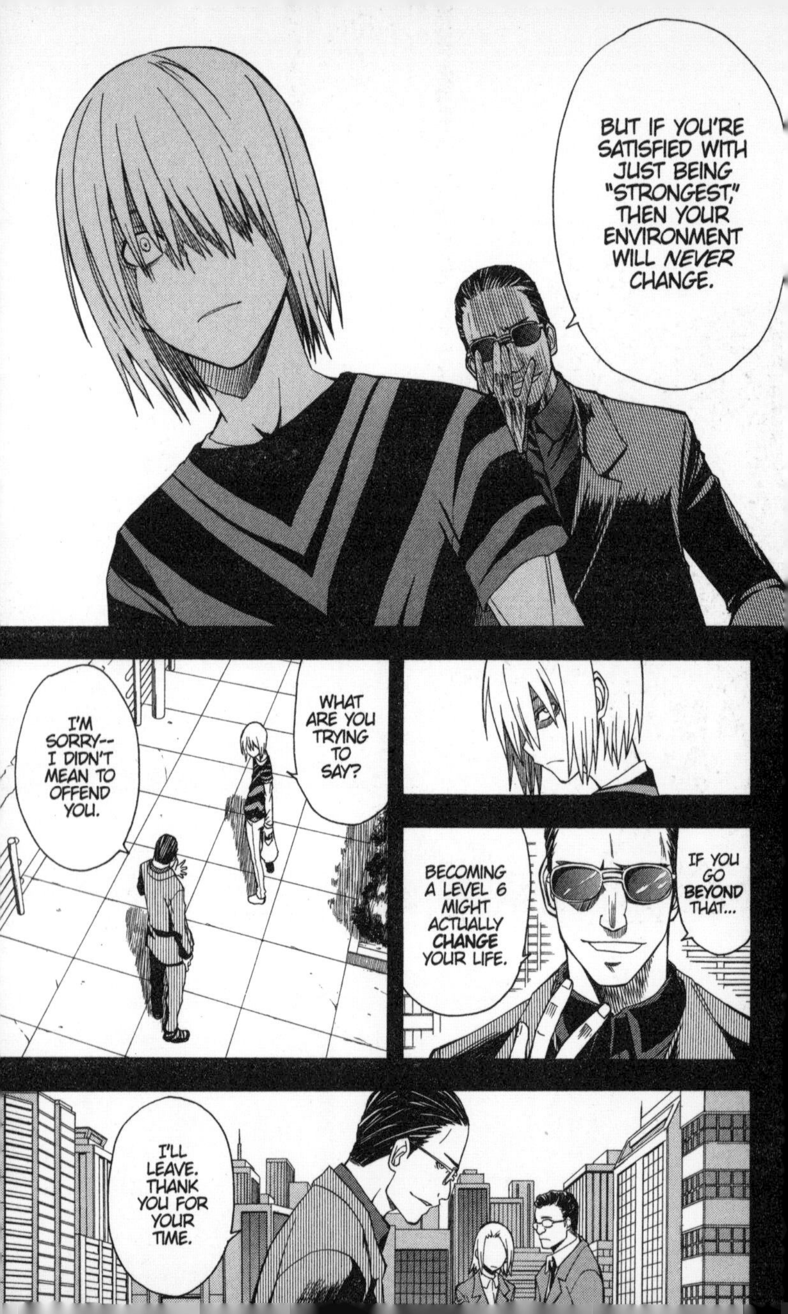
BUT IF YOU'RE SATISFIED WITH JUST BEING "STRONGEST," THEN YOUR ENVIRONMENT WILL NEVER CHANGE.
IF YOU GO BEYOND THAT...
BECOMING A LEVEL 6 MIGHT ACTUALLY CHANGE YOUR LIFE.
WHAT ARE YOU TRYING TO SAY?
I'M SORRY-- I DIDN'T MEAN TO OFFEND YOU.
I'LL LEAVE. THANK YOU FOR YOUR TIME.

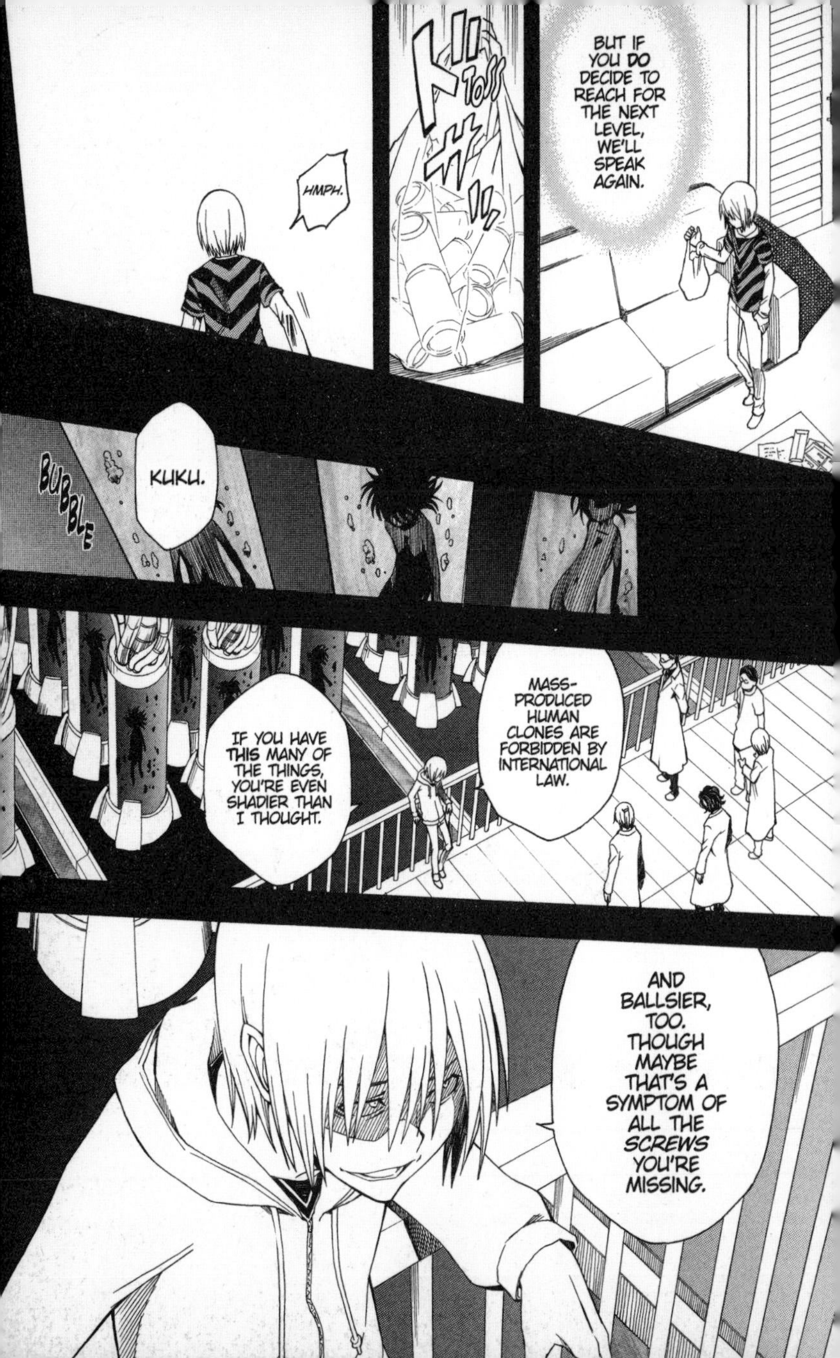
BUT IF YOU DO DECIDE TO REACH FOR THE NEXT LEVEL, WE'LL SPEAK AGAIN.
TOSS
HMPH.
KUKU.
BUBBLE
MASS-PRODUCED HUMAN CLONES ARE FORBIDDEN BY INTERNATIONAL LAW.
IF YOU HAVE THIS MANY OF THE THINGS, YOU'RE EVEN SHADIER THAN I THOUGHT.
AND BALLSIER, TOO. THOUGH MAYBE THAT'S A SYMPTOM OF ALL THE SCREWS YOU'RE MISSING.

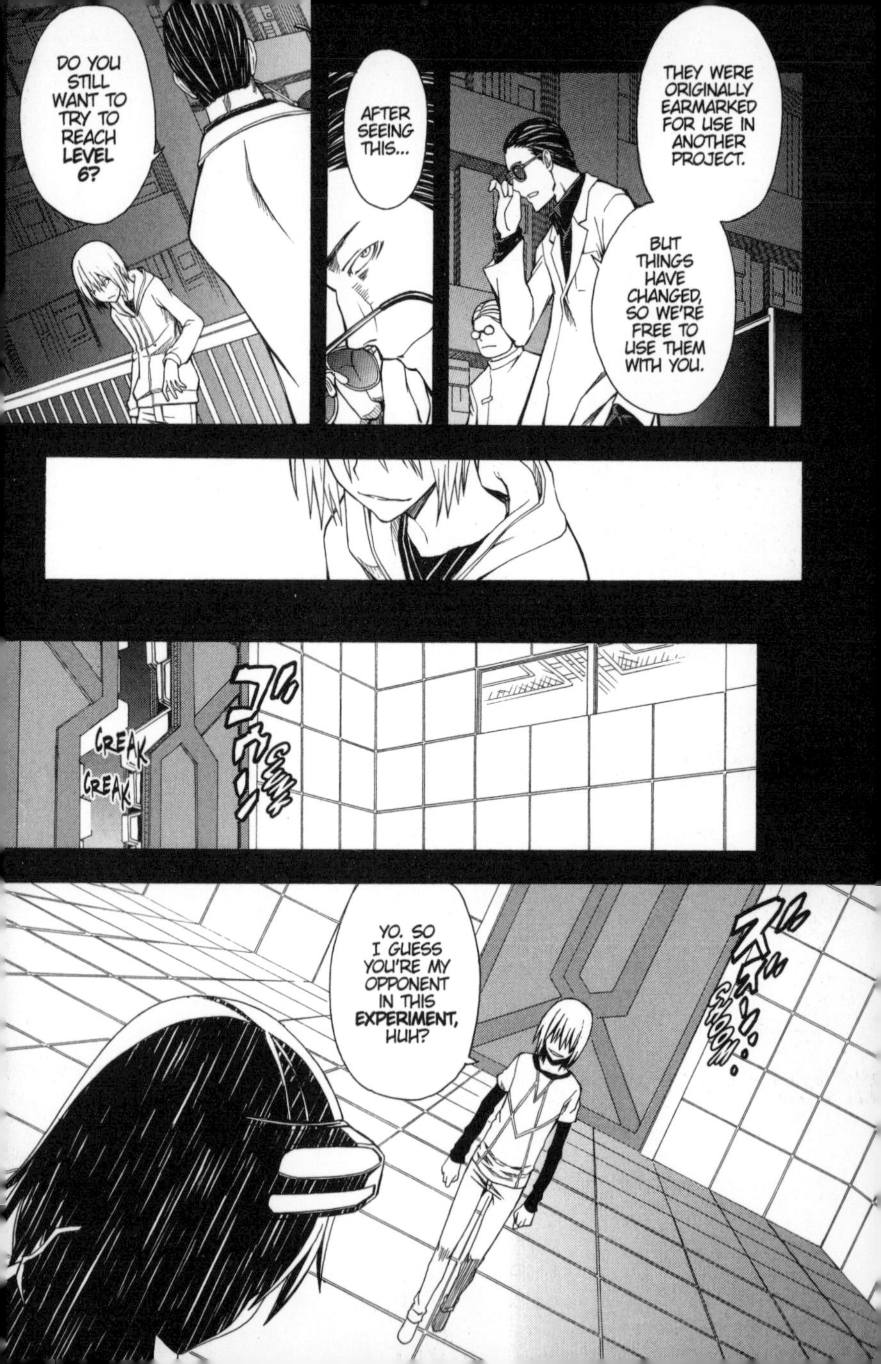
THEY WERE ORIGINALLY EARMARKED FOR USE IN ANOTHER PROJECT.
BUT THINGS HAVE CHANGED, SO WE'RE FREE TO USE THEM WITH YOU.
AFTER SEEING THIS...
DO YOU STILL WANT TO TRY TO REACH LEVEL 6?
CREAK
CREAK
YO. SO I GUESS YOU'RE MY OPPONENT IN THIS EXPERIMENT, HUH?

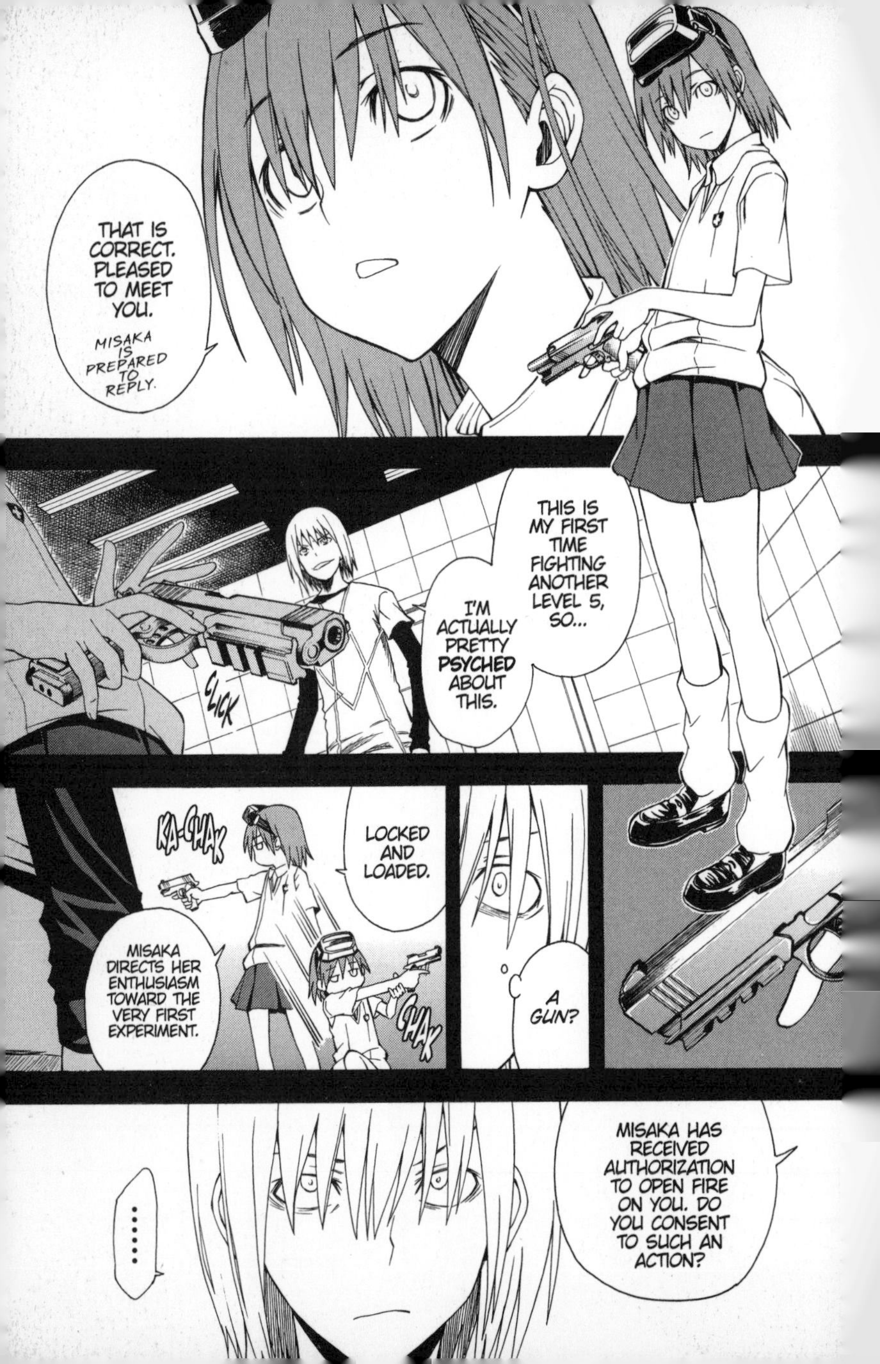
THAT IS CORRECT. PLEASED TO MEET YOU.
MISAKA IS PREPARED TO REPLY.
THIS IS MY FIRST TIME FIGHTING ANOTHER LEVEL 5, SO...
I'M ACTUALLY PRETTY PSYCHED ABOUT THIS.
CLICK
A GUN?
LOCKED AND LOADED.
KA-CHAK
MISAKA DIRECTS HER ENTHUSIASM TOWARD THE VERY FIRST EXPERIMENT.
CHAK
MISAKA HAS RECEIVED AUTHORIZATION TO OPEN FIRE ON YOU. DO YOU CONSENT TO SUCH AN ACTION?
......

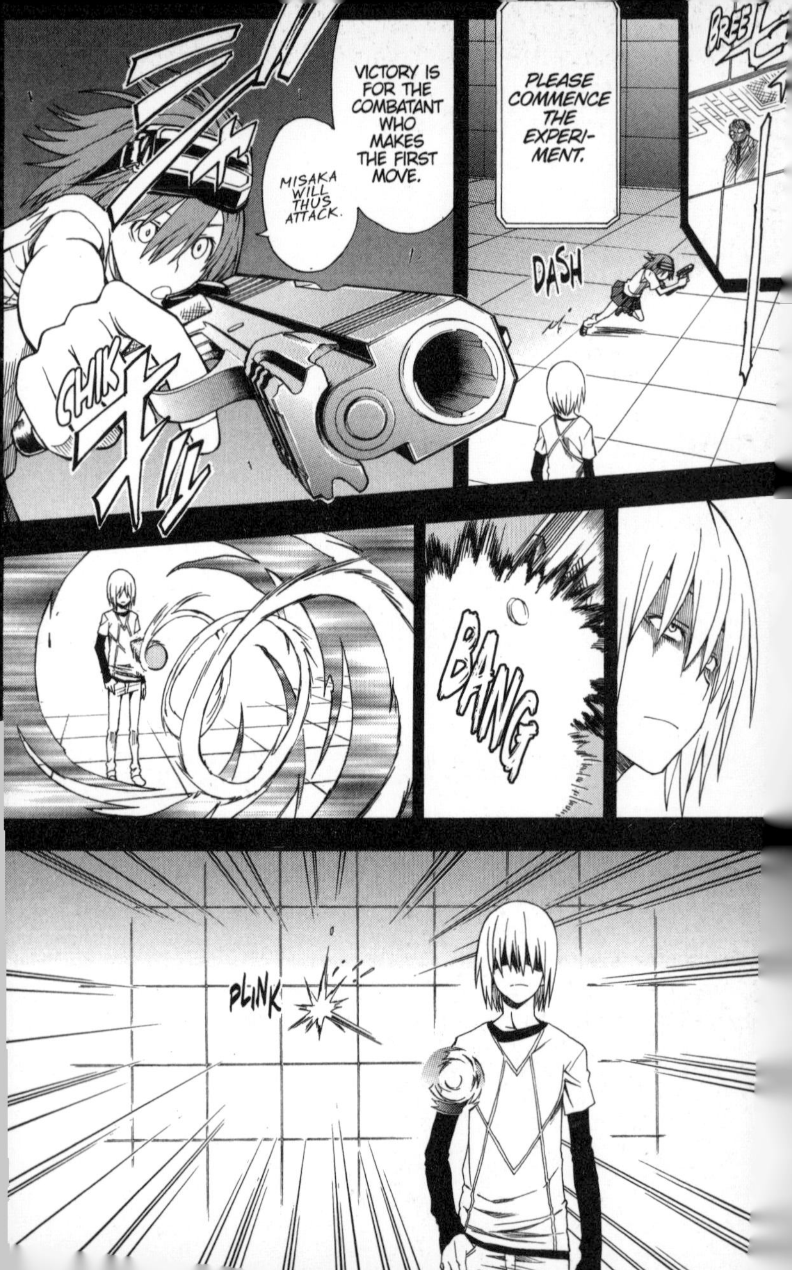
BREE
PLEASE COMMENCE THE EXPERIMENT.
DASH
VICTORY IS FOR THE COMBATANT WHO MAKES THE FIRST MOVE.
MISAKA WILL THUS ATTACK.
CHIK
BANG
PLINK

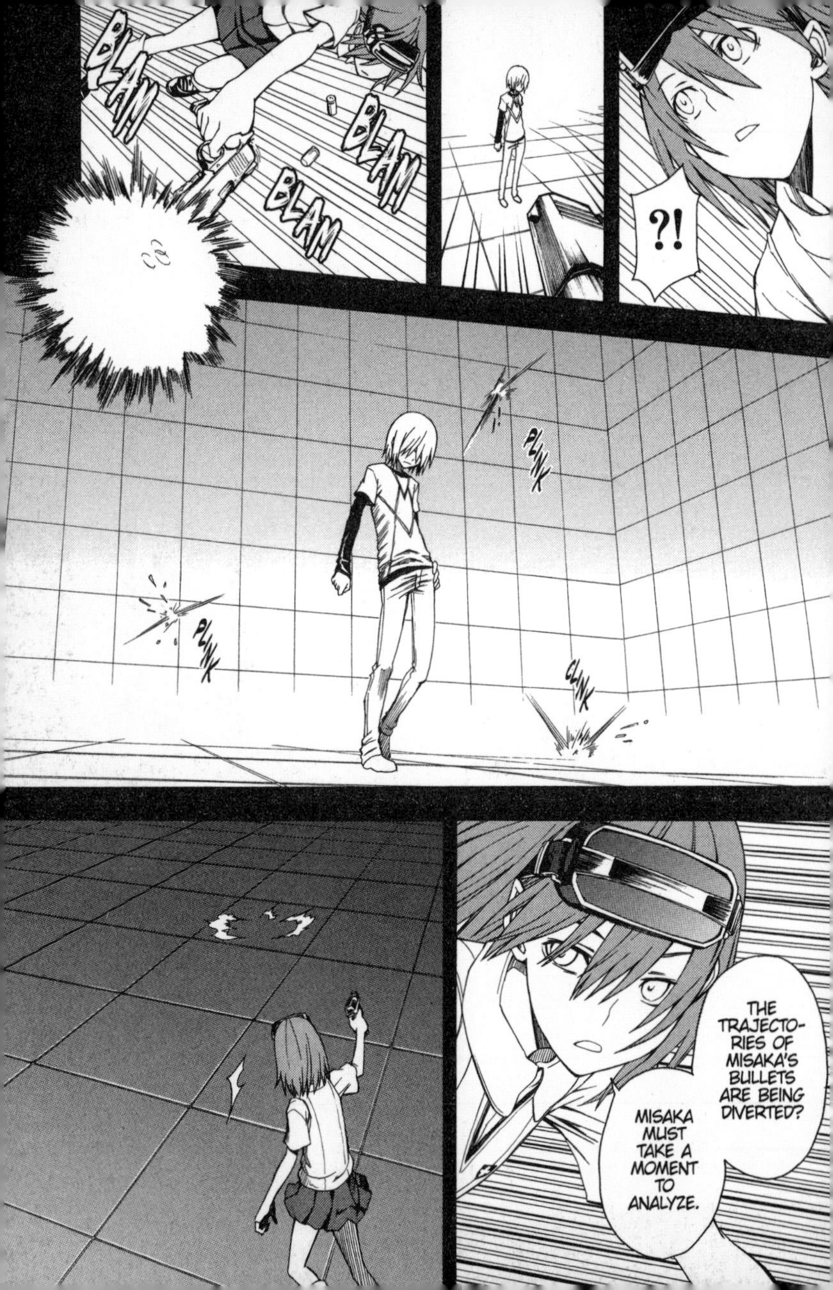
?!
BLAM
BLAM
BLAM
BLAM
PLINK
PLINK
CLINK
THE TRAJECTORIES OF MISAKA'S BULLETS ARE BEING DIVERTED?
MISAKA MUST TAKE A MOMENT TO ANALYZE.

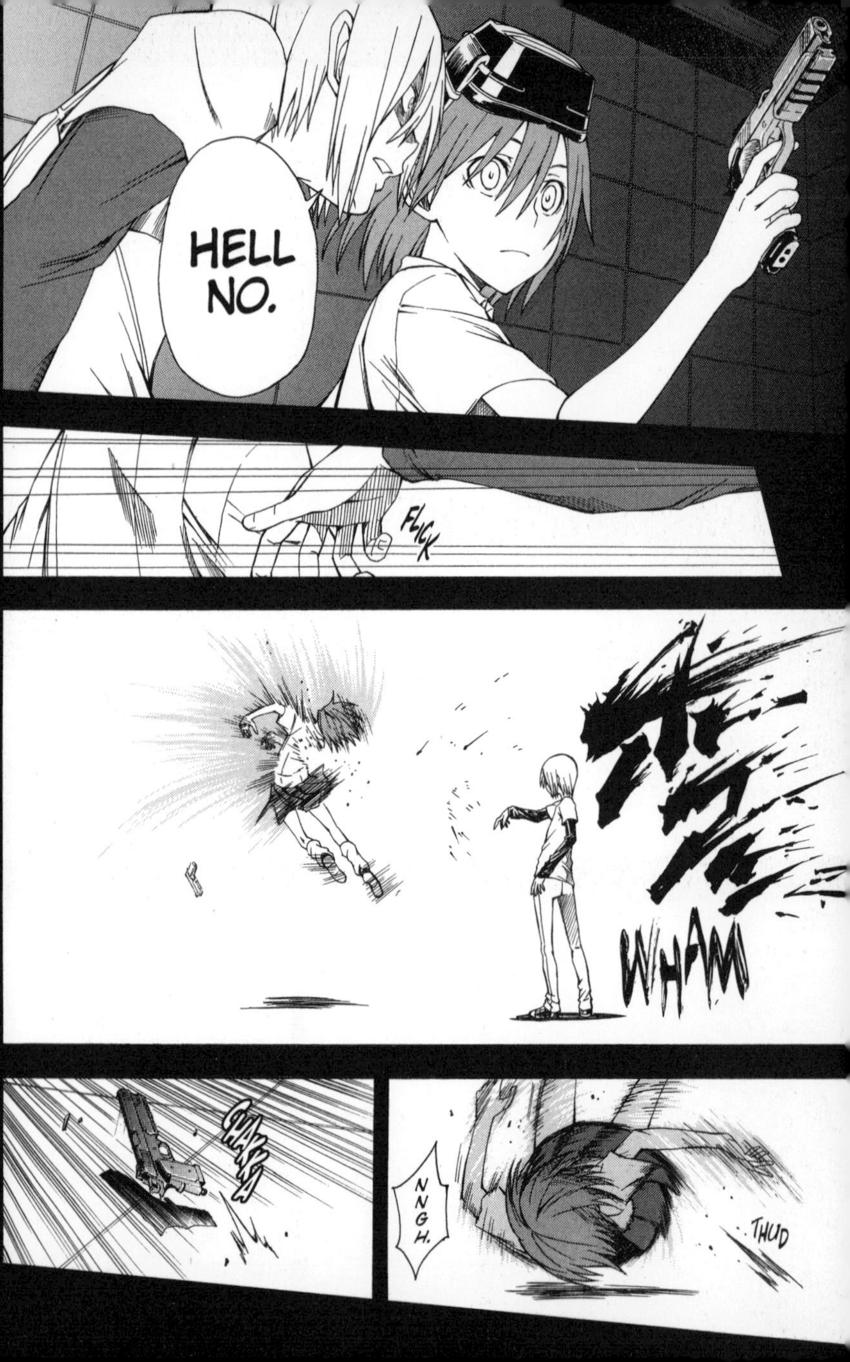
HELL NO.
FLICK
WHAM
NNGH.
THUD
CHAKA

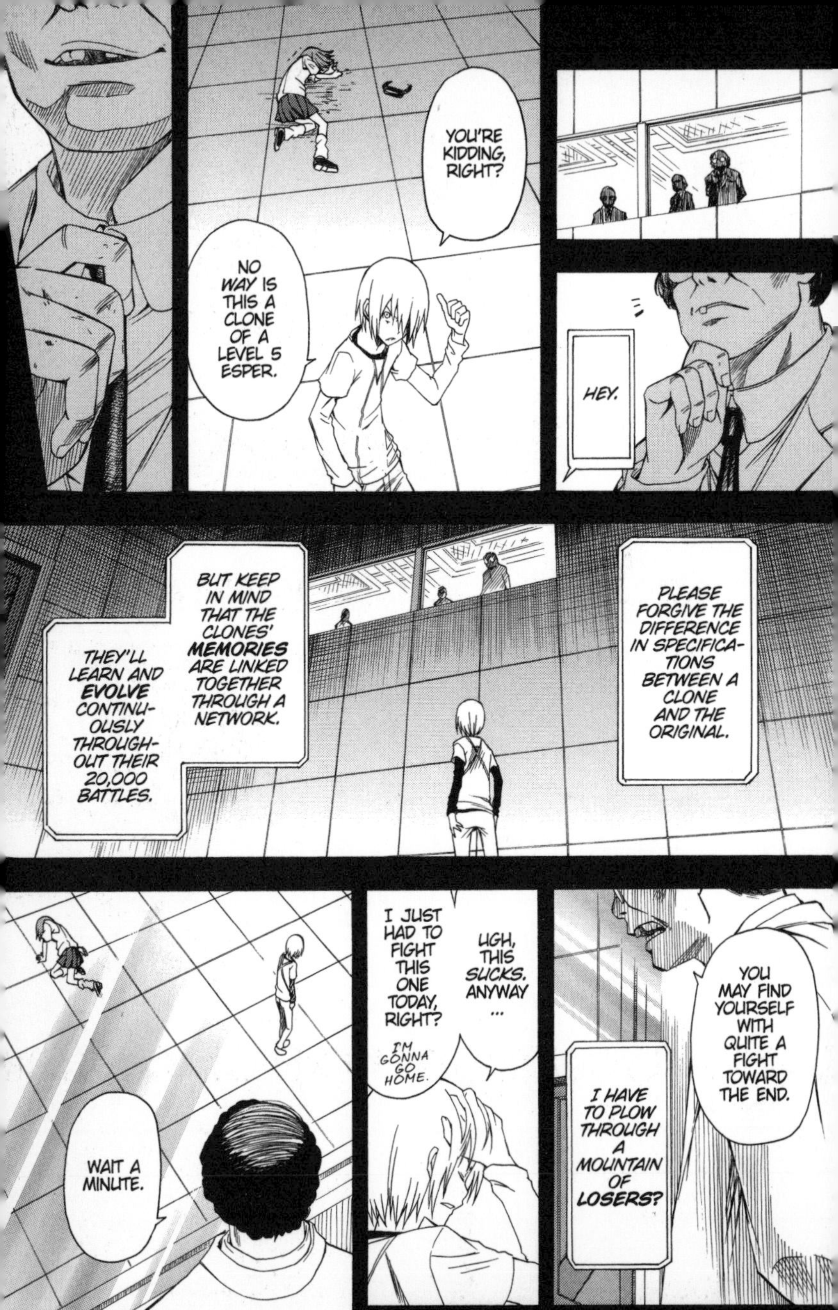
HEY.
YOU'RE KIDDING, RIGHT?
NO WAY IS THIS A CLONE OF A LEVEL 5 ESPER.
PLEASE FORGIVE THE DIFFERENCE IN SPECIFICATIONS BETWEEN A CLONE AND THE ORIGINAL.
BUT KEEP IN MIND THAT THE CLONES' **MEMORIES** ARE LINKED TOGETHER THROUGH A NETWORK.
THEY'LL LEARN AND **EVOLVE** CONTINUOUSLY THROUGHOUT THEIR 20,000 BATTLES.
YOU MAY FIND YOURSELF WITH QUITE A FIGHT TOWARD THE END.
I HAVE TO PLOW THROUGH A MOUNTAIN OF **LOSERS?**
UGH, THIS SUCKS. ANYWAY...
I JUST HAD TO FIGHT THIS ONE TODAY, RIGHT?
I'M GONNA GO HOME.
WAIT A MINUTE.

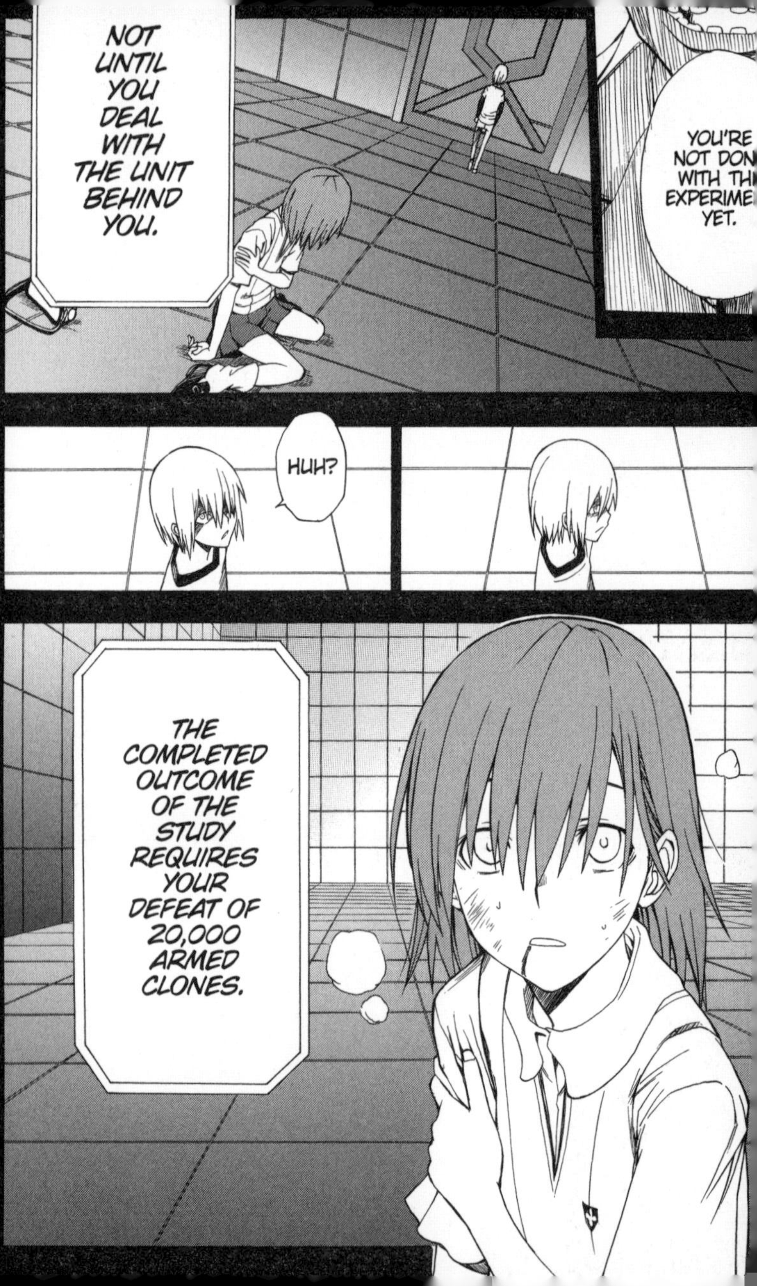
YOU'RE NOT DON WITH TH EXPERIME YET.
NOT UNTIL YOU DEAL WITH THE UNIT BEHIND YOU.
HUH?
THE COMPLETED OUTCOME OF THE STUDY REQUIRES YOUR DEFEAT OF 20,000 ARMED CLONES.

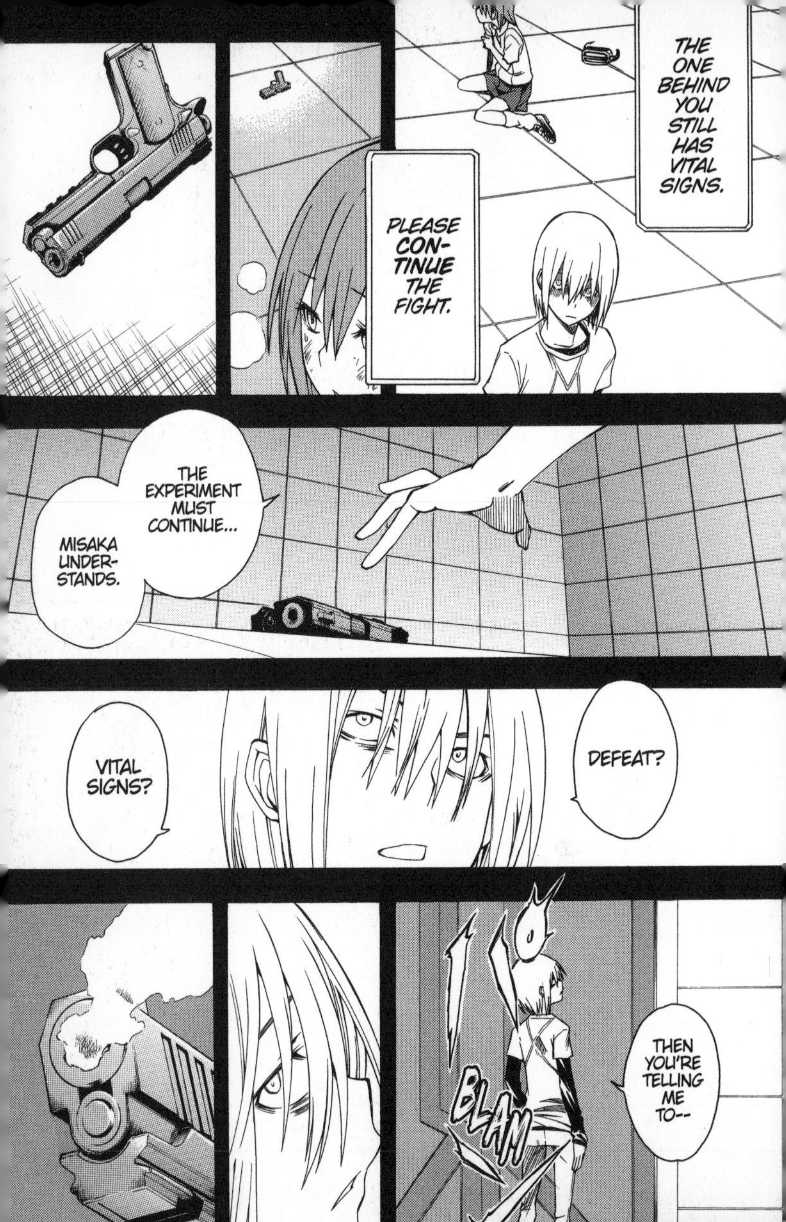
THE ONE BEHIND YOU STILL HAS VITAL SIGNS.
PLEASE CON-TINUE THE FIGHT.
THE EXPERIMENT MUST CONTINUE...
MISAKA UNDER-STANDS.
DEFEAT?
VITAL SIGNS?
THEN YOU'RE TELLING ME TO--
BLAM

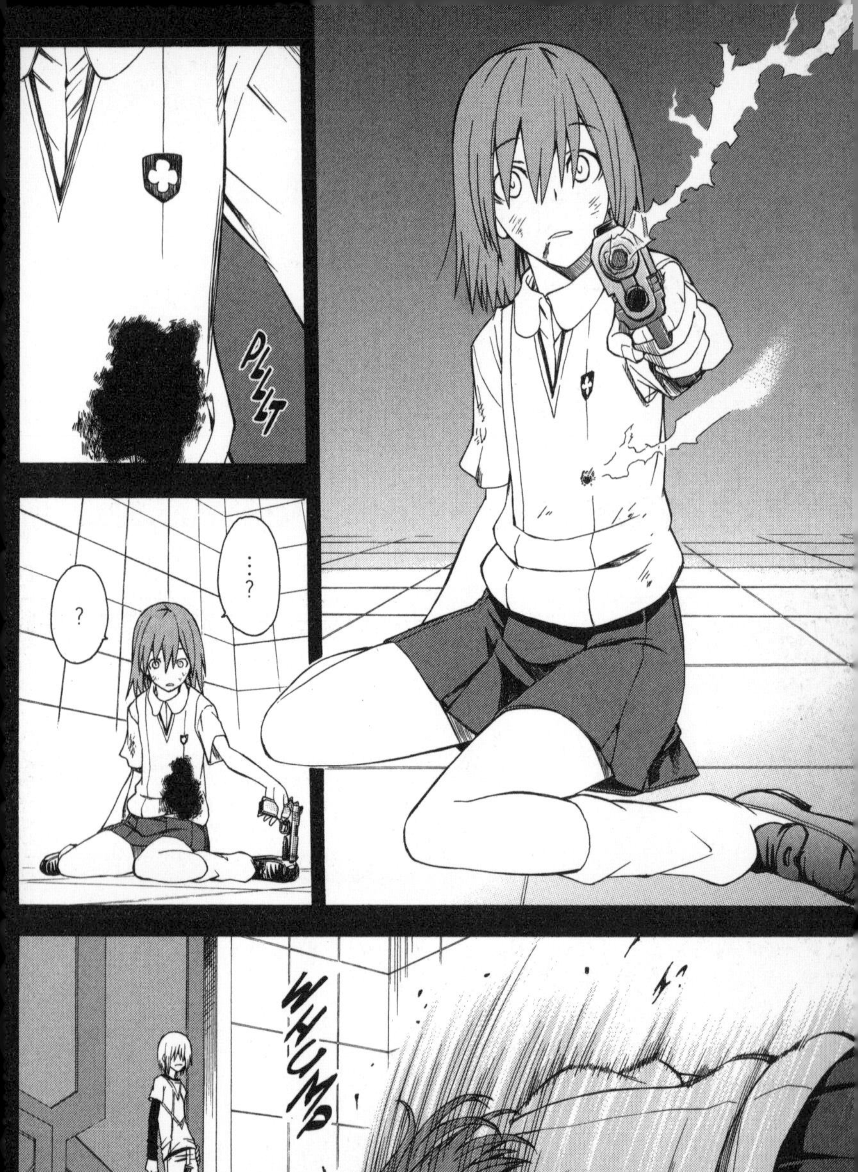
PLLT
...?
?
WHUMP

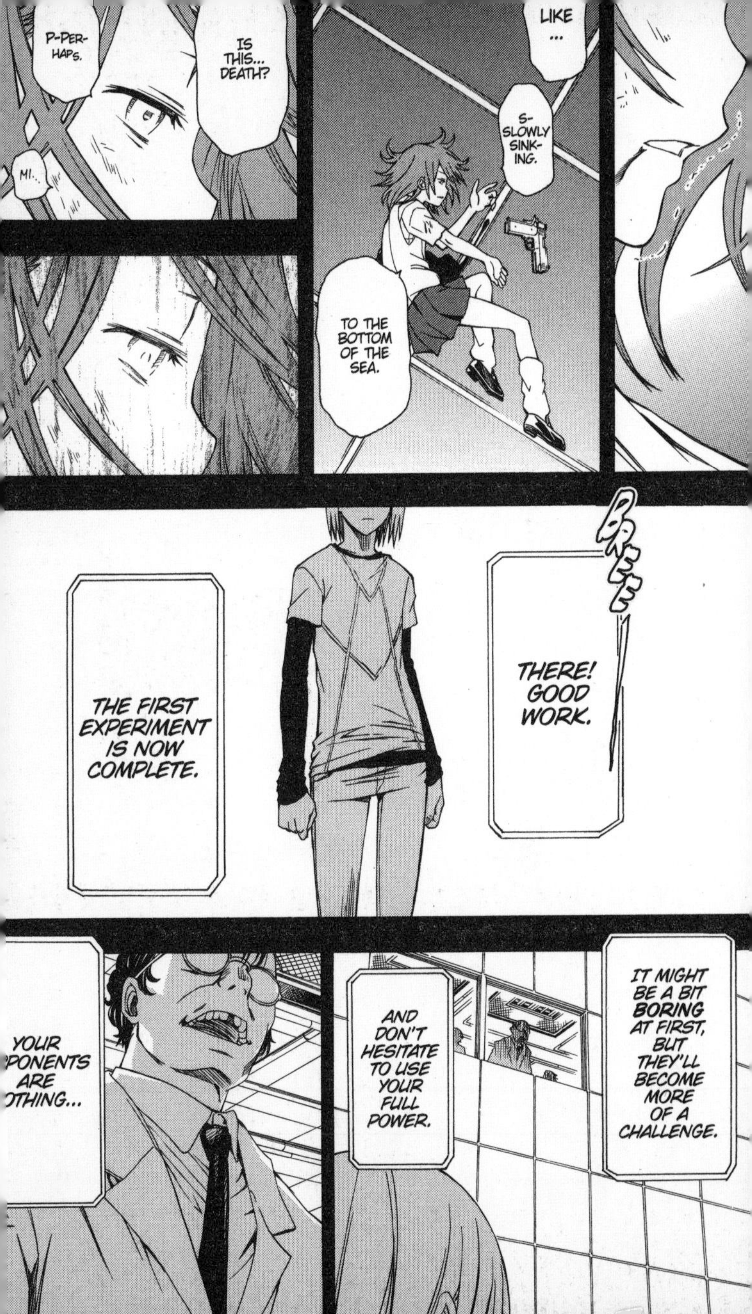
LIKE...
S-SLOWLY SINKING.
TO THE BOTTOM OF THE SEA.
IS THIS... DEATH?
P-PER-HAPS.
MI...
BREEE
THERE! GOOD WORK.
THE FIRST EXPERIMENT IS NOW COMPLETE.
IT MIGHT BE A BIT BORING AT FIRST, BUT THEY'LL BECOME MORE OF A CHALLENGE.
AND DON'T HESITATE TO USE YOUR FULL POWER.
YOUR PPONENTS ARE OTHING...

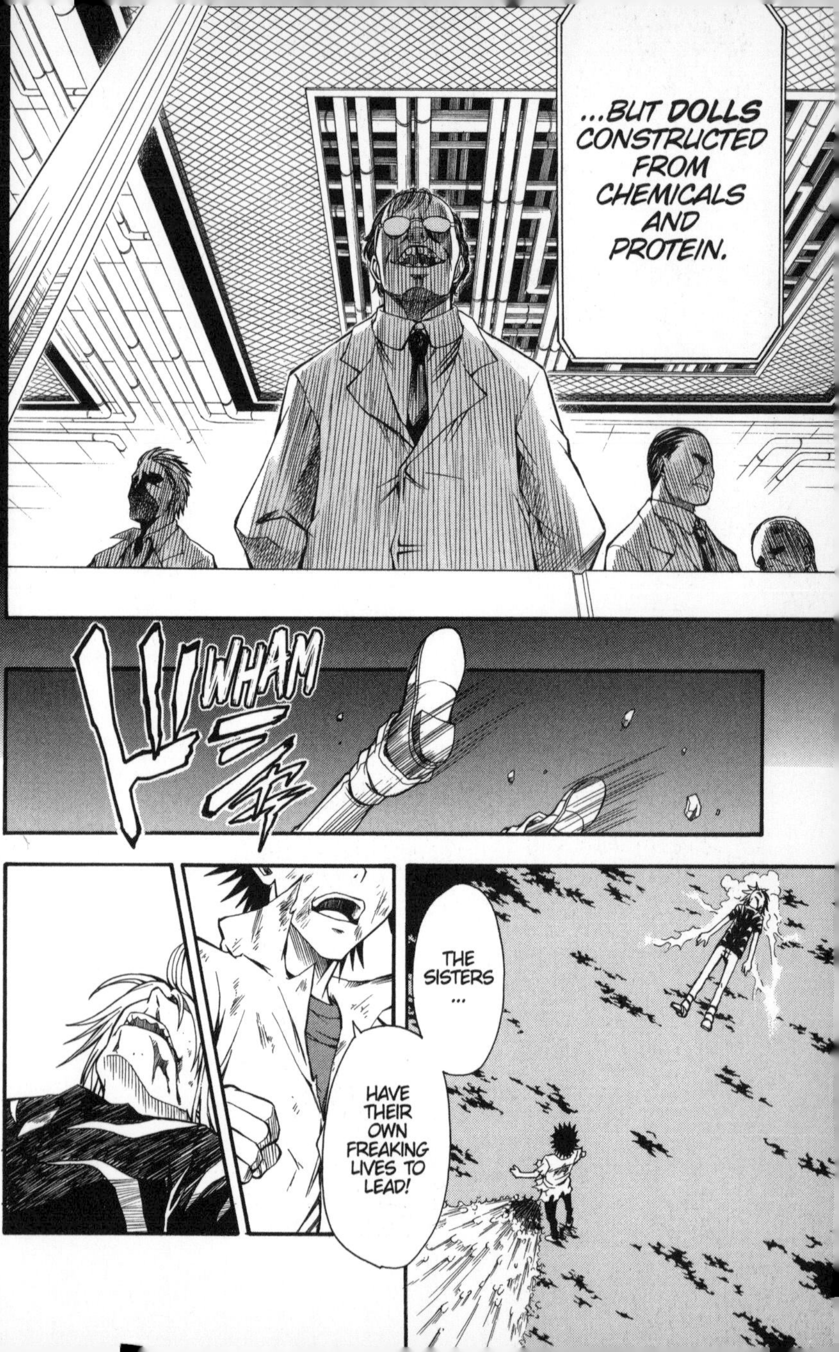
...BUT DOLLS CONSTRUCTED FROM CHEMICALS AND PROTEIN.
WHAM
THE SISTERS...
HAVE THEIR OWN FREAKING LIVES TO LEAD!

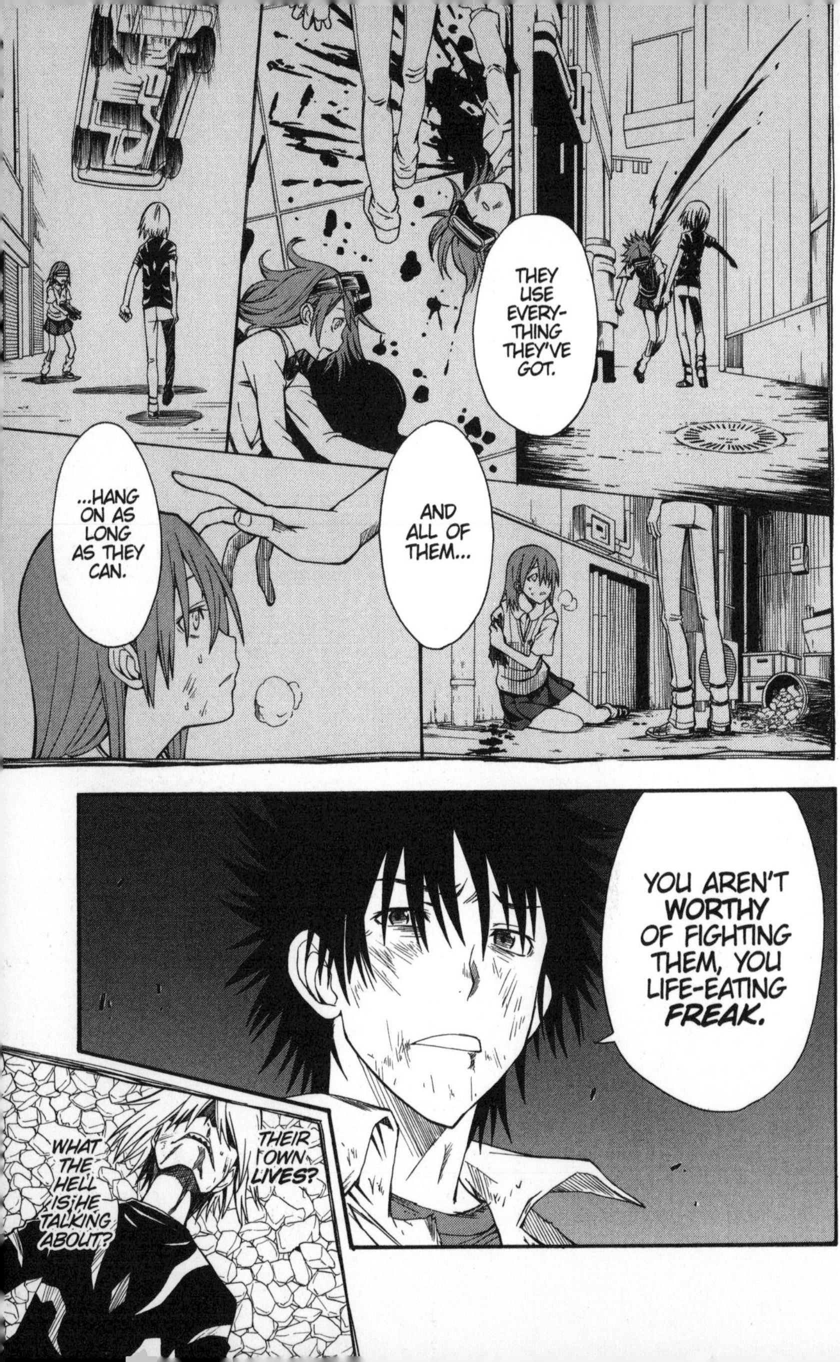
THEY USE EVERYTHING THEY'VE GOT.
AND ALL OF THEM...
...HANG ON AS LONG AS THEY CAN.
YOU AREN'T WORTHY OF FIGHTING THEM, YOU LIFE-EATING *FREAK.*
THEIR OWN LIVES?
WHAT THE HELL IS HE TALKING ABOUT?

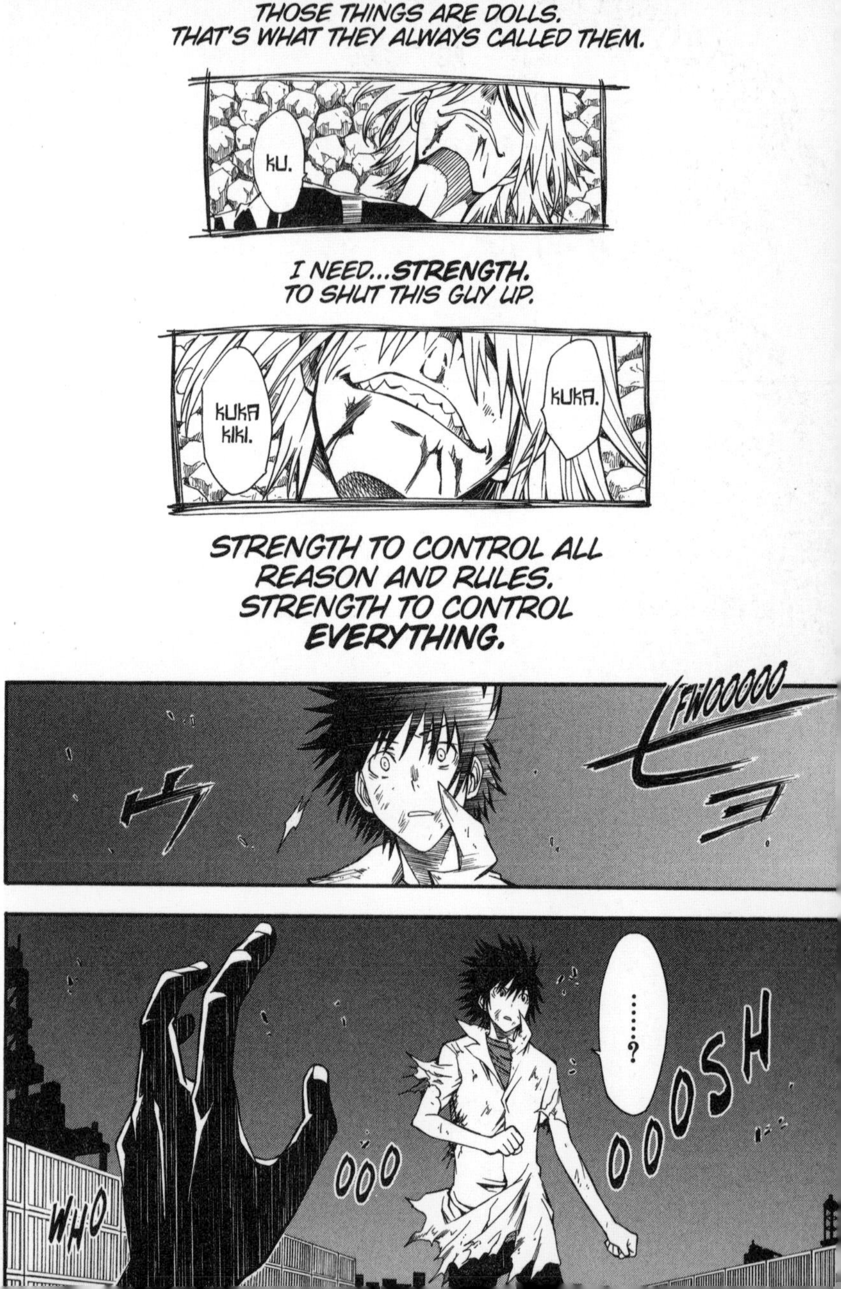
THOSE THINGS ARE DOLLS.
THAT'S WHAT THEY ALWAYS CALLED THEM.
KU.
I NEED...STRENGTH.
TO SHUT THIS GUY UP.
KUKA.
KUKA KIKI.
STRENGTH TO CONTROL ALL REASON AND RULES. STRENGTH TO CONTROL EVERYTHING.
FWOOOOO
......?
OOOSH
OOO
WHO

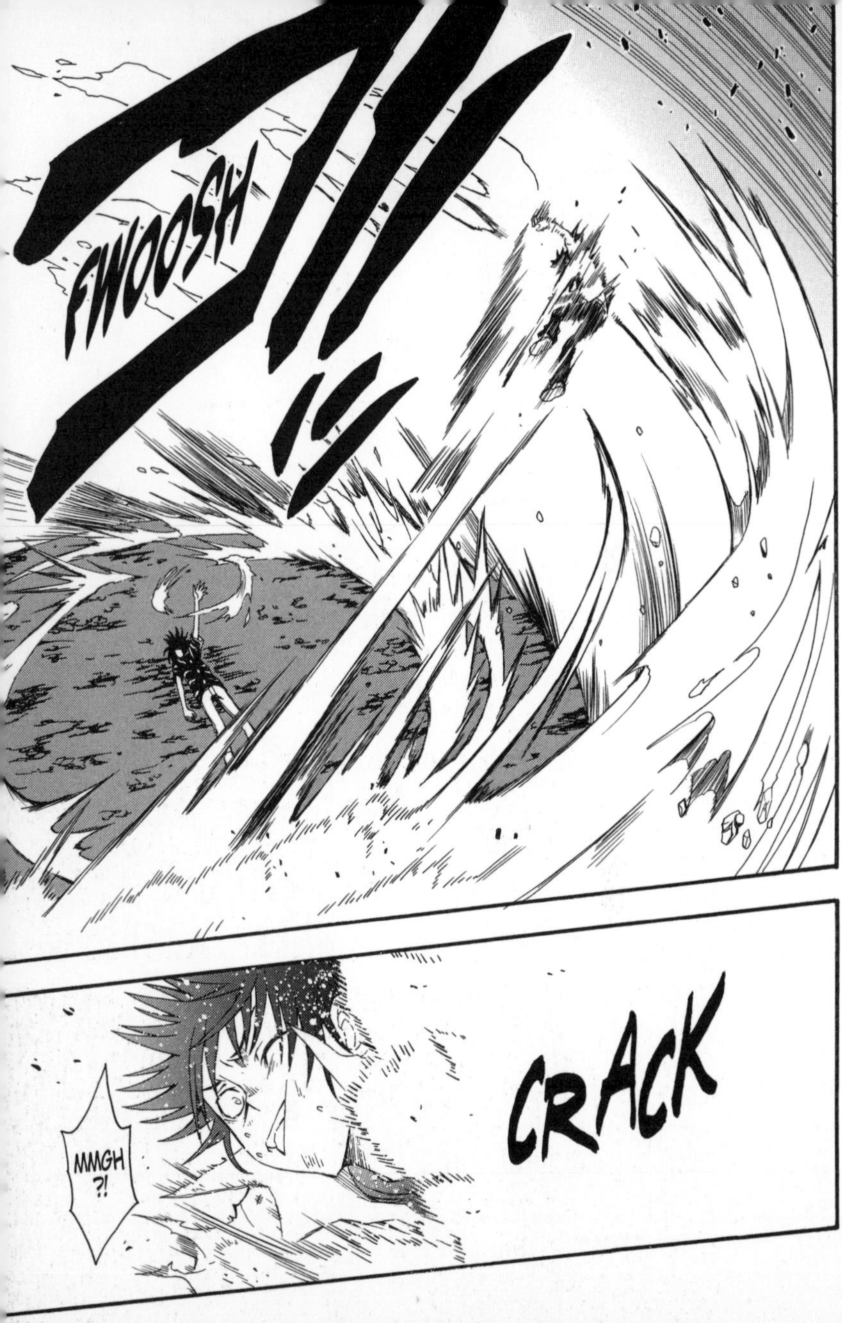
FWOOSH
CRACK
MMGH ?!

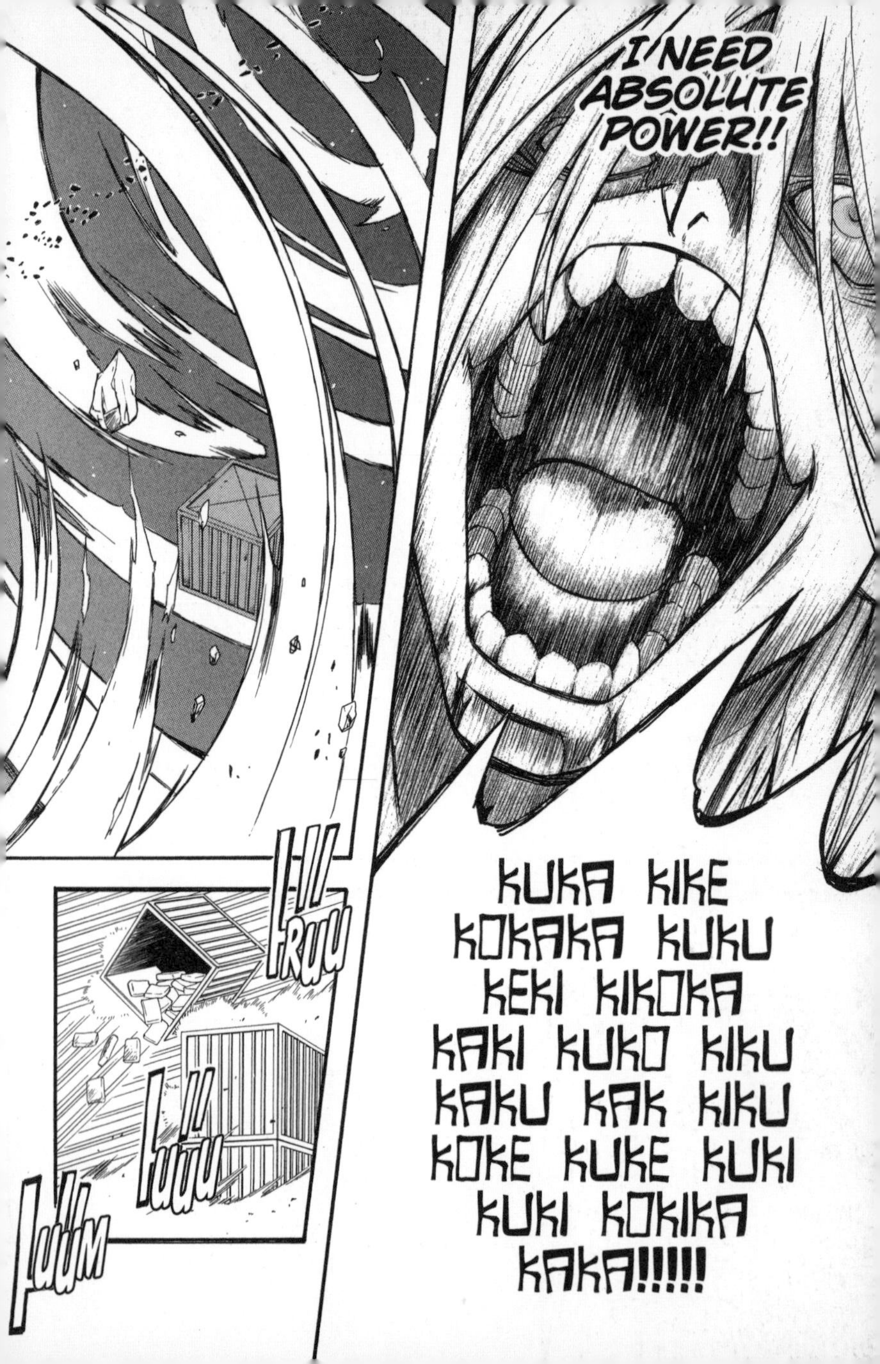
I NEED ABSOLUTE POWER!!
KUKA KIKE KOKAKA KUKU KEKI KIKOKA KAKI KUKO KIKU KAKU KAK KIKU KOKE KUKE KUKI KUKI KOKIKA KAKA!!!!!
FRUU
FUUU
FUUM

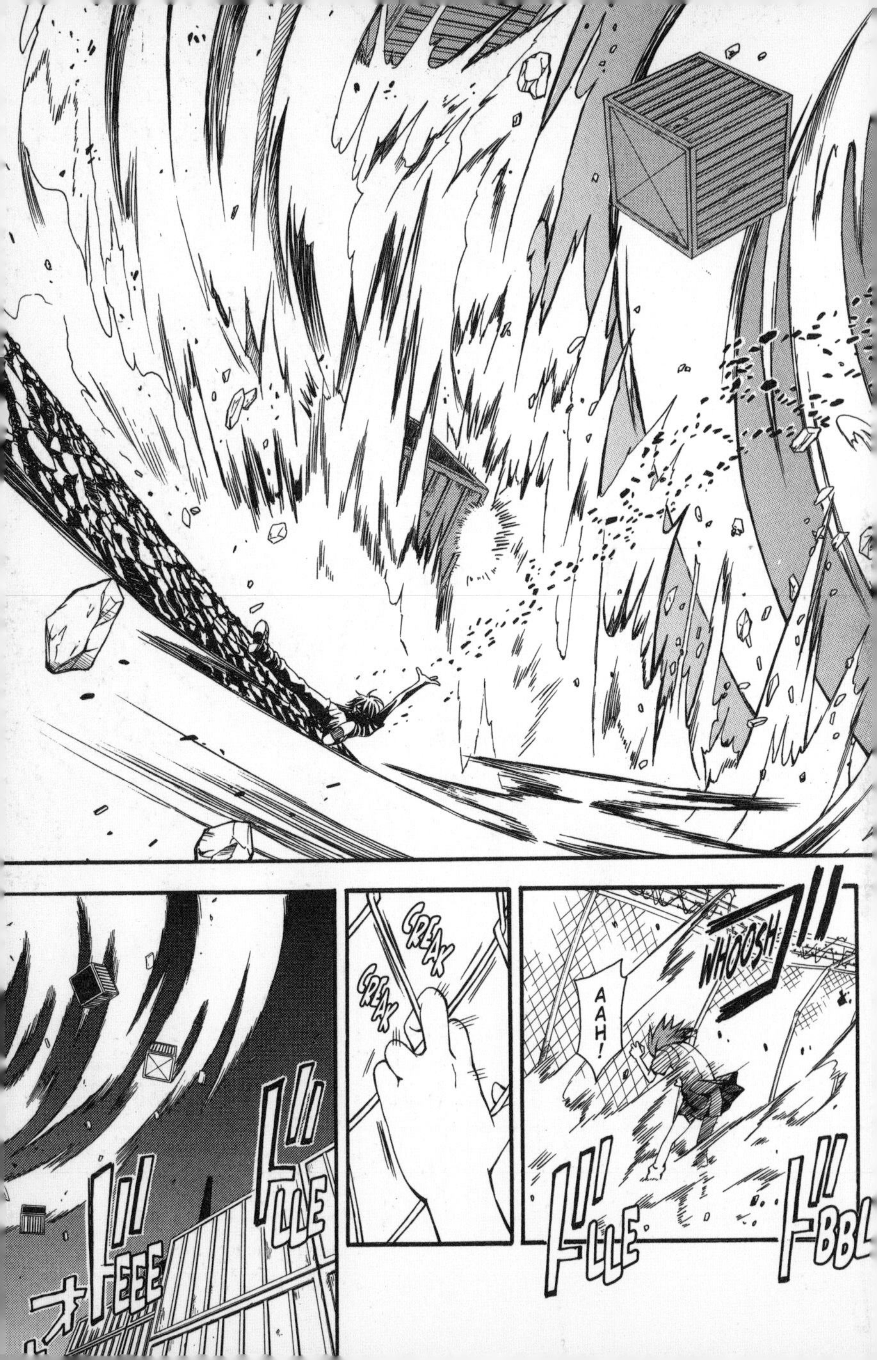
WHOOSH!!
AAH!
CREAK
CREAK

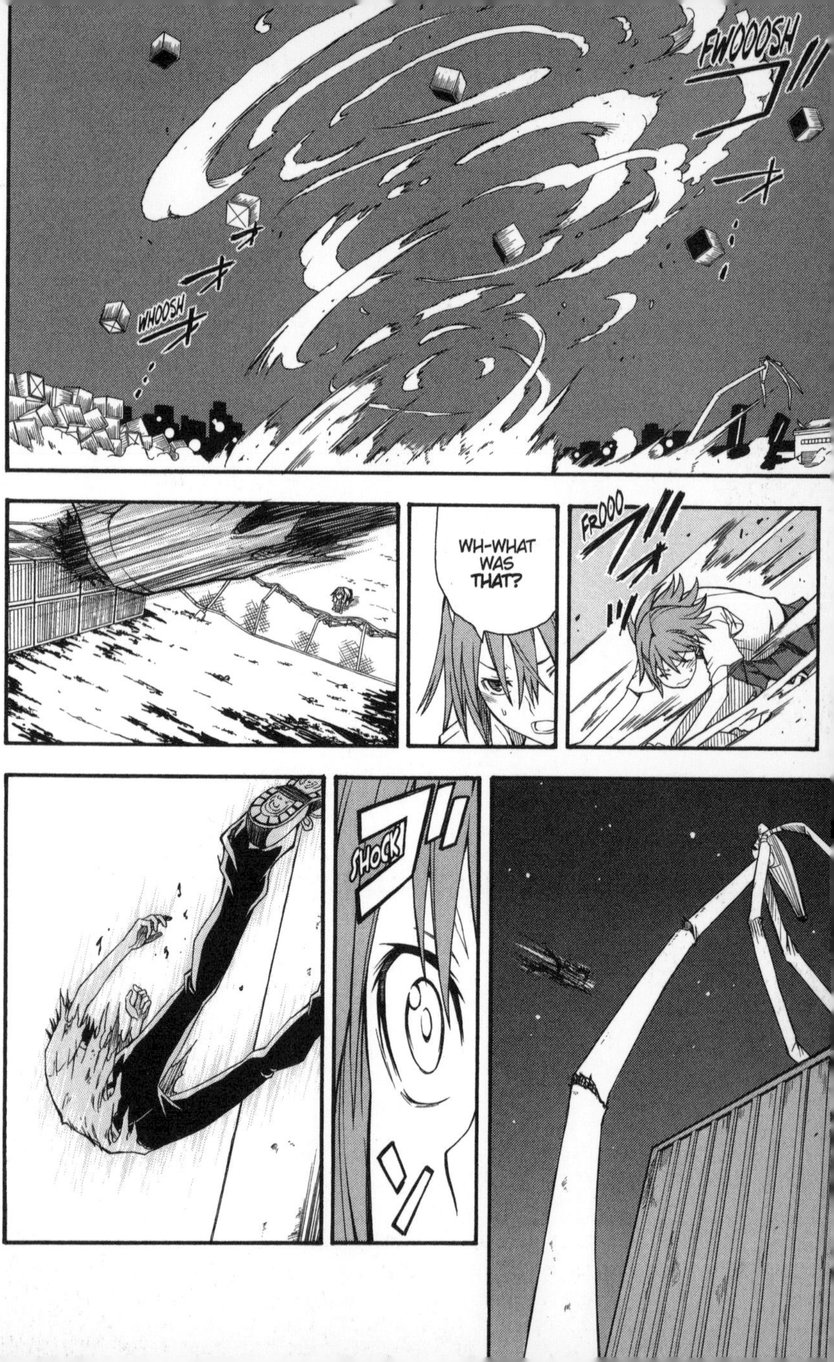
FWOOOSH
WHOOSH
FROOO
WH-WHAT WAS THAT?
SHOCK

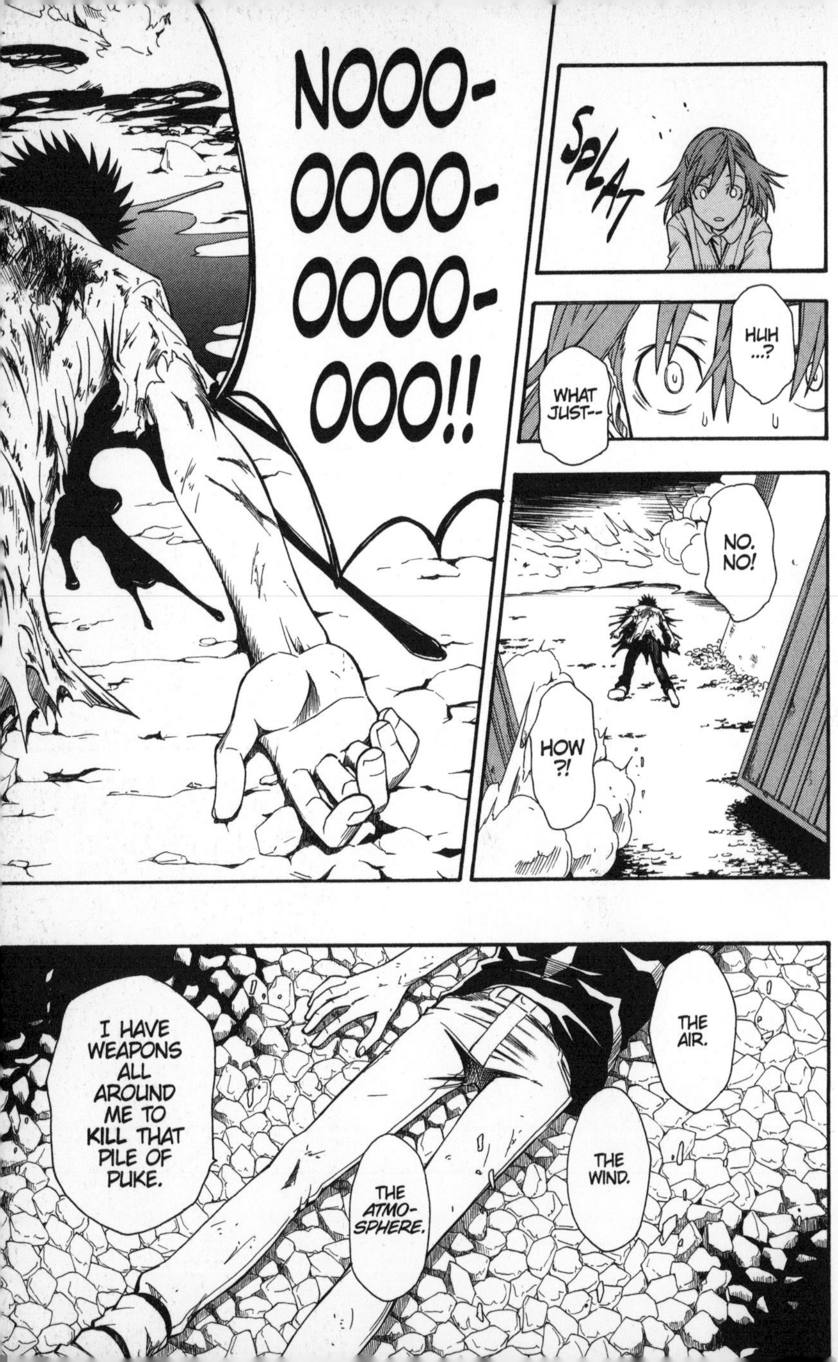
SPLAT
HUH ...?
WHAT JUST--
NO. NO!
HOW ?!
NOOOO-OOOO-OOOO-OOO!!
THE AIR.
THE WIND.
THE ATMO-SPHERE.
I HAVE WEAPONS ALL AROUND ME TO KILL THAT PILE OF PUKE.

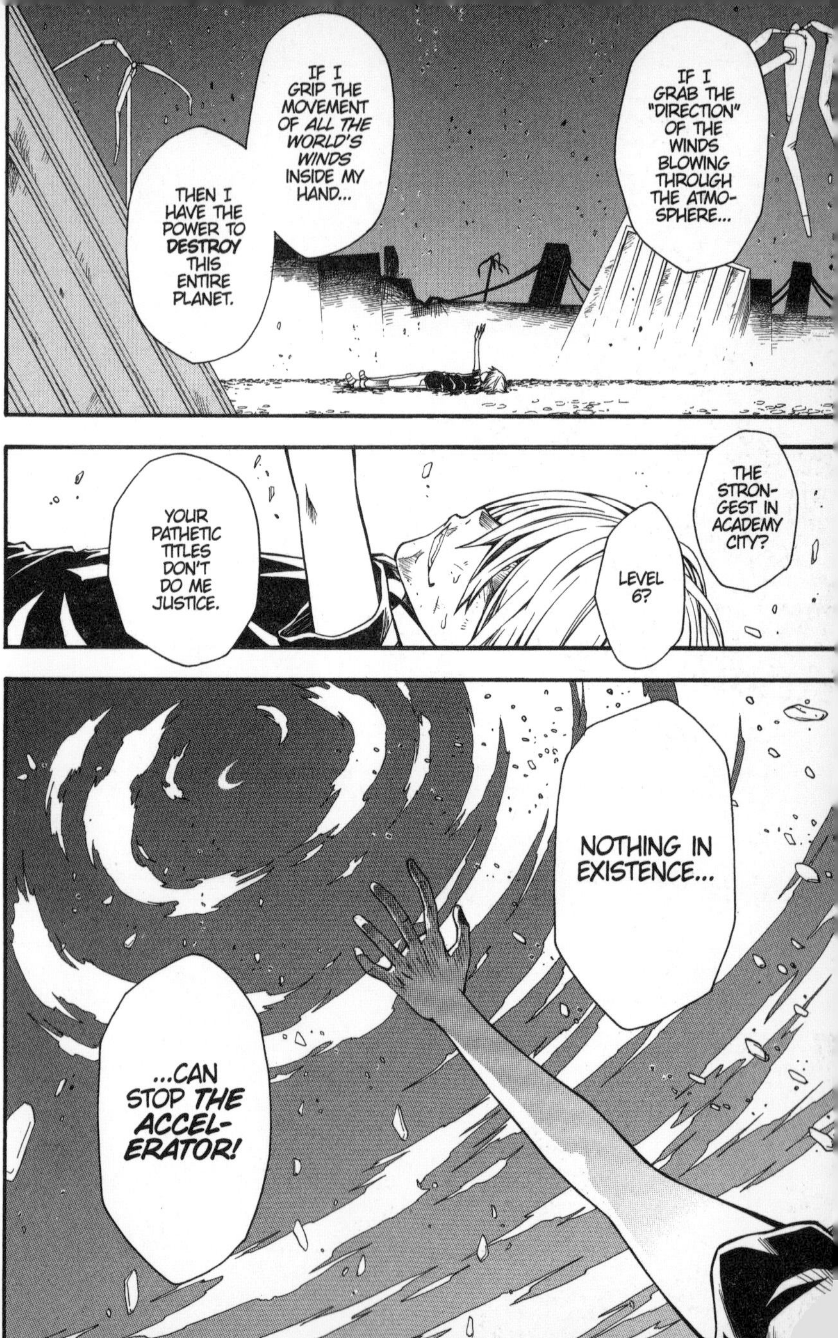
IF I GRAB THE "DIRECTION" OF THE WINDS BLOWING THROUGH THE ATMO-SPHERE...
IF I GRIP THE MOVEMENT OF *ALL THE WORLD'S WINDS* INSIDE MY HAND...
THEN I HAVE THE POWER TO **DESTROY** THIS ENTIRE PLANET.
THE STRON-GEST IN ACADEMY CITY?
LEVEL 6?
YOUR PATHETIC TITLES DON'T DO ME JUSTICE.
NOTHING IN EXISTENCE...
...CAN STOP ***THE ACCEL-ERATOR!***

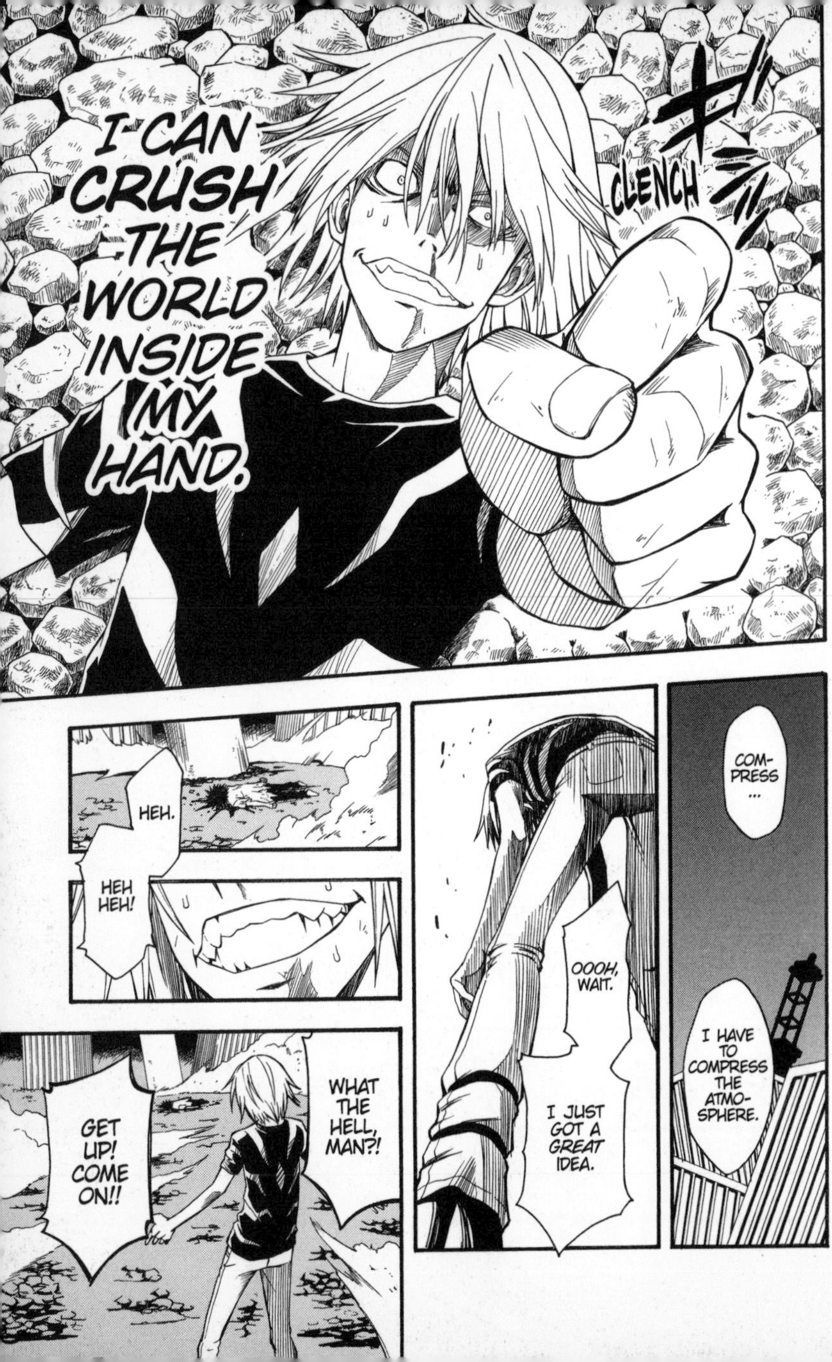
CLENCH
I CAN CRUSH THE WORLD INSIDE MY HAND.
COM-PRESS ...
I HAVE TO COMPRESS THE ATMO-SPHERE.
OOOH, WAIT.
I JUST GOT A GREAT IDEA.
HEH.
HEH HEH!
WHAT THE HELL, MAN?!
GET UP! COME ON!!

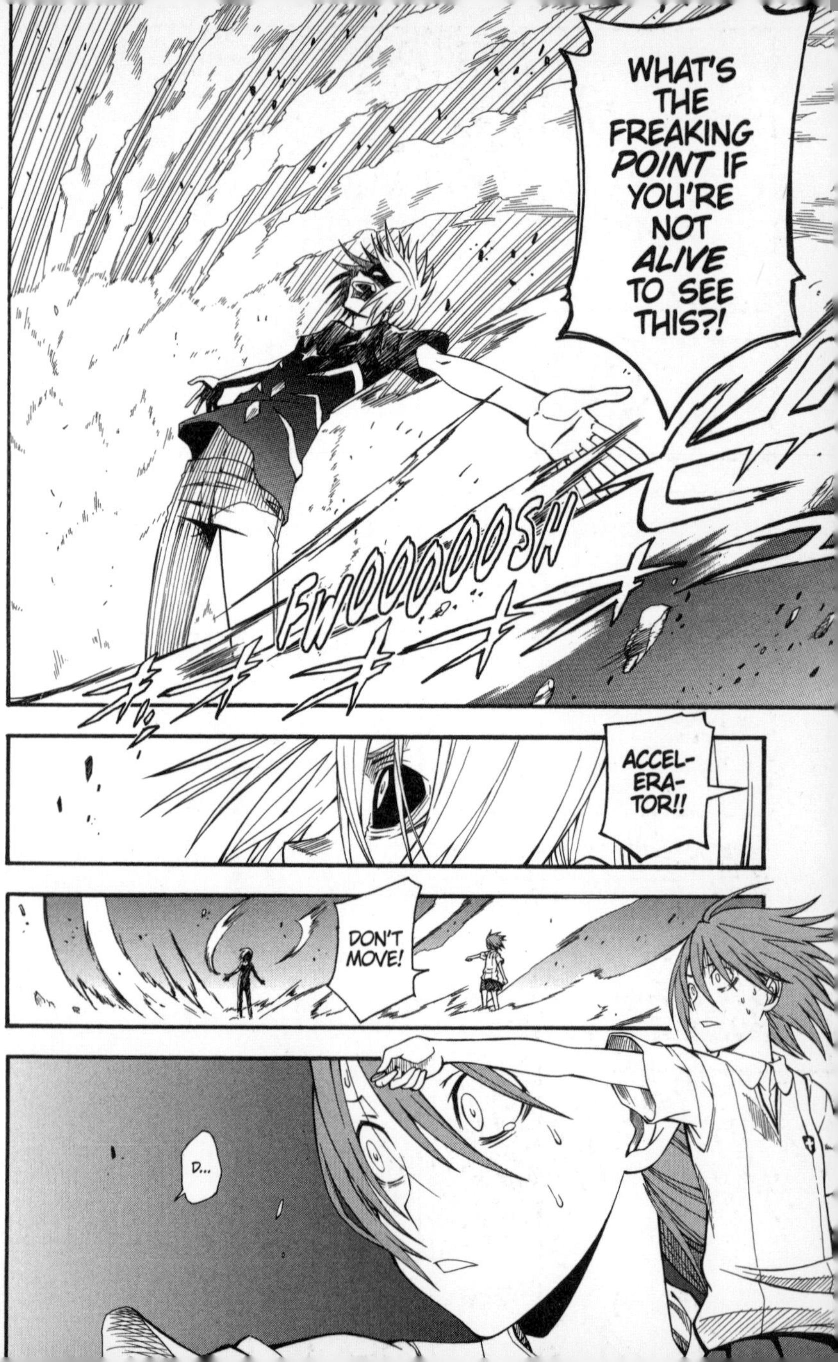
WHAT'S THE FREAKING *POINT* IF YOU'RE NOT *ALIVE* TO SEE THIS?!
FWOOOOOOSH
ACCEL-ERA-TOR!!
DON'T MOVE!
D...

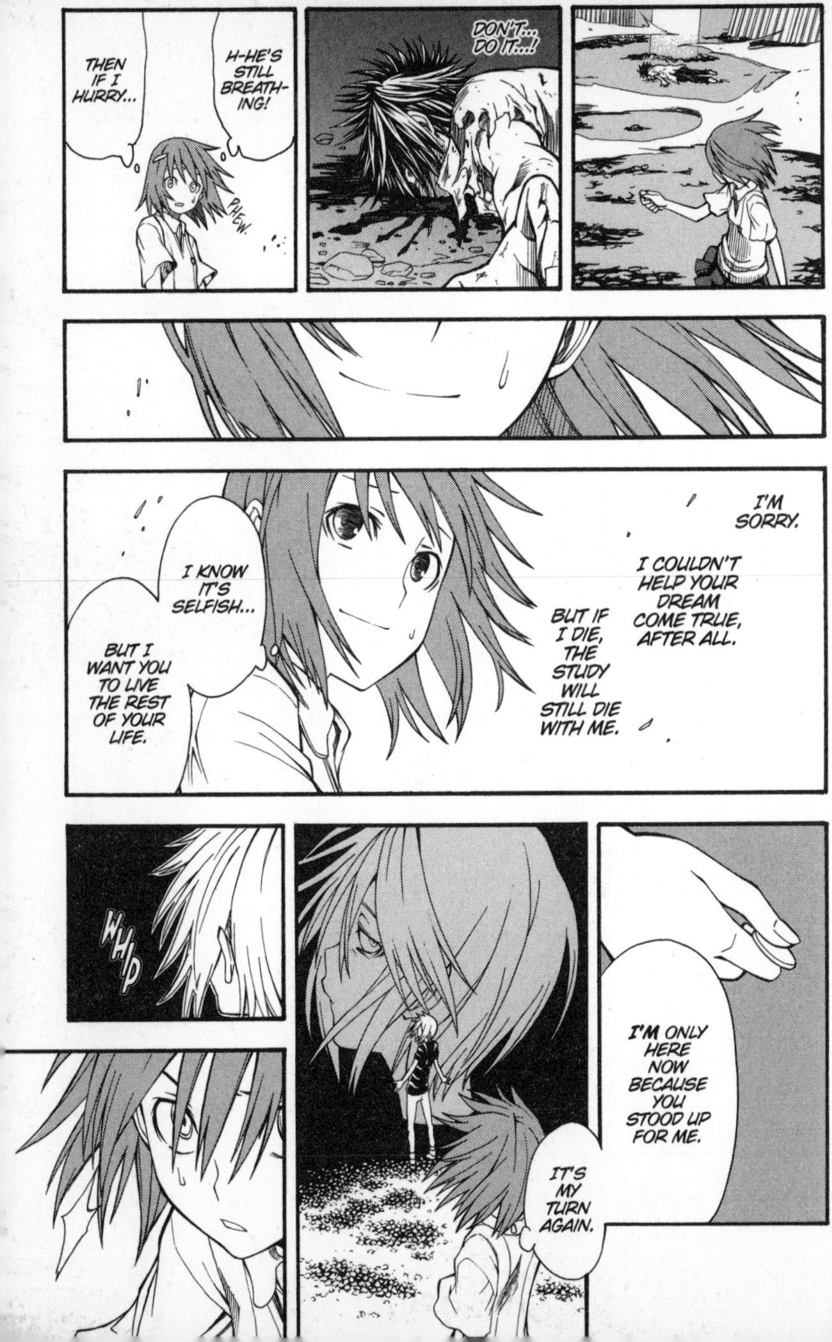
DON'T... DO IT...!
H-HE'S STILL BREATHING!
THEN IF I HURRY...
PHEW.
I'M SORRY.
I COULDN'T HELP YOUR DREAM COME TRUE, AFTER ALL.
BUT IF I DIE, THE STUDY WILL STILL DIE WITH ME.
I KNOW IT'S SELFISH...
BUT I WANT YOU TO LIVE THE REST OF YOUR LIFE.
I'M ONLY HERE NOW BECAUSE YOU STOOD UP FOR ME.
IT'S MY TURN AGAIN.
WHIP

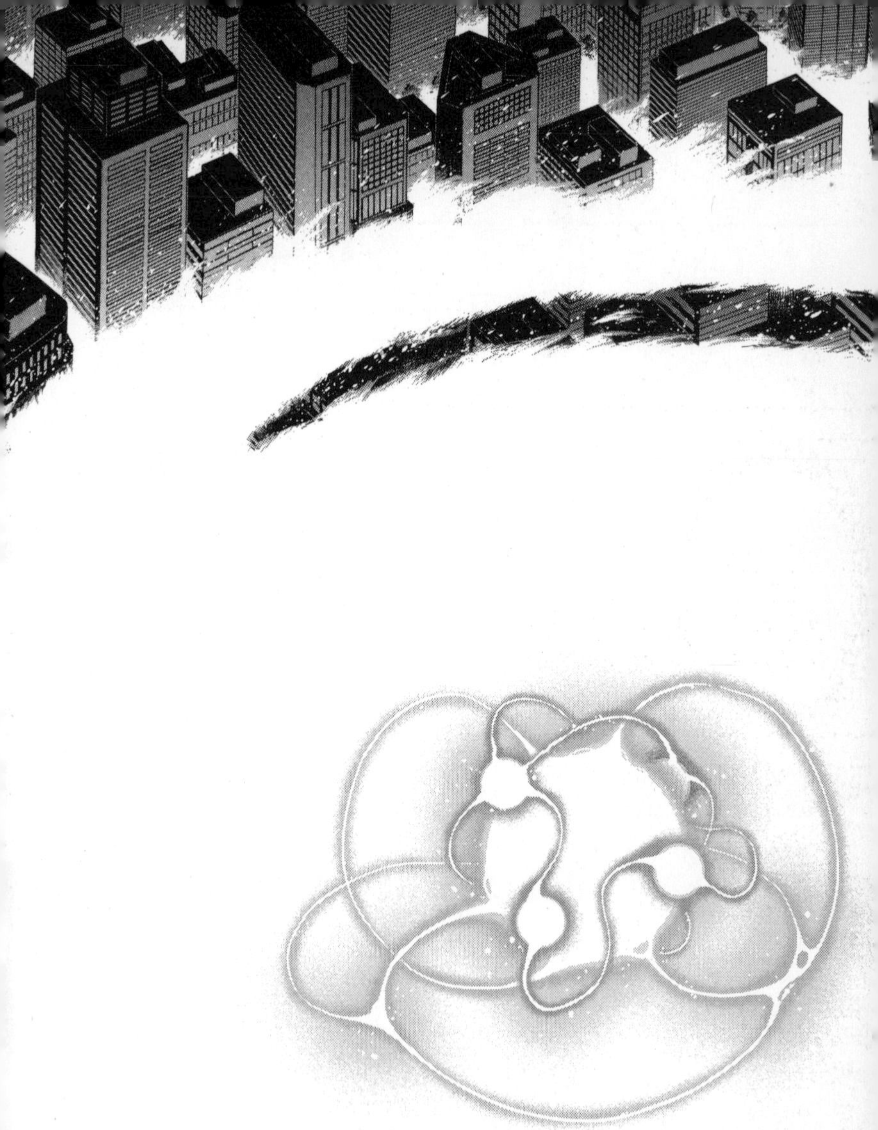

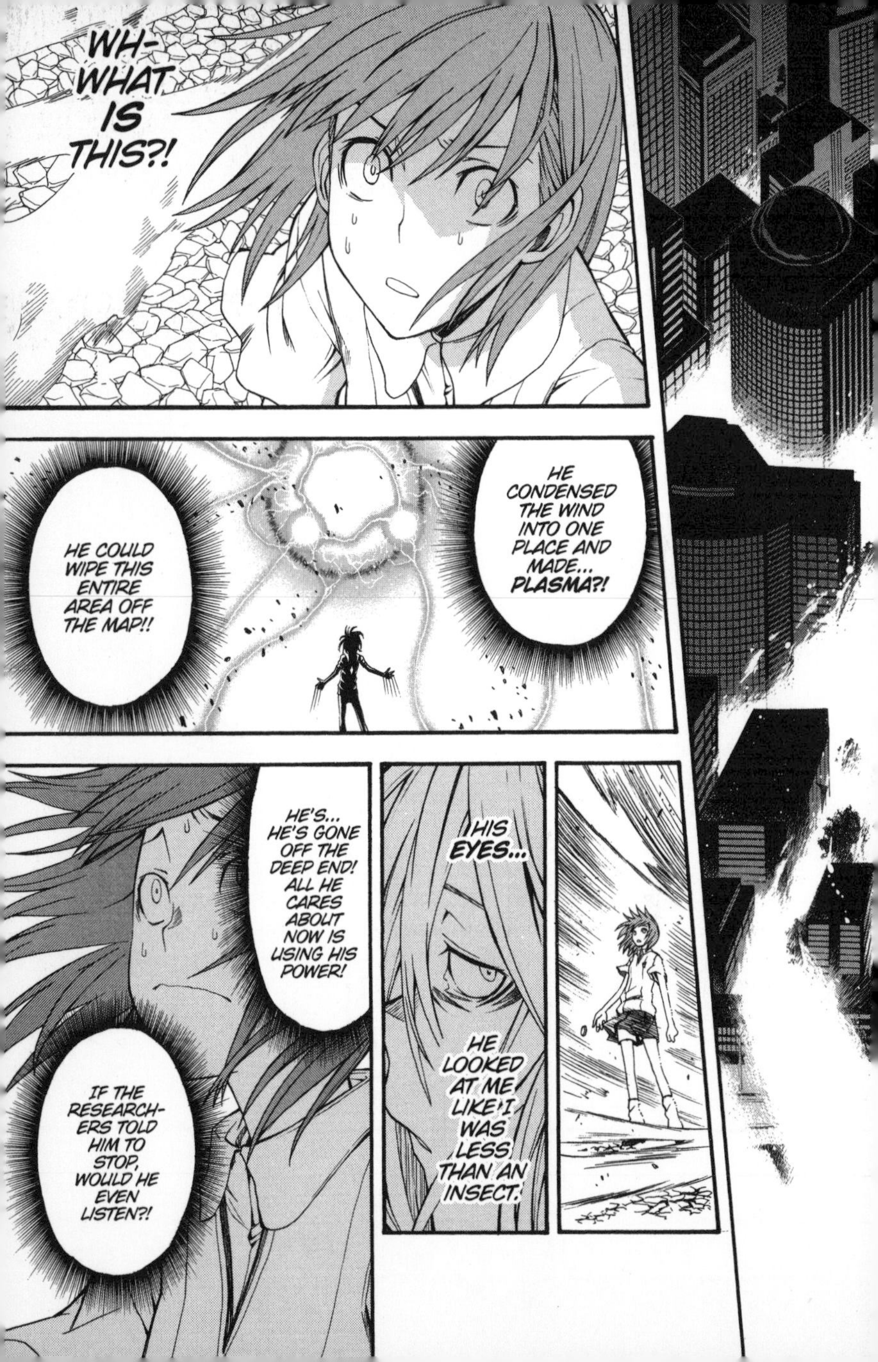
WH- WHAT IS THIS?!
HE CONDENSED THE WIND INTO ONE PLACE AND MADE... PLASMA?!
HE COULD WIPE THIS ENTIRE AREA OFF THE MAP!!
HIS EYES...
HE LOOKED AT ME LIKE I WAS LESS THAN AN INSECT.
HE'S... HE'S GONE OFF THE DEEP END! ALL HE CARES ABOUT NOW IS USING HIS POWER!
IF THE RESEARCH- ERS TOLD HIM TO STOP, WOULD HE EVEN LISTEN?!

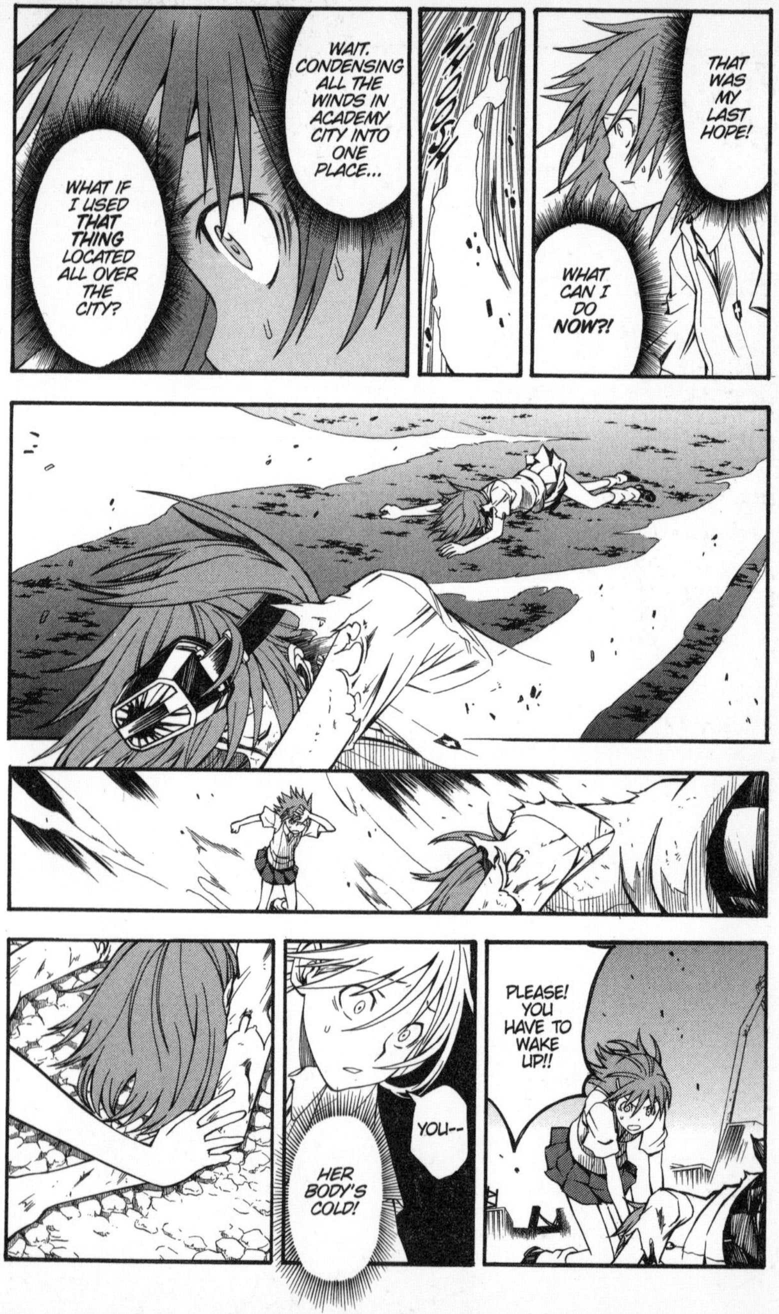
THAT WAS MY LAST HOPE!
WHAT CAN I DO NOW?!
WHOOSH
WAIT. CONDENSING ALL THE WINDS IN ACADEMY CITY INTO ONE PLACE...
WHAT IF I USED THAT THING LOCATED ALL OVER THE CITY?
PLEASE! YOU HAVE TO WAKE UP!!
YOU--
HER BODY'S COLD!

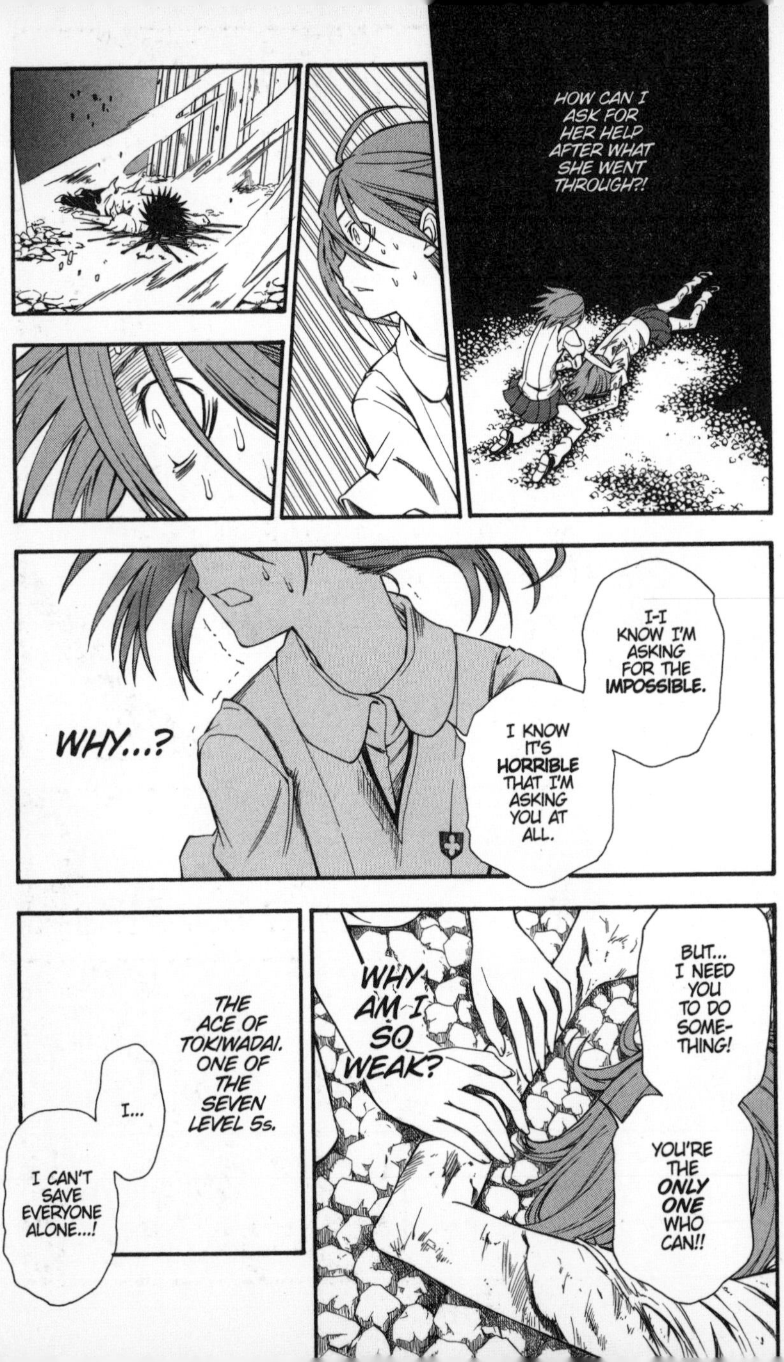
HOW CAN I ASK FOR HER HELP AFTER WHAT SHE WENT THROUGH?!
I-I KNOW I'M ASKING FOR THE IMPOSSIBLE.
I KNOW IT'S HORRIBLE THAT I'M ASKING YOU AT ALL.
WHY...?
BUT... I NEED YOU TO DO SOMETHING!
YOU'RE THE ONLY ONE WHO CAN!!
WHY AM I SO WEAK?
THE ACE OF TOKIWADAI. ONE OF THE SEVEN LEVEL 5s.
I...
I CAN'T SAVE EVERYONE ALONE...!

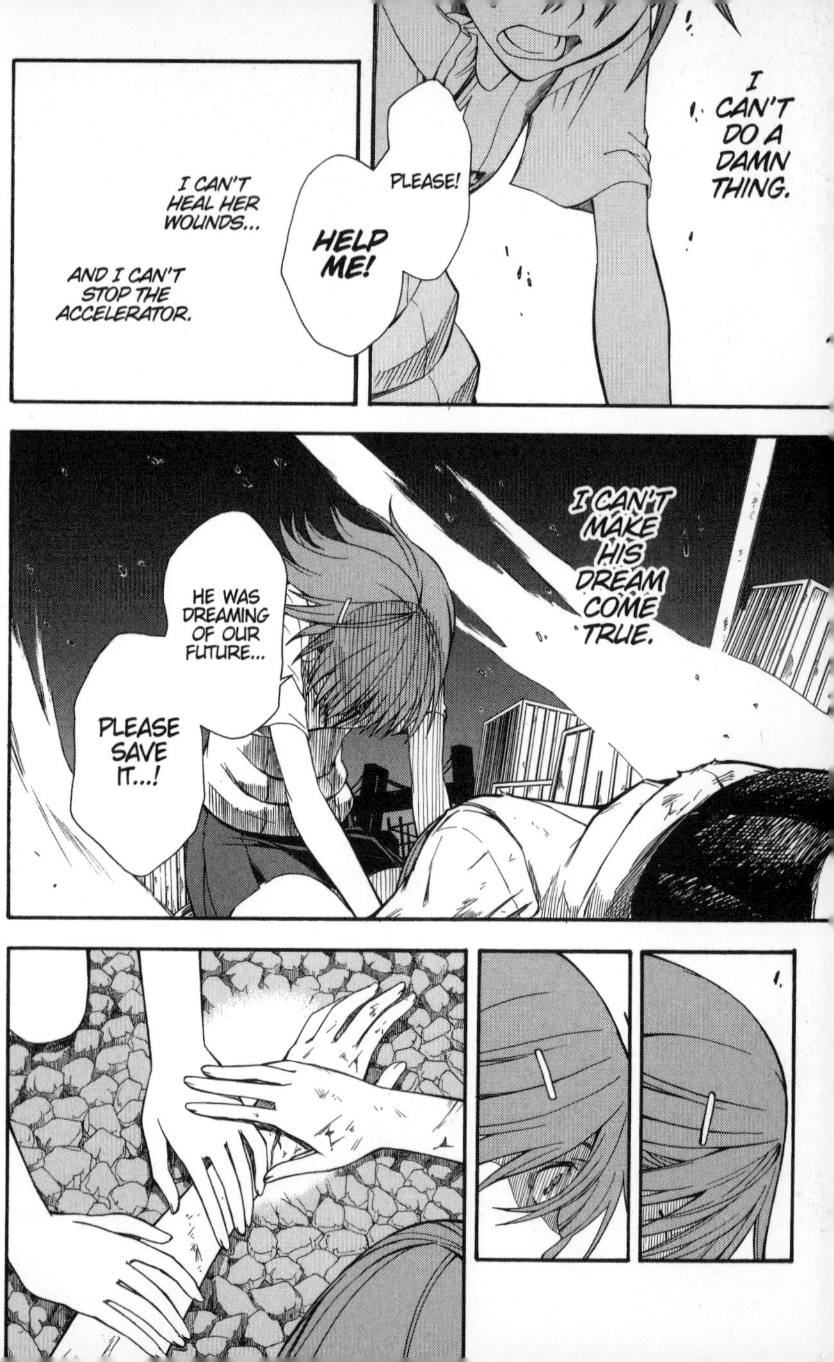
I CAN'T DO A DAMN THING.
PLEASE!
HELP ME!
I CAN'T HEAL HER WOUNDS...
AND I CAN'T STOP THE ACCELERATOR.
I CAN'T MAKE HIS DREAM COME TRUE.
HE WAS DREAMING OF OUR FUTURE...
PLEASE SAVE IT...!

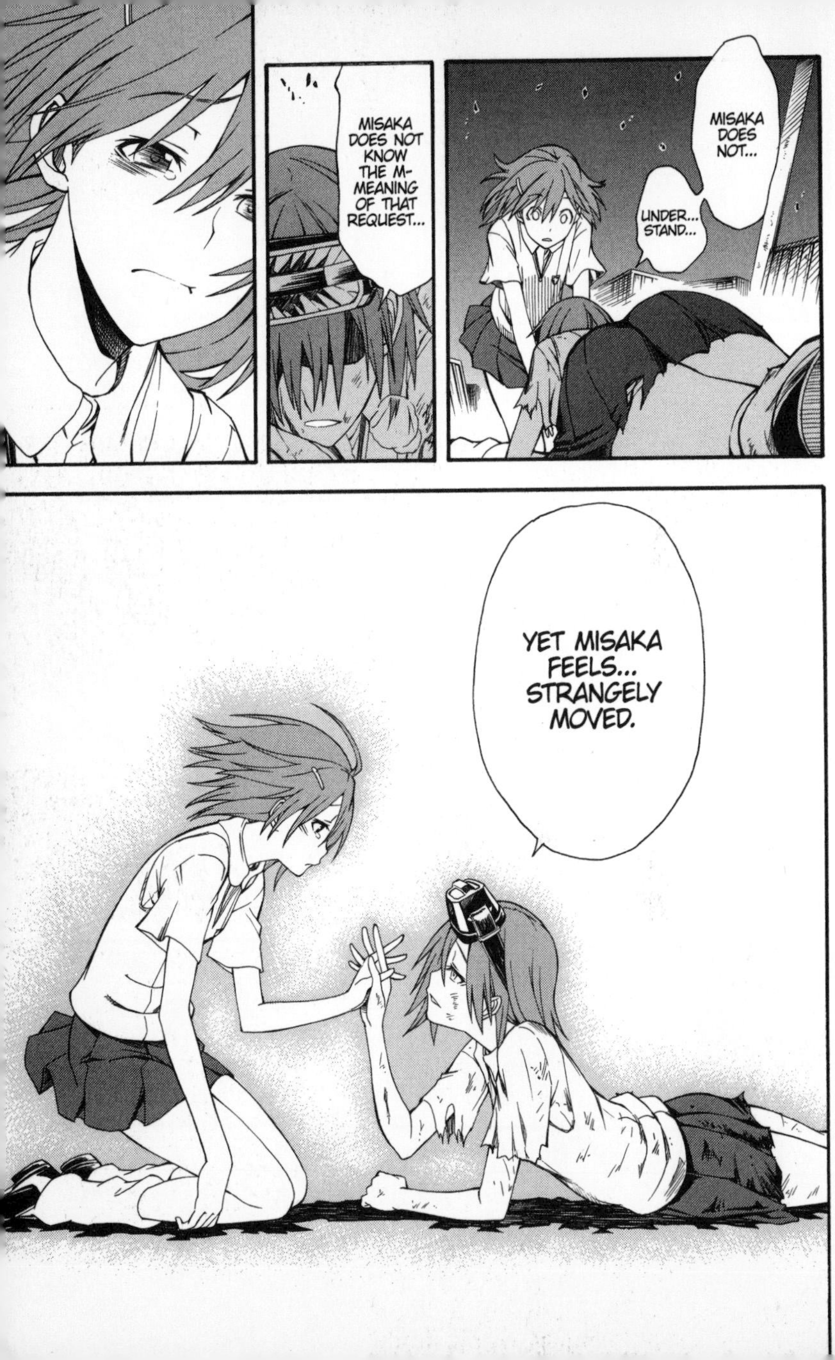
MISAKA DOES NOT...
UNDER... STAND...
MISAKA DOES NOT KNOW THE M-MEANING OF THAT REQUEST...
YET MISAKA FEELS... STRANGELY MOVED.

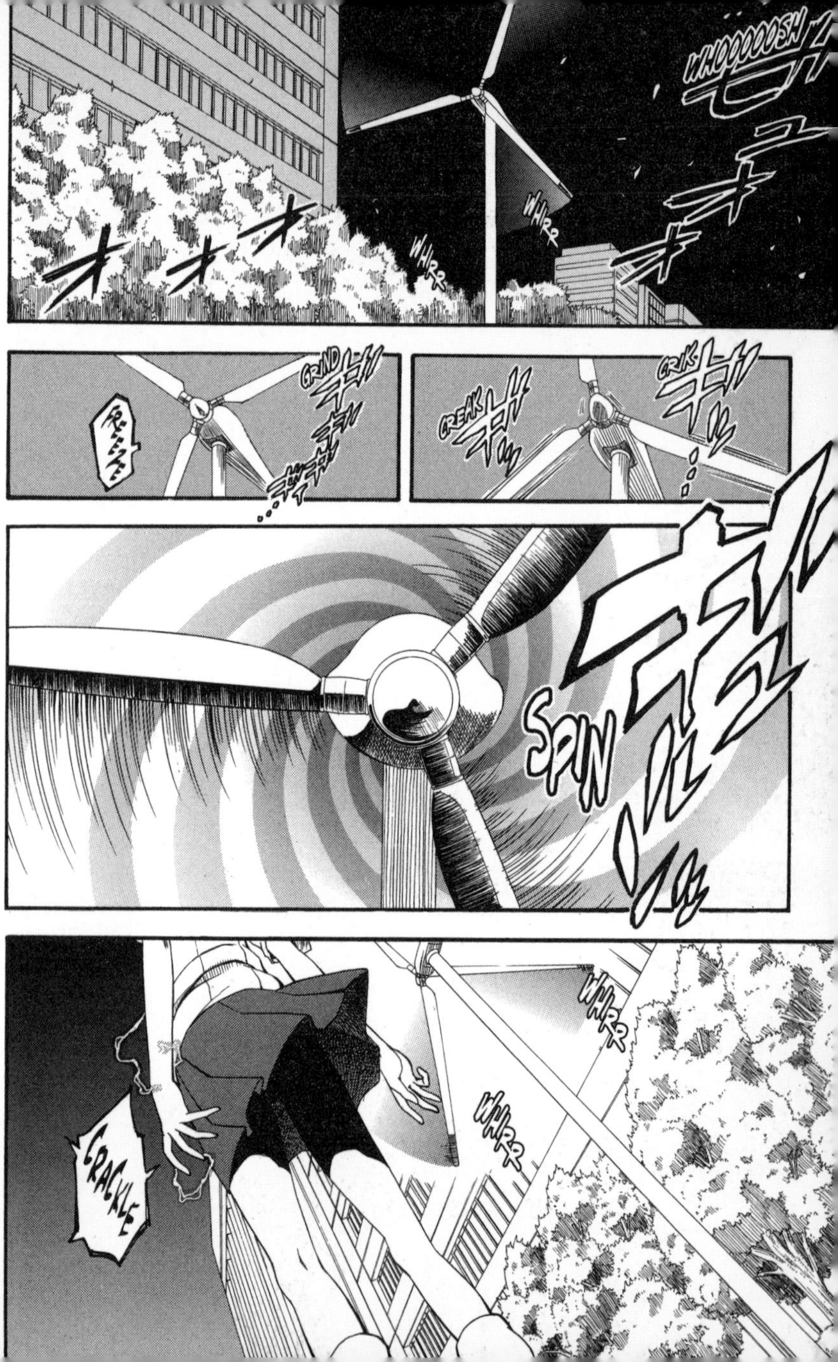
WHOOOOOOSH
WHIRR
WHIRR
GRIK
CREAK
GRIND
SPIN
WHIRR
WHIRR
CRACKLE

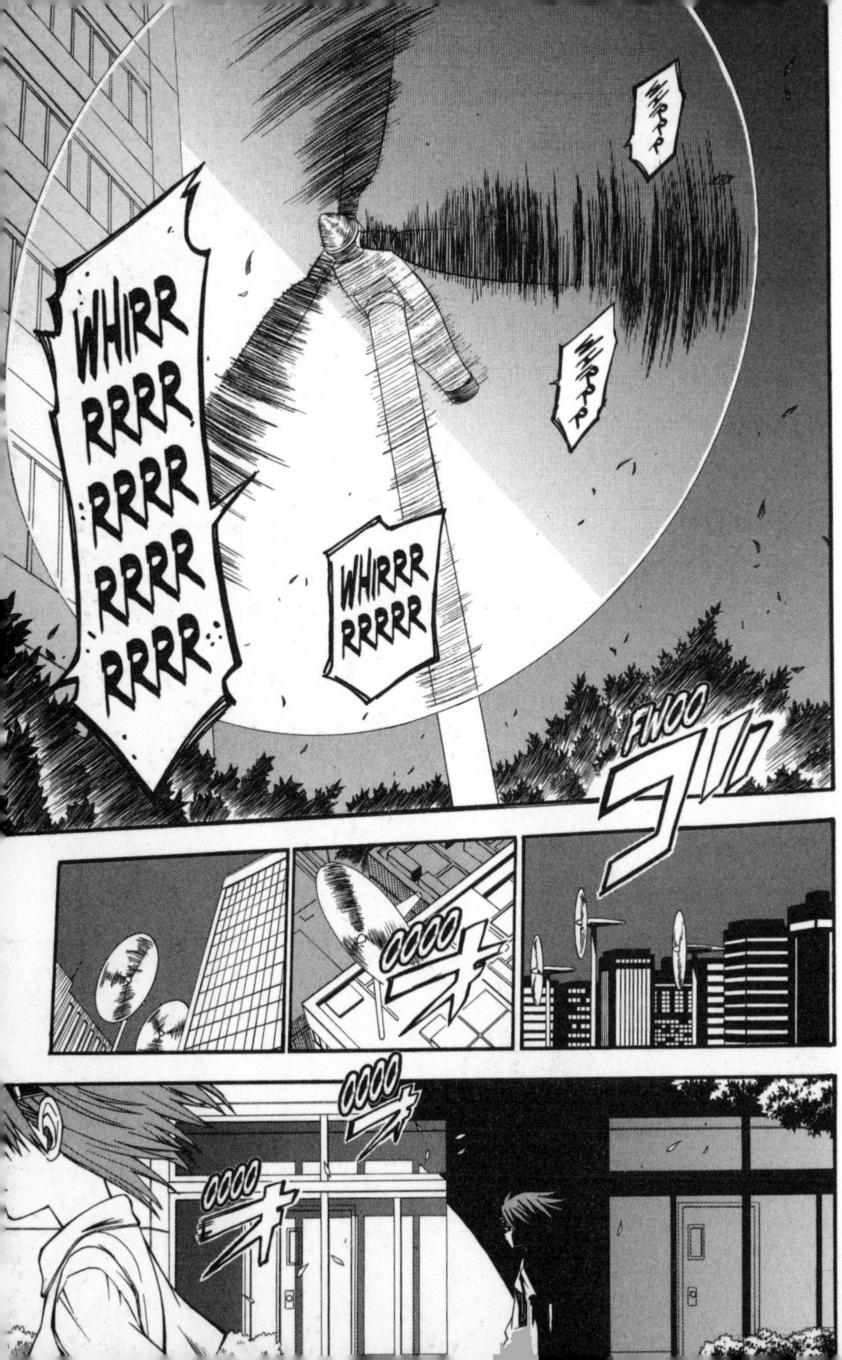
WHRRR
WHRRR
WHIRR RRRR RRRR RRRR RRRR RRRR
WHIRRR RRRRR
FWOO
OOOO
OOOO
OOOO

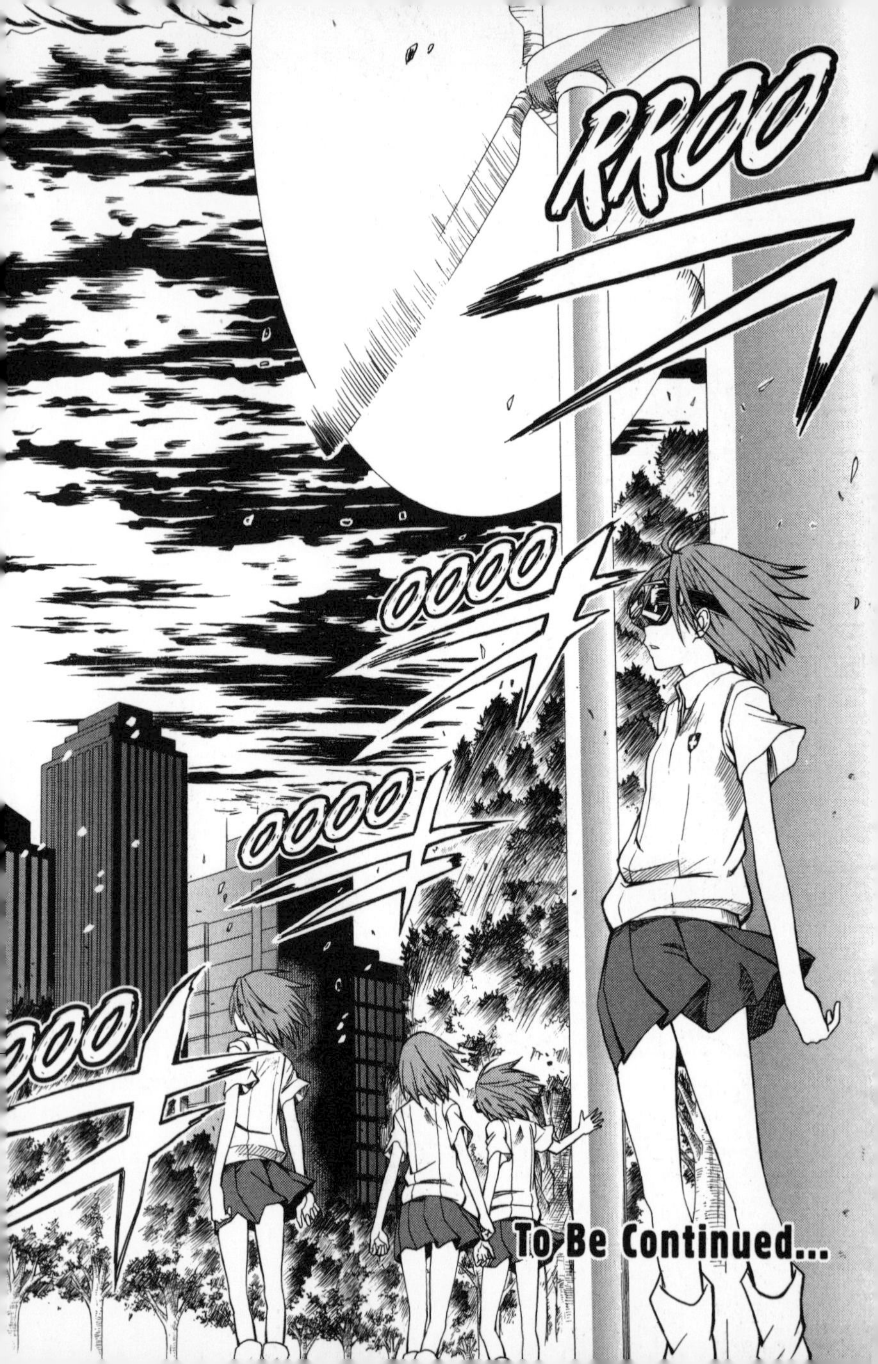
RROO
OOOO
OOOO
OOO
To Be Continued...

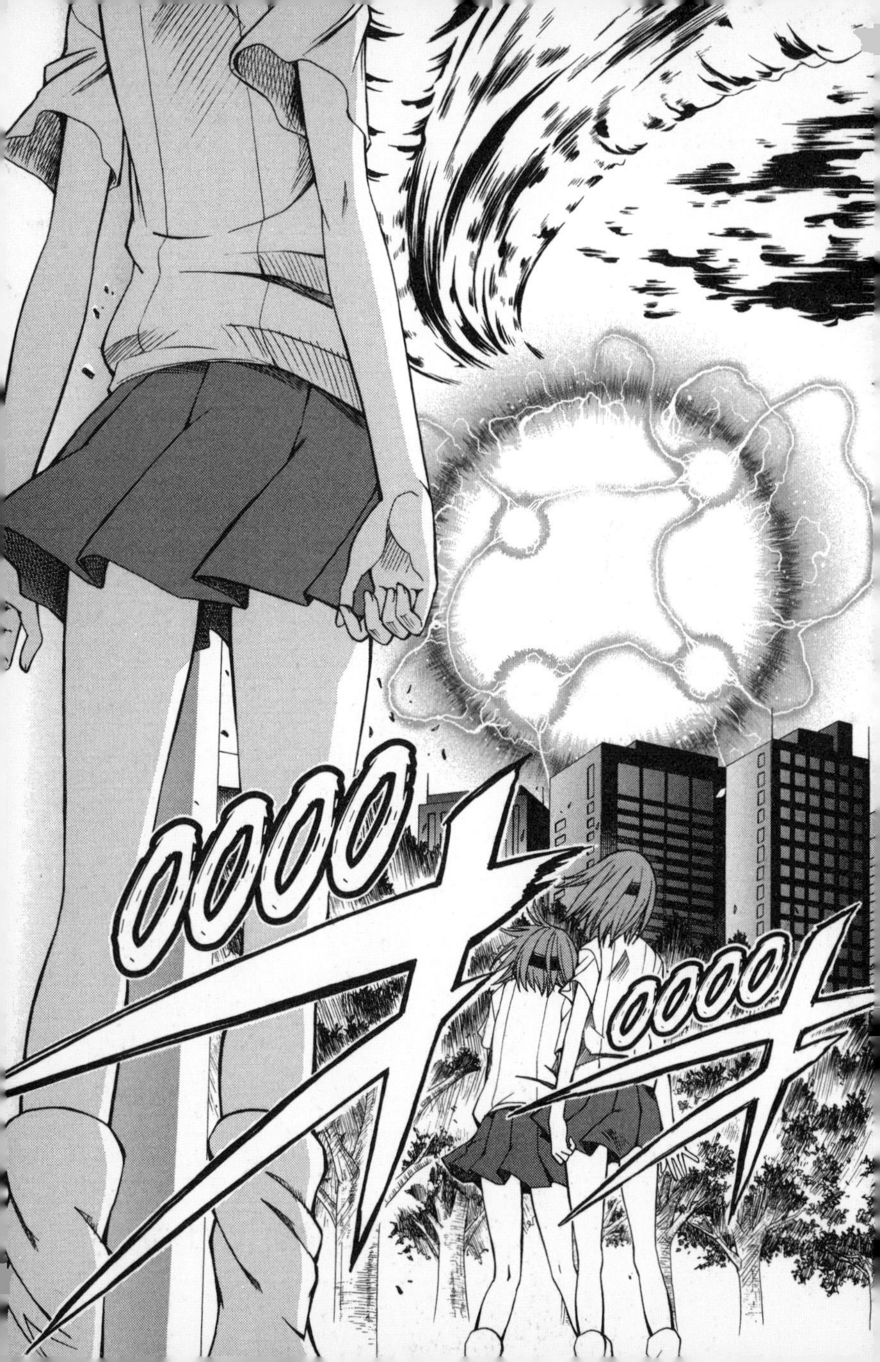
OOOO
OOOO

A Certain Gentleman-like Accelerator

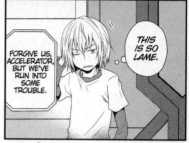

THIS IS SO LAME.
FORGIVE US, ACCELERATOR, BUT WE'VE RUN INTO SOME TROUBLE.
DUE TO AN EQUIPMENT MALFUNCTION, WE COULDN'T CULTURE OUR UNIT IN TIME.
WHA?
BUT DON'T WORRY.
GLARE
BLIP
BLIP
WE HAVE A RUSH UNIT WE BRED TO FUNCTIONALITY.
......
TINY
PLEASE FORGIVE THE DIFFERENT SPECIFICATIONS.
NO CAN DO!
BLUNT
!!
WHY NOT?!

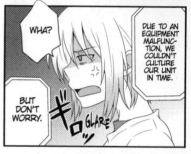

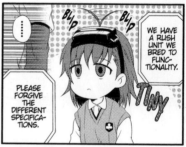

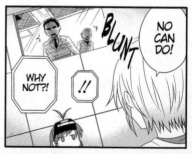

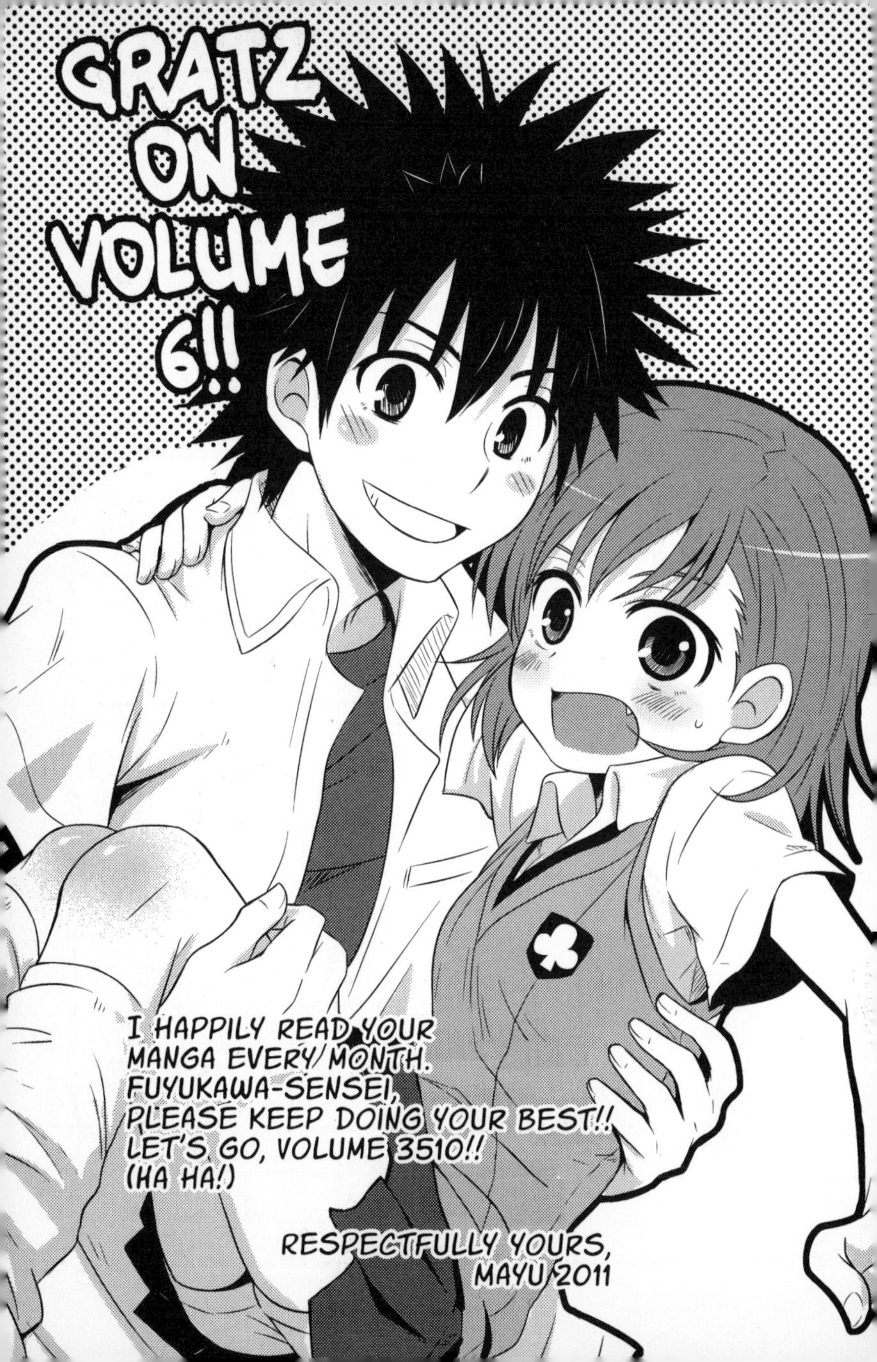
GRATZ ON VOLUME 6!!
I HAPPILY READ YOUR MANGA EVERY MONTH. FUYUKAWA-SENSEI, PLEASE KEEP DOING YOUR BEST!! LET'S GO, VOLUME 3510!! (HA HA!)
RESPECTFULLY YOURS, MAYU 2011

What Actually Took Place

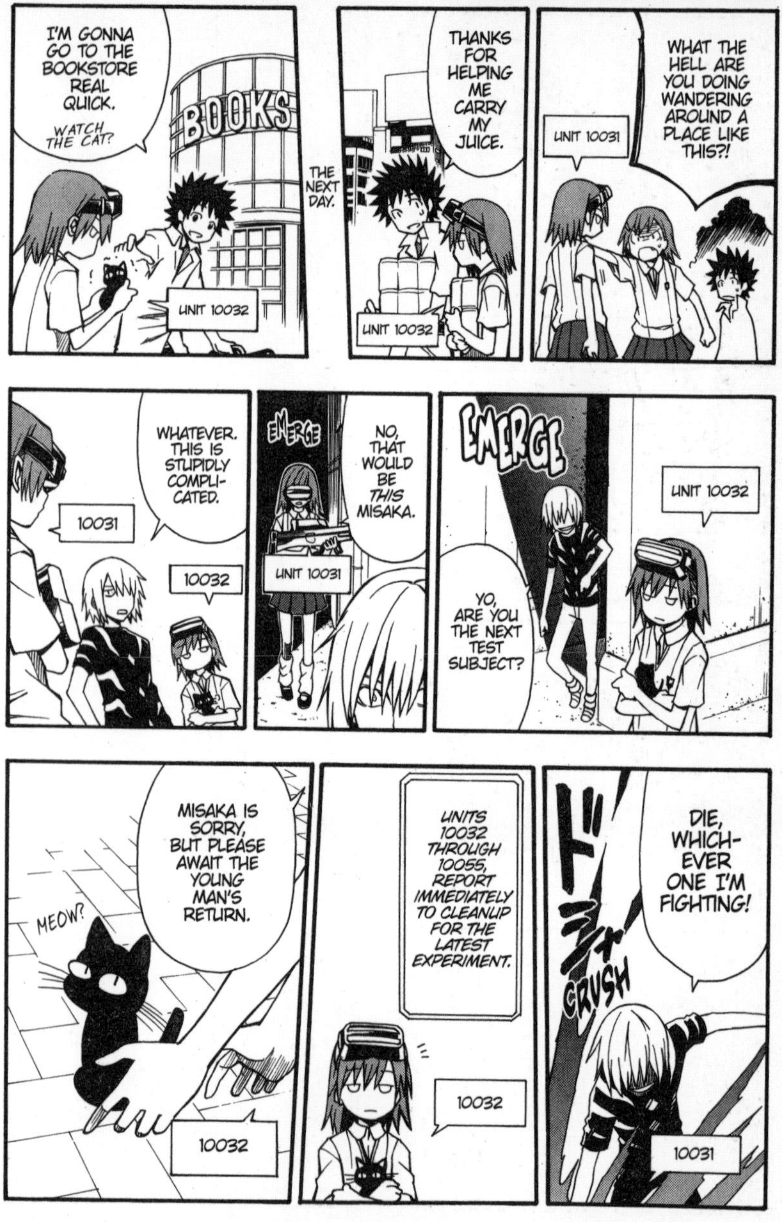

WHAT THE HELL ARE YOU DOING WANDERING AROUND A PLACE LIKE THIS?!
UNIT 10031
THANKS FOR HELPING ME CARRY MY JUICE.
THE NEXT DAY.
UNIT 10032
I'M GONNA GO TO THE BOOKSTORE REAL QUICK.
WATCH THE CAT?
BOOKS
UNIT 10032
EMERGE
UNIT 10032
YO, ARE YOU THE NEXT TEST SUBJECT?
EMERGE
NO, THAT WOULD BE *THIS* MISAKA.
UNIT 10031
WHATEVER. THIS IS STUPIDLY COMPLICATED.
10031
10032
ド
DIE, WHICH-EVER ONE I'M FIGHTING!
CRUSH
10031
UNITS 10032 THROUGH 10055, REPORT IMMEDIATELY TO CLEANUP FOR THE LATEST EXPERIMENT.
10032
MISAKA IS SORRY, BUT PLEASE AWAIT THE YOUNG MAN'S RETURN.
MEOW?
10032

Behind the Scenes

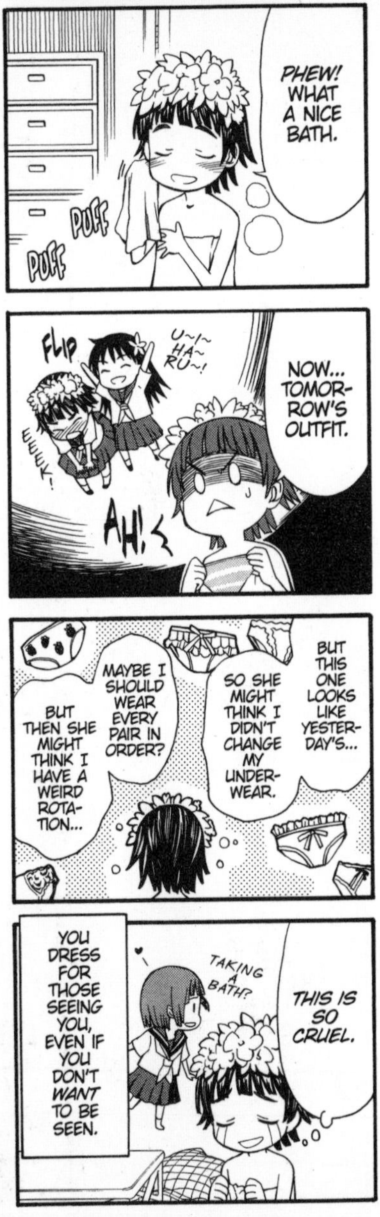
PHEW! WHAT A NICE BATH.
PUFF
PUFF
NOW... TOMOR-ROW'S OUTFIT.
U~I~ HA~ RU~!
FLIP
EEEEK!
AH!
BUT THIS ONE LOOKS LIKE YESTER-DAY'S...
SO SHE MIGHT THINK I DIDN'T CHANGE MY UNDER-WEAR.
MAYBE I SHOULD WEAR EVERY PAIR IN ORDER?
BUT THEN SHE MIGHT THINK I HAVE A WEIRD ROTA-TION...
THIS IS SO CRUEL.
TAKING A BATH?
YOU DRESS FOR THOSE SEEING YOU, EVEN IF YOU DON'T WANT TO BE SEEN.

10031 Hits

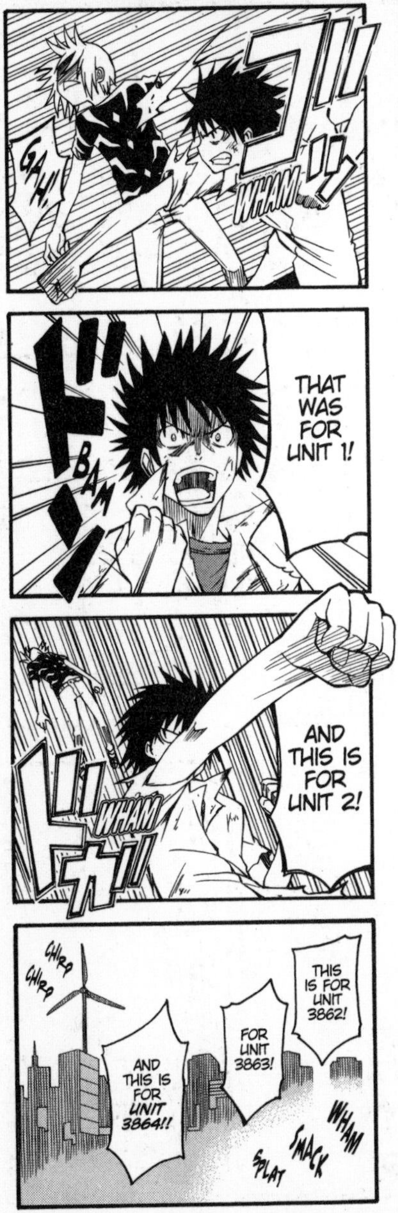
WHAM
GAH!!
THAT WAS FOR UNIT 1!
BAM
AND THIS IS FOR UNIT 2!
WHAM
THIS IS FOR UNIT 3862!
FOR UNIT 3863!
AND THIS IS FOR UNIT 3864!!
WHAM
SMACK
SPLAT
CHIRP
CHIRP

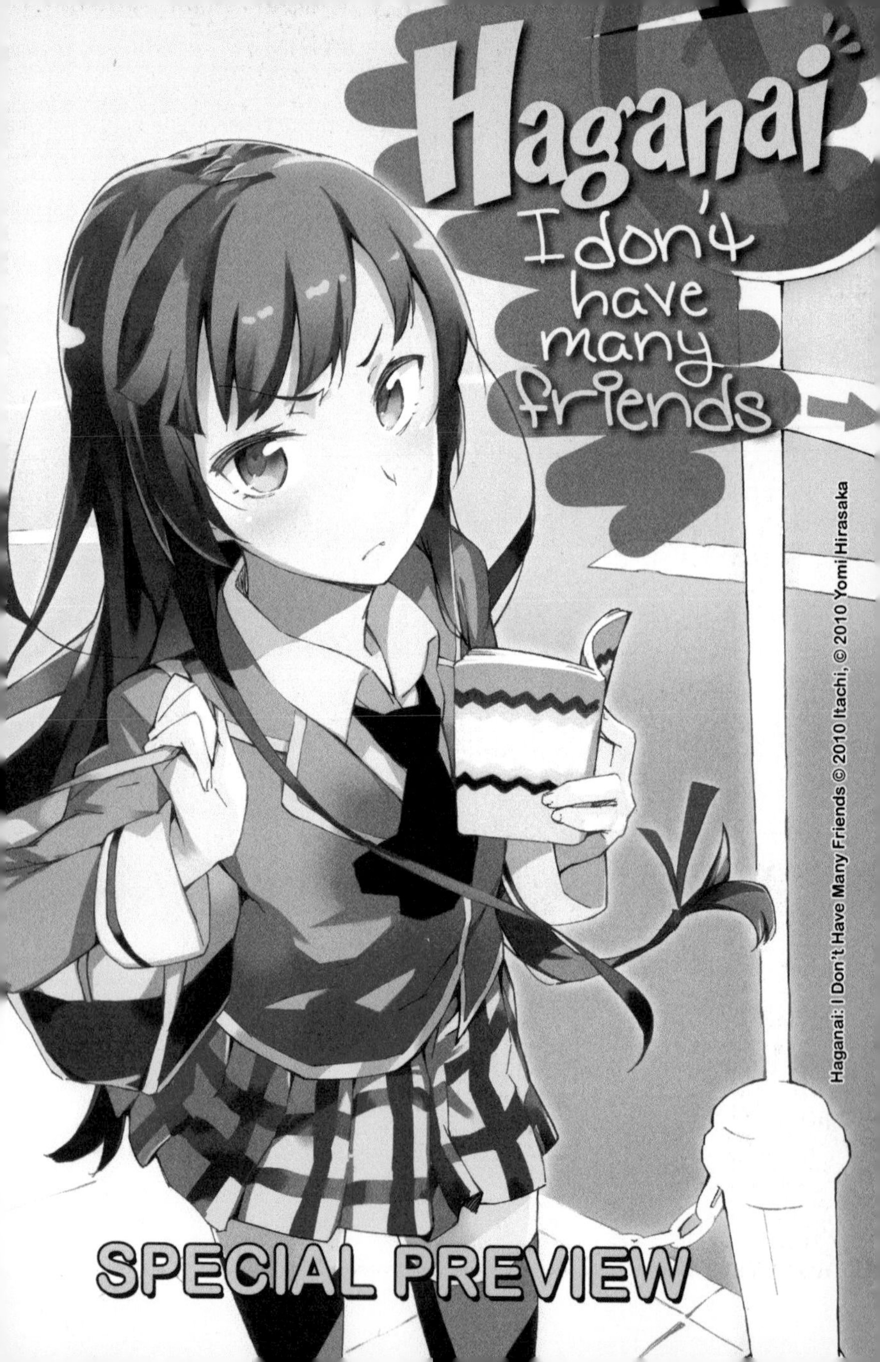
Haganai
I don't have many friends
SPECIAL PREVIEW
Haganai: I Don't Have Many Friends © 2010 Itachi, © 2010 Yomi Hirasaka

SAINT CHRONICA ACADEMY. A ROOM IN THE CHAPEL.

SPECIFI-CALLY, COMMON ROOM 4.

LOOK, GET ON WITH IT.

YOU HAVE TO TAKE SOME TOO.

LET'S GET THIS COMPETI-TION ROLLING.

...WHERE THE NEIGH-BORS CLUB MEETS.

IT'S THE ROOM...

UGH...

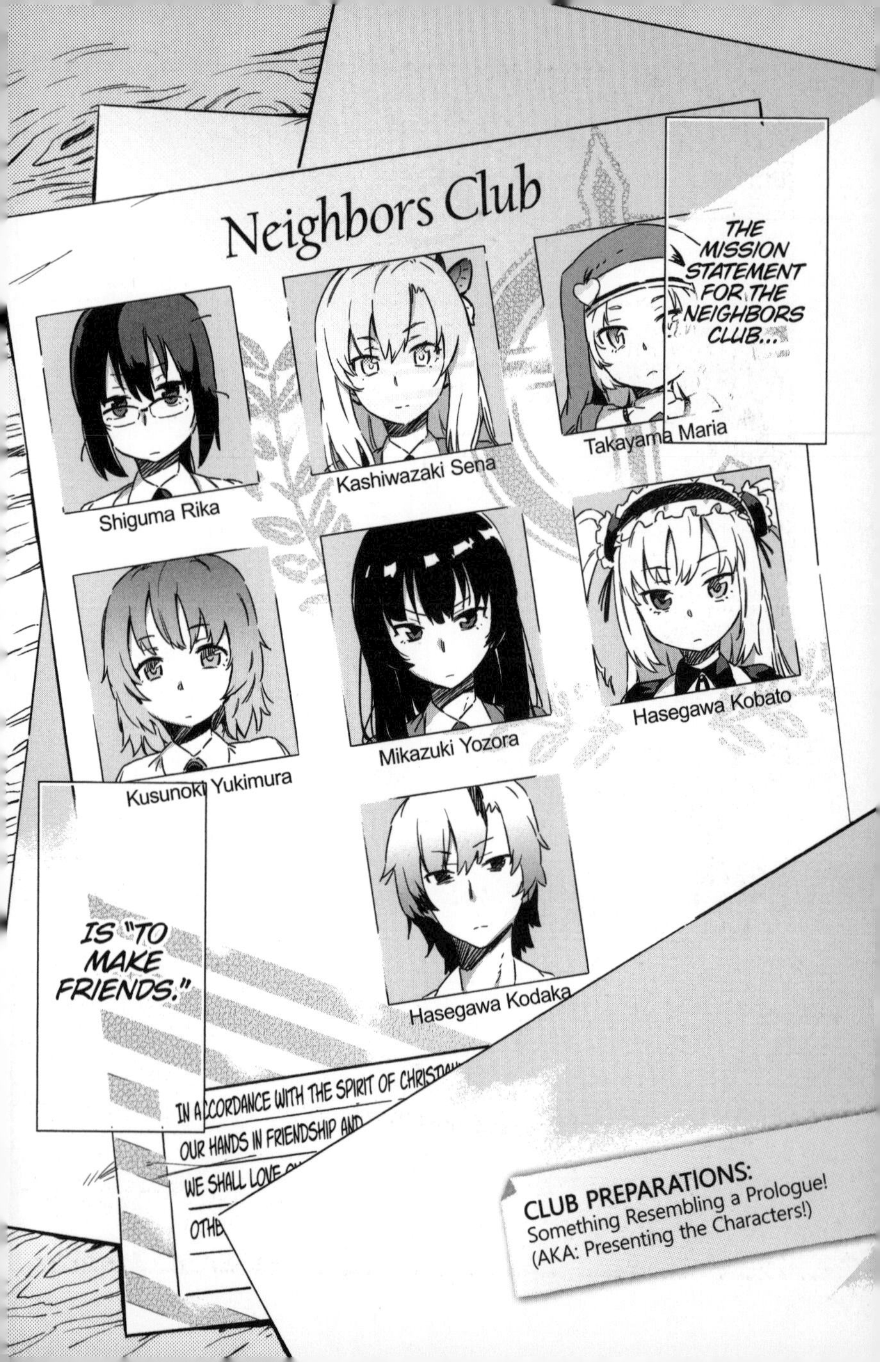
THE MISSION STATEMENT FOR THE NEIGHBORS CLUB...
Neighbors Club
Takayama Maria
Kashiwazaki Sena
Shiguma Rika
Hasegawa Kobato
Mikazuki Yozora
Kusunoki Yukimura
Hasegawa Kodaka
IS "TO MAKE FRIENDS."
IN ACCORDANCE WITH THE SPIRIT OF CHRISTI
OUR HANDS IN FRIENDSHIP AND
WE SHALL LOVE O
OTHE
CLUB PREPARATIONS:
Something Resembling a Prologue!
(AKA: Presenting the Characters!)

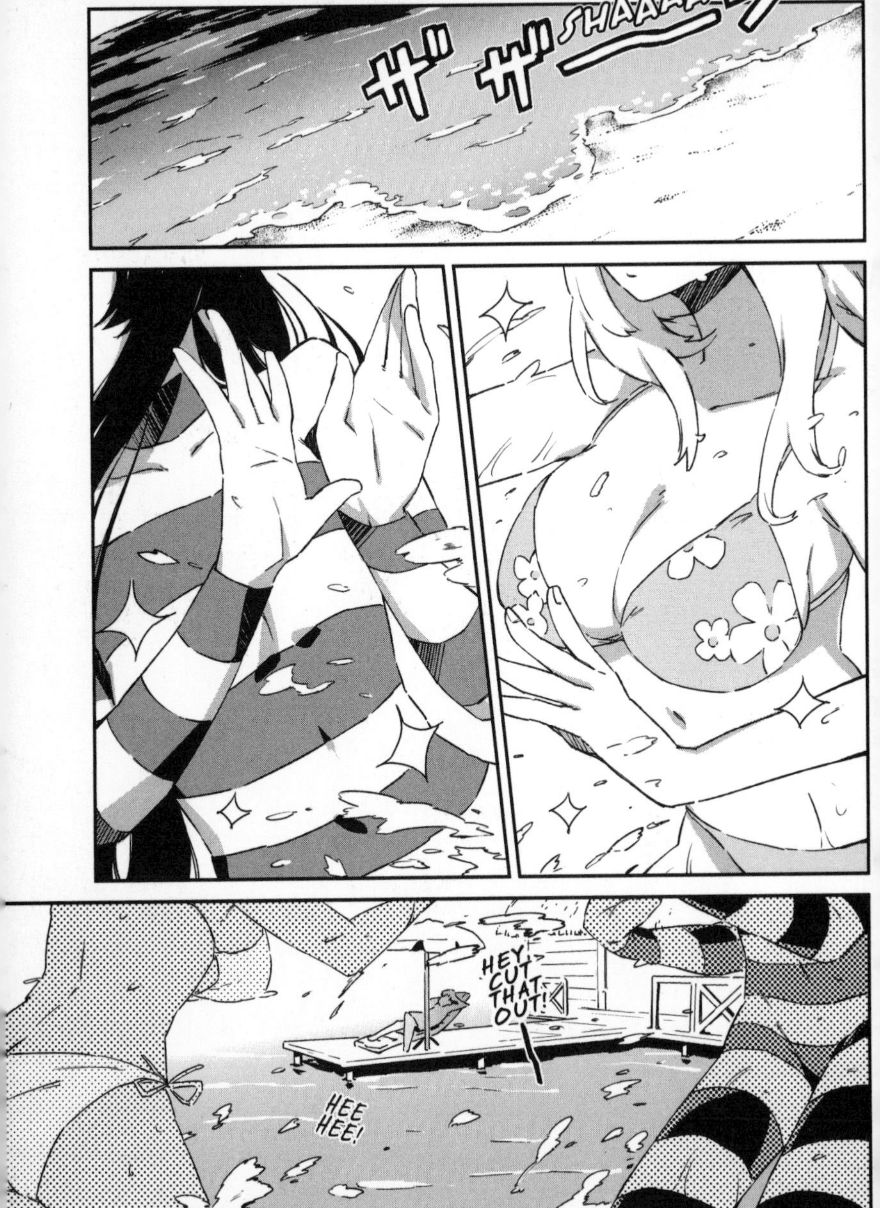
ザザ SHAAAA
HEY CUT THAT OUT!
HEE HEE!

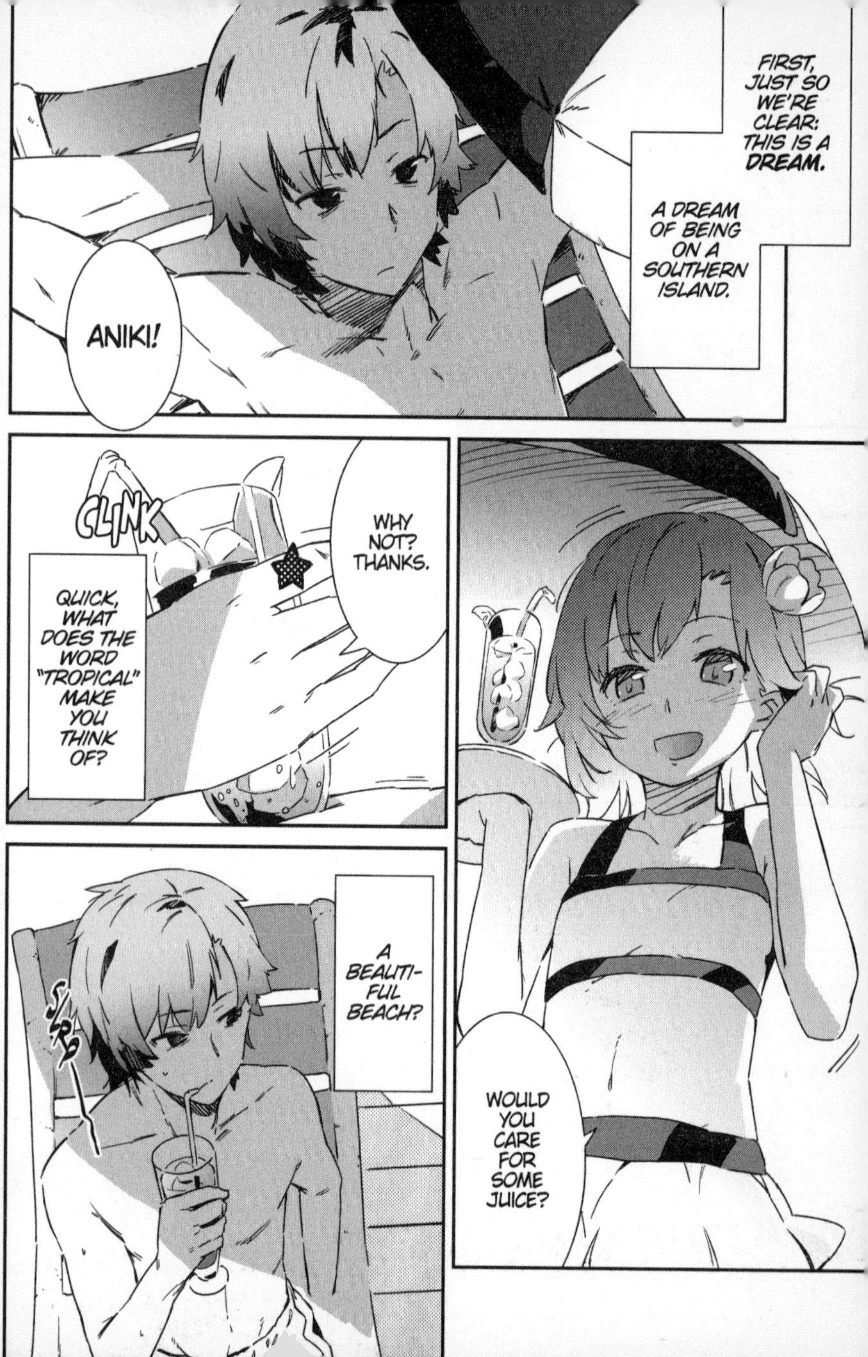
FIRST, JUST SO WE'RE CLEAR: THIS IS A DREAM.
A DREAM OF BEING ON A SOUTHERN ISLAND.
ANIKI!
WOULD YOU CARE FOR SOME JUICE?
WHY NOT? THANKS.
CLINK
QUICK, WHAT DOES THE WORD "TROPICAL" MAKE YOU THINK OF?
A BEAUTIFUL BEACH?
SLRP

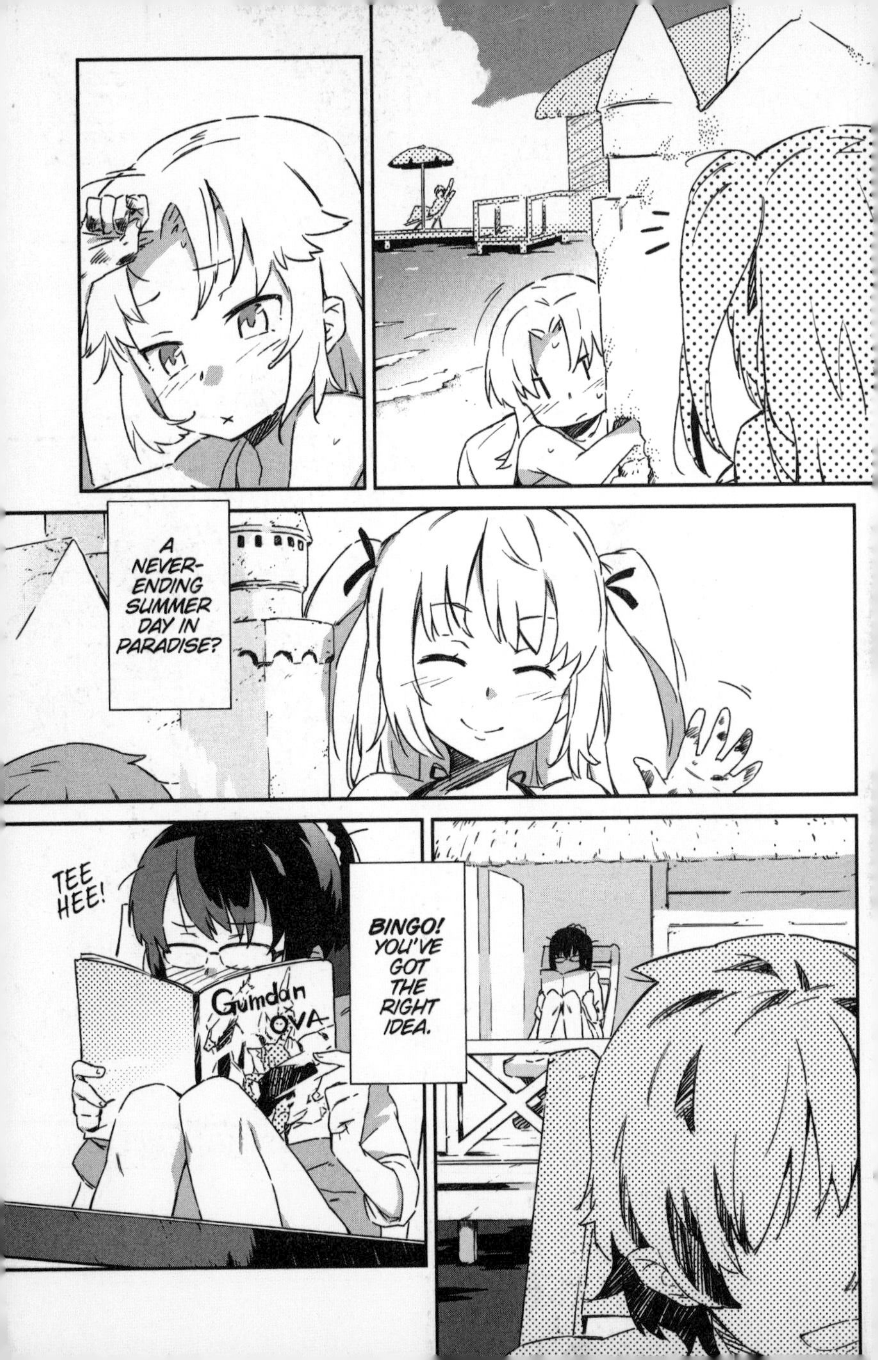
A NEVER-ENDING SUMMER DAY IN PARADISE?
BINGO! YOU'VE GOT THE RIGHT IDEA.
TEE HEE!
Gumdan OVA

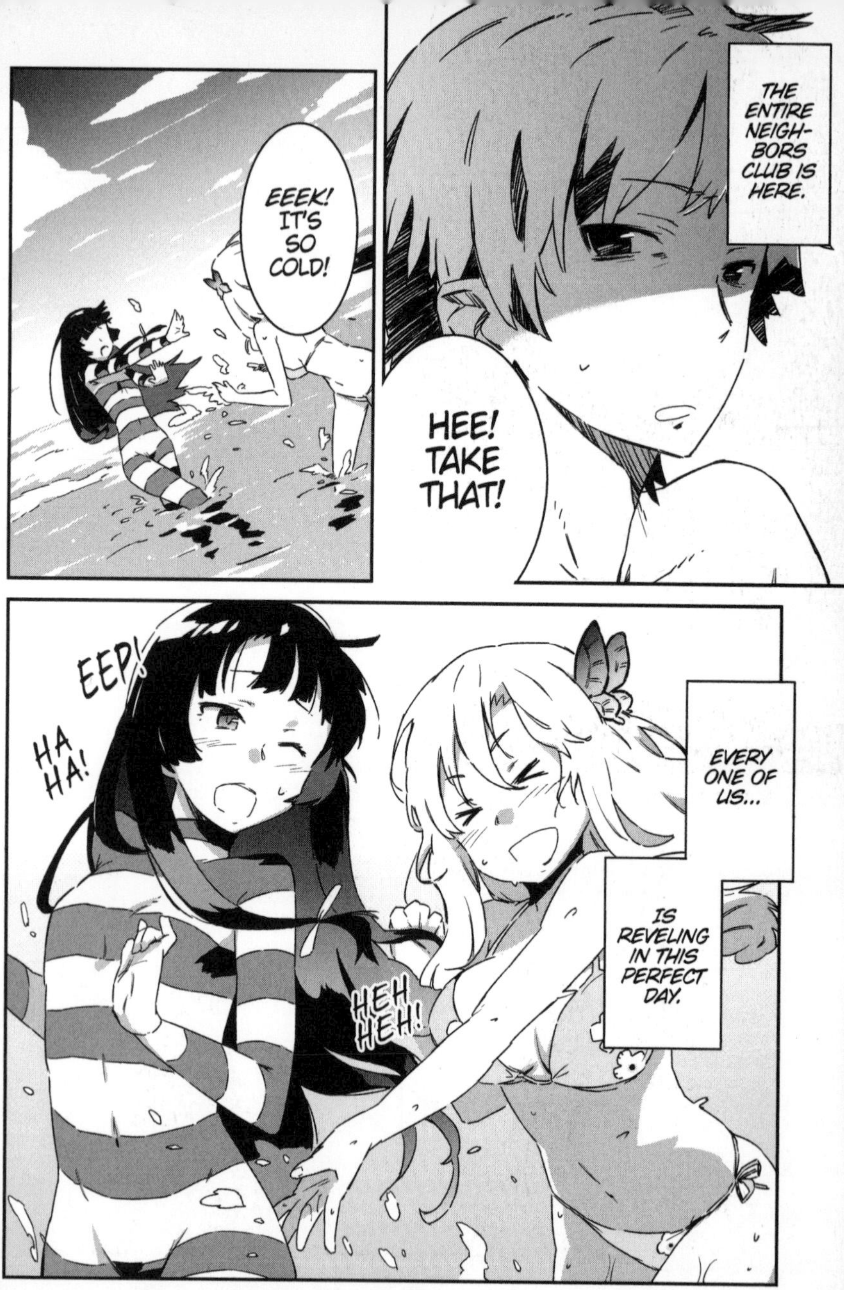
THE ENTIRE NEIGHBORS CLUB IS HERE.
HEE! TAKE THAT!
EEEK! IT'S SO COLD!
EVERY ONE OF US...
IS REVELING IN THIS PERFECT DAY.
HEH HEH!
EEP!
HA HA!

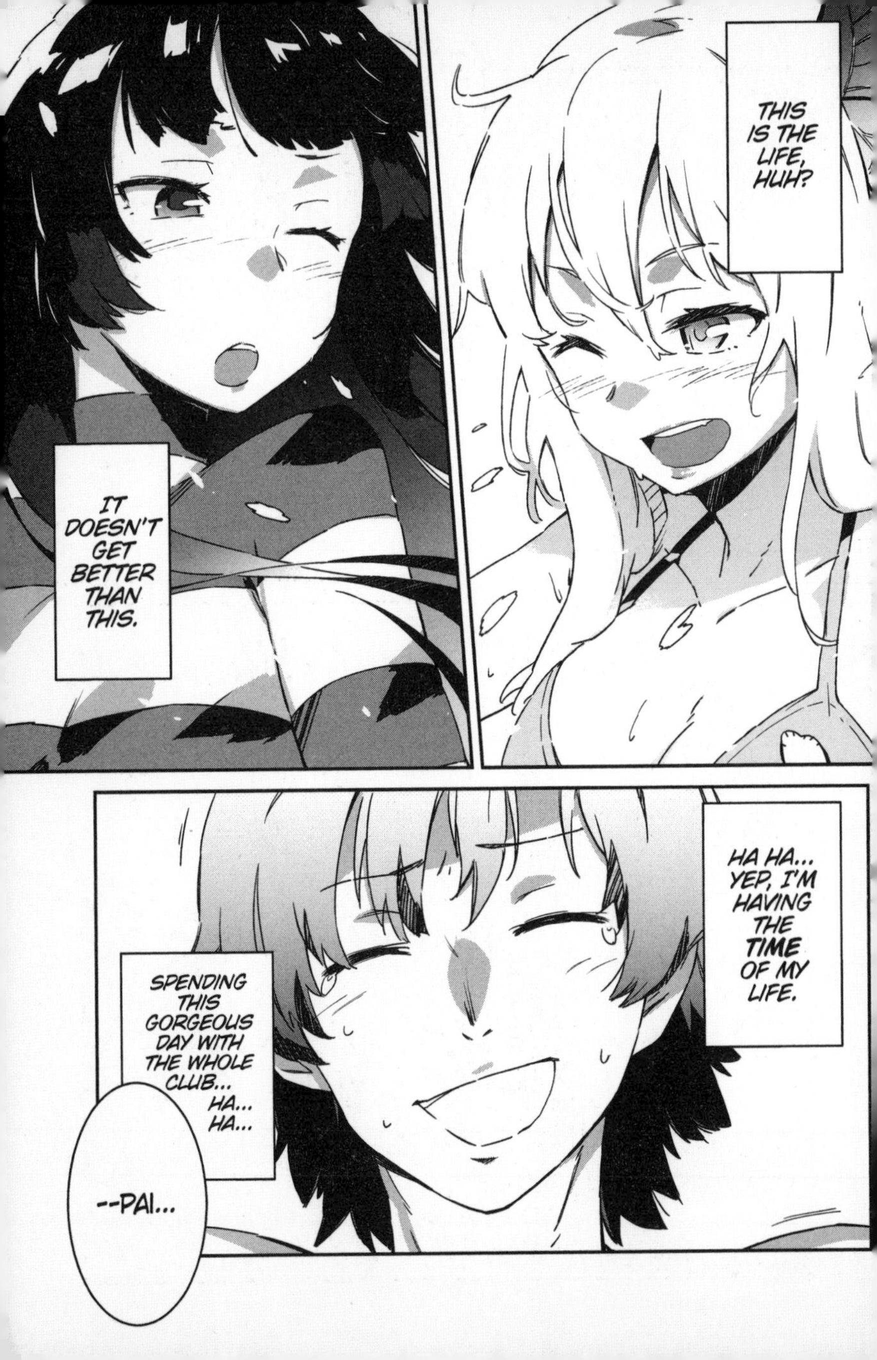
THIS IS THE LIFE, HUH?
IT DOESN'T GET BETTER THAN THIS.
HA HA... YEP, I'M HAVING THE TIME OF MY LIFE.
SPENDING THIS GORGEOUS DAY WITH THE WHOLE CLUB... HA... HA...
--PAI...

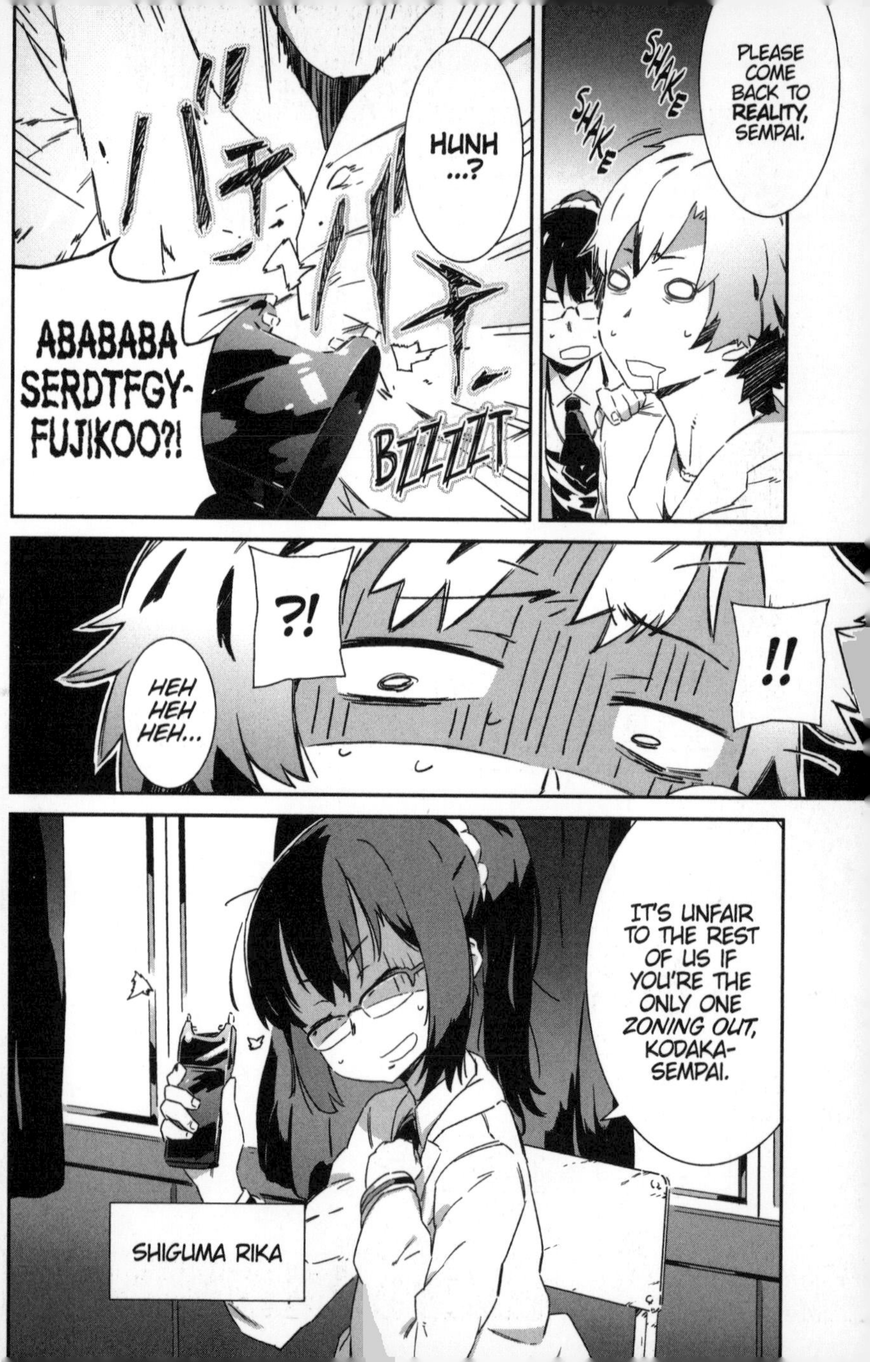
PLEASE COME BACK TO REALITY, SEMPAI.
SHAKE
SHAKE
HUNH ...?
ABABABA SERDTFGY-FUJIKOO?!
BZZZZT
!!
?!
HEH HEH HEH...
IT'S UNFAIR TO THE REST OF US IF YOU'RE THE ONLY ONE ZONING OUT, KODAKA-SEMPAI.
SHIGUMA RIKA

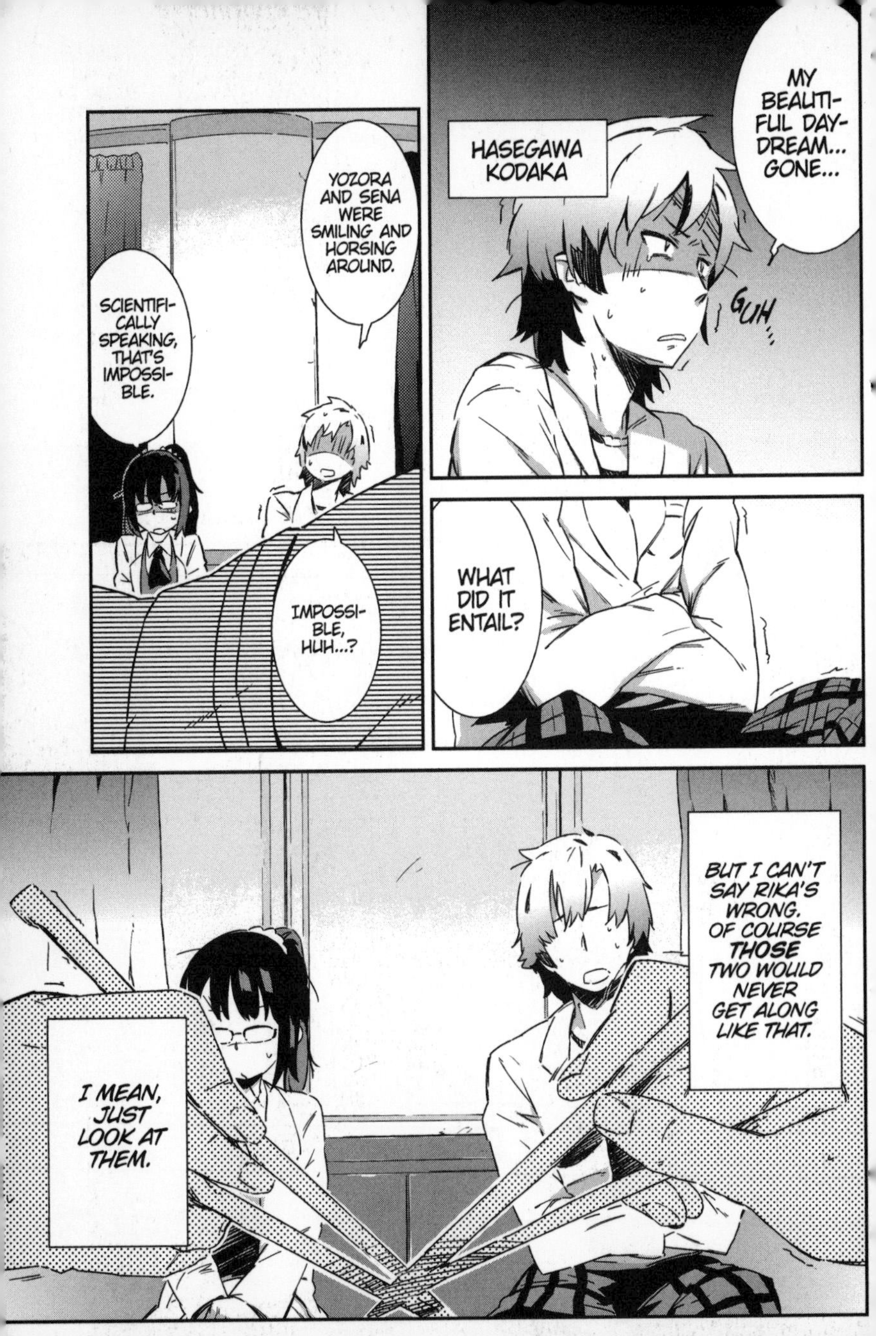
MY BEAUTIFUL DAYDREAM... GONE...
HASEGAWA KODAKA
GUH...
WHAT DID IT ENTAIL?
YOZORA AND SENA WERE SMILING AND HORSING AROUND.
SCIENTIFICALLY SPEAKING, THAT'S IMPOSSIBLE.
IMPOSSIBLE, HUH...?
BUT I CAN'T SAY RIKA'S WRONG. OF COURSE THOSE TWO WOULD NEVER GET ALONG LIKE THAT.
I MEAN, JUST LOOK AT THEM.

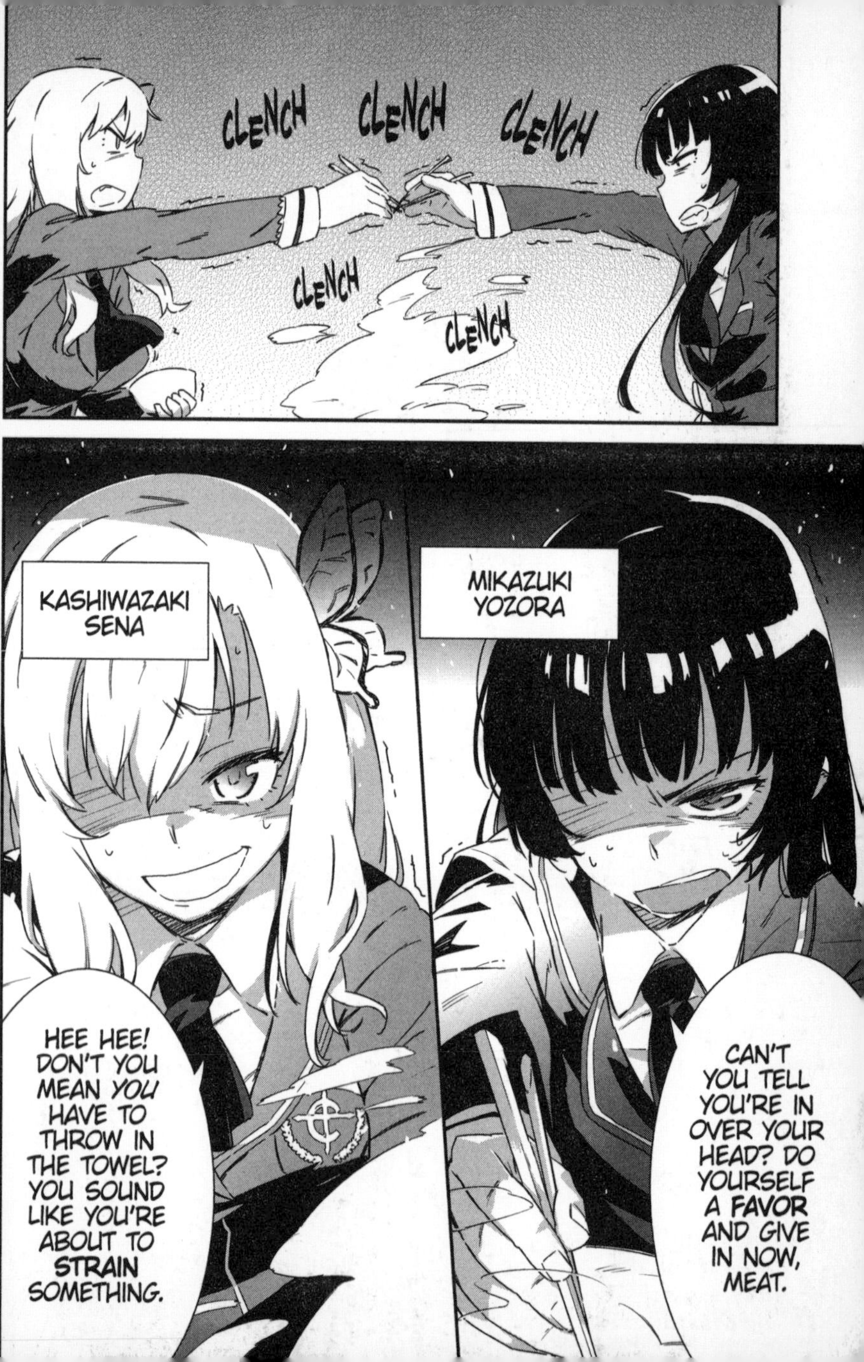
CLENCH
CLENCH
CLENCH
CLENCH
CLENCH
MIKAZUKI YOZORA
CAN'T YOU TELL YOU'RE IN OVER YOUR HEAD? DO YOURSELF A FAVOR AND GIVE IN NOW, MEAT.
KASHIWAZAKI SENA
HEE HEE! DON'T YOU MEAN YOU HAVE TO THROW IN THE TOWEL? YOU SOUND LIKE YOU'RE ABOUT TO STRAIN SOMETHING.

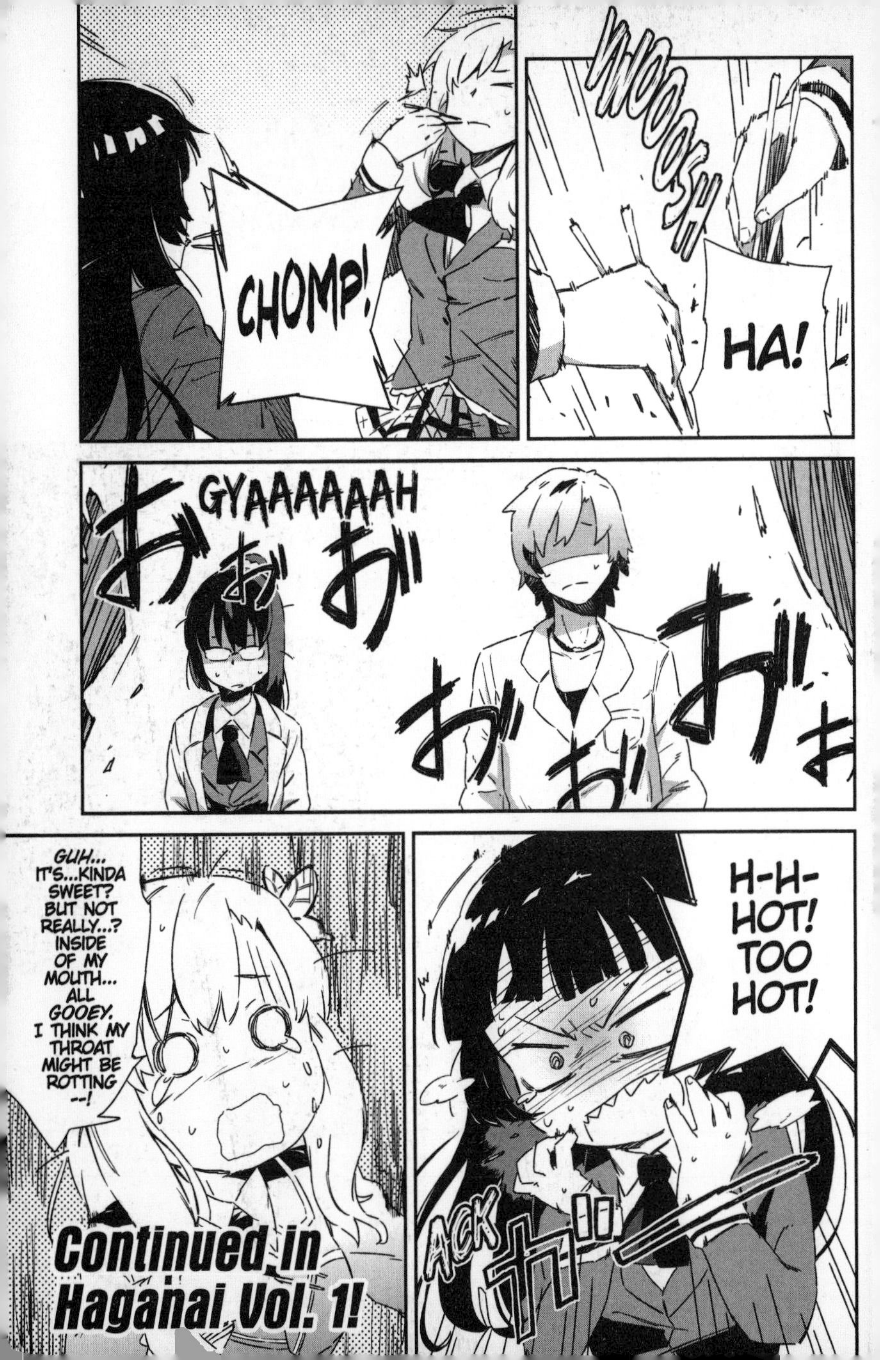
WHOOOSH
HA!
CHOMP!
GYAAAAAAH
H-H-HOT! TOO HOT!
ACK
GUH... IT'S...KINDA SWEET? BUT NOT REALLY...? INSIDE OF MY MOUTH... ALL GOOEY. I THINK MY THROAT MIGHT BE ROTTING--!
Continued in Haganai Vol. 1!